Religion and Materi␣

Religious belief is rooted in and sustained by material practice, and this book provides an extraordinary insight into how it works on the ground. David Morgan has brought together a lively group of writers from religious studies, anthropology, history of art, and other disciplines, to investigate belief in everyday practices; in the objects, images, and spaces of religious devotion and in the sensations and feelings that are the medium of experience. By avoiding mind/body dualism, the study of religion can break new ground by examining embodiment, sensation, space, and performance.

Materializing belief means taking a close look at what people do, how they feel, the objects they exchange and display, and the spaces in which they perform, whether spontaneously or with scripted ceremony. Contributions to the volume examine religions around the world—from Korea and Brazil to North America, Europe, and Africa. Belief is explored in a wealth of contexts, including Tibetan Buddhism, the Hajj, American suburbia and the world of dreams, visions, and UFOs.

David Morgan is Professor of Religion at Duke University, USA, where he also holds an appointment in the Department of Art, Art History, and Visual Studies. He is the author of *Visual Piety* (1998), *Protestants and Pictures* (1999), *The Sacred Gaze* (2005), and *The Lure of Images* (2007) and is an editor of the journal *Material Religion*.

Religion and Material Culture

The matter of belief

Edited by

David Morgan

Routledge
Taylor & Francis Group

LONDON AND NEW YORK

First published 2010
by Routledge
2 Park Square, Milton Park, Abingdon, Oxon, OX14 4RN

Simultaneously published in the USA and Canada
by Routledge
711 Third Ave, New York, NY 10017

*Routledge is an imprint of the Taylor & Francis Group,
an informa business*

Typeset in Sabon by
Book Now Ltd, London

British Library Cataloguing in Publication Data
A catalogue record for this book is available from the British
Library

Library of Congress Cataloging in Publication Data
Religion and material culture: the matter of belief / edited by David Morgan. p.
cm.
Includes bibliographical references and index.
1. Religious life. 2. Religion. 3. Religions. 4. Faith. 5. Material
culture—Religious aspects. I. Morgan, David, 1957–
BL624.R425 2009
202′.2—dc22   2009016868

ISBN10: 0–415–48115–5 (hbk)
ISBN10: 0–415–48116–3 (pbk)

ISBN13: 978–0–415–48115–1 (hbk)
ISBN13: 978–0–415–48116–8 (pbk)

Contents

Illustrations

Contributors

Editor

David Morgan is Professor of Religion at Duke University, North Carolina, where he also holds an appointment in the Department of Art, Art History, and Visual Studies. Author of *Visual Piety* (1998), *Protestants and Pictures* (1999), *The Sacred Gaze* (2005), and *The Lure of Images* (2007), Morgan has also edited several volumes, written widely on religion and visual theory as well as media and religion, and is an editor of the journal *Material Religion*.

Contributors

Jens Baumgarten is Adjunct Professor of Art History at the Universidade Federal de São Paulo (Federal University of São Paulo). He specializes in early modern art history of Latin America and Europe as well as in historiography of art, visual culture, and its theoretical and methodological contexts. He is the author of *Image, Confession, and Power* (*Konfession, Bild und Macht*, 2004) and several articles, and editor of two volumes, *Images and War* and *Visualization and Cultural Transfer*.

Jeremy Biles is an instructor at the School of the Art Institute of Chicago. He is the author of *Ecce Monstrum: Georges Bataille and the Sacrifice of Form* (Fordham University Press, 2007) and the editor of *Prompt*, a journal of visual art.

Gretchen T. Buggeln holds the Phyllis and Richard Duesenberg Chair in Christianity and the Arts in Christ College, Valparaiso University. She is the author of *Temples of Grace: The Material Transformation of Connecticut's Churches, 1790-1840* (2003) and numerous articles on religious architecture, American material culture, and museums. Her current book project is *Churches for Today: Modernism and Suburban Expansion in Post-World War II America.*

Insoo Cho is an Assistant Professor of Art Theory at Korea National University of Arts, and received his Ph.D. in Chinese art history from the University of Kansas in 2002. He is the co-author of *Geurimege mureun sadaebuui saenghwalgwa pungnyu* (Confucian Visual Culture in Joseon Korea, 2007) and has published articles on Korean and Chinese visual culture. He is an editor of *Korean Journal of Art History.*

Inge Daniels is a Lecturer in Visual and Material Culture at the Institute of Social and Cultural Anthropology, University of Oxford. Her research interests include everyday religious practices, consumption, and the anthropology of space. Daniels has published several articles on the material culture of luck and domestic practices in Japan, and a monograph entitled *The Japanese House: Material Culture in the Modern Home* will be published by Berg in 2010.

Laura Harrington is currently a Research Assistant at Harvard University. She is the contributing editor of *Kalacakra Tantra* (1999) and *Tibetan Astro Science* (2000), and the author of several articles on Buddhist thought and art. Her current project is a crossover work on Buddhist visual culture, designed to be of use to students and scholars of Buddhist Studies, religious visual culture, and Asian religious traditions.

Anna-Karina Hermkens is an anthropologist working as a postdoctoral researcher at the Faculty of Religious Studies at Radboud University Nijmegen. She is co-editor of *Moved by Mary* (2009). Her fields of interest are material culture studies, gender, religion, and conflict and her most recent research concerns the relation between religion, ritual, violence, and the (female) body in Papua New Guinea and Indonesia.

Gordon Lynch is Professor of Sociology of Religion and Director of the Centre for Religion and Contemporary Society at Birkbeck College, University of London. He has authored and edited several books, including *Understanding Theology and Popular Culture* (2005), *The New Spirituality* (2007) and *Between Sacred and Profane: Researching Religion and Popular Culture* (2007). His current research interests include theorizing the sacred in contemporary Western society.

Richard McGregor is Assistant Professor of Religious Studies and Islamic Studies at Vanderbilt University. His primary field of research is the

Middle East, with particular emphasis on religious practice and intra-Islamic discourses on religion. He is the author of *Sanctity and Mysticism in Medieval Egypt* (2004), and co-editor of *The Development of Sufism in Mamluk Egypt* (2006), and *The Case of the Animals versus Humans: A Tenth Century Fable from Iraq* (2009).

Jon P. Mitchell is Reader in Anthropology at the University of Sussex. His published work examines the anthropology of religion, ritual, politics, history and popular culture in Malta. His books include *Ambivalent Europeans* (2002), *Powers of Good and Evil* (edited with Paul Clough) (2002), *Global and Local Football* (with Gary Armstrong) (2008), and a special issue of *Journal of Mediterranean Studies* on "Modernity and the Mediterranean," which he edited in 2002.

Allen F. Roberts is Professor of World Arts and Cultures at the University of California, Los Angeles. A socio-cultural anthropologist, Roberts specializes in African systems of thought and expression, local-level politics, and cultural history. He conducts research, mounts exhibitions, and writes with his spouse, Mary Nooter Roberts. Their projects include "A Saint in the City: Sufi Arts of Urban Senegal," funded by the National Endowment for the Humanities and seen in six US museums, 2003–2008.

Mary Nooter Roberts is Professor of Culture and Performance in UCLA's Department of World Arts and Cultures. She studies philosophical dimensions of African visual and performance-based arts and the politics of representation. Her exhibitions and books include *Secrecy: African Art that Conceals and Reveals* (1993); *Memory: Luba Art and the Making of History* (with A.F. Roberts) (1996); *Inscribing Meaning: Writing and Graphic Systems in African Art* (2007), and *Luba: Visions of Africa* (2007).

Jojada Verrips is emeritus professor of European Anthropology at the University of Amsterdam. He has written and edited a number of books in Dutch and is currently working on a book entitled *The Wild (in the) West*. His main interests are anthropology and religion, anthropology and (abject) art, *aisthesis* or aesthetics as an embodied and embedded phenomenon, anthropology of the senses, blasphemy, cannibalism in the Western world, maritime anthropology, vandalism and violence.

Preface

Interest in the relevance of non-textual sources for the study of religions has been developing for many years. Indeed, ethnographers, art historians, musicologists, and archeologists have long relied on other kinds of evidence. But over the past few decades scholars of religions have looked to ritual, daily practice, imagery, objects, spaces, and bodies as promising ways of enriching and expanding the evidence for studying religions—not as systems of ideas or laws, but as lived, as intuited, as inconsistent, as adaptive. But this development is not without its problems. If the ethnographic, qualitative, and humanistic study of religion runs a grave risk, it is surely the temptation to overemphasize the local and to transform everything it sees into some form of personal or collective meaning. The same is true of material culture studies, which can fall prey to the assumption that often prevails in iconographical analysis—that everything must mean something.

A realization informing the work of many scholars in recent years has been the consideration that human beings do not translate everything significant or compelling into words or engage in a public or private discourse on the matter. They do not need to do so, because the locus of salience is not limited to discursive reasoning. We may speak of other forms of forging meaning or value such as aesthetic intelligence or sensuous cognition. The study of the material cultures of religions is one powerful way of taking that elusive dimension of human experience much more seriously because this approach deploys a set of tools that are able to recognize the nuances of felt-life and to discern its importance for people. The use of things, the sensation of things, the cultivation of feelings that objects, spaces, and performances induce and are in turn colored by—this is the felt-life or aesthetic dimension of human behavior that this book seeks to examine as a vital aspect of religions over time and around the world.

Beliefs have generally been understood, especially by Christian theologians and scholars shaped by Christianity, to consist of ideas or doctrines, the formal teachings of religious institutions. The argument of this book, however, is that beliefs may be much more productively understood as emerging from and enfolded within the practices, things, and feelings that shape individuals and communities over time. Beliefs are what people do, how they do it, where, and when. Not just why, which is the traditional framing of the contents of belief. In addition to everything else they are, religions, the essays in this book argue, are also characteristically the patterns of feelings and sensations bound up with performances, objects, and spaces. These domains have been widely ignored or regarded as inarticulate or inchoate, but that is only because scholars have not focused their analytical attention on them and have been directed by strongly creedal or dogmatic notions of what "real" religion is, that is, what Christianity or Judaism or Buddhism or Hinduism is, on the arch assumption that such abstractions may be satisfactorily defined by crystallizing their world of belief into clear tenets concerning more or less universal categories of God or gods, afterlife, scriptures, revelation, transcendence, and so forth. Over the last generation this approach has been widely and shrewdly critiqued by anthropologists, historians, and scholars of religion. But in spite of the critique, the bias persists, and the resource of materiality has not fully been recognized or put to effect. We hope this book helps advance that project.

This is a book for students and scholars in any number of disciplines who work on religion and are interested in the study of materiality as a fundamental aspect of their subject. The book offers a wide range of original case studies that explore under key rubrics how religious life is intimately, robustly material. An opening section examines the history of intellectual frameworks and how they have either facilitated or precluded progress in the investigation of religious material culture. Yet, throughout, the assumption is that theory is a tool for doing the scholarly investigation of religions better. In this regard, the aim of the book is to help *materialize* Religious Studies as a field of inquiry.

I wish to thank Lesley Riddle for her encouragement to produce this book and Amy Grant for her collegial assistance and initiative in making it happen. The contributors have labored valiantly to produce readable, substantive essays, and have done so while juggling personal and professional commitments. They have each been a pleasure to work with and have exceeded my expectations for original and progressive scholarship in their subfields and in the larger, much less well-defined precinct called "the material culture of religions." Special thanks to Jojada Verrips and to Larissa Grau for patiently reading drafts and commenting on them. And I express my gratitude to Duke University for a well-timed semester's leave, which was happily invested in writing my contributions and to assembling this volume.

Introduction
The matter of belief

David Morgan

The matter of belief
Overview of the book

The academic study of religion in the modern West has been shaped by the idea that a religion is what someone believes, which consists of a discrete, subjective experience of assent to propositions concerning the origin of the cosmos, the nature of humanity, the existence of deities, or the purpose of life. When seeking to understand a religion, scholars have long tended to ask: what are its teachings? Focus on "belief" as a set of teachings derives from the creedal tradition of Christianity, which was intensified by Protestantism. From there, belief passed beyond the realm of religion into the philosophy of language, where it came to be strictly defined in terms of the truth-value of a proposition. Anthropologists and others have challenged "the generally unquestioned assumption that adherents of a given religion, any religion, understand that adherence in terms of belief" (Lopez 1998: 21). Some have strongly urged scholars not to regard belief as a universal mental or "inner state" that might serve as a frame for the study of religion (Needham 1972). In an examination of the ethnographer's use of "belief," anthropologist Rodney Needham concluded that the concept "does not constitute a natural resemblance among men, and it does not belong to 'the common behaviour of mankind'" (ibid.: 188). He scrutinized the Christian legacy shaping the English verb, "believe," which he maintained had shifted from the older Jewish idea of trust to the New Testament idea of accepting the *kerygma* or message of Jesus Christ (ibid.: 48). Talal Asad famously argued that:

> [Clifford] Geertz's treatment of religious belief, which lies at the core of his conception of religion, is a modern, privatized Christian one because and to the extent that it emphasizes the priority of belief as a state of mind rather than a constituting activity in the world.
>
> (1993: 47; and see Keane 2008).

Yet another anthropologist, Malcolm Ruel, conducted a more detailed survey of the history of Christian thought regarding belief, showing how it had evolved from the New Testament to the modern period. Ruel found that the

Christian idea of belief began as the practice of trust or faith in the event of the messiah, then, in a series of shifts, became the declaration of initiates, the declaration of the orthodox party, the inward experience of the believer, and finally the affirmation of values common to all humanity (Ruel 1997: 50–1). Trust, declaration, inwardness, and affirmation. Ruel showed that all of these are embedded in their historical traditions and shaped distinctively by Christian cultural contexts. To universalize any of them as characteristic of religions anywhere and at any time is what anthropologists and philosophers and scholars of religion have prudently warned against.

A range of meanings comparable to what Ruel described was found in the linguistic history of "believe" undertaken by Wilfred Cantwell Smith. Tracing the meaning of the word and its antecedents from Indo-European roots to the present, Smith demonstrated that the word and closely related terms evolved from meaning "to love" or "to cherish or hold dear" to the medieval significance of a ceremonial declaration of faith or loyalty, to the modern notion of holding an opinion or conviction (Smith 1979: 105–27; also Needham 1972: 40–50 and Pagels 2003: 3–29). Smith's overriding concern was to resist the conflation of "faith" and "belief" in the present by recovering the older range of meanings and affixing them to the idea of faith, which he then opposed to belief understood as the considerably less engaging practice of "the holding of certain ideas" (Smith 1979: 12). Faith he defined as:

> an orientation of the personality, to oneself, to one's neighbour, to the universe; a total response; a way of seeing whatever one sees and of handling whatever one handles; a capacity to live at a more than mundane level; to see, to feel, to act in terms of, a transcendent dimension.
>
> (ibid.)

The problem with faith, however, as many of the writers mentioned above pointed out, is that it is even more attached to its Christian genealogy than is belief. One might speak of Hindu "beliefs" such as the ideas of karma and rebirth, but could one speak meaningfully about "the Hindu faith"? Indeed, the very doctrines of karma and rebirth render the Christian sense of "faith" inoperative or unnecessary within a Hindu view of human existence. If belief tends in the modern ear to invoke the avowal of doctrines or creeds, faith invariably hauls in the covenant and trust that animate Christianity.[1]

The problem of belief qua prescription is that it reduces a religion to a body of assertions demanding assent. In fact, religions are rarely describable as this. Even the most prescriptive or Fundamentalist versions of Protestantism, Islam, or Judaism are much more than that. Their embodied forms of practice such as prayer, liturgy, and pilgrimage, their sensations of sound in corporate worship, their visual articulations of sacred writ, their creation of spaces that sculpt sound and shape living architectures of human bodies—all these vastly exceed the narrow idea of a religion as the profession of creeds or catechetical formulae singularly understood to represent an inner state of volition. Insisting that any religion consists of the affirmation of a salient corpus of beliefs is a reductionism that does violence to the particularity and diversity of human religions by imposing a rigid template on them. By the same token, setting up "faith" or "trust" or "covenant" as the norm is no less presumptuous.

And yet I submit that we need to be able to compare accounts of different religions in a way that allows for similarities no less than fundamental differences. Belief may be serviceable if understood in broad, but also somatic or material terms. People report the reality of UFOs, the presence of angels, hearing the voice of God, the power of spirits to work for good or ill, the ability of Quranic text to bestow *baraka*, of passages of Torah bundled in a mezuzah to do the same, of the Bible opened randomly to reveal a pertinent scripture verse. Describing these as beliefs in the thin sense of affirmed dogmas fails miserably to help us understand what is happening in the lives of those in which these practices may be observed. These examples evince knowledge, conviction, memory, imagination, sensation, emotion, ritual action. Under what terms could the single word 'belief' be meaningfully applied to mark out their family resemblances without compromising their necessary and irreducible peculiarities?

In a fascinating essay entitled "The Fixation of Belief," American philosopher Charles Sanders Peirce described belief not as a linguistic phenomenon, but as a psychological and physiological one. "Our beliefs guide our desires and shape our actions," he wrote. "The feeling of believing is a more or less sure indication of there being established in our nature some habit which will determine our actions" (Peirce 1992: 1:114). Belief was feeling and habit linked intimately to action. He went on to contrast the experience of belief with the feeling of doubt:

> Doubt is an uneasy and dissatisfied state from which we struggle to free ourselves and pass into the state of belief; while the latter is a calm and satisfactory state which we do not wish to avoid, or to change to a belief in anything else. On the contrary, we cling tenaciously, not merely to believing, but to believing just what we do believe.
>
> (ibid.)

Belief as active clinging or holding to, as habit, as feeling suggests that even when people do utter religious creeds, they are doing far more than affirming the truth of a proposition. It also suggests that religion need not involve propositions and affirmations whatsoever. Belief is much more than a linguistic event. Let us consider a hypothetical instance drawn from the area of my own scholarly expertise, the history of Christianity. I do so not to privilege that religion, which, indeed, I have been attempting to de-privilege, but to show that the very religion from which the bias arose regarding belief itself offers grounds for re-conceiving belief.[2]

When someone says, "I believe in God" and is asked what he intends by that, he may reply, "I affirm the existence of the creator and sustainer of the universe," in effect, elaborating what he means by "God." But if asked what "believe" means, he may frown at being asked something so obvious. Then he may move to the affective register of the experience of believing and say, "I feel certain that God exists" or "I am convinced with all of my heart" or "There is no doubt in my mind regarding the proposition." If he is asked how he is so sure, he might reply that the belief matters to him more than anything else. Why? Because he has always believed this, ever since his youngest days, and has never found himself to be in error for doing so.

At this point our believer has revealed something very important. He brings Peirce's insights to mind by suggesting that belief is a practice and that it was absorbed in childhood. The habit of feeling certain is something he has practiced over and over. There was not a time when he did not believe. From the beginning, his parents and siblings and extended family have believed. What does that mean? By focusing on the practices of belief, we can have a very concrete notion of what this means: They sat with him at dinner and prayed; they attended church on Sundays, perhaps gathering in the same order in the same pew week after week; he was a member of a church choir or an acolyte or participated in a youth group that prayed and read the Bible and gathered regularly to engage in Christian activities; he and his family sang hymns at Christmas, ate foods peculiar to that holiday and others on Easter; read scripture in the evenings around the kitchen table. Were these cognitive exercises? Marginally, but primarily they were the iteration of familiar feelings packaged and evoked and regularly rehearsed in the techniques of the body that he acquired from the earliest moments of his family and communal life. He was taught how to fold his hands when praying, to close his eyes, to sit still and erect, to kneel at bedside, what voice to use as he prayed, as well as the archaic verbiage of prayers and snippets of pious diction; he learned when and how to stand and kneel and genuflect (if Catholic) during worship, how loud to sing, how to blend his voice with those around him.

All of this is the slowly sedimentary practice of belief, built up over the course of his life and inflected with the feelings toward his family and friends and community, endlessly repeated, tirelessly educating the ear, the eye, the palette, the body's schemes of posture and gesture. So when our interlocutor says that he believes in God, we must listen for the silent speech beneath his words, the habits and felt-life of old practices. We must learn to hear his sighs, his gritted teeth, the murmur of nostalgia, the distant gaze of eyes searching the memory of folded hands, sore knees, and the lingering melody of the Eucharistic liturgy. He says he believes, but what he really does is feel, smell, hear, and see.

There is, then, another way of thinking about belief. What if belief were about more than faith in things unseen, trust in divine promises, or the declaration of the truth of certain teachings? What if believing were not fundamentally different from seeing or smelling or dressing or arranging space? People need not recite creedal statements to be described as believers. In other words, a narrow version of Christian practice should not dictate the terms for defining "belief." What is belief? In Christianity it commonly involves an act of volition and a symbolic expression in speech, but it need not exhibit either feature prominently, or perhaps not at all. Our reflections on Peirce's observations imply that belief is not best understood as a discrete linguistic event. "The essence of belief," he proclaimed in another essay, "is the establishment of a habit." A belief acts as "a rule for action" (Pierce 1992: vol. 1, p. 129). Accordingly, an utterance of belief properly regarded is but the visible tip of an entire iceberg. Limning the girth and structure of the submerged body of belief is the purpose of this book.

So if it is advisable to look for religion along broader avenues than creedal utterances, and it certainly is, then we do well to look for ways of believing that engage more of a human being than discursive performance alone. This will mean examining how people behave, feel, intuit, and imagine as ways of belief. This will mean regarding utterances as symbolic events that are anchored to much larger processes. Belief is not merely the symbolic act of representation, but the symbol as well as all that it evokes and draws on. The acting, feeling, intuiting, and imagining absorbed and practiced over time are signified by a proposition of belief. But belief is more than the linguistic act of signification. These activities are implicit in a statement like "She believes that she should behave thus and so because her god expects it of her." To understand or apprehend the nature and content of her belief, we must examine far more than the utterance as a proposition within a system of propositions.

The deep shape of the belief, in other words, is everything that issues in the utterance, for it is the history and momentum of embodied practices that engage her person in a duty or practice or feeling enjoined by her deity. Religious and ethical belief is a holding to a practice and a tradition of that practice. Such holding may be represented in statements of belief, or tenets, from the Latin *tenere*, to hold, but should not be reduced to them. Moreover, such statements may not be even remotely creedal. The connections cherished by believers are to the elders, ancestors, or founders, whose ways they remember ritually and devotionally as forms of reverence. John of Damascus insisted on venerating icons because it is "the tradition of the Church," which he reminded the iconoclasts came down in written form as well as non-written. "Therefore, since so much that is unwritten has been handed down in the Church and is still observed now, why do you despise images?" (Damascus 2000: 31–2). A Cheyenne account of the origin of the sun dance revealed that the dance "was conceived and taught to the people by the Creator, Maheo, and his helper, Great Roaring thunder" through the intermediary of a legendary medicine man named Horns Standing Up (Erdoes and Ortiz 1984: 34). The shaman was told by Maheo to teach it to the people, and that "if they perform the ceremonies in the right way, they will be favored for generations to come" (ibid.: 36). Or consider the countless myths that explain physical circumstances, infusing the physical world with the traces of the sacred such as the Hui Muslim story that the angel in paradise grabbed Adan (the biblical Adam) by his throat as he ate the apple, though Haowa (Eve) entirely swallowed the fruit. The result was an Adam's apple in his throat and her body's menstruation (Li and Luckert 1994: 78). The first deeds were registered in the body, and remembered somatically through the ages. This is not to suggest, of course, that religionists do not avail themselves of polemic or reason. John of Damascus readily provided theological deductions to support his practice of icon veneration, but reason did not have the final say. The authority of belief lay in the tradition of authority, which consisted of a lineage of practices traced back to the apostles and to Jesus himself (whose endorsement of icons was evident to John of Damascus in the legend of the messiah's contemporary, King Abgar, who received a cloth bearing the features of Jesus' face[3]). Rather than weighting religion in favor of doctrines and propositions, scholars of lived religion may understand teachings as ways of framing, securing, and disseminating habits and practices. In other words, to say "I believe" might be understood to mean that one holds to a particular habit of feeling, willing, thinking, and practice. When believers do utter abstract statements like "I believe my God is the only God," we can know what that means by asking the difference it makes in their behavior, e.g. that they object to the use of images for fear of inciting God's jealousy.

Therefore, instead of asking "what does a religion teach?" we might focus on the social and interpersonal relations that characterize practitioners of a religion. We might ask alternatively: what is it that people teach their children? Yet even that question remains in the orbit of content, reducing religion to the delivery of sacred information. *What* they teach their children certainly matters, but in what manner and on what occasions they teach them will be no less important to consider. Thus, a better approach might inquire: *how*, *when*, and *where* do people teach their children *what* they teach them? This moves the inquiry to the register of material culture by examining the conditions that shape the feelings, senses, spaces, and performances of belief, that is, the material coordinates or forms of religious practice. By shifting attention to what people do, and understanding belief as grounded in practice, we open the door for substantive analysis of the materiality of religion since making, exchanging, displaying, and using artifacts are principal aspects of human doing.

Wilfred Cantwell Smith's eloquent definition of faith quoted above, "an orientation of the personality, to oneself, to one's neighbour, to the universe, ... ," captures something fundamental, though it is imbued with the humanistic ideals of personalism. Belief is a broad orientation that emerges from the habits absorbed in childhood or at other times in life such as conversionary periods when, like learning a new language, the mind is powerfully opened under conditions of duress or crisis to absorbing fundamental new patterns. Belief is a shared imaginary, a communal set of practices that structure life in powerfully aesthetic terms. Belief is perhaps best framed as a pervasive community of feeling because the holding that it involves is public and verifiable when it consists of holding to other people and the institutions they share.

Belief, this book will argue, is much more than assent or conviction if we understand it as a disposition that engages diverse aspects of a human being. Belief may be defined in many ways: *dogmatically*, as the affirmation of tenets; *affectively*, as the experience of certain feelings and emotions; *voluntaristically*, as the necessary or willful performance of certain duties; and *practically*, as participation in a group's discrete or definitive practices. The voluntaristic and the practical are distinguished by virtue of conscious determination, on the one hand, and the shaping effect of repetition, on the other, though the two are clearly related to one another. In his comprehensive *Critique of Religion and Philosophy*, a systematic résumé of theories and definitions of religious and philosophical domains and their relations to one another, Walter Kaufmann concluded that reductionist approaches to religion failed consistently. He prudently urged an integrated approach, which will be the framework for this book:

> The chief lesson of a survey of attempted definitions of religion is that, in religion, practice, feeling, and belief are intertwined, and every definition that would see the essence of religion in just one of these three facets is too partial.
>
> (Kaufmann 1961: 103)

The matter of belief

Rather than marginalizing belief, we need a more capacious account of it, one that looks to the embodied, material features of lived religion. A recent collection of essays entitled *Materializing Religion* put the matter quite nicely: "the idea of religion itself is largely unintelligible outside its incarnation in material expressions" (Arweck and Keenan 2006: 2–3). Anthropologist Webb Keane has aptly observed that "Religions may not always demand beliefs, but they will always involve material forms" (Keane 2008: 124). Forms of materiality—sensations, things, spaces, and performance—are a matrix in which belief happens as touching and seeing, hearing and tasting, feeling and emotion, as will and action, as imagination and intuition. Moreover, religion happens not *in* spaces and performances as indifferent containers, but *as* them, carved out of, overlaid, or running against prevailing modes of place and time. Materiality refers to more than a concrete object or to this or that feeling. Sensation is an integrated process, interweaving the different senses and incorporating memory, and emotion into the relationships human beings have with the physical world.

Materiality is a compelling register in which to examine belief because feeling, acting, interacting, and sensation embody human relations to the powers whose invocation structures social life. Most believers live their religion in the grit and strain of a felt-life that embodies their relation to the divine as well as to one another. The transcendent does not come to them as pure light or sublime sensations in most cases, but in the odor of musty shrines or moldering robes or the pantry where they pray. Thus, medieval European pilgrimage tasted of the dust of roads headed toward Santiago de Compostella; its sound was the din of the crowds mulling in markets on cobbled squares before cathedrals; its look and feel were the colored light piercing the dark coolness housed within; it smelled of sweaty bodies, baked bread, and incense. And all of these sensations intermingled to embody contrition, petition, offering, pledge, and redemption. The saints themselves returned the gaze of the penitent. They looked at the devout and expected a response. So the pilgrims uttered prayers, offered what they could, made their promises, heard the mass in its inscrutable Latin, glimpsed the Host, gazed on the reliquary in which resided a precious bit of sacred matter, and then returned home to await the work of the saint.

Belief is the felt expectation that the world works in a particular way. In order to understand belief, the scholar is not content with lapidary professions from the believer, but looks at what the person does and feels, how he rears his children, how (as well as what) she teaches them, how believers parse time, organize space, how they train, regard, and decorate their bodies. In each of these are evident the material conditions under which they seek certain ends. By assaying the felt-life of belief, the scholar aims to understand how belief shapes or colors human consciousness, how it operates as a way of knowing, or, perhaps better put, as a way of feeling, by which I do not mean a thoughtless state of emotion, but something like the domain of practical reason. What I have in mind is an approach to religion that attends to belief as an embodied epistemology, the sensuous and material routines that produce an integrated (and culturally particular) sense of self, community, and cosmos. It is not only to systematic theology or sacred philosophy that we look to learn this, but to the lived world of belief. In particular, to the forms of materiality which organize the world.

It makes sense therefore to turn to the history of epistemology and phenomenology in modern philosophical thought as one way to expand the framework for thinking about belief. These traditions take sensation and the structure of consciousness very seriously. An ample conception of belief is at work, for example, in the way the word was used by philosopher David Hume to describe the most quotidian assumption of what one might call the minded body: the belief that the table at which I write will continue to exist into the next moment. Sitting at the table, resting my arms on it, is a *corporeal practice of belief* that seldom becomes conscious, except in moments of artistic or meditative experience or those junctures in practice when the body's pain or pleasure or the flow of experience congeal into states of awareness. But my belief in the endurance of this table does not rely on a particular state of consciousness. It consists in what my body does.

The persistence of the material world is a belief no less than the willed assumption that gods exist or that pouring a libation in honor of a spirit will secure good fortune. Indeed, the two forms of belief are one in the same for religious believers. Is the divine any less real, any less relevant, than the duration of a table? In both cases, belief is the glue that holds the world together. My belief that the table will continue to exist is not, strictly speaking, a rational assertion. Indeed, as Hume argued, it's not an operation of reason at all, but the effect of custom, which led him to argue that "all probable reasoning is nothing but a species of sensation. 'Tis not solely in poetry and music, we must follow our taste and sentiment, but likewise in philosophy" (Hume 2000: 72). And for this reason Hume spoke in sensuous terms of discriminating one opinion or belief from another species of idea. An idea we believe "feels different from a fictitious idea, that the fancy alone presents to us: And this different feeling I endeavour to explain by calling it a superior *force*, or *vivacity*, or *solidity*, or *firmness*, or *steadiness*" (ibid.: 68; italics in original). Belief that X is the cause of Y is an idea that results from the impression or sensation of the repeated association of Y following X. As a mental phenomenon, belief is always traceable to sensation.

In this manner, belief shows itself to be a corporeal assumption or expectation, the cognitive predisposition of an embodied epistemology. Belief is what I know with my body. I feel the world enduring, I address its endurance with my gesture, the distribution of my body's mass, with a robust leap of expectation as I push against the floor and the chair and rest my elbows on the hard surface of the table. If it were not there and the world did not behave the way it does, I would not only think and feel differently, I would act otherwise. The pressure in my ears tells me that the world is there, welcoming my balanced gesture or rhythmic gait. The sidewalk will not abruptly jump into the air when I step on it. I believe that because my body tells me it is so—not in words, but in feelings, in the minute intuitions of sensation confirmed by the body's archives of long experience. Belief begins as the material fit between body and habitat, the delicate sensory loop arcing from body–mind to environment and back.

All ideas, Hume asserted, begin with sensation. In the twentieth century, the phenomenological philosopher Maurice Merleau-Ponty expressed very well the intimate relation of body and world. Though he did not discuss belief in the way that Hume did, he carefully distinguished the consciousness of the body's construction of the world from the scientific knowledge of the Cartesian cogito, the domain of propositional or logical discourse:

> The identity of the thing through perceptual experience is only another aspect of the identity of one's own body throughout exploratory movements ... I am involved in things with my body, they co-exist with me as an incarnate subject, and this life among things has nothing in common with the elaboration of scientifically conceived things.
>
> (Merleau-Ponty 1962: 215)

Merleau-Ponty moved beyond Hume's association of ideas approach to the relation of body and meaning by developing a much more intricate account of the integral relationship between perception and abstract cognition. He spoke of the "natural self" (*un moi naturel*) as distinct from the intellectual self.[4] The natural self, the sentient subject, was that aspect of consciousness that exists in sensation and "enters into a sympathetic relation with" the qualities of things (ibid.: 248).

The self does not simply create representations of the world, but participates in the world such that "the sensible ... is nothing other than a certain way of being in the world ... so that sensation is literally a form of communion" (by which Merleau-Ponty explicitly alluded to the Christian sacrament of the Eucharist (ibid.: 246)). He characterized the human body as the interface with the world: "My body is the fabric into which all objects are woven, and it is, at least in relation to the perceived world, the general instrument of my 'comprehension'" (ibid.: 273). The body is both part of the world and the means by which the world is understood. Even words, he pointed out, are sensible to the body:

> It is my body which gives significance not only to the natural object, but also to cultural objects like words. If a word is shown to a subject for too short a time for him to be able to read it, the word "warm," for example, induces a kind of experience of warmth which surrounds him with something in the nature of a meaningful halo ... Before becoming the indication of a concept [the word] is first of all an event which grips my body.
>
> (ibid.)

Merleau-Ponty did not wish to reduce words or percepts to bodily sensations, but to recognize the body's powerful role in crafting the apprehension and understanding of the world. The body, he asserted, "is that strange object which uses its own parts as a general system of symbols for the world, and through which we can consequently 'be at home in' the world, 'understand' it and find significance in it" (ibid.: 275).

Merleau-Ponty's philosophical work is largely corroborated by neurobiological studies since his day. Antonio Damasio's important work on emotion and feeling makes many of the same points summarized from Merleau-Ponty. Damasio points out that the neural patterns or mental maps that constitute the brain's response to external stimuli are "based on changes which occur [*sic*] in our organisms ... when the physical structure of the object interacts with the body" (Damasio 1999: 320). Consciousness is "the unified mental pattern that brings together the object and the self" (ibid.: 11). Damasio stresses the monistic plane that joins brain and world, and he stringently avoids any kind of dualism that segregates thought as a separate substance. In a way that recalls Merleau-Ponty's discussion of the natural self and the cogito or intellectual self, Damasio describes levels of consciousness. There is what he calls "core consciousness," which:

> occurs when the brain's representation devices generate an imaged, nonverbal account of how the organism's own state is affected by the organism's processing of an object, and when this process enhances the image of the causative object, thus placing it saliently in a spatial and temporal context.
>
> (ibid.: 169)

Core consciousness only renders a sense of the present. What Damasio calls "extended consciousness" introduces the sense of past and future, the broader range of time allowing greater articulation of sequence for narration, computation, and subtle determinations of change, causation, and reasoning (ibid.: 195–202). This corresponds to Merleau-Ponty's description of the cogito, that higher sense of self that seems distant from what it contemplates. Yet for both philosopher and neuroscientist, all consciousness is grounded in the body.

Both philosophical and scientific considerations suggest that we do not understand the embodied nature of religious belief until we reckon the intimate way in which felt expectations bind together imagined and physical universes for believers. The aim driving the chapters in this book is to demonstrate in various ways that belief should be studied as taking place in material practices. Belief should not be understood as coming only before such things as the veneration of relics or the ecstatic drudgery of pilgrimage, but as being constituted by them. People do what they want to believe. They make belief in the things they do. This book argues that materiality *mediates* belief, that material objects and practices both enable it and enact it. Handling objects, dressing in a particular way, buying, displaying, and making gifts of particular commodities, attending certain events are all activities that engage people in the social relations and forms of sacred imagination that structure their relations to the divine. Each of these activities and countless others, whether performed by Christians or Hindus or Wiccans, construct particular bodies of belief. If we are to understand that, we must attend to a set of rubrics that will ground the study of religions in materiality.

Overview of the book

The chapters are divided into five areas of focus: theory, sensation, things, spaces, and performance. Their common task is to demonstrate how belief is the structuring, dynamic activity of material practices in particular historical and cultural circumstances. Emerging from embodied experience or sensation, from engagement with things, unfolding and defining sacred spaces, and activated by many forms of performance, belief owes far more to the body than Religious Studies has often allowed. In every case, the account of materiality will argue that the study of the material cultures of religions is not the study of objects *per se,* nor a neurological approach to belief, nor even in the first instance a new chapter in body studies. Instead, the argument is that the study of religions will benefit from an approach that undertakes an abundant account of social life mediated in feelings, things, places, and performances. It is not a new art history or a new material culture, but is framed by the social construction of the sacred. The approach takes the human body not as an irreducible essence, not as a universal language, not as the material substrate of soul or spiritual essence, but as something made and self-making.

It has become customary to open scholarly books with chapters on theory. This is a useful practice when theoretical vistas are made to shed light on analytical practice, to inform interpretation with its history of thought, its assumptions, limits, and opportunities. But theory-wonking—stressing theory for its own sake—is not useful, in my estimation, if the task at hand is to illuminate analysis and interpretation. So the book begins with a section devoted to theory, but we hope theory as a tool for improving the practice of critical thinking about the study of religious material culture. Chapter 1, by Jojada Verrips, is an intellectual history of how the social sciences have approached the study of religion, and what limitations and advantages are important to recognize by scrutinizing conceptual orientations that have directed scholarship. From the vantage point of a distinguished career as a social and economic anthropologist, Verrips provides a subtle reflection, framed autobiographically, on the quest among social scientists, in particular anthropologists, to overcome the mind/body split, a tenacious dualism that has long compromised the need to give the body its due as a constitutive participant in the experience, valuation, and meaning-making of human culture, especially religion.

In Chapter 2, Gordon Lynch turns to object relations theory in the psycho-analytic tradition in order to explore how scholarship can understand better the power of beliefs as affixed to mental objects, and by extension, to their material counterparts. As a result, objects take on a life and allure, even an agency that anthropologists and art historians have observed at work in religious devotion and ritual. Lynch's attention to the psychological dimension also underscores how terms like "material culture" and "visual culture" should not be restricted to their physical objects, but understood in the broader register of mind, body, sociality, and culture. I bring Part I to a close with a survey of a large body of work in order to discern major categories of thought that have cleared the way in recent decades for thinking substantively about the materiality of religion. The categories that I identify are reflected in the subsequent organization of the book's chapters.

The range of themes raised in the first three chapters will resonate through-out the rest of the book, which consists of case studies that focus on discrete religious traditions and histories. These chapters cluster around the themes of sensation, things, spaces, and performance. At the heart of all of these are two interwoven topics: embodiment and belief. Each of these essays argues in its own way that the two are in fact inseparable. Understanding how, in view of considerable differences and variations from one moment and tradition to another, is the overarching concern of this book.

Sensation is a broad assortment of human experiences—physical contact with the worlds within and beyond the body's material envelope as these are defined by touch, sight, smell, and sound, but also memory, intuition, and imagination, what might be called inner sensation. Sensation, in other words, is part of a single continuum stretching from the senses to the brain's emotional coding, intuition, memory, feeling, and ratiocination. The inherent instability of the world and the body consists of their own transience as systems of energy relentlessly passing into one state and out of another; of the various sensory thresholds of the human body and the conceptual registers and cultural imaginaries of different human groups, times, and places. Sensation touches on all of these by recording, translating, interpreting, compensating, and transforming what may be ambivalently referred to as "experience."

If Gordon Lynch reminds us of the broader register in sensation's conceptual and social aspects, Mary Nooter Roberts' chapter demonstrates how objects are situated within encompassing sensoria. Seeing is not an isolated human activity, but part of movement and touch. This suggests that the study of materiality invites scholars to emerge from the tight hold of disciplines that focus attention on one sense (such as seeing or hearing) or one form of information (such as texts or language) in order the better to match their analyses to the object of their study. It also suggests that the "meanings" we seek to grasp are not exhausted by conventional concepts of scholarship. The challenge is to develop ways of study and understanding that recognize that such things as feeling, time, social configuration, and sensations or the experience of compound artifacts such as image/texts or sound/motion or touch/narrative are the principal and compelling shapes of meaning for many religious practitioners. Laura Harrington's chapter on Tibetan Buddhist meditation practice shows how sensation and the experience of embodiment are a fundamental means of overcoming the body–mind's tenacious hold on the illusion of Self. By placing themselves in the grisly midst of the cremation grounds, Tantric Buddhist practitioners confront the very sensations and feelings and conceptual patterns that secure the hold that fear exerts and that keeps people clinging to selfhood.

Things are as unstable as sensations because things arise from sensation. But one of the things cultures do is seek to discern and produce relative stabilities for the sake of constructing and maintaining life-worlds. Things are manufactured as sensory objects, as socially shared and circulating, and as apprehended through the lens or grip or scent of culturally defined practices and templates. A person's sense of something, in other words, is biologically, socially, and culturally constructed. Things circulate through a variety of protocols of exchange. They are displayed, hidden, disguised, forgotten, destroyed, re-created. They exhibit biographies and are often best studied over time.

In Chapter 6, Allen Roberts examines the restless lives of images as they migrate from one setting to the next, showing how meaning is inconstant and best understood within the itinerary of an object's travel. This throws considerable light on the importance of the relations that people enter with images, on the agency that images can exhibit, on the transience of meanings, on the way in which images becomes 'sites of contestation' between rival parties, and how interdependent images, narratives, and physical and social contexts are in the experience of an image's value. In Chapter 7, Jeremy Biles directs our attention to the problem of visualizing the supernatural, the unknown, the mystical—the very things whose existence threatens the stability of the ordinary. Fascinated by apparitions, Biles considers the key role that visual media play in mediating or capturing what may be otherwise invisible or unseeable. Photographs occupy a kind of liminal place because they reproduce what is physical but also register what is unseen without their intervention. Media, therefore, make things and play a fundamental part in making the sacred.

Inge Daniels' ethnographic study of dolls in contemporary Japanese homes in Chapter 8 shows how deeply engaged people become with objects, including even those they do not wish to possess. People are tied to objects by the obligation of the gift economy, but also by the economy of luck, which governs the circulation of fortune and misfortune. Owners conceal some dolls because by seeing them and living with them, they would activate the dolls' tendency to respond to them. By the same token, disposing of the dolls improperly can invite bad luck. The world of things is animated with a viscosity and momentum that restricts human autonomy since agency comes at a price. To live in a world that responds to human presence means accepting the consequences of a world in which things are able to act with an agency of their own.

Spaces are the arenas erected in different times and places for certain things to happen, for performances to take place, for the sacred to become sensible, for discrete modes of possibility to prevail. But spaces are not the empty opposite of things, for the two come attached to one another. Things imply a certain kind of space; spaces allow for certain kinds of things. Spaces and things are cultural realities that belong to one another. Spaces are often presumed universal, but encoded in them are various hierarchies, concepts of public, private, and semi-private, or family, clan, and nation—all of which amount to the coordinates of belonging. They make visible, but also render other things or people invisible. They are made to contain but also to make possible the existence of objects. Spaces are structures created by circulation, patterns of movement, cycles of activity, hierarchies, and series that are maintained by religious narratives and rites, in the wilderness or bush, on pilgrimage, in home, village, city, and in transnational migrations. Spaces render worlds from the environment, making the unknown familiar and wresting order from chaos.

In Chapter 9, Jens Baumgarten investigates the theatrical wherewithal of Baroque and Neo-Baroque churches in Brazil as stages for performing revelation, sainthood, authority, and national identity. The spaces of twentieth-century churches build on their seventeenth-century predecessors by orchestrating the visual piety of Brazilian Catholicism, in particular by providing the *mise-en-scène*, or stage setting for paintings and sculptures that enact sacred history. The power, and the failure, of spaces to embody identity, to create or fail to create community ideals, to materialize a desired aim are the subject of Gretchen Buggeln's examination of mid-twentieth-century American construction of instructional spaces by Protestant congregations. In Chapter 10, she considers the confident claim of Protestant educators and architects that the physical environment of the Sunday School exerted a powerful influence on the moral and intellectual formation of children. And yet, Buggeln is struck by the cavalcade of changes inserted during actual planning and construction that compromised the faith in material forms to shape spiritual constitution. Did environment influence children or did it not? Or did mundane finances intervene to curtail the ideals of a tradition commonly dismissed for its aesthetic frugality? On the other side of the world, in an entirely different religious context and historical tradition, Insoo Cho shows in Chapter 11 how objects and spaces are mutually engaged in Korean ancestral shrines. He stresses the important relation that images and sacred objects have to ritual practices and spaces such as funerals, commemorative rites, and shrines, thus resisting the tendency among some art historians to separate the artifact from its milieu in accord with a Western aesthetic of disinterested contemplation. Not only are object and space knit together by ritual practice, they structure seeing as a form of engagement with space and time that may not be abstracted from the context without changing the meaning of the artifact.

Performance is not limited to formal, scripted ceremony or official rite, but includes how people perform different roles in the settings of daily life. Everyday performance is not theatrical or artistic in a formal sense, but the quotidian dramaturgy of social life. Performance puts things and spaces together to accomplish a wide range of cultural work. Essays in this section of the book consider many ways in which things participate in performances and how performances both presuppose and generate spaces and sensations. Performances are not only enactments of rigidly prescribed scripts, but, whether improvised or carefully planned, they are actions that achieve their purpose (or not) by being conducted. The chapters each demonstrate how thinking about performance and ritual practice returns us to the materiality of things, the character of bodies as gendered, sexed, and otherwise culturally constructed, and the sacred as a relational process that constellates people, spaces, objects, and the divine.

In Chapter 12, Anna-Karina Hermkens considers how clothing enters into the performance of personal and social identity, allowing the body/person to perform roles that bring new accents or meanings. Cloth mediates the living and the dead, drawing value from the remains of the ancestors and then distributing it among family or clan members. Spirits enter the living in part through the ritual clothing they wear. In a powerfully corporeal way, clothing changes the person, becoming the body and touching all aspects of the wearer. In no minor way we are what we wear. Clothing is not only a social form of communication, although it certainly is that, but also operates in a more visceral manner as a way of embodiment. The power of dress comes into another view with Richard McGregor's study of the clothing of the Ka'ba, which Muslim practice has long animated as a feminine personality that draws pilgrims to Mecca. The Ka'ba enjoys the special devotion of residents of Cairo, where the *kiswa*, the elaborate black and embroidered clothing of the structure, is fabricated and sent to Mecca for the stately adornment of the stone pivot of the Muslim devotional universe. In Chapter 13, McGregor traces the fascinating history of the pilgrimage that delivers the sacred clothing, showing how the transmission of the *kiswa* has never enjoyed a place of prominence in scholarship. By retraining the focus on the practice of carrying and displaying the *kiswa*, his chapter demonstrates how the study of the Hajj is affected by materializing it and how performance can distribute the sacred over time and space rather than locating it only in one place.

Jon Mitchell brings the book to an eloquent close with his ethnographic investigation of the communal performance of statues of the Virgin, St. Paul, and the Crucified Jesus during annual *festas* in their honor on the island of Malta. Mitchell is especially good at showing how images for Maltese Catholics are not merely symbols, placeholders for ideas, but forms of presence grounded in centuries of Catholic practice and thought. The procession of images is one of the ways in which saintly or divine presence happens for devotees. This activity brings the images to life by removing them from their usual situation within the church interior, by allowing participants to interact with the sacred personages, and by allowing the saints or Jesus themselves to respond to the local setting. For example, a large statue of St. Paul pauses at side streets as he proceeds in order to bless them with his glance. The engagement of the devotee with the image is intimately embodied and best understood in the category of presence that Mitchell articulates, an experience that cannot be understood without careful attention to the ritual and spatial setting and the devotee's performative engagement with the imagery.

Readers will be struck by the diversity of topics and I hope welcome their historical, geographical, and religious variance from one another. But throughout the range of essays, the book will achieve its principal purpose if readers discern that belief is a useful framework for analysis when it is understood as what people do to encounter in things, bodies, spaces, and action the realities that would amount to nothing if their mystery were not mediated by human practice.

Notes

1 Smith's passionate project to universalize faith as a human phenomenon has been carefully criticized by Ruel (1997: 54–6).

2 One might step far beyond the Christian world to examine the intricate organization of practices and spaces in the Berber house as described by Pierre Bourdieu in a now classic essay that explored the intimate integration of the structure of the interior of a Berber house in North Africa into the landscape and cosmos, delineating the interior spatial structure of life (especially of girls and women) from birth to maturity (Bourdieu 1970).

3 Damascus (2000: 35). He also frequently quoted Pseudo-Dionysius the Areopagite, who was long believed to have been the man whom Paul converted while preaching in Athens, mentioned in Acts 17: 34.

4 Merleau-Ponty (1962: 251); cf. Merleau-Ponty (1945: 249). For more recent phenomenological analysis of embodiment, particularly the "embodied self," see Csordas (1990); Gallagher (2005: 78–84); and Thomas (2006).

Part I

THEORY

1

Body and mind
Material for a never-ending intellectual odyssey

Jojada Verrips

Religion and the body
Body–mind in anthropology
Religion and belief

Once upon a time I thought that the distinction between body and mind was as useless as that made by Marx between *Unterbau* and *Überbau*. As a matter of fact, I ended my dissertation on the role of religion in a small Calvinist Dutch village with a sentence in which I aired this rather radical materialist viewpoint (Verrips 1978). In order to be able to defend my bold opinion against attacks, I collected quotes from a host of scholars working in various disciplines and active in different epochs that seemed to support it in an unambiguous way (see Thomson 2008). Of course, the famous statement "*ohne Phospor keine Gedanken,*" by the nineteenth-century Dutch physiologist Moleschott, was among my top ten. The absolute number one, however, was the statement by anthropologist Charles Laughlin and psychiatrist-and-anthropologist Eugene d'Aquili:

> There is no level of reality intervening between *Homo sapiens* as a biological phenomenon and that organism's environment. In other words, human behaviour is the result of a dialectic between the central nervous system, primarily the higher cortical functions, and the environment. All other asserted or posited levels of reality have analytic status only.
>
> (1974: 196)

Both scholars propounded that the days of the traditional concept of culture were numbered: that it had to be drastically redefined, if not disappear altogether, for it inhibited the development of cultural anthropology into a nomothetic social science based on a unitary theory of human evolution and behavior. Heavily influenced by modern structuralism, as developed by Lévi-Strauss and others, social scientists envisioned a theoretical synthesis based on insights gained in a series of disciplines, such as anthropology, linguistics, cognitive psychology and neurophysiology. I was fascinated by their new approach, which they baptized *biogenetic structuralism*, for it seemed to imply, at least in my view, a farewell to the kind of disappointing "culturological" and mentalistic perspectives that had dominated anthropology in the 1960s and 1970s, which completely ignored the relevance of the physical body and what went on inside this entity for what went on between bodies. At long last, some anthropologists seemed to have taken Marcel Mauss' call to take (the techniques of) the (physiological functioning) body seriously by placing it center stage.[1] It is true that a few years before Laughlin and d'Aquili launched their outspoken materialist theoretical views, Mary Douglas had already presented her ideas about the relevance of the body in society and, even more importantly, as a symbol for society. However, she did not really take into consideration what the biogenetic structuralists emphasized: that is, the neuro-anatomical and neurophysiological make-up of the body and how this was related to the behavior of human beings towards each other and the environment in which they lived. The latter wanted to discard such "unscientific" superorganic notions as "mind" or "reason," because they were misleading, and instead directly concentrate on the study of neuroanatomical (or more specifically: "dendritic-axonic-synaptic") configurations in the brain. "Great," I thought, "at long last we will get rid of the Cartesian split that has haunted us for so long, and work in the direction of a much more realistic monistic stand!" What was especially appealing in this connection was that Laughlin and d'Aquili stated that not only modes of "thought," "reason," "cognition" and "sciencing," but also "mythologizing" and "magical causation," i.e. religious phenomena *pur sang*, are "actually the behavioural equivalents of internal, neurophysiologically structured, and systematic channels of sensory association and processing of the human brain, as well as of the brains of other organisms" (1974: 196). In my enthusiasm I even forgave them for overlooking an article by Lévi-Strauss on shamanistic curing in which he dealt with a "rapid oscillation between mythical and physiological themes, as if to abolish in the mind of [a] sick woman the distinction which separates them" ([1949] 1967: 188), an issue to which I will return in Section II.[2]

Though I soon developed doubts with regard to the reductionist perspective sketched by Laughlin and d'Aquili, I cannot deny that it held me in a firm grip for some time. The main reason for my enthusiasm was the fact that I was raised in a staunch orthodox Calvinist milieu, like so many people in the Netherlands, where a sharp distinction was made between body and mind: where the flesh, on the one hand, was associated with a lack of reason, with distracting and therefore negative emotions, and in its wake with abject practices called "sinful"; and where the mind or spirit, on the other hand, was associated with the promising presence of reason and rationality, the imprisonment of all kinds of irrational feelings, especially sexual and aggressive ones, and the inclination to behave as if these feelings did not exist. Though I managed to say goodbye to this rather depressing type of Protestantism, I guess that it was due to this strongly dualistic, ocular-centric and reason-oriented religious background that I later developed a keen interest in alternative ways of perceiving the relationship between body and mind, especially monistic ones. So, my temporary embrace of the materialist approach of the biogenetic structuralists was rooted in my religious background and my wish to find an alternative to the gloomy dualistic and morally loaded world-view with which I had grown up. I had had enough of the idea that the body and the mind were separate entities, that the former was inferior and the latter superior, and I started to look for scientific perspectives that emphasized a more balanced and integrated relationship, preferably a monistic one, such as that of the biogenetic structuralists. This quest, which brought home to me that there are many varieties of dualistic and monistic thinking with regard to the relationship between body and mind based on the Bible and/or the work of philosophers such as Descartes, is still in progress, as the remainder of this chapter will show. It sometimes reminds me of the quest for the Holy Grail—but this time not outside but inside our bodies.

Though it is tempting to sketch right now the nature of the doubts that I developed with regard to biogenetic viewpoints in particular, and radically monistic perspectives in general, I will first present a short section in which I will describe how such approaches, in spite of their evident flaws, inspired me to look in a different but fruitful way at certain religious phenomena by placing the whole body, and not only the brain, at center stage. Thereafter I will concentrate more or less chronologically upon the work of a specific number of scholars, both anthropologists and others, who have over the past four decades tried to tackle the body–mind problem in one way or another. Finally, I will try to make clear what I think or feel with regard to this long-standing yet unresolved issue, the possible consequences that it might have for the kind of research we engage in, especially in the field of religion, the maintenance of borders (between disciplines, for example), and the (im)possibility of adequately reporting about what we study.

Religion and the body

At the end of the 1970s, a number of biogenetic structuralists published a volume called *The Spectrum of Ritual: A Biogenetic Structural Analysis* (d'Aquili *et al.* 1979), which contained a solid article by anthropologist Barbara Lex on the neurobiological aspects of ritual trance. Like a few others at that time, such as Erika Bourguignon (1973), Lex was interested in religion and so-called altered states of consciousness (i.e. possession and trance). She had written, for example, a most intriguing essay on the phenomenon of voodoo death in which, according to her, bodily processes played a dominant role (Lex 1974). In a sense, Lex was following in the footsteps of scholars such as Neher, Needham, Jackson and Sturtevant, who in the 1960s had studied the effects of rhythmic stimulation during rituals on the functioning of the brain, or the ways in which sounds might trigger altered states of consciousness. However, Lex's approach is much more elaborate, for alongside the functioning of the central nervous system she also took into consideration that of the autonomous nervous system and how both systems through particular "driving behaviors," for example, drumming, singing, dancing, etc., might get bodily tuned in specific ways so that persons start to think, feel, and act in a totally deviant manner. What other anthropologists at the time tended to take as fact needing no further physical exploration and explanation was turned into a problem by Lex, on the basis of her conviction that the behavior of people cannot be fully understood if one ignores the role of (ir)regularities in the neurophysiological functioning of their bodies.

Fascinated by her ideas about the origins and effects of trance, I decided to find out what I might discover by doing a restudy of a spectacular religious movement in the Netherlands in the middle of the eighteenth century (Verrips 1980). This movement, which occurred between 1749 and 1752, had Nijkerk in the province of Gelderland as its epicenter, whence it seemed to have spread to other regions of the country. One of its striking features was that it started with people (especially children, women and elderly persons belonging to the lower classes) behaving as if they were the victims of serious epileptic attacks. They would seem to suffocate, breathe in strange ways, suddenly fall asleep, have spasms, tremble, fall down as if dying, and were subject to all kinds of visions. These were but a few of the physical symptoms from which they suffered, and which caused a huge disturbance in their communities. They stopped eating, cried, sang hymns, and prayed to Jesus, begging him to forgive them their sins and save their souls. Soon this mysterious malfunctioning of the body went hand-in-hand with a kind of religious revival, which was supported by several preachers in the country. They started writing pamphlets in which they interpreted the turmoil taking a religious turn as an exceptional but nevertheless fully acceptable consequence of the dawning insight that a sinner could not gain access to the kingdom of the Lord without believing in the savior Jesus Christ. Many preachers did not consider it abnormal that people should get physically upset when they realized that they might be lost forever. In order to support their viewpoint, they pointed out that people often trembled and sweated all over after receiving bad news. That this realization that if they did not accept the gospel they would go to hell should come to so many people at the same time had to be understood as one of the Lord's unfathomable acts.

Of course, Satan could not stand aside doing nothing, so he also was involved. The result was a gigantic struggle within a great many people to avoid his attacks and be saved. Who ever had heard of the knowledge of misery, salvation and thankfulness ensuing from a "dikbloedig gestel" (thick-blooded constitution) or "beroerde harsenen" (disturbed brains) as some cynics suggested? No, according to the many preachers and theologians who tried to interpret these mysterious happenings in several regions of the Netherlands, this knowledge was the immediate outflow of the Holy Spirit working on the minds of sinners and of the workings of their minds on their bodies. In fact, however, they neglected the many cases in which these physical symptoms obviously preceded rather than succeeded a heightened religious consciousness. In other words, there were and still are good grounds to seriously doubt the one-sided interpretation of contemporary preachers and theologians (as well as that of later scholars who studied the movement from a similar perspective), emphasizing the unique role of the Holy Spirit and mind disturbing the bodies of so many people, and to at least consider the possibility that they were actually suffering from a specific illness. As a matter of fact, the hypothesis that the religious upheaval might have been caused by an illness was even put forward at the time. Skeptical observers suggested, for example, that a serious disturbance of the nervous system—possibly as a consequence of having eaten spoiled meat— had functioned as a trigger for the religious effervescence.

One can imagine that I, who very much sympathized with Lex's neurophysiological approach to trance and altered states of consciousness, felt supported in my quest for an answer to the question of what kind of illness might have troubled so many people. After a careful study of all the physical symptoms reported by contemporary observers, I concluded that ergot poisoning might be a very convincing candidate.[3] An article by Williams (1923) on the *Vailala Madness* among the inhabitants of the Gulf and Purari District (former Australian New Guinea) in 1919, made me think of this possibility. Williams quotes an official who compared the spasms and bodily contortions of the people involved in this famous iconoclastic movement with the St Vitus's Dance (or chorea), later interpreted as a convulsive nervous disease caused by spurred rye (*claviceps purpurea*). Interesting in this connection is that later interpreters of the *Vailala Madness*, such as Peter Worsley, refused to take seriously the suggestion that there might be a direct relationship between the outbreak of a huge influenza epidemic in the area and the sudden upsurge of the movement shortly thereafter. In this case the significance of malfunctioning bodies for the feverish rise of a social body was swept aside in favor of an explanation in terms of native resentment at a social and political position.

This tendency not to take into consideration the biological make-up of human beings and the extremely complex neurophysiological processes taking place in their bodies, in normal or abnormal ways, when studying their mindscapes, humanscapes, and landscapes, has been dominant for decades in the social sciences. In a sense it was (and as a matter of fact still is) a consequence of the division of labor between the different disciplines within academia. When I concentrated on the biogenesis (or perhaps it is better to say the pathogenesis) of a religious movement, it was not so much my goal to solve the riddle of its occurrence by launching the hypothesis that this was exclusively due to eating fungus-infected rye bread. Rather, I desired attention to be paid to the concept that thinking, feeling, and acting are phenomena that cannot be properly understood if one neglects or even denies that they are in the first and last instance bodily-based processes. Moreover, I wanted to emphasize the necessity of at least attempting to get rid of the Cartesian heritage of leaving the study of the objective (mal)functioning body to the medical sciences and that of the subjective (mal)functioning mind to the humanities (see Strathern 1996: 5). In fact, I dreamt of the advent of a really holistic and ultimately materialistic approach to the variety of human life on planet Earth, which would put an end to the frustrating reign of the deficient and therefore unsatisfactory distinction between mind and matter. This dream has not died, but it has become much tamer and milder over time.

This change is in the first place related to the fact that more and more social scientists in the past decades have developed an interest in studying the role played by both healthy and sick bodies in (trans)forming societies and cultures, as well as in trying to elaborate new perspectives on the body–mind distinction. Reasons for this interesting trend are, for example, the upsurge of new feminisms, changing sexual patterns and the emergence of AIDS, the increasing cyborgization of humans, the decoding of our genetic makeup, gene-therapy and cloning, xeno-transplantation, new reproduction technologies, as well as the development of ever more advanced instruments to scan the body, especially the brain, and the progress in the realm of artificial intelligence.

A second reason for the taming of the dream was a slowly dawning insight that the wish to get rid of the concept of mind might mean throwing out the baby with the bathwater. I will address this later. First, however, I want briefly to sketch how other social scientists have tried to pay more attention to the importance of the body and bodily processes so as to better understand social and cultural phenomena in, for instance, the religious realm pre-eminently associated with the mind and the metaphysical.

Body–mind in anthropology

To my knowledge, Claude Lévi-Strauss was one of the first anthropologists to seek to relate body and mind in a way that foreshadowed the manner in which certain anthropologists are currently trying to connect them: that is, by taking into consideration what is going on at the deep level of the central and autonomous nervous system. In the thought-provoking article I referred to earlier, on the shamanistic cure of a sick woman by a Cuna Indian (Panama), he not only argues that this cure can be compared with a psycho-analytic session, but also that, just like such a session, it might stimulate

> an organic transformation which would consist essentially in a structural reorganization, by inducing the patient intensively to live out a myth—either received or created by him—whose structure would be, at the unconscious level, analogous to the structure whose genesis is sought at the organic level.
>
> ([1949] 1967: 197)

What Lévi-Strauss tried to make clear is that a pre-eminently symbolic phenomenon such as a myth, here presented to a patient by a shaman, (probably) has an "… 'inductive property,' by which formally homologous structures, built out of different materials at different levels of life—organic processes, unconscious mind, rational thought— are related to one another" (ibid.). He got the inspiration for this idea about the possible effectiveness of particular symbolic constellations at a physiological (even biochemical) level from Freud, who suggested that one day neuroses and psychoses might no longer be understood in psychological terms, as well as from research done by neuroscientists in Sweden. What I found and still find striking is the fact that Lévi-Strauss apparently had no problems whatsoever in moving between the different levels that many scholars (both social scientists and philosophers)—afraid of unacceptable reductionism—want(ed) to keep as separate fields of research.

More than twenty years later, Lévi-Strauss wrote a kind of sequel to the article published in 1949: "Structuralism and Ecology." In this piece he explicitly stated that structuralists wanted to reunite perspectives that due to "the narrow scientific outlook of the last centuries" had been considered to be mutually exclusive. To judge from the following excerpt, alongside Hegel, it was Descartes whom he had in mind (*excusez le mot*) as responsible for this outlook:

> [S]tructuralism recovers and brings up to awareness deeper truths that are already latent in the body itself. By reconciling soul and body, mind and ecology, thought and the world, structuralism tends toward the only kind of materialism consistent with the ways in which science is developing. Nothing could be farther from Hegel; and even Descartes, whose dualism we try to overcome while keeping in line with his rationalist faith.
>
> (1973: 23)

Though Lévi-Strauss here explicitly expressed the wish to overcome "dualism," one cannot but conclude that his terminology remained dualistic in the sense that he kept reasoning in terms of a mind–body dichotomy (not only in this article but also in other publications). For, on the one hand, he uses such terms as "mind," "soul," "mental constraints," "mental laws," "thought," "intellect," "perception," "inner logic," "intelligibility," and, on the other, "body," "brains," "senses," "sensibility," "nervous system," "anatomy," "physiology" and "natural foundations" (both of our thinking and perception as well as of the "world," "ecology" or "reality"). So, the kind of language game with which he confronted his readers did not excel in clarity, especially given his failure to define the concepts presented. His use of so many concepts without specification illustrates how difficult it is for anyone interested in integrating levels that have for such a long time been studied separately by different disciplines to express oneself properly. I will return to this issue in the final section.

However, Lévi-Strauss's rather imprecise language use did not diminish my sympathy for his fundamental message. He posits that two determinisms exist: (1) the determinism of the "mind" that structures everything that it receives through both the perceiving senses and the recording "brains," and (2) the determinism of the "environment," "ecology" or more precisely "techno-economical activities" and "socio-political conditions." In other words, Lévi-Strauss is interested in the two-way process between what goes on within the body and what surrounds it. According to him, it concerns a *collusion* that is based on the outside and the inside being structured in a similar way and therefore structuring in a similar way too. In his own words:

> [N]ature appears more and more made up of structural properties undoubtedly richer although not different in kind from the structural codes into which *the nervous system* translates them, and from the structural properties elaborated by *the understanding* in order to go back, as much as it can do so, to the original structures of *reality*. It is not being mentalist or idealist to acknowledge that *the mind* is only able to understand *the world around us* because *the mind* is itself part and product of this same *world*. Therefore *the mind* in trying to understand it, only applies operations which do not differ in kind from those going on in *the natural world* itself.
>
> (ibid.: 22, my italics)

I think that it is important to stress that the collusion between inside and outside has not so much to do with content, but rather with the "fact" that both operate according to the same formal properties. The content, or what exactly enters the mind/body, is embodied, and is retrieved when necessary, differs in terms of context and time. It is exactly this idea that formed the starting point for Lévi-Strauss's gigantic intellectual odyssey through the myths of the South and North American indigenous populations and that enabled him to discover their underlying (binary) logic, a logic that he saw grounded in specific properties of both the body or human nature and the nature with which it is surrounded. That is why structural analysis is not a kind of "gratuitous and decadent game," for it "can only appear in the mind because its model is already present in the body" (Lévi-Strauss 1981: 692). Moreover, it brings to the one who practices it sensations of immense fulfillment "through making the mind feel itself to be truly in communion with the body" (ibid.). Thus, a structural analysis as envisaged by Lévi-Strauss not only reveals in the last instance "profound organic truths," but also generates, in so doing, a series of most agreeable bodily experiences.

I find these observations interesting for two reasons. In the first place, because they show that the concept of mind as used by Lévi-Strauss is just a designation for the potential of the body to generate and process what one calls knowledge about, for example, itself and the world of which it is a part, what to think and feel about these entities as well as about how to behave towards them. It is not a ghost in a machine, but a not-yet-decoded powerful and crucial facet of specific physiological and biochemical processes which we call "mind" and about which we reason, for the time being, in psychological terms and as if it were something ethereal. In the second place, I deem Lévi-Strauss's observations with regard to the sensation of unity of mind and body when he engaged in structural analyses very interesting, for they remind me of what some scholars have said about religious sensations, namely that they temporarily erase the distinction or gap between subject and object, in this case not so much between mind and body, as between self and world.[4]

To conclude my short exposé on the thoughts of the godfather of structuralism, I want to stress the fact that he developed a perspective on the relation between body and mind that implied no clear-cut distinction, but rather their complete integration at a physical level. Moreover, I want to underline that he, contrary to popular belief, took the body and especially what goes on within it more seriously than many anthropologists and sociologist who also placed the body on center stage.[5]

A case in point is Bourdieu. Bourdieu was interested in the question of how "systems of objective relations" or the "observed order" are produced, and therefore designed "the theory of the mode of generation of practices" to enable him to study "the *dialectic of the internalization of externality and the externalization of internality,* or, more simply, of incorporation and objectification" ([1972] 1977: 72). As part of this theory, he launched the notion of *habitus,* i.e. "systems of durable, transposable *dispositions,*" that were the result of the internalization, incorporation or embodiment of external social structures. Though the body figures large in Bourdieu's work —for it is with the body that people read the "book" from which they learn their vision of the world, to use his own metaphor—it contains no passages in which he tries, as Lévi-Strauss did, to include knowledge about the (mal)functioning body at organic levels. One looks in vain for sections dealing with how the physical body is (un)able to incorporate externality first and to externalize it later. That is all taken for granted by Bourdieu.

Significant in this connection is a footnote in his famous book *Outline of a Theory of Practice* in which he (ibid.: 202–03) contrasts his own position in a succinct but revealing way with that of Lévi-Strauss. The latter is, in Bourdieu's view, not the kind of radical materialist one might think, for his philosophy of mind (claiming that it is a functioning *thing* with an architecture in which images of the world are inscribed) turns out to be nothing other than a kind of idealism stressing the universality of logical categories. The crucial difference between him and Lévi-Strauss, so he states, consists of the fact that he is interested in the dialectic relation between the embodied "structured, structuring dispositions," or the habitus, and social structures, whereas Lévi-Strauss ignores this, because he is focused on "establishing a direct, unmediated identity between mind and nature" and therefore neglects "everything covered by the concept of habitus." Schemes of thought and logical categories are not universal, for they correspond to the social world and not to the natural world.

What I find striking is the emphasis in Bourdieu's sketch on differences between his outlook and that of Lévi-Strauss's, and the lack of any effort to look for possibilities to expand his theory by integrating certain elements from Lévi-Strauss. One reason to do this would be the fact that both scholars were heavily influenced by the ideas of Durkheim and Mauss on the origin of classifications and the role of the social and physical body. Where Lévi-Strauss became interested in the formal operations of the mind, brain or minded body without which the disturbing socio-cultural variety in the world might never be properly understood, Bourdieu instead concentrated on the ways in which the interplay between bodies and different social structures resulted in different kinds of habitus (and thought schemes). Both scholars placed the body center stage, but with one fundamental difference: Lévi-Strauss included its physical functioning in his studies and tried to relate mind with matter, while Bourdieu excluded this biological dimension and did not bother much with matter and mind. To formulate it in a somewhat exaggerated way: whereas the former tried to build bridges between the language games of different disciplines, the latter developed no serious efforts in that direction. This is a pity, for it might have led to a more encompassing theory of practice.[6] In a certain way, one is left in the case of Bourdieu with the somewhat uncomfortable idea of a socially-molded body that molds in its turn without having the slightest notion of how the body as a physical entity influences, directs, or limits this double molding process. In this respect he missed a chance to supplement his theory with certain elements from that of his counterpart, for instance, the idea that the physical body (also) seems to structure what it embodies: that is, the social structure.

However, this criticism does not mean that I do not appreciate Bourdieu's ideas about embodiment and habitus. On the contrary, they have a great heuristic value, not least for scholars with an interest in religious ideas and practices, for these ideas and practices get embodied, anchored in the flesh in such a way that one sometimes can recognize certain believers (such as staunch Calvinists or orthodox Muslims) from a distance and make prognoses about their behavior in all kinds of contexts. Their bodily tuning, for instance, in a kinetic and proxemic sense, represents, so to say, a specific Gestalt that can trigger implicit knowledge and feelings—both negative and positive—about less visible forms of such a tuning, for example, of their emotional make-up and ways of thinking, even of the nature of their sensorium. The wide variety of condensations of spiritual matters in the body and the manner in which they might function as beacons for others in society form an almost inexhaustible field of research. That, however, is another point.

Both Lévi-Strauss and Bourdieu have inspired many social scientists to pay more attention to the role of the body and its relation to what we call mind in socio-cultural settings.[7] Together with others, the former, for example, gave the impetus to the rise of biogenetic structuralism that once fascinated me so much, whereas the latter stimulated several sociologists and anthropologists to elaborate his ideas of embodiment and habitus. Csordas (1990), for instance, wrote an influential article in which he presented embodiment as a paradigm for anthropology. Alongside Bourdieu's theory of practice, Merleau-Ponty's theory on perception formed his source of inspiration in developing this paradigm. According to Csordas, the former had been successful in letting collapse the duality between structure and practice, and the latter that between subject and object, by invoking embodiment as a "methodological principle." This collapsing, so he states, "requires that the body as a methodological figure must itself be nondualistic, that is, not distinct from or in interaction with an opposed principle of mind." Merleau-Ponty solved this problem by seeing the *body* as "a setting in relation to the world" and *consciousness* as "the body projecting itself in the world," whereas Bourdieu solved it by seeing the (socially informed) *body* as the "principle generating and unifying all practices" and *consciousness* as "a form of strategic calculation fused with a system of objective potentialities." The former summarized this collapse of body and mind in the concept of *preobjective* and the latter in that of the *habitus*. Though both scholars shared the paradigm of embodiment, they articulated their positions "in the methodologically incompatible discourse of phenomenology and ... dialectical structuralism," according to Csordas, whereupon he starts with the *tour de force* of developing "a nondualistic paradigm of embodiment for the study of culture," making use of the two concepts mentioned in analyzing "the empirical domains of religious experience and practice" (Csordas 1990: 8–13).

However, contrary to the expectations raised, his article does not end with the presentation of a convincing nondualistic paradigm. Csordas' text raises serious doubts as to whether he has actually solved the Cartesian split. First, because Csordas seems to overlook the fact that his source of inspiration Bourdieu, in just being silent about the mind when writing about embodiment and habitus, only creates the impression that the mind disappeared in or merged with the body (or the habitus), where, on closer inspection, it does not. In fact, the mind emerges in such expressions as "schemes of thought." It is further revealing that the index of Bourdieu's book does not contain an entry "mind" and that the already mentioned footnote which I addressed above can be read in such a way that one might even think that "mind" is the equivalent of either "the social structures" or the "structured, structuring dispositions" (alias, the habitus).[8] In the second place Csordas' claim is debatable because he frequently uses expressions that immediately remind one of the split: of the mind *and* the body.

Though he emphasizes the relevance of the body and embodiment, the body he writes about is certainly not the material, biological body, but just a peculiar mixture of a philosophically conceived and a socially informed body. His interest in the material body is limited to a series of visible and audible corporeal expressions and does not include the deep structures and processes that make these expressions possible. For he explicitly states that physiological explanations of, for example, glossolalia, in terms of trance or altered states of consciousness do not take us very far, if we want to understand these bodily states "as *modus operandi* for the work of culture" (ibid: 32). However, the fact that without physiological processes this work of culture would not be possible at all seems a logical reason not to set them aside so easily. Moreover, their genesis is often triggered by cultural means (e.g. culturally specific driving behaviors or manipulations of the sensorium, such as the production of certain types of sounds and rhythms that tune the body) and with the explicit intention of losing oneself for a while in a world in which normal feeling, thinking, and acting are replaced by something different. A kind of temporary ritual rebellion against "what thought has made of life" (Lévi-Strauss 1981: 681).

Though I am impressed by Csordas' effort to launch embodiment as a paradigm for anthropology (why not for other social sciences?), I regret his putting the physical body between brackets. I therefore doubt his claim of succeeding in collapsing the duality of body and mind—at least in the sense of Descartes' *res extensa* (material body) and *res cogitans* (immaterial soul, mind)[9]—by introducing the concepts preobjective and habitus. We are left with the riddle of the role of the physical body in packing and unpacking all kinds of so-called cultural stuff at the deep level of physiological and biochemical structures and processes. One might even say that Csordas' denial of the relevance of these processes and structures for a better understanding of cultural phenomena is just another "proof" of the fact that this packing and unpacking is of a binary nature, as Lévi-Strauss suggested. We seem each and every time to be the victims of the dualist tricks of our physical body, for if we replace a dualism for a monism we are left with a new dualism: in Csordas' case with *physical body: bodymind*.[10]

A splendid illustration of this new type of dualism in anthropological circles is, for instance, presented by Michael Lambek in his illuminating article: "Body and mind in mind, body and mind in body: some anthropological interventions in a long conversation" (1998). He makes it clear that the Cartesian split remains, if one reasons from the perspective of the mind about the relationship between body and mind, but that it collapses if one starts reasoning from the body with regard to this relationship, for there is then a sort of "split unity," that is, a mindful body or bodymind. This view is very much inspired by Csordas' ideas about embodiment, thus indirectly by Merleau-Ponty's notion of the preobjective and Bourdieu's habitus concept. Lambek illustrates the usefulness of Csordas' paradigm with a case history on the possession of one of his informants, Ali, who switches from Ali to The Sailor and behaves during his possession by this demon according to his habitus. Like Csordas, Lambek also neglects in the analysis of this case the physical manipulation or specific tuning of the body as an effect of heavy smoking and drinking. He also ends up with a culturalist view on the in- and ex-corporation of a specific model of performance during a possession session. No attempt is made to consider the riddle of how the physical body makes this temporary transformation in identity possible. It is just assumed that the body (or better: the mindful body) is able to do such things: that is, retrieve stored information and store it again in its dark crevices until it is retrieved again. The body is nothing less and nothing more than a molded–molding instrument (agent or even actor) producing culture, whose constantly transforming make-up is left as an object for study to other disciplines, such as the neurosciences. Though I can understand this attitude, which rests on a deep fear of being accused of unacceptable reductionism, I consider this to be a pity, for it means that one robs oneself of an opportunity to include previously neglected facets of human feeling, thinking, and acting.

Over the past two decades ever more social scientists have developed an interest in the inner workings of the body, more especially of the brain, and have wondered how the insights of neuroscientists can be integrated into their discourses on social and cultural phenomena. After the rise of the sick body, the socially informed body, the temporarily differently tuned body, the nonverbal or proxemic and kinesthetic body, the sensorial body and the tattooed body as fields of interest, it now seems to be the turn of the neurobiological body to appear in the universe of social scientific discourse.

After the pioneering efforts of scholars such as Lévi-Strauss, Laughlin, d'Aquili, Lex, and Hufford to direct attention to this kind of body, it now enjoys a rapidly increasing popularity among anthropologists (see Reyna 2002) and sociologists (see Watson 1998),[11] not least among those with an interest in religion.[12] It may be that this remarkable trend has something to do with the fact that neuroscientists conduct research on the effects of drugs (both legal and illegal) and physical damage on the (mal)functioning of the body, especially of the brain, and every now and then engage in seeking materialistic explanations for so-called spiritual phenomena such as Out of Body and Near Death Experiences.[13] However, what is more important is the question of what kind of enriching insights this heightened attention for the neurobiological body has brought us so far, for instance, with regard to the process of embodiment of cultural phenomena or the good old Cartesian split. In the first place, it has led to a lot of debates between "believers" in a neurobiological turn of the social sciences and "skeptics."

A good example of such a debate is that between Edward Slingerland, on the one hand, and Francisca Cho and Richard K. Squier, on the other, in the *Journal of the American Academy of Religion* (2008, 76[2]: 375–457).[14] The former is of the opinion, that "the mind is the body, and the body is permeated through-and-through with mind" and that "consciousness, under this understanding, is not a mysterious substance distinct from matter, but rather an emergent property of matter put together in a sufficiently complicated way" (Slingerland 2008a: 378). He criticizes social constructivism, because it accepts "human-level structures of meaning … as possessing ontological status," instead of conceiving them as "grounded in the lower levels of meaning studied by the natural sciences" (ibid.). For this reason, he defends "a vertically integrated approach" or reductionism and a return to Darwinism. Thirty years ago the biogenetic structuralists aired similar views, but Slingerland does not refer to their work. Cho and Squier agree with Slingerland that it can be useful to apply the tools of cognitive science to, for instance, religious phenomena and that human beings can be seen as integrated mind–body systems, but they have great difficulty in accepting the idea that physical reductionism and/or the philosophical assumption that the world consists of nothing but matter. They point out that the language of many scientists including that of Slingerland often suffers from vagueness and lack of content and that the idea that we are nothing but matter is "irrelevant, at best, or an *a priori* justification for killing people, at worst" (Cho and Squier 2008a: 413).

The linguistic critique of Cho and Squier shows a great family resemblance to that of neuroscientist Bennett and philosopher Hacker on the language use of modern brain neuroscientists (as well as that of many psychologists and cognitive scientists). According to Bennett and Hacker, the members of the first two generations were still working in a Cartesian tradition distinguishing a body and a mind and ascribing psychological attributes to the mind, but the members of the third ascribed these attributes to (parts of) the brain (Bennett *et al.* 2007: 15). This third generation is fond of showing via neuro-imaging and related techniques, how specific cells of the brain "do things," "interpret," "interact," etc., as if they were conscious little human beings. In their discourse, the cells have taken the place of the homunculus once invoked to make clear what went on in our brains. Bennett and Hacker argue that this ascription of psychological properties to the brain is senseless, for in their Wittgensteinian vision only human beings as a whole, and not their parts, can feel, think and (inter)act. Anyone who does not understand that *"The brain is not a logically appropriate subject for psychological predicates,"* is falling prey to "the mereological fallacy," that is, the tendency to ascribe attributes to parts that only are valid for a whole, and is therefore producing strictly speaking … nonsense (ibid.: 21ff.).

Though I find the radical critique of scholars such as Cho, Squier, Bennett and Hacker interesting, it does not convince me in several respects. Let me briefly touch on one point: that is, the fact that we will never be able to escape from the insufficiency of our language to designate exactly our experiences of and insights into ourselves and the world that surrounds us. In the meantime, we can only try to find less inadequate or more precise words and sentences to describe and analyze them. In this respect, social scientists with an interest in incorporating the knowledge of the neurosciences find themselves faced with the problem of how to integrate the often imperfect language in which this knowledge is phrased into their own imperfect language games or discourses.[15] However, the fact that such an endeavor is an inherently risky and tricky one and may lead to inadequacies should not prevent us from at least engaging in it. Otherwise we will miss a chance to develop a more complete view on how socially (in)formed bodies function in both negative and positive ways as parts of the social bodies to which they belong. In this respect I fully agree with Watson's advice addressed to sociologists, "that they will need to understand, at a general level, how culture comes to inhabit a biological organism" (1998: 24).

So much for the debates and my view on the sides taken. What about the Cartesian split? Where are we with regard to this old and fundamental problem since the advance of the cognitive and neurosciences? Is it gone, as I once wished and Csordas seems to claim, or is it still alive and kicking? If one looks at the terminology deployed, such as the mindful body, and the language used by scholars with different disciplinary backgrounds propagating materialist perspectives, one cannot but conclude that the split is still with us. It is there, however, in a changed sense, for the mind is by many of them no longer perceived as a kind of immaterial property of a living body, but under the influence of technologically very advanced neurological research, especially of the brain, as solidly grounded in the physical body of human beings. The word "mind," has, in other words, become a term that refers to not yet decoded, extremely complex material processes in our bodies that regulate the transformation of physiological and biochemical events, in, for example, our brain, into thoughts, memories, stereo-metrical images and language and vice versa. It has become a term that is not yet fragmented into components of the material complexities to which it refers, but that will not disappear because we need it in order to denote the chain of processes as a whole. In order to convey a somewhat clearer idea of what kind of processes I am hinting at, the best comparison I can make is to the inextricable relationship between invisible binary digits and visible images. So I end up maintaining the concept of mind because I realize that we need it to speak of those not-yet-deciphered intricate material processes responsible for our consciousness of ourselves and the world in which we live. It now even seems silly to me that I once wanted to get rid of the concept because I felt that it referred to something immaterial, metaphysical, and even of divine origin. Doing away with the mind would have robbed me of the possibility of denoting the awe-inspiring, complex material processes that were foreshadowed in the immaterial meaning of the concept so familiar to us, and that perhaps at some future point will be decoded.

Religion and belief

Having made clear my view with regard to the mind–body problem, I want to sketch briefly what this might imply for the study of religion from a more materialistic perspective. My main point is that the great interest of social scientists in the body so far has not led to many serious efforts to include the physical body in their perspectives. In fact, the physical body is generally speaking still put between brackets by them: mostly out of fear of falling into a reductionist trap, which might eventually mean the disappearance of the identity of their discipline. If one reads their work, one is struck by the fact that they stop short just where the real challenge begins: that is, in understanding more of the physical embodiment process, the ways in which the dispositions one talks about become anchored in the flesh and what that might mean for their malleability, transformability, and durability over time. Everybody acknowledges the fact that the deterioration of the physical bodies of elderly people can lead to serious disturbances in their ways of thinking, feeling, and acting, in short to an increasingly messy socially informed body with increasingly messy behavior in its wake. However, as long as deterioration processes do not explicitly manifest themselves in these fields, the physical functioning of socially (in)formed bodies is overlooked as irrelevant for social and cultural behavior. What can come into focus, if one follows my view, is that certain types and manifestations of so-called social and cultural behavior, for example, when they significantly deviate from those which people have learned to in-corporate, might trigger serious disturbances at a physical level in socially (in)formed bodies to such a degree that their owners become unreasonably intolerant, even outspokenly aggressive and violent on the rebound.

This can be observed in *optima forma* in the sphere of religion and belief, phenomena associated as almost no others with the world of the immaterial, metaphysical, and the divine or the mind, the soul and the sacred. I think that this kind of lopsided classification and evaluation of religion and belief at the side of an immaterially conceived mind, at least in the Western world, is one of the big mistakes of our time. It would also be better to perceive religion and belief as physically embodied phenomena and the sometimes very violent reactions to confrontations with deviant representations of dogmas and imagery as efforts both to defend bodily grounded metaphysical truths and, in doing so, to maintain a socially informed physical integrity of self and society. That belief is firmly ingrained in the body (or the mind understood in a material sense) comes in a telling way to the fore in the case of blasphemy, when offended people talk in terms of feeling ill or being hurt in such a way that they have to vomit. When they use such expressions this is not just metaphorical language, but language that hints at fundamental experiences in the flesh as a consequence of being touched by, for instance, imagery outside the body that is entirely in opposition to imagery stored inside their bodies (see Verrips 2008). If we want, for example, to develop more encompassing insights into the physical background of this kind of language use by believers as well as that of mystics trying to express their often very physical experiences with divine entities, we need to cross the borders between disciplines. Then it is necessary to retune ourselves or to "exorcize" from our bodies the idea that consulting the work of scientists who try to solve the riddles of the mind and body in a materialist fashion cannot be relevant for social scientists and will eventually lead to a misplaced use of their technical language and unacceptable forms of reductionism. Neither needs to be the case, if we remain critical with regard to both. In this respect I fully agree with Ozawa-de Silva, who wrote: "If one shifts the boundaries and expands the conceptual possibilities, ... the nature of the field itself changes, not necessarily to deconstruct its very real achievements, but to show other and fresh directions beyond those so far pioneered" (2002: 37).

Notes

1   Though Mauss emphasized the necessity of the socio-psycho-biological study of certain phenomena, such as the techniques of breathing in generating mystical states, he himself never made such a study (see Lyon 1997: 90/91). For further discussion of his essay, see chapter 1 in Lyon (1997).
2   In their later publications the biogenetic structuralists even developed an outspokenly negative attitude towards Lévi-Strauss's work, because they saw him

as a representative of "semiotic structuralism," which was considered to be "essentially dualistic" and denying "the role of action (associated, of course, with the body and the physical) in the ontogenesis of structures" (Laughlin *et al.* 1993: 161). If they had read his work better, they might not have written this, as Lévi-Strauss provides much evidence that he takes the physical body very seriously.

3   This approach shows a great family resemblance to the experience-centered study of supernatural assault traditions in North America by Hufford (1982).

4   Noteworthy in this connection is Lévi-Strauss's perspective on the relationship between thought and ritual. Whereas thought "creates an ever-increasing gap between the intellect and life ... ritual is ... a reaction to what thought has made of life," a way back to reality (1981: 681). Against this background one might say that carrying out a structural analysis was for him as much an intellectual as a ritual activity.

5   I need to emphasize here that Lévi-Strauss's attention is focused almost exclusively on the mind or the brain as an instrument of reasoning; he does not pay much attention to the role and influence of emotions in co-shaping the thought and life of human beings as do some contemporary philosophers (see Nussbaum 2001).

6   By his efforts to occasionally cross the boundaries of language games, Lévi-Strauss showed that he was not afraid of a careful kind of reductionism, whereas Bourdieu seemed to shun such efforts (see Bourdieu [1972] 1977: 120), which is why he remained in a certain sense the prisoner of what neuro-philosoper Churchland has called "folk psychology" (1986: 299).

7   See, for overviews of the diverse range of studies of the body that sprang up in the social sciences in the twentieth century, Synnott (1993: Ch 9) and Strathern (1996).

8   He writes: "the dialectic of the social structures and structured, structuring dispositions – or, in a more eighteenth-century language, of mind and nature" ([1972] 1977: 202).

9   See Descartes ([1649] 1996) for a succinct overview of the distinction between body ("corps") and mind ("l'âme"), their different functions ("fonctions") and the manner in which they act on each other ("Comment l'âme et le corps agissent l'un contre l'autre").

10   See for a similar kind of critique, Strathern (1996: 177–86). Though Strathern devotes much attention to scholars who seriously tried to take the physical body more seriously, such as Ernest Rossi and Mark Johnson, he also ends up with a rather empty body as far as its internal functioning is concerned.

11   See Fabrega (1977) for an overview of early work on the relation between culture, behavior and the nervous system. "*ZYGON Journal of Religion and Science*" is an important platform for articles on the neuro-scientific study of religious and spiritual phenomena.

12   See, e.g., the œuvre of Harvey Whitehouse.

13   However, see McCauley and Whitehouse (2005) who suggest that it was due to calls from anthropologists and others that neuroscientists developed an interest in studying religious phenomena.

14   The correspondence in the order it occurred is as shown below:

Slingerland, Edward (2008a) "Who's Afraid of Reductionism? The Study of Religion in the Age of Cognitive Science," *Journal of the American Academy of Religion* 76(2): 375–412.

Cho Francisca, and Richard K. Squier (2008a) "Reductionism: Be Afraid, Be Very Afraid," *Journal of the American Academy of Religion* 76(2): 412–18.

Slingerland, Edward (2008b) "Reply to Cho and Squier," *Journal of the American Academy of Religion* 76(2): 418–20.

Cho, Francisca, and Richard K. Squier (2008b) 'He Blinded Me with Science': Science Chauvinism in the Study of Religion," *Journal of the American Academy of Religion* 76(2): 420–49.

Slingerland, Edward (2008c) "Response to Cho and Squier," *Journal of the American Academy of Religion* 76(2): 449–55.

Cho, Francisca, and Richard K. Squier (2008c) "Reply to Slingerland," *Journal of the American Academy of Religion* 76(2): 455–57.

15 See Lévi-Strauss (1971: 642/43) for an interesting view on the relation between the natural and physical sciences, on the one hand, and the social sciences, on the other, concerning their different dependency on symbols in their "apprehension of reality."

2

Object theory
Toward an intersubjective, mediated, and dynamic theory of religion

Gordon Lynch

The relational nature of personhood
The sacred object
Sacred objects, sacred subjects?
Between heaven and earth

In the Introduction to this book, David Morgan proposes an understanding of belief as "a shared imaginary, a communal set of practices that structure life in powerfully aesthetic terms" and as "a pervasive community of feeling" (p. 7). Morgan's challenge to the preoccupation with narrowly confessional and propositional understandings of 'belief' in the study of religion reflects an established critique of such notions of belief within anthropology (see, e.g., Lindquist and Coleman 2008). But in my own discipline of the sociology of religion, such narrow conceptions of belief persist both in terms of the emphasis on survey data measuring respondents' attitudes to creedal statements (see, e.g., Voas and Crockett 2005), and the use of interviews to try to elicit the core beliefs and spirituality of those within and beyond institutional religion (see, e.g., Hunt 2003; Smith and Denton 2005). The persistence of such propositional understandings of belief—even in the face of evidence that they make little sense to research respondents (see, e.g., Smith and Denton 2005: 131)—makes David Morgan's grounding of belief in socially shared practices and aesthetic regimes a welcome corrective. For those involved in the sociological study of religion, this current volume offers important concepts and methods for taking seriously the significance of embodiment, aesthetics, space, practice, and materiality for religious belief. This has the potential of helping us to build much richer accounts of religious and secular subjectivity than accounts of religious meaning-making based on the personal creeds that research participants are able (or often not able) to narrate to us. Morgan's concept of belief as a "pervasive community of feeling" generated through the sedimentation of practices through time can also be usefully linked to other concepts in social and cultural theory such as Raymond Williams' view of culture as a "structure of feeling" (Williams and Orrom 1954), Pierre Bourdieu's (1984) concept of "habitus" and Anthony Giddens' (1984) theory of the recursive reproduction of social structures. Engaging with these wider theories can generate further conceptual tools for thinking about how modes of belief are contested and change through time, the relationship between belief, social distinctions and social capital, and the relationship between agency, practice, and structure.

There are also important questions still to explore in relation to Morgan's understanding of belief. Thinking about belief as emerging out of sedimented material, social and aesthetic practices does not account for forms of belief which are disconnected from any practical religious life. Abby Day's (in press) qualitative study of belief among people in northern towns in the UK has provided evidence of respondents who claimed to believe in Christianity, while not adhering to orthodox Christian beliefs or engaging in any form of ritual Christian practice. In this context, professions of Christian belief were a particular kind of identity-work, connected to wider assumptions about what it meant to be white, morally decent or part of a particular family tradition. In the complex circulation of ideas about religion in contemporary culture, "belief" can therefore become detached from the practices and aesthetic regimes of particular religious communities, and become a tool for constructing a particular kind of identity. Such uses of religious belief are still grounded in a particular embodied and situated life-world—for example, the experience of growing up as a white teenager in a former mill town in which there is a large, segregated Muslim population. But these life-worlds may involve little, and often no, contact with what we would conventionally think of as religious communities and practices. We may therefore need to remain open to alternative forms of belief to those identified in Morgan's framework.

Regardless of this minor qualification, Morgan's theory of belief represents a valuable approach for making sense of the formation and performance of religious subjectivities across a range of historical and cultural contexts. This chapter builds on his model by paying particular attention to the role of embodied, mediated, and dynamic relationships with sacred others (gods, spirits, saints) in the practice of religious belief. More specifically, I want to examine how concepts drawn from psychoanalytic theory might help us to take these relationships more seriously as social and cultural phenomena, in ways that help us to make connections between the psychological worlds of individual religious adherents, their social, material and cultural context, and the sacred others with whom they relate. Before exploring these ideas in more depth, though, it will be useful to think briefly about the failure to take seriously this relational dimension of religion within the sociology of religion.

The relational nature of personhood

The unquestioned status of propositional models of belief within the sociology of religion arguably reflects a lack of theoretical discussion within this field about the nature of the person as a social agent. A common default position is to emphasize the autonomous, reflexive individuals striving to construct their own religious belief-system and lifestyle which becomes the center for their way of acting in the world (see Berger 1967; Luckmann 1967; Wuthnow 1998; Roof 1999; Hoover 2003; see also Giddens 1991). From this perspective, the autonomous, reflexive self is an expression of particular structures and processes in late modernity, which include the effects of cultural pluralism in promoting awareness of choice, the possibilities presented by the expansion of higher education and media and the emergence of a lifestyle, consumer culture. Yet at the same time, a slippage can occur within these discourses of the autonomous, reflexive "spiritual consumer" in which it is implied that this form of selfhood is such an inevitable and universal consequence of the all-pervasive effects of late modernity that it becomes the ontological condition of the contemporary self. The observation that, under certain quite specific historical and cultural conditions, some people find themselves needing to make reflexive choices about the meaning and structure of their lives shifts to the Sartrean existential claim that we are all condemned to freedom and choice.

The ontological claim that we exist as autonomous individual selves, acting out of the meaning-systems that we reflexively construct, fails to do justice to significant aspects of our personhood. An emphasis on individuality fails to recognize the ways in which our lives are embedded and negotiated through networks of relationships with family, partners, colleagues and friends, as well as through face-to-face, mediated or imagined relations with other communities and groups. The exercise of choice—removed from the commitments, emotions, memories, possibilities, aspirations and constraints associated with these relationships—is a rare phenomenon. We are—quite literally, in developmental terms—relational beings before being autonomous, and whatever autonomy we experience in our lives is always nested within our relationships. Similarly, the idea that we act as social agents from the center of our belief-systems fails to do justice to the more complex motive-forces that shape the conduct of our everyday lives. These include the unconscious, desire, habit, the logics of local practices (i.e. our practical consciousness of how to act in specific contexts), our need to maintain acceptable performances of self-presentation, cultural norms, and the ways in which our material environment shapes our imaginations and actions. "Belief"—in the sense of propositional beliefs about the meaning of life—may therefore play little role in the practical conduct of our lives from when we get up in the morning until we go to bed at night. Claims about the ontological status of the autonomous, reflexive self may be powerfully buttressed by neo-liberal discourses that valorize individual choice in political, economic, and social life, by legal structures protecting individual human rights, and by longer movements and traditions that have generated the subjective turn in cultural life.[1] But these larger ideological, cultural and political movements represent interventions in the broader normative question of what kind of society and culture we should seek to build rather than necessarily providing adequate descriptive models of how we practically live as social agents. Relational models of the self that provide richer accounts of the nature and basis of human agency beyond notions of individual reflexivity and autonomy are therefore needed if we are to understand more clearly the nature of lived religion.

The sacred object

The theory of relations with sacred others that I will explore here forms part of this project of trying to develop a richer understanding of the significance of subjectivity and relationship in lived religion. My starting point with this is the idea that some forms of religious belief entail faithful interaction with, or in relation to, sacred objects. This idea involves a dual understanding of the meaning of "object". The sacred object is, on one hand, an object in a material sense, encountered by the adherent through processes of social and aesthetic mediation. As Birgit Meyer (2006: 15–16) puts it, "Mediation objectifies a spiritual power that is otherwise invisible to the naked eye ... thereby making its appearance via a particular sensational form dependent on currently available media and modes of representation." Without such everyday mediation of the sacred through material and sensory forms, sacred objects experience a social and cultural death like the old gods who formerly inhabited the Pantheon in Rome. At the same time, the sacred object is also an object in a psychological sense, more specifically as understood within psychoanalytic object relations theory. This is to say that a sacred object is a dynamic focus for subjective associations and feelings in the mental world of the religious adherent and that the relationship with the sacred object can affect the psychological structures and feeling-states of the adherent. The chapters in this volume already give considerable attention to the material forms of the sacred object, and so I will focus more here on the psychological understanding of the sacred object, as well as saying something about how the psychological and material connect.

To think of the sacred object in terms of object relations theory opens up both significant possibilities as well as complexities for our theorizing of lived religion. Object relations theory—or more accurately, object relations theories—have played an increasingly central role in psychoanalytic theory and clinical practice in recent decades, marking a shift away from classical Freudian drive theory towards a focus on the psychological significance of our experiences of inter-personal relationships. The diversity of theoretical approaches within the object relations school, however, means that the concept of the "object" can have different meanings in the work of different theorists. These concepts also function within wider theoretical narratives which offer sometimes different, sometimes overlapping, accounts of the process of psychological development in early childhood and the significance of such early processes for later adult functioning. Given this complexity, it is unrealistic to imagine that an object relations perspective on the sacred object is easily defined at present. While there has been a growing literature exploring religious belief and experience from an object relations perspective, much of this provides a somewhat problematic basis for any approach to the study of lived religion which takes seriously historical processes of social and cultural mediation (as we shall explore shortly). This means that a more developed object relations framework for theorizing sacred objects may well need to go beyond those writers who have undertaken more explicit and detailed work on object relations and religion, to examine the work of other object relations theorists whose attention to religion is less well developed. The contribution of object relations theory to the sociological and cultural study of religion therefore requires much further clarification, and the following observations are intended as preliminary markers for this project.

Within object relations perspectives on sacred objects, a broad distinction may be made between approaches that understand the sacred object as a transferential phenomenon and those which think about the sacred object as a transitional phenomenon. Transferential theories of sacred objects interpret such objects in the context of broader patterns and structures of transference that individuals demonstrate in their relations with others and which they have learned through their early experiences with care-givers. For example, James Jones (1991) argues that the way in which individuals experience their relationship with God reflects patterns of transference deriving from early childhood, which will also be evident in their other current relationships. The experience of a childhood lived with a dominating and controlling care-giver may then produce patterns of passivity and dependency in a person's adult relations, as well as a sense of passivity in relation to a dominating and critical God. In this sense, the God-object can function as the blank screen *par excellence*, upon which an individual's patterns of transference are most clearly projected. Although the individual's imagined relationship with a sacred object may reflect one's wider patterns of transference, some theorists would also argue that the God-object has particular properties which mark it out as different from the other object relations that a person forms. Ana-Maria Rizzuto (1979), for example, argues that a person's understanding of God may indeed be initially constructed out of fragments of early experiences of relations with care-givers, but that the God-object plays an important, on-going role in grounding a person's sense of self and purpose. Furthermore, Rizzuto argues that the God-object is not necessarily unchanging, but can be subject to different understandings and patterns of relationship throughout an individual's life-course. Indeed, if a person's imagined construct of God remains inflexible, it is likely to become problematic as that individual negotiates new psychological or developmental crises, and without some adaptation, a person may abandon an image of God as too painful or irrelevant.

Another model for a transferential understanding of sacred objects, based on the self psychology developed by Heinz Kohut (1984), examines the ways in which a relationship with a divine "selfobject" might affect the psychological structures and feeling-states of an individual. Kohut proposed that selfobject transference was activated in relationships in which an individual experiences the other as a powerful source of mirroring, kinship or focus for idealization, and that such transference was important both in childhood and adult life in shoring up the healthy psychological "self." Within this transferential theory, then, it is possible to ask how a person's relation with God functions in such selfobject terms, both in his or her childhood development and his or her ability to negotiate psychological tensions in later life. How might, for example, an understanding of an empathic, mirroring God act as a source of consolation, or a powerful idealization of God serve as an inspiration and source of energy, in the face of a person's sense of depression or anxiety?

What these transferential models of the sacred object share in common is an interest in the ways in which a person's object relations with God are similar to, and in some respects different from, object relations with other people. Given the psychoanalytic emphasis on the importance of early experience in establishing patterns of transference, they also focus on how such early experiences shape subsequent experiences of God, both in terms of providing the content for images of God as well as generating psychological conditions in which a God-object might later be experienced as persecutory, irrelevant or consoling.

The interest that such transferential models show in thinking about the sacred object in person-like ways is potentially of considerable value for understanding lived religion. There are, however, significant limitations with such models at present. A common concern within this literature is with object-representations of, and transferential relations with, God. While case material in this literature offers rich accounts of individuals' early family experiences, their subsequent life histories and significant relations, and the feelings and meanings they attach to God, only negligible accounts are given of the religious communities and practices through which relations with that God have been formed. This literature typically treats 'God' as a self-evident religious category, failing to reflect in what ways this assumed notion of God is a culturally and historically-specific concept deriving from Christianity or natural philosophy—or indeed from the traditional Freudian critique of religion.[2] For approaches to the study of lived religion that take seriously the specificities of the contexts in which people form relations with sacred objects, as well as the specificities of those sacred objects themselves, the concept of a generalized, de-historicized, and de-contextualized "God-object" is problematic. To treat "God" or the sacred object simply as an analytic blank screen to receive the individual's transference projections is to neglect the ways in which the meanings and associations attached to a particular sacred object are inscribed by historical and social conventions or, as we shall see later, shaped by wider institutional projects and operations of power. Similarly, to suggest that the content of a person's image of and relationship with a sacred object is determined by their experiences of early care-givers risks a reductionist emphasis on early experience that neglects the ways in which an individual's understanding of their relationship with a sacred object may be informed primarily through interactions in adulthood (see Miller 2008: 290ff.).

An alternative object relations framework for thinking about the sacred object is to conceive of it as a transitional phenomenon. This approach is particularly influenced by the work of Donald Winnicott on the significance of transitional objects and transitional space for the child's developmental process of perceiving and engaging with the external world. The transitional object is a material object in the external world—such as a soft toy or blanket—onto which the child projects an imagined bond that serves as a source of continuity and soothing. Importantly, though, the materiality of the object ("it must seem to the infant to give warmth, or to move, or to have texture, or to do something that seems to show it has vitality or reality of its own," Winnicott 1971: 7) gives the child an experience of a meaningful connection within their inner world with an object that is recognized as being, in some sense, not them and offers an early experience of a form of subjectivity beyond the self. The transitional object does not represent a wholesale engagement with the external world "as it is" by the child, but the creation of a particular kind of object that is at the same time both external and infused with imagination and which therefore occupies a distinctive transitional space that is neither wholly within or wholly external to the child. Writers such as Rizzuto (1979) and Meissner (1984) have argued that the God-object can be understood as such a form of transitional object which unlike soft toys or comfort blankets can retain a particular kind of emotional significance throughout adult life. This is a significant distortion of Winnicott's ideas, however, in which the transitional object functions only at a particular stage in early childhood development before becoming de-animated. Winnicott's work does provide another way of thinking about sacred objects as transitional phenomena, however, in which religious life is seen as a later expression of the human capacity for infusing external objects with intense creativity and imagination which was originally forged through encounters with transitional objects. In Winnicott's own words:

Its [the transitional object's] fate is to be gradually allowed to be decathected, so that in the course of years it becomes not so much forgotten as relegated to limbo. By this I mean that in health the transitional object does not 'go inside' nor does the feeling about it necessarily undergo repression. It is not forgotten and it is not mourned. It loses meaning, and this is because the transitional phenomena have become diffused, have become spread over the whole intermediate territory between 'inner psychic reality' and 'the external world as perceived by two persons in common,' that is to say, over the whole cultural field.

(ibid.: 7)

Winnicott therefore suggests that religious life stands in direct continuity with the capacity for illusion learned in childhood, where the term "illusion" does not mean "false" but a state in which external reality is infused with subjective imagination. He comments:

I am therefore studying the substance of *illusion*, that which is allowed to the infant, and which in adult life is inherent in art and religion, and yet becomes a hallmark of madness when an adult puts too powerful a claim on the credulity of others, forcing them to acknowledge a sharing of illusion that is not their own. We can share a respect for *illusory experience*, and if we wish we may collect together and form a group on the basis of the similarity of our illusory experiences. This is a natural root of grouping among human beings ... It is assumed here that the task of reality-acceptance is never completed, that no human being is free from the strain of relating inner and outer reality, and that relief from this strain is provided by an intermediate are of experience which is not challenged (arts, religion, etc.). This intermediate area is in direct continuity with the play area of the small child who is "lost" in play.

(ibid.: 3, 18)

In Winnicott's terms, then, the capacity for relationship with a sacred other in adult life might be understood not so much in terms of transferential patterns of relationship formed through interactions with early care-givers, but in terms of the human capacity for deep imaginative engagement with external objects which remains part of the unresolved task of negotiating external reality beyond the self. Significantly, Winnicott also recognizes the social dimension of such imaginative processes, thus providing a conceptual framework that might help us to connect inner experiences of relations with sacred others and processes of social mediation with other people which help to maintain such "illusory experience." The important role that material culture (toys, blankets) play in the early development of such an imaginative capacity also points to the way in which the imaginative engagement with sacred others in adult life might also be materially mediated (see also Meissner 1984: 180–1), as well as the ways in which material objects might play an active role in evoking psychological states within the individual (Bollas 2009). Such a transitional model offers a potential basis for enquiring how this imaginative capacity is enacted and mediated in specific historical and social contexts through particular media and practices. This makes it more possible to analyse the relationships between adherents and their sacred objects in ways that are more contextually sensitive than purely intra-psychic models of the God-object rooted in early experience.

With some critical revisions, transferential and transitional models of sacred objects may therefore both illuminate our understanding of belief as faithful interaction with a sacred other. Moving beyond the propositional beliefs of the autonomous and reflexive self, a theory of the sacred object can therefore help us to understand the everyday constructions of religious life-worlds as fundamentally relational (involving interactions with sacred objects and other adherents), mediated (both materially and socially) and dynamic (in that they have direct effects on participants' psyches).

Sacred objects, sacred subjects?

If object relations theory offers potentially valuable insights for making sense of lived religion, then more recent developments in psychoanalytic thought raise further questions about how we think about sacred objects. Since the early 1980s, there has been a growing interest among some theorists and clinicians in the development of a relational model of psychoanalysis which takes more seriously the intersubjective nature of the analytic relationship (Mitchell 1988; Skolnick and Warshaw 1992; Mitchell and Aron 1999). This relational turn has focused on the significance of the analyst's own subjectivity for the therapeutic process, rather than thinking about the analyst simply as recipient of the patient's transference. Clearly this raises particular issues in relation to clinical practice. But some theorists have used this relational turn in psycho-analysis to ask wider questions about the nature and implications of the individual's capacity to recognize another person as an equivalent yet separate center of subjectivity, "a mind that is fundamentally like our own but unfathomably different, and outside our control" (Benjamin 1995: xii). This has opened up new ways of thinking about human ontology which attempt to examine how human subjectivity is fundamentally constituted through intersubjective interactions, an interest shared by others working in philosophy, social theory and developmental psychology.

We noted earlier in our discussion that to see the sacred object simply as a blank screen *par excellence* for the psychological projections of the religious adherent is problematic because it fails to recognize the meanings that have been inscribed on sacred objects in particular institutional and cultural contexts. But it may be possible to move even further beyond this point. The relational turn in psychoanalysis rejects the notion of the analyst as blank screen because it fails to recognize the significance of the analyst's own subjectivity. But is it possible that sacred objects, with whom adherents form emotionally charged relationships, could also be thought of as having some form of subjectivity? Could we think not so much in terms of sacred objects, as sacred subjects with whom some form of intersubjective encounter is possible? To raise these questions might appear to open up only a metaphysical conversation which is the professional domain of philosophers and theologians. But questions of the subjectivity of sacred others can also be explored to some extent within the framework of social and cultural theory, and in doing so, may generate concepts that are more attentive to the intersubjective ground of lived religion.

Attempts to theorize subjectivity have become increasingly important for a range of academic disciplines with the turn to new forms of critical social and cultural thought since the late 1960s (Blackman *et al.* 2008). While this theoretical debate is contested and unresolved, it is increasingly structured around three concerns: subjectivity as a site of subjection or engagement with subject-positions available in a given context, subjectivity as a site of experience, and subjectivity as a site of agency. Contemporary theoretical accounts of subjectivity are therefore often attempts to understand how individuals interact with discourses of self-hood available to them in a given context, how such interactions relate to embodied, aesthetic experiences of being in the world, and what kind of agency underlies the distinctive ways in which individuals engage with their social context and experience their worlds.

Does this broad framework for thinking about subjectivity give us any grounds for conceiving of sacred others as subjects in their own right? This will require a fuller discussion than is possible here, but in brief I would argue that it is possible to think in terms of some form of sacred subjectivity demonstrated by gods, spirits, ancestors, and saints, and to think of these sacred others as sites of subjection, imagined experience, and agency. As we have discussed, sacred others are subject to the ways in which adherents symbolize them, and different social and institutional mechanisms legitimize and perpetuate particular ways of talking about and interacting with that sacred other. The nature of what subject-positions are legitimate for a sacred subject can clearly be contested among their adherents, as histories of religious orthodoxy and heresy demonstrate. But sacred others remain subject to the ways in which adherents narrate them through sedimented and evolving structures of religious discourse recursively reproduced through various religious practices.

At the same time, sacred subjects might also be thought of as exerting a form of agency. This is not the same kind of agency demonstrated by empirically observable human beings, but then there are reasonable grounds for arguing that our concepts of agency need greater refinement than the intentional actions of individuals and groups. As Bruno Latour has argued, in the context of actor-network theory, anything that "modifies a state of affairs by making a difference is an actor", and agency can be attributed to anything that "might authorize, allow, afford, encourage, permit, suggest, influence, block, render possible, forbid, and so on" (Latour 2005: 71–2). Although Latour is thinking here about seeing material objects and environments as exerting agency in social life, there is no reason in principle why such agency might not also be attributed to sacred subjects. The sedimentation of religious narratives and discourses around particular sacred subjects means that adherents learn to encounter these subjects with the expectation that the sacred other will relate to them in certain ways—as a source of healing, moral challenge, forgiveness, power, hope, blessing, and so on.

The experience of the sacred subject acting in these ways is not generated simply within the imagination of the individual adherent, but is made possible by the ways in which a wider group of adherents narrates and interacts with the sacred subject. Similarly, the collective of adherents is not free to narrate the sacred subject in any way that they wish, but encounters that subject through sedimented and evolving patterns of discourse that extend back into the past and into a wider imagined community of faith in the present. As a consequence, the individual adherent experiences the sacred subject as having a life and reality beyond themselves. As Durkheim ([1912] 2001) observed, this sense of being addressed by a reality beyond the self is an intrinsic element of the human experience of participation in society, and thus of the social mediation of the sacred subject. Following Latour, the material forms through which the sacred subject is mediated also set their own possibilities for adherents' interactions with them. Again, the contemporary community of the faithful encounters the sacred subject as a force beyond itself, because the sacred subject is made real through the historical sedimentation of spaces, practices, and discourses about that sacred other that stretch beyond it (ibid.: 18). The significance of (and anxieties around) forging a relationship with that past are demonstrated both in the importance of claims about the authentic maintenance of that past as a key rhetorical tool of religious legitimation (see, e.g., McCutcheon 2005), as well as the energies that religious communities invest in imagining and reconstructing that past through ritual, pilgrimage and narrative.

Through the energizing effects of history, materiality, and society, channelled through the expectations and interactions made possible through particular patterns and media of religious discourse and practice, the sacred subject is encountered as a force and presence beyond the immediate lives of the individual adherent or gathered community of the faithful. The sacred subject brings with it its own conditions of encounter, thus authorizing, allowing, encouraging, suggesting, influencing, blocking, making possible, forbidding, in ways that are not simply under the control of adherents. Sacred subjects are subject to the ways in which adherents narrate and interact with them, but sacred subjects also set conditions in which such

narrations and interactions take place. This agency is not simply the property of the sacred subject, then, but emerges through the interactions
between adherents and the sacred subject. This might encourage us, as
Schofield Clark (in press) has suggested in another context, to think about
agency not so much as the property of specific individuals or technologies
but of complex social systems in which limits, possibilities, stasis, and
changes occur through cycles of interaction and feedback involving people
and their relational, material, and imagined environments.

The question of whether the sacred subject can be understood as a distinctive site of experience is perhaps hardest to think about in social scientific rather
than metaphysical terms. But even here there is scope for reflection. It may
make little sense for the social scientist to speculate on whether Jesus or the
orisha is feeling or thinking something in a particular religious interaction, but
it is important in this context to note that adherents can work hard to generate
a sense of the contents of the inner world of the sacred subject. For example,
the public discourse of Evangelical prayer meetings places a strong emphasis on
painting a picture of what God is thinking and feeling in the immediacy of that
gathering of the faithful (Campbell *et al.* 2009). As social scientists, we may not
think of sacred others as possessing subjectivity analogous to human subjectivity, but we should be interested in the fact that adherents imaginatively construct those sacred others as separate centers of subjectivity and think about the
implications of such experiences of religious intersubjectivity.

In summary, it may be helpful not to think of sacred others as sacred objects
or as sacred subjects, but as both objects and subjects. As Jessica Benjamin (1995:
7ff.) has suggested, both theories of object and subject relations can be valuable
in understanding different kinds of psycho-social process rather than us necessarily being forced to choose between one framework or the other. Sacred
others, therefore, can be understood as objects in the sense of being the focus
of adherents' transference, as internalized and dynamic representations within
adherents' psyches, or as animated through the human capacity for deep
imaginative engagement with external objects. At the same time, sacred others
may be thought of as subjects in that the subject-positions they occupy and the
kinds of influence they exert on adherents' lives are not simply the product of
the immediate projections brought to the sacred other by a specific individual
or group. Sacred others therefore have a kind of separate life, formed through
past histories of discourse and mediation, which pre-exists the contemporary
adherent and provides the context within which any relational encounter with
that sacred other is possible.

Between heaven and earth

This discussion so far has been theoretical, noting omissions in understandings of the person as social agent within the sociology of religion and

exploring the value of psychoanalytic concepts for a relational model of lived religion. In the final part of this chapter, I will build on these theoretical observations further by discussing them in relation to one of the most important recent books to have adopted an intersubjective approach to the study of religion, Robert Orsi's *Between Heaven and Earth* (2007).

A cultural history of twentieth-century American Catholicism, Orsi's book innovatively weaves together narratives about members of his own family with broader narratives about social, cultural, and religious changes during that period. It also breaks important ground in reflecting on the significance of the relationships that American Catholics forged with sacred others—various saints, guardian angels, Mary and Jesus—suggesting that "one challenge of writing about religion is to figure out how to include figures of special power as agents in history and actors of consequence in historical persons' lives and experiences" (ibid.: 2). Such relationships, he adds, "have all the complexities – all the hopes, evasions, love, fear, denial, projections, misunderstandings, and so on – of relations between humans" (ibid.: 2), and attention to concrete examples of such relations demonstrates the ambiguous and ambivalent effects of such sacred figures in the lives of their adherents.

Orsi's work clearly demonstrates how the trajectory of individual biographies leads people to form intense attachments to particular sacred others. One of his uncles, Sal, who suffered from cerebral palsy, became attached to Blessed Margaret of Castello, who was born in 1287 with a number of physical disabilities, and abandoned by her family, only to be adopted eventually into a Dominican order of lay-women. Orsi's grandmother, Giulia, was similarly said to have a special love for the Tuscan saint, Gemma Galgani. In both instances we can see the emotional work that is being done through such relations with sacred objects. In Kohut's terms, Sal and Giulia find in their respective saints an experience of mirroring and kinship—Sal in Margaret's experience of disability and disempowerment and Giulia in Gemma's suffering at the hands of the men to whom she was bound—in which their own suffering is understood and held by a more powerful, sacred presence. These are not simply private psychological experiences, however, but socially and materially mediated. The experience of Margaret and Gemma as living sacred subjects in Sal and Giulia's lives was made possible by the material mediation of these saints through pamphlets and pictures which could be kept in special places in the home. Such experiences of relationship with sacred subjects also rely on wider forms of social mediation, for example, in the groups of people who campaigned for Margaret and Gemma to be canonized and who commemorated them through different media. These identifications are not therefore private, inner experiences, nor, despite their potentially beneficial emotional effects, are they necessarily wholly healthy. As Giulia's case demonstrates, devotion to Gemma Galgani brings not only the comfort of identification with a sacred other, but also subjection to the role of passive, pious female suffering at the hands of more powerful men.

Orsi also demonstrates how the formation of such relations with sacred others takes place in the context of wider institutional projects. One case in point is the conscious attempt to nurture children's relations with sacred subjects. Childhood relations with sacred others were not then, simply, an outworking of an intrinsic instinct for a "God-object" (or other sacred intermediaries), but produced in an institutional context in which children were disciplined into relations with sacred others through the use of particular material objects, spaces, and bodily practices. In part, such disciplining took the form of the training of the imagination, the social construction of transitional phenomena identified by Winnicott, through encouragement by priests, nuns, and other teachers, enabling children to engage imaginatively with their own chosen patron saint, or their guardian angel. Such disciplining also made use of material objects through structured religious play such as building a Christmas crib or make-believe masses using props bought from specialist Catholic suppliers, again designed to evoke a particular kind of sacred imagination. Such disciplining also took material form in children's own bodies through careful training for their participation in sacred ritual (e.g. children being rehearsed in incomprehensible lists of sins to perform in the confessional, or being taught how to comport themselves during Mass), itself supported by a range of material media such as magazines, posters, and cartoons that sought to encourage correct behavior.

The energies poured into forming children in relations with sacred others reflect the particular significance that children held as being themselves material media of sacred presence for the wider Church. As symbols of innocence and dependence, children were taken to be emblematic of the human condition before God, and physically displayed as such in ritual settings (e.g. through the display of altar boys). Orsi observes that this reflects a wider tendency in the Church to make use of those who are vulnerable and dependent—whether children, women, or "cripples"—as suffering symbols of God's grace. In this context, then, people were not simply encouraged and enabled to forge relations with sacred others through material objects. But some kinds of bodies were themselves constructed as material media of divine presence to the supposed edification of the wider community of the faithful (e.g. the faithful, patient suffering of the "cripple," given by God to show the shallowness of this life compared to the world to come) and therefore became particularly important sites for interiorizing relations with sacred subjects. The forging of relations with sacred others is not, therefore, some kind of personal psychological process, shaped only by experience of early care-givers, but also framed by wider institutional projects. The interiorization of relations with sacred others, made possible through material objects, spaces, and bodily practices, is thus run through both with personal significance—of individuals' hopes, anxieties, fears and desires—and wider institutional practices of power.

As Orsi is careful to observe, though, such intersubjective relations between heaven and earth are neither simply good or bad, but ambiguous and ambivalent, and provide examples both of the deployment of institutional power and successful resistance against this. The care and interest shown to Sal by other Catholics in his neighborhood, which gave him some kind of social life, were also run through with the project of constructing those with physical disabilities as "faithful cripples." Yet in his devotion to Margaret of Castello, Sal also found a connection with a sacred presence that allowed him to resist this project to some degree, allowing him the opportunity to express his anger at the social marginalization that Margaret and others had suffered at the hands of the Church and wider society. Similarly, having one's body positioned as a special site of sacred significance—for example, in the case of children displayed at Mass—also conferred on such people the capacity to disrupt these sacred imaginaries, spaces, and practices. The plentiful media on training children to participate in Mass was therefore also accompanied by articles and cartoons devoted to deploring the bad behaviour and dishevelled appearance of children in sacred rites.

Orsi's work therefore provides a rich account of the intersubjective, material and dynamic nature of the construction of American Catholic life-worlds, demonstrating the value of careful fieldwork for developing and refining our theoretical concepts. His work shows the complex interplay between personal biographies, particular networks, spaces, and practices of social and material mediation, and wider social and institutional structures and power. As such, it provides a model for future work that is more attentive to the intersubjective nature of lived religion, and demonstrates how taking seriously the experience and construction of relations with sacred others can form an integral part of the social and cultural study of religion.

Notes

1 We could also add to this list the powerful status that cognitive theories continue to occupy within the human sciences (see, e.g., Henriques *et al.* 1998: xff.)

2 The attempts by writers such as Rizzuto and Meissner to develop psychoanalytic accounts of how a God-object might form part of healthy psychological functioning are explicit attempts to critique Freud's understanding of the pathological roots of religion and the illusion of God. It is also worth noting, in passing, that in Meissner's (1984: 182) work there is also a post-Vatican II disdain for popular uses and meanings of Catholic material and visual culture and a preference for a more universal concepts of God.

3

Materiality, social analysis, and the study of religions

David Morgan

Leading themes in the study of religions and their material cultures
Material culture as an approach to the study of religion

The study of religion has always included attention to the material traces of the past. Western archeologists and art historians since the eighteenth century, for example, have carefully scrutinized pottery shards, coins, figurines, jewelry, architectural ruins, frescoes, and altarpieces. The interpretation of things is not new in the study of religion. Yet what has changed among scholars is the reason for studying religion as well as the practice of defining religion(s). Anthropologists and sociologists in the nineteenth and early twentieth centuries focused on "primitive" or "archaic" societies for the study of religion since they took a generally evolutionary approach, famously championed by David Hume in his study of the history of natural religion.[1] The premise was that human history evinced a universal tendency to progress from simple toward complex forms of belief, specifically from animism to monotheism. It was a model that favored the present and, not incidentally, underscored the Western imagination's regard for its superior role in a colonial global landscape (Masuzawa 2005).

Not only has the cultural politics of the study of religions shifted, so too has the object of study and the interpretive frame deployed to scrutinize the object. Victor Turner noted a very telling turn in anthropology that is, I believe, symptomatic of several disciplines and fields in the humanities and social sciences over the past forty years or so. The emphasis in anthropological theory, he observed shortly before he died in 1983, had moved "from structure to process, from competence to performance" (1988: 21). And, one might add, from rational cognition to embodied practice. It is not difficult to discern in the sentiment his approval of turning the corner on the intellectualism of structuralist accounts of ritual and myth, where knowledge makes people cultural participants, establishing their "competence," that is, the ability to act meaningfully in a society. Turner elaborated on his observation in formulating an anthropology of performance:

Performances are never amorphous or openended, they have diachronic structure, a beginning, a sequence of overlapping but isolable phases, and an end. But their structure is not that of an abstract system; it is generated out of the dialectical oppositions of processes and levels of process. In the modern consciousness, cognition, idea, rationality, were paramount. In the postmodern turn, cognition is not dethroned but rather takes its place on an equal footing with volition and affect.

(ibid.: 80)

Turner was convinced that the dynamic character of social experience was lost to the approach that stressed rationality as the key to human sociality. He did not propose an irrationalist scheme to replace modernity. For him, postmodernism represented a change in sensibility that would allow anthropologists to strike an appropriate balance between thought, will, and feeling. Setting aside the nomenclature of the postmodern, I would like to affirm his quest for integrating cognition with the other dimensions of human existence. Indeed, cognition itself is more than intellection. As we will see, studies in neurobiology, which Turner himself hailed at the end of his career, have suggested that emotions, movement, and gesture are integral aspects of human cognition (ibid.: 156–78). We think and remember with feelings and with our bodies. And performance, as Turner argued, is one of the most fundamental ways in which cultures operate. But what does this mean for the study of religious material culture?

Leading themes in the study of religions and their material cultures

Changes in why scholars study religions and what they understand themselves to be studying have accented a variety of themes in scholarship. I would like to summarize them here, not with the intention of treating them exhaustively, but to sketch their principal characteristics and to indicate their significance for the study of religious material culture. I denote five discrete, but clearly interrelated themes in scholarship that have come gradually to the fore in recent decades: (1) the felt-life of belief; (2) embodiment; (3) space and ritual; (4) performance and practice; and (5) aesthetics. Examining each of these will allow us to make a few summary remarks about material culture as an approach to the study of religions. I propose to examine each topic by discussing select primary studies and arguments associated with each. I make no attempt at a comprehensive review of literature nor even at enumerating the major contributors to each niche of research.

The felt-life of belief: emotion, feeling, sensation

Interest in the relationship between emotion, or the passions, and religion is old. In the eighteenth century, David Hume noted the connection in his *Natural*

History of Religion, where he argued that the first glimmer of a divinity occurred when humankind considered the prospect of life beyond "the present course of things." This realization was propelled by hopes and fears such as "the anxious concern for happiness, the dread of future misery, the terror of death, the thirst of revenge, the appetite for food and other necessaries" (Hume 2007: 38–9). William James also discerned the powerful interweaving of belief and emotion. In *Varieties of Religious Experience* he wrote that feeling was "the deeper source of religion" than "philosophic and theological formulas" and he devoted an entire chapter to "Religion and Neurology" (1961: 337). Psychologically framed views of religion and emotion such as those offered by Hume and James were designed to explain the utility of belief, to help account for the work it performs in human psyche or society. Modern neuro-science has continued along this path in a number of ways such as measuring states of consciousness during meditation, as in the case of Buddhist monks.

But for the study of religious material culture, it is important to begin with the scientific claim that emotions are not an ornament of consciousness, but are inseparable from it. Rather than something added to the bare facts of empirical sensations, like frosting on a cake, emotion is intrinsic. For example, researchers have found that "when consciousness is impaired so is emotion" (Damasio 1999: 16). Indeed, emotions participate in the most basic mechanisms of human consciousness, serving two fundamental functions: producing a reaction to a stimulus and regulating the state of the organism in order to respond to the stimulus (ibid.: 53–4). Emotions code memories and are intimately associated with their recall. Moreover, Antonio Damasio cites investigations that show how "emotion is integral to the process of reasoning and decision making."[2] He also points out that emotions are fundamental to the experiences that exert the greatest influence on human behavior: pain and pleasure, reward and punishment, approach and withdrawal. On the basis of these, he unsurprisingly suggests that emotions are "inseparable from the idea of good and evil."[3]

This suggests that human beings exist within landscapes of feeling. By feeling is meant an emotional state of awareness, an internal sensation of sadness, happiness, fear, anger, surprise, or disgust. Damasio adds to this list what he calls the secondary or social emotions of embarrassment, jealousy, guilt, and pride; and the background emotions of well-being, malaise, calm, and tension, which are manifest as mood because they color an object rather than serve as one themselves (Damasio 1999: 50–1). He distinguishes feelings and emotions, arguing that feeling an emotion is the experience of emotions "in juxtaposition to the mental images that initiated" the neurobiological process (Damasio 1994: 145). So feelings arise from consciousness of emotions, and are therefore discrete states of awareness. When they see, hear, touch, or taste, human beings experience emotion, use emotion to evaluate and remember their experience, and rely on it in their social engagements as

forms of intelligence. If we fail to recognize this, we miss something fundamental in religions. Many traditions of thought rank feeling and emotion as
inferior or even unreliable, but careful scrutiny of such views, such as the
position articulated by Plato in his *Republic*, shows that emotions *per se* were
not banned, only those considered a threat to the governance of the soul.
Plato had Socrates explicitly endorse musical modes and poetic forms that
indulged the emotional gravitas that promoted solemn submission to the
greater good of the state (Plato 1992: 75, 399b–c). The same must be said of
religious traditions conventionally regarded as unemotional. In fact, the emotional range may be comparatively narrow and staunchly policed, but it is
rudimentary to the personal and social practices that characterize Puritanism,
for example. By denying feeling, humans change their relationship to a person, place, or thing, and construct a practice of selfhood that is grounded in
a characteristic pattern of feeling closely associated with time, place, and
people. Feeling is something that powerfully joins people into communities
(Harré 1986; Lyon and Barbalet 1994; Brennan 2004).

All societies invest a great deal in teaching their members to feel similarly. They rely on collective rituals and practices such as ceremonies,
parades, entertainment, and religious rites to do so. Emotions bridge public
and private because the neural networks that constitute the internal anatomy of an emotion are linked directly to muscular-skeletal systems. To feel
happy, in other words, means to smile; to feel anger is to grimace. We rely
on muscles in the face, shoulders, and chest to confirm that we feel happy.
This intimate organic connection is the visual basis for communicating feeling, and works to such a degree that seeing a gesture or expression in another
person can trigger the same emotion in us.[4] Being in the overwhelming presence of dozens, hundreds, or thousands of other people who are cheering,
weeping, ruminating, fervently praying or singing easily elicits the same
feeling, or at least a shared disposition toward the public display of a feeling
considered appropriate for the occasion. By the same token, images or
objects that circulate among many can serve to unify public feeling or sentiment.[5] What has been aptly termed "emotional contagion" consists of the
transmission of feeling by virtue of the "unconscious imitation of physical
states" perceived among other humans (Thagard 2006: 244; see also
Lundquist and Dimberg 1995). This extends to things in the form of imagery portraying the human face or gesture or to any object that is anthropo-
morphized such that its emotional quality affects a person who touches or
sees the object.

Feelings not only join human beings to one another, but also join them
to animals, to living things, to places, and to objects.[6] Feelings can become
so intimately associated with external inducers of emotions that the two
appear virtually indistinguishable, like Pavlov's dog, which responded to a bell
as neurologically identical to the promise of reward. Of course, behaviorist

reductions of human beings to the simplicity of stimulus-response routines are not appealing to humanists engaged in the study of complex cultural phenomena such as religious belief. The point is not to treat humans in simplistic terms, but to recognize the importance of emotion in the connections, indeed, the relationships that people develop with objects, animals, and places. The study of the materiality of religion finds here one of its richest domains of inquiry, especially since traditional approaches have tended to dismiss the cultural biography of things in religious belief as superstitious, idolatrous, low-brow, or primitive. A great deal of research has clearly shown how things matter to believers (McDannell 1995; Hermkens 2005; Pattison 2007).

Embodiment: the body in belief

Bodies convey feeling not as a set of abstract signs, but by a more immediate connection, one that enables emotional contagion. The movement or expression of emotion in a body is conveyed intuitively to companions, often unconsciously and unintentionally. Feeling shapes consciousness at a somatic level, operating in human beings socially as a medium that is not fully subject to rational or intentional control. Panic is only an extreme example of this. More prosaic, but no less efficacious is the way children and students imitate the gestures, expressions, and voices of their parents and teachers without thinking of it. Or the way a massive stream of pedestrians flows down a sidewalk and across a street, able quite intuitively to maintain a collective rhythm, rate, and distance among one another, creating a transient but real social body. This somatic capacity for collective behavior is one reason why corporate worship and ritual are effective; or one might say that they are effective because they are affective. People feel like one body because they are feeling together, conveying attitudes, emotions, and dispositions by means of standing, sitting, kneeling, chanting, singing, or praying together. The body in such cases does more than signify belief: it hosts belief. More than passively enabling it, the body shapes, colors, tunes, tastes, and performs belief. Believers receive belief intuitively from others as embodied forms of imitation, intimidation, and empathy, and then adapt the bodily routine to suit their situation—perhaps to deepen a social bond or to negotiate some degree of resistance or difference. The most obvious example of this complex and varied process is the training of children, whose bodies are the site of instruction no less than their intellects. Seating order, processions, uniform or formal dress, corporate exercises like standing at attention or kneeling in prayer, group recitations, musical and vocal performance, public punishment and praise—all serve as techniques for disciplining the individual body to participate in the social body of belief. The body becomes how individuals and group do belief.[7]

The history of body practices may be studied as constituting ways of believing. How people dress, gather, greet, amuse themselves, eat, and organize their homes reveal their class, their perceived status, their economic aspirations, and what they do that joins them to others. In addition to the preservation of social structure, belief affords the opportunity to study agency in restructuring it. Belief is not only what people do to conform to the limitations of gender roles as set by the prevailing economic demands of producing heirs, promoting authority and social order, or amassing capital. Belief is also what people do to expand their options, to wiggle from strict prescriptions of behavior, or to imagine themselves beyond what they are told they must do or think or feel. When we consider the role of religious beliefs in campaigns for social justice, for example, it becomes clear that belief can assist people in re-creating themselves by seeking new roles, new narratives, by reimaging their social presence, by changing their place within the communities in which they circulate. The body plays a fundamental role in this since it is a principal form of social signage, the public face that people present to their fellows. But it is also always more than signage. It is the seat of experience in the sense that the body registers in feelings and moods what it experiences beyond itself. The body entertains what the face may not expose. Dissimulation and concealment are possible because expression of feeling is not hardwired. This means that the body serves as a hidden interior, which is where many cultures locate an inner self as opposed to a more publicly accessible self or selves.

Bodies also carry history in them, intermingling previous states with the present, intermingling language with feeling. Religious historian Marie Griffith has studied the history of American body cultures and the place that religion has played in the conception of the body and the practices that have shaped and envisioned it (Griffith 2004). In many religions the body is regarded as an index of the individual's relation to the deity or spirit world. Among the Evangelicals whom Griffith has studied, illness and the ailing body are evidence of vice or unbelief; health and beauty the blessing of divine approval. If we are to avoid the pervasive influence of dualism, scholars must attempt not to limit the body to the status of a sign about something else, but scrutinize ways in which it can be the very medium of meaning-making, the site of religion, not only its signification. Griffith's driving concern is to ask how body type "has come to seem a virtually infallible touchstone of the worth of persons about whom one knows nothing else, as well as the value—indeed, the deepest truths—of one's own self: a vital component of subjectivity" (ibid.: 7). The body has become the self, or at least its most fundamental, socially accessible manifestation.

A primary claim in the study of the body today is that there is no essential body, that bodies are historically, culturally constructed. If this is so, then religions have taken an often important part in making bodies. "You are what you eat," "you are what you look like"—these truisms are abetted by modern advertisement's driving but generally tacit pitch: "you need this commodity in order to be what you really want to be." Religions such as Christianity and Judaism commonly say the same thing couched in the normative discourse of ethical imperatives: "you ought to do this or affirm that in order to be the person whom God meant you to be," which is one reason why many versions of these religions and capitalism cooperate so well (Moore 1994; Einstein 2008). For example, Christian diet and fitness gurus since the later twentieth century have taught that God empowers believers to reduce their weight. Prayer and Christian association bring this about. Moreover, as Griffith argues, "ideal bodies ... perform indispensable work as effective agents of devotional intimacy," that is, being slender and fit are ways in which some Christians achieve and cultivate their relationship with the divine (2004: 161). Their god calls them to be thin and by becoming so, they enjoy a new intimacy with him. At the same time, of course, thin bodies remain key aspects of the social capital of sexual allure, class status, and the arch propriety of gender roles. Religion and power are inextricable.

Space and ritual

As a category of analysis and interpretation, "sacred space" received special attention in the work of Mircea Eliade. In "Sacred Space and Making the World Sacred," the opening chapter of *The Sacred and Profane*, which appeared in English in 1959, Eliade presented a conception of sacred space that he set in diametric opposition to what he held to be the desacralized or profane world-view of the modern, industrial, post-religious age. Durkheim had treated the arch distinction of sacred and profane as a local structuring of difference that was arbitrary but absolute, a compulsory pairing that enforced the difference by taboo (Durkheim 1995: 36–8). Social order was the result. A related narrative construction of signs informed the structuralist understanding of the sign worked out in continental theory most importantly by Ferdinand de Saussure, Roman Jakobson, and Claude Lévi-Strauss. Eliade had something else in mind. For him, entire world-views were either sacred or profane. He spoke in sweeping generalizations of long ages of humanity: "religious man" as primitive or archaic societies, and "profane man" as the inhabitants of modern, Western society. And yet Eliade considered each form of humanity to be suffering from loss, which it was driven to reverse. So-called archaic societies conducted religious ritual as a way of returning to the cosmogonic moment, the gods' creation of the universe, which ritual reenacted in order to effect a return to the mythic origin.

Eliade's approach has been repeatedly criticized in several respects, most especially perhaps his tendency to universalize symbols as common elements in very different, widely separated religious traditions, lifting them from their immediate circumstances in order to say something about human nature, about "religious man" or "profane man," as if such nebulous essences adequately represented the diversity of the human record. Jonathan Z. Smith wrote one of the most memorable critiques of Eliade in his widely read collection of essays, *To Take Place: Toward Theory in Ritual* (1987), where he argued against universalizing particularities and, following Durkheim, pushed the analysis of place toward the far more sociological conception of location within hierarchy than the understanding of space as ritual response to the irruption of the sacred into time and space (Smith 1987: 45). Place for Smith is not a reply to the sacred, but the very construction of it. Place is neither what god or nature do, but is rather the product of human thought. "Human beings are not placed," he contends, "they bring place into being" (ibid.: 28). This means that Smith returns the understanding of sacred and profane to the Durkheimian sense of difference:

> A ritual object or action becomes sacred by having attention focused on it in a highly marked way. From such a point of view, there is nothing that is inherently sacred or profane. These are not substantive categories, but rather situational ones. Sacrality is, above all, a category of emplacement.
>
> (ibid.: 104)

Prohibition or taboo not only enforced the difference between sacred and profane, but constituted it.

But in this concept of place, or emplacement, the sensory, the bodily dimension of experience, suffers. Smith glosses Durkheim's view that the indices of the sacred "are to be derived from social rather than sensory experience" (ibid.: 106). Place is not sensory, but rather the scaffolding on which to hang the stipulative message of social organization: "the sacred is here and know your place accordingly." The sacred is a form of information, structuring the social field hierarchically. For this reason, Smith adduces several schematic diagrams, culled from various sources, and interprets them as social maps that the sacred is designed to enforce. This social analysis of ritual is clearly important and unquestionably useful in locating sacred space within the coordinates of time and place. But one must ask what happens to materiality in an approach in which place, or better, social location, is finally not about space but serves as a metaphor of difference, is, in fact, never more than an empty signifier. Place for Smith is a dramatizing of a linguistic system of difference. He remains a structuralist for whom things are symbols in cultural systems.

I do not wish to polarize this approach and one that seeks to maintain the relevance of materiality in the understanding of ritual. Ideally, one would not need to choose between analyzing power as an ontological transformation and power as social construct organizing the field of human relations. People locate power in things, enter into and cultivate relations with things and places, organize their lives around the experience of things and places. While doing so is always a social activity working within economies and cultural politics, that is not all that religious spaces and things do. Reductionist interpretation threatens to squash particularity no less than does universalist interpretation, and both compromise the robust character of life-worlds, tending to cast them as allegories within the hermeneutic of the interpreter, who presumes to tell us what the rituals "really" mean.

In his brief discussion of "sacred space," Gerardus van der Leeuw expressed the opposite view of the Durkheimian approach:

> Before building is begun it must be quite definitely ascertained whether the place selected is suitable for the "position." This really means that we cannot make shrines and cannot select their "positions," but can never do more than merely "find" them.
>
> (1963: vol. 2: 398)

Finding them means locating their manifestation of what van der Leeuw called the sacred: "Power." The sacred is not constructed by acts of consecration, but exists first as a manifestation of power. According to van der Leeuw, who surveyed ancient religions from around the world, people seek the issue or generation of power for the work it can perform. One cannot say, according to his analysis, that a taboo or ritual consecration creates the sacred by charging an object with power, by setting it off from the ordinary, because the taboo and the consecration are applied to what *already has power*. He used a telling analogy, comparing the taboo in primitive societies to the warning "Danger! High Voltage" (ibid.: vol. 1: 44). The warning sign does not invent the electricity, but is there to draw attention to its power. Cultural analysts need to take religious ritual and material culture with comparable seriousness. Christians, therefore, regard an image of Jesus as compelling or impressive not only because a priest has blessed it or because it was given to them on a ritual occasion, but because they recognize the image as Jesus. His power reaches them in his gaze. Jesus looks at them and they feel his look as a tangible contact. Likewise, an apparition of Mary appears on the side of a building spontaneously. The devout respond by erecting makeshift elements of a shrine, by depositing candles and gifts. In order to understand why, we need to examine the mobility of the sacred, its dynamics of appearance, the role of memory, the unconscious, and the place of feeling in religious life. All of this fleshes out the cultural construction of the sacred in ways that authoritarian acts of taboo and consecration only begin to capture. What we need is the history of practice that people bring to things in order to understand the depth in which their experience of the sacred is rooted.

In a very helpful overview of leading and conflicting accounts of sacred space, David Chidester and Edward Linenthal identified the "divergence between a substantial and situational definition of the sacred," characterizing it as a "contrast between what might be called the poetics and the politics of sacred space" (1995: 6). Without entering into polemics, it is compelling to venture, even only in passing, what an integration of these forms of interpretation might entail. Consider, for example, the *USS Arizona* Memorial, the national monument in Hawaii, discussed by Chidester and Linenthal in their introduction to *American Sacred Space* (ibid.: 3–5). The situational analysis of sacred space would contend that the Arizona is sacred because ritual consecration sets it off from ordinary space, an act of differentiation that is enforced by the prohibition of its desecration. Stress on site as empty signification of difference will rely on prohibition rather than on ethnography and material analysis of what visitors actually experience because the difference itself is telling them what to experience: difference. The real point is *meaning*, not textured or varied experience. Political analysis of sacred space will be much more interested in contestation of control and ownership than in what people report they experience or what the material organization of space inclines them to feel, think, or see. For the politics of sacred space, place is a demarcation, a line in the sand, not a place experienced. But in an approach that integrates poetics and politics (which Chidester and Linenthal urge), sacred space is studied as host to human/divine encounter, aesthetic or felt-knowledge, ritual perception, the tangible experience of nationhood, the affirmation of authority, or, possibly the transformation or realignment of power. The patriotic monument is where American history meets the bodies of visitors, where narrative touches them, where memory becomes personal, where individuality contributes its energy and interests to national stories in order that they may enter into daily life to be remembered, or re-cast. Particular and general meet, changing one another in a renewing synthesis. The social life of things and places is not ignored, nor is the material dimension subordinated to cultural politics. More than political allegory, there is actual content to the sacred that merits analysis and interpretation. And that content is grounded in the body and material practice, where politics and poetics were always already set in tandem.

Performance and practice

Social and psychological thought since the late nineteenth century has made use of the idea of performance as a kind of social dramaturgy of the self, where human selves are understood to play various roles of themselves. For William James, for instance, the human self consisted of three major aspects—the material, the social, and the spiritual "me." James defined the material me as the body and the clothes, but also those people and places with which one bears intimate physical connection: family, home, and property. The social self is a multitude of roles since "a man has as many social selves as there are individuals who recognize him and carry an image of him in their mind. To wound any one of these his images is to wound him" (James [1892] 1985: 46). According to James, we perform a slightly or dramatically different self-role in the various settings and with different friends or associates each day.

The presentation of self dominated the study of performance among sociologists and social psychologists through the twentieth century and has long been of interest to anthropologists. Likely the most influential writer in this domain has been Erving Goffman, whose major book, *The Presentation of the Self in Everyday Life* (1959), developed the dramaturgical approach in a very broad and instructive way. Goffman approached human interactions as collaborative encounters in which several things tend to happen. A person will project "a definition of the situation when he appears before others," though others, "however passive their role may seem to be, will themselves effectively project a definition of the situation by virtue of their response to the individual and by virtue of any lines of action they initiate to him" (1959: 9). In other words, the participants cooperate more or less (some parties must be coerced, others coaxed, cued, or enjoined by flattery) in working out the framework in which their interaction will take shape. "Together the participants contribute to a single over-all definition which involves not so much a real agreement as to what exists but rather a real agreement as to whose claims concerning what issues will be temporarily honored." This "working consensus" operates as a felt or intuited convention that may with effort be amended, broken, or replaced, though in most encounters, a single agreement governs relations.

Goffman's analysis of performance may be productively applied to the study of belief and materiality, especially with a view to working out an integration of the poetics and politics of the sacred. Because he did not assume that a human self is a unitary essence, but rather, like James, a repertoire of roles regularly performed, his account socializes the understanding of belief, removing it from the domain of abstract doctrine and assent. Belief might be characterized instead as the formation and maintenance of a consensus or community of feeling, in which the self one performs with the community is the self one wishes to be recognized by the deity, spirit, or ancestor. Worship is a presentation of the self—personal and collective—to the divine. As liturgy and most forms of religious ritual clearly show, the divine is not just a passive audience for the performance, but also a participant, even if one beseeched, invoked, conjured, or lamented. Belief is not simply the affirmation of teaching, but the performance of self before the divine other and the community of feeling.

In the final several decades of the twentieth century, performance emerged as a new context for social analysis. For both Goffman and anthropologist Victor Turner:

> The basic stuff of social life is performance … Self is presented through the performance of roles, through performance that breaks roles, and through declaring to a given public that one has undergone a transformation of state and status, been saved or damned, elevated or released.[8]

Turner sharply distinguished what he considered modernity's spatial imaginary, in which the Cartesian cogito legislated a rationalization of space, regulating time as a linear sequence and organizing space into a homogeneous display of discrete objects, best represented in the visual logic of linear perspective (Turner 1988: 72–4). To this regime he contrasted postmodernity's multi-perspectival consciousness of time:

> The notion of society as an endless crisscrossing of processes of various kinds and intensities is congruent with this view. Time is coming to be seen as an essential dimension of being as well as multi-perspectival, no longer as a linear continuum in spatial terms.
>
> (ibid.: 79–80).[9]

The emphasis on time made performance a powerful lens for studying culture and it facilitated understanding materiality as a process.

Whether or not one wishes to associate the shift from space to time in social analysis with the move from modern to postmodern, Turner rightly draws attention to the paradigm of performance as a way of framing the study of social life that has engaged many scholars in the past several decades. Performance has encouraged the development of a much more robust, less intellectualized understanding of the social construction of reality. Social performance is understood to make public attitudes, to create shared consciousness, to order social fields, to circulate feelings, and thereby to help establish consensus, which may be thought of as the social body of a group. Turner stressed that social dramas are not unilateral, but "crisscrossing," engaging in dissent, opposition, variety, multiplicity. Performances can affirm the status quo or attack it. They may be creative and disruptive no less than routine and reassuring. And a member maintains a felt, embodied connection to the social body by means of performative experience:

> There is a living and growing body of experience, a tradition of communitas, so to speak, which embodies the response of our whole collective mind to our entire collective experience. We acquire this wisdom

not by abstract solitary thought, but by participating immediately or vicariously through the performance genres in sociocultural dramas.

(ibid.: 84)

Emphasis on participation rather than abstract thought is characteristic of the study of performance and practice, which are comparable, if not quite identical. A widely influential source in thinking about the social dynamics of human behavior, one keyed to the study of practice rather than specifically to performance, has been Pierre Bourdieu. Practice may be very closely related to performance, even almost indistinguishable, if by practice we mean discrete routines of behavior that accomplish a variety of forms of cultural work, including the production and maintenance of social bodies. Perhaps Bourdieu's most important consideration has been the idea of habitus (developed from Marcel Mauss—see Mauss 1973—but as old as Plato and Aristotle), which he understood as "a system of dispositions" acquired over the course of a lifetime, but especially and most influentially in childhood (Bourdieu 1977: 82). By disposition he meant body-practices and sensibilities that incline people to act in a particular way. They are felt-orientations taken up in daily experience by a kind of archive of habits on which people draw in routines and performances. Children are especially active in manufacturing habits. As Socrates asked an interlocutor, "Haven't you noticed that imitations practiced from youth become part of nature and settle into habits of gesture, voice, and thought?" (Plato 1992: 72). Bourdieu certainly agreed, observing that by imitating the bodily actions of others, children produce

a pattern of postures that is both individual and systematic, because linked to a whole system of techniques involving the body and tools, and charged with a host of social meanings and values: in all societies, children are particularly attentive to the gestures and postures which, in their eyes, express everything that goes to make an accomplished adult—a way of walking, a tilt of the head, facial expressions, ways of sitting and of using implements, always associated with a tone of voice, a style of speech.

(Bourdieu 1977: 87)

The result is a living repository of body schemes or habits that "pass from practice to practice without going through discourse or consciousness." Moreover, given the fundamental lessons of socialization that occur in childhood, during which time the body and self of the child are shaped by the techniques and structures of the life-world in which it has come to exist, Bourdieu believed that the house was "the principal locus for the objectification of the generative schemes."[10]

By focusing on the material organization of the house as the most important site for the formative effects of habitus, Bourdieu helps us think once
again about the parameters of objects, props, scenography, body practices,
and space (Bourdieu 1970). Although his analysis of a Berber house teeters
on the structuralist play of ideas, his study intermingles body and space with
language and sign (ibid.: 169). It is becoming clear, and the chapters of this
book will confirm it, that the focus of material analysis is not merely the
object itself or space understood as the enclosure occupied by objects. Time
and action, performance and practice make the study of material culture
much more dynamic, stressing both the changes in objects over time, their
own biographies, and the role that placement, use, and reception each play in
understanding what an object does. It is *material practice* that becomes the
actual focal point of study. Objects and spaces are not static, with abstract
meanings encoded within them. Indeed, their "meanings" are often not singular or intellectual meanings at all, but rather the stories of their travels
through time.[11] The experience of material practice is frequently uninten-
tional, unarticulated, and felt. Often its significance is performance itself, the
ritualized sensation of seeing, touching, hearing, or feeling. Asking how to
study sensation and how to think of it as broader forms of cognition and
social experience brings us to the new instantiation of aesthetics.

Aesthetics

Aesthetics has long been considered the science or philosophy of beauty.
But that definition lacks the original, more expansive understanding of the
word. In 1735, Alexander Baumgarten coined the term "aesthetic," which
he took from the Greek word for perception, *aisthesis*, and in his major
work, *Aesthetica*, he defined his new "science of aesthetics" as "the perfection of sensual cognition as such, which is beauty" (Baumgarten 1983: 10).
He saw in poetry (and the other arts by extension) the refinement of sensation, inferior to reason, but still a form of thought. Baumgarten contended
that the utility of aesthetics would be:

> to make available appropriate materials to the sciences, to adapt scien-
> tific knowledge to the intellectual capacity of anyone, to press the
> improvement of knowledge even beyond the limits of the clearly known,
> to lay solid foundations for contemplative and spiritual activities and for
> the liberal arts, [and] to grant a certain superiority in common life under
> equal conditions to all other people.
>
> (ibid.)

The clearly moral character of Baumgarten's aesthetics and the practical
nature of beauty as distilled perception fell by the wayside in the course
of the eighteenth century as conceptions of the faculty of taste came to

dominate aesthetic discourse. Insistence on the disinterested nature of aesthetic judgments pushed away from Baumgarten's idea of the useful and pleasing refinement of sensation and toward the social distinction of taste.

Yet in recent years a number of scholars have questioned the post-Baumgarten understanding of "aesthetic" in regard to the study of religious material culture. In each case, they have sought to recognize the role of the body in religious material practice. For example, Simon Colman distinguished the classical notion of aesthetic value from the aesthetic practices of speaking and the use of imagery among the Pentecostals whom he studied in Sweden, contending that "a powerful 'aesthetic' sensibility, a coherent system of recognizing the presence of divinity in the visual and material" was at work in their worship practices (Coleman 1996: 108). In *Visual Piety* (Morgan 1998), I undertook the description and interpretation of an alternative aesthetic of lived religion (ibid.: 22–58; 2003). This aesthetic was not grounded in a disinterested relation of viewers to the image or figure of a deity, for example, but in the very embodied interests of viewers for what the deity can offer them:

> Those who venerate the saint or savior of popular images bring broken bodies to be mended, shattered nerves, and sick children to be healed. The body of the believer is explicitly engaged in what we may call the visual piety of popular religious images.[12]

Encouraged by Michael Taussig's re-reading of Walter Benjamin on mechanical reproducibility, Christopher Pinney has argued that the "disembodied, unidirectional and disinterested vision" at work in Western aesthetics misses the dynamics of visual practices among Indian peasants engaged by mass-produced images of Hindu deities. In order to recover the "mutuality and corporeality in spaces as varied as those of religious devotion and cinematic pleasure" among Indian viewers, Pinney has suggested an alternative critical practice he calls "corpothetics."[13] Brent Plate has aptly urged that the study of religious aesthetics be clearly distinguished from Christian theology and be practiced under the banner of religious studies in order to understand the creative, artistic construction of religious worlds (Plate 2005: viii).

Birgit Meyer has urged the scrutiny of what she calls "sensational forms," by which she means the structures that organize, evoke, and transmit feelings of the transcendent, especially awe and wonder (2006: 10). These are not analogous to the universal forms of intuition described by Immanuel Kant concerning time and space, but culturally constructed forms of sensation or "objectifications" that are especially amenable to mediation, that is, transmission and staging in different media. (This treatment of time and space is in fact indebted to Hegel, not Kant, as Daniel

Miller's description of objectification makes clear: "a process in time by which the very act of creating form creates consciousness" (Miller 2005: 9)). How the forms shape feeling, what manner of experience they stimulate and frame, how different media affect their performance, how the forms change among different audiences and over time are all matters for aesthetic analysis as it is being described here. Meyer encourages critical development in this domain for the study of religious experience in order to "account for its material, bodily, sensational and sensory dimension."[14] In so doing, she is careful to underscore the need for a reconstructed notion of the aesthetic.

Material culture as an approach to the study of religion

Having defined a number of key words (feeling, body, space, practice, performance), I have deferred until now the task of framing what may be the most rudimentary term for this book: material culture. What is it? We might begin with "matter," which may be a bit less vexing than "culture" to define. Western philosophers since the ancient Greeks have often begun with a prime distinction: the difference between knower and known, which is premised on the notion of soul as a substance apart from the material world. Ideas and the act of knowing are immaterial and therefore superior to the material world of things, the realm of shifting, impermanent appearances. What we have discussed in the concept of habitus and the role of objectification, however, suggests that this dualist split is not the only way to think about materiality. By recognizing the body and its engagement in spaces and things as integrally engaged in the production of experience, we are urged to recast the understanding of matter. Body, mind, and thing are not as discrete as classical philosophy often portrayed them to be.

So what is a thing? What goes into our experience and evaluation of a material object? Certainly its physical properties—its weight, texture, size, shape, and color. But also its relationship to other objects and its placement in the space we ourselves may inhabit next to it, above or below it, or from afar. And there is the object's change over time that is always at work making it what it is. All of these qualities of a thing, even its changing states, bear directly on its physical connection to our bodies. This suggests that a thing is, in part, what it offers us physically—pleasure, pain, or threat of harm. Already we see that a thing is more than a thing, more than itself. A thing is a thing-for-us. But its thingness has only begun to become apparent. We find that a thing's physical characteristics may be rivaled, even eclipsed by the intentions and desires of our fellows who may want it for themselves. Children often argue over a toy as if it answers to their deepest longing, yet the winner may abandon it as soon as she sees her playmates directing their attention to another toy. Things are social.

Adults are hardly different. We want what others want. It is not the thing so much as the social rivalry that infuses the thing with desirability. The presence of a thing, its presentation to consciousness, depends on more than its physicality. Things exist within spaces of value, the cultural marketplace of desire. In addition to desire, use enfolds a thing into a register of value that is what we see or touch when we apprehend a thing. If I have a use for a thing, I am especially aware of it. If I do not require it for some purpose at hand, the thing may fade away on a shelf of stuff or submerge into the oblivion of a drawer of odds-and-ends. Things also exist for human beings within taxonomies, set within schemes of kinship. A hammer is a hammer because its objectness bears a relation to the class of things known as hammers. When we see a hammer, it may be that we see that relation as much as this particular hammer. This is often the case with persons: we see a woman, a man, a black man, a rich man—not individuals, but examples of classes. And we also encounter histories in things. Things come to us with genealogies and biographies such that we see in the thing more than what is there physically—we see evidence of its previous states, of its itinerary, of it trajectory to the present moment. This may change our estimation of the thing, our use for it, our care or disregard for the thing. Finally, we see ourselves and others in things. The letter from a lover is more than mere paper; the photograph of one's parent or child is more than an image; the souvenir from a vacation is more than a bit of clay or wood. Embedded in these things is something that matters to us—our relationship to the person, time, or place from which the object issues.

And yet, in spite of the social or political career of things, there is to consider the life of a thing beyond the human uses for it. The brief consideration of things so far has been clearly slanted toward the network of human consciousness because I have framed the definition of things in terms of their relevance for human beings, especially as related to the human body and human sociality. Most conceptions of "material culture" incline in this direction since whatever such a term may mean, it clearly favors the significance of material things as culture or shaped by human beings. But it is important to bear in mind that this anthropocentric approach need not be in force. One might frame the study of things in terms of non-human materiality, that is, as the editors of *Handbook of Material Culture* summarized one major theme in the study of materiality, "Things as materially existing and having a significance in the world independent of any human action or intervention" (Tilley *et al.* 2006: 4). Although thingness is a concept, a product of human ideation, it remains baldly true that things were here long before human beings arrived.

But framed within the study of religion, the study of things assumes they are an important and almost infinitely varied means by which human beings feel their way into their worlds, feel themselves, feel the past, anticipate the future, feel together. Yet we must distinguish two dimensions to this framework. There is the politics of things, their inflection within social fields, and there is the poetics of things, that is, their capacity to act upon us, to assert agency, to make rather than only to be made. Several chapters in this book consider the power that images and objects exert in human life. It is important not to collapse the poetics of things into the politics if we are to be able to discern both their materiality and human corporeality.

Is there a way to conduct a balanced or integrated investigation? Anthropologist Webb Keane raises the possibility when he alerts us to the need to avoid isolating cultural representations:

> Even the most transcendental images occur in particular social and onto-logical spaces, facing audiences, making use of performers and their skills, presupposing certain assumptions about how actions occur and what sorts of beings inhabit the world, and requiring economic and social resources.
>
> (1997: 11)

Seeking an integrated account may begin with recognizing the degree to which things are the scaffolding by which the body extends itself, the avenues by which the mind travels as a physical structure in time and space. Things are the medium of various forms of social exchange that structure human relations, create and maintain systems of value. Things may operate as mere tokens in exchange, as with coins, or, as Annette Weiner argued in an important essay, they may bear far greater "symbolic density" by being kept out of exchange, held in the possession of individuals, families, clans, institutions, peoples, or nations—such as rare coins collected and left to family members (Weiner 1994). Some things perform as the passive instruments of a putatively autonomous human consciousness (think of disposable pens, lawn tools, admission tickets, empty soda bottles); others possess individual stories and are part of a genealogy prized by those who admire them (such as religious relics, works of art, antiques, or heirlooms). The former facilitate the operation of daily life; the latter expand and enable thought, feeling, and sensation. In both cases, however differently, objects act on us. Instrumental objects enable humans to imagine and practice agency; objects of intrinsic value enable people to imagine their relation to those people, institutions, histories, or gods whom they experience as sacred. By exerting themselves, people build the world about them, acting on objects, which in turn offer them a world in which to live. Objectification is the process of human activity returning to itself from the world around it, or rather, allowing people to be subjects that apprehend an ordered, valued world of their making. The dialectical process is the self-making of human consciousness, the work of culture.[15] Things both show and tell human beings who they are, or who they want to be. I say "show" *and* "tell" because people rely on things both as information (the language or coded operation of things) and as agents. There is not a deep ontological split between the universe and human beings. And this point enables us to venture an attempt at defining material culture.

Material culture consists of the things, the practices of using things, and the forms directing their uses on which we build and maintain the worlds about us, and thereby encounter and value ourselves and others. The three dimensions of material culture are things, uses, and paradigms. Material culture is not just objects, not just architectural foundations or jewelry or paintings because, as we saw above, things are more than things. Their edges fade into the systems of value we rely on to recognize and deploy them. Their boundaries fade as they are deployed in practices, merging into bodies and spaces in the medium of feeling. Things are present or absent according to the purposes and needs that drive our activities. But things are also recalcitrant, resistant forces that challenge the schemata or paradigms of culture, the expectations or dispositions that shape human perception. Materiality is also the push-back of physical regimes that culture must grapple within in its world-making activity. Things are powerful, compelling, living agents that touch us, scare us, calm us, protect us. Moving throughout our engagement with them is a complex array of embodied assumptions, which stitch together the patchwork fabric of order into worlds, which are the stage on which a social actor, a person, a human being takes her place.

With that said, what may we offer as a working definition of the material culture of religion? In short, religious material culture consists of the objects, spaces, practices, and ideas in which belief takes shape. Belief, as argued in the Introduction, is not merely discursive assent to a proposition or teaching, but the entire body of human activities that makes a force, an event, or a place sacred. Belief is manifest as an oriented consciousness, but it is also the means of orientation, that is, belief is to be found subtly rooted in what orients people to act as they do. Belief takes the shape of bodies, individual and social, contributing to and drawing from the formative reservoir of habits. Considered as an emergent or temporal phenomenon, belief begins to happen long before an individual may ever affirm a creed. Discerning the life of belief as the stories of things, of bodies, of spaces, and of practices is therefore the business of the scholar of religious material culture.

Notes

1 Hume (2007). Hume traced the rise of religion from its inception in polytheism, arguing for an upward tendency "from the statue or material image to the invisible power; and from the invisible power to an infinitely perfect deity, the creator and sovereign of the universe" (ibid.: 59).

2 Damasio (1999: 41). For consideration of the cognitive function of emotion in religion, see Thagard (2006: 237–49).

3 Damasio (1999: 55). Hume opened his study of the passions with the same claim (Hume 2007: 3).

4 For a biological study of the human face and communication, see Lundqvist and Öhman (2005).

5 See for instance Corrigan (2002: 82–103); Morgan (2007: 165–95; 2009); and Meyer (2006).

6 Two of the most original and influential studies on the felt connections between things and people are Freedberg (1989) and Gell (1998).

7 A pioneering essay in the study of the cultural literacy of the body is Mauss (1973).

8 Turner (1988: 81). Turner explicitly included Goffman in the passage quoted; see also Schieffelin (1998: 194).

9 Influenced by the tradition of Van Gennep and Turner, the ritual theorist Ronald Grimes has criticized Eliade and Jonathan Smith for the disproportionate stress on space in the study of ritual (Grimes 2006: 101–13).

10 Bourdieu ([1972] 1977: 89). For more recent considerations of Bourdieu's concept of practice and habitus as it relates to ritual and the body, see Schieffelin (1998: 199–200); Crossley (2001: 91–119); and Miller (1987: 103–06).

11 See Davis (1997), who carried into art historical investigation the biographical approach to objects set out by Kopytoff (1986).

12 Morgan (1998: 31). For a sustained argument for returning physicality and emotion to the experience of art and the study of aesthetics, see Dissanayake (1992: 24–32).

13 Pinney (2004: 193). For a collection of essays that takes up Alfred Gell's argument that "In so far as there can be an anthropological theory of 'aesthetics', such a theory would try to explain why social agents, in particular settings, produced the responses they do to particular works of art" (Gell 1998: 4), see Pinney and Thomas (2001).

14 Meyer (2006: 19). For an insightful discussion of the task of aesthetics for the study of religious mediation, see Meyer and Verrips (2008).

15 For a classical discussion of objectification (or objectivation) in the social constructivist tradition see Berger (1967: 3–29); for the application of the idea to material culture, see Miller (1987), Myers (2001: 20–21), and Tilley (2006).

Part II

SENSATION

4

Tactility and transcendence
Epistemologies of touch in African arts and spiritualities

Mary Nooter Roberts

Haptic visuality and visual tactility: knowledge based upon touch
Touching to remember
Touching for spiritual validation and spiritual mediation
A blessing touch
Touching the untouchable

A man wearing an elaborately beaded headdress looks intently at the small wooden board in his left hand. It is bedecked with multicolored beads, as well as a few cowry shells, buttons, and a large metal pin. He gently traces a path along a line of beads with his right index finger, pointing to details while reciting a lengthy account of a Luba king's exploits in the early twentieth century (Figure 4.1). His fingers brush across the surface of the board as if he were reading Braille, yet this man is not visually impaired. On the contrary, he is visually empowered because he is in a state of spirit possession. The donning of his headdress indicates that he has been "mounted" by one of the Bavidye of the Luba spiritual pantheon of twinned tutelary spirits of king-ship. Only in a state of trance can the man decipher the complex and deeply layered references encoded in the colors and patterns of the beads and other features of the board, and only through touch can he trace a path through this spiritual maze of meaning. It is this *visual tactility* that gives him the insight to translate, transmit, and apply the secrets of Luba royal culture.

In keeping with art history more broadly, in African art history there has been a bias toward the visual to the neglect of other sensory inputs that constitute the total experience of a work of art. Such approaches reflect the ocularcentric nature of modern Western experience. As David Chidester states (2005b: 61), "the modern world is supposedly a domain of visibility, constituted by the hegemony of the gaze, governed by panoptic surveillance (Foucault 1979), and ruled by the 'scopic regimes of modernity'" (Jay 1988). Descriptions of the aesthetic qualities of African objects have tended to focus upon visually ascertained formal attributes. And yet, anyone who participates in the contexts of African arts or has conducted extended research

Figure 4.1   A court historian touches the beads on a Luba mnemonic device to
activate remembrance

Source: Photo by Mary Nooter Roberts, Democratic Republic of
the Congo (DRC), 1989.

on them in Africa has noted the importance of multisensory experience.
Whether emblems to be held, masks to be worn, altars for supplicating
divine intervention, or objects that require anointing, consecration, and/or
other kinds of devotional or therapeutic contact, African art is almost
invariably an art of touch.

Although studied in the context of art history and anthropology and
exhibited in museums of art and natural history, many of the works that we
include in this broad and arbitrary category of "African arts" are spiritual or
religious in nature, and often were intended for ritual or ceremonial uses that
resulted in progressive transformations of the surface and appearance of the
object. Objects have "careers" and "lives," that is (M. Roberts 1994). For
example, among Bamana peoples of Mali, the enigmatic sculptural forms
known as *boli* were reservoirs of knowledge for members of the Komo association, whose culmination ceremonies were marked by the initiates' patting
of substances onto the surface of such figures to signify ascension to the ranks

of knowledge and esoteric abilities. The changing shapes and forms of *boli* were indices of generational accumulations of wisdom and agency. As an associated proverb states of related material and performance arts, "the Komo mask is made to look like an animal. But it is not an animal, it is a secret" (McNaughton 1979: 44).

Scholars of African masquerades have demonstrated the rich synaesthetic dimensions of performance (Drewal and Drewal 1983; Lawal 1996; Strother 1998, Lamp 2004; among others). Sound, smell, sight, touch, and taste are all integral parts of something greater than any single mode or result of sensory input. Nor are masquerades to be viewed passively, as though masks may be removed from performers' clothing ensembles, that may be auditory (e.g. ankle bells) or kinetic—only to be experienced in complex choreographies. Accompanying orchestras may complement visual impacts with their mnemonic or riffed rhythms. An aromatic register is provided as food is prepared or dust is kicked up—sometimes quite purposefully as an ephemeral screen. Shouts of encouragement and appreciative laughter or derision, should a performer falter, prove that audiences are integral to masquerade experience. And an extra frisson of fear mixed with taunting challenge may occur when spirit maskers or their attendants brandish whips or other weapons to keep crowds at bay. As one Yoruba proverb has it in allusion to annual Gelede masquerades honoring women of the community, "The eyes that have seen Gelede have seen the ultimate spectacle" (Drewal and Drewal 1983: 1), implying that "seen" is a far more inclusive multisensory experience than may meet the eye.

While African sensory experiences in plastic and performance arts have been well documented, touch and tactility have received less attention and yet are integral to the experience of many kinds of objects. Tucked within the descriptive commentaries concerning virtually every kind of object used for spiritual mediation in African cultural contexts are references to tactility. This may be manifested as physical engagement with an object, producing patina and traces of wear, or as accretions of offerings upon surfaces of things and places. Visual effects of such engagement may be smooth or worn surfaces (Blier 2004), or accumulated and "integumented" ones—that is, "skins" of or thresholds to powers within (Rubin 1974). Tactility may be more mimetic but no less real, as a "haptic visuality" in which "the eyes themselves function like organs of touch," as one experiences relationships of embodied sensation linking viewer and image (Marks 2000: 22; 2002: 3).

Among Luba peoples of the Democratic Republic of the Congo (DRC), with whom I conducted research in the late 1980s,[1] every object valued in the West for its formal attributes of aesthetic achievement was an object of tactility—whether a throne to support one's weight, a staff of office gripped in the hand, a headrest to dream upon, a cup from which to imbibe palm wine, an axe worn ceremonially over the shoulder, or an ivory pendant borne on the chest of a noble. Luba royal emblems interact with human bodies. Furthermore, most objects of wood and ivory have been and are anointed regularly with palm oil and other organic substances. Luba divination objects are similarly dependent upon manipulation by a diviner and sometimes a client, as well. Only through such intimate and enduring physical contact can such objects mediate with the spirit world (Roberts and Roberts 1996: 177–209).[2]

While these things involve direct touch and manipulation, spiritual modes of viewing are dependent on a different sort of touch. Indeed, spirits are sometimes the most important intended audience for African works of art, and the manner in which spirits *behold* the objects may be through intangible tactile relationships residing in the mind's eye. For Luba, a haptic gaze may be asserted by humans embodied by spirits (spirit mediums, diviners, and other ritual practitioners), or spirits may need no such transaction with the living; but in both cases, the act of visual touching links the spirit and human realms in transcendent intersubjectivities that enable insight and efficacy.

Despite the crucial importance of human and spiritual contact with objects, it has not been customary to focus on the sensory dimensions of African art, especially in museums as the locations where African objects are most readily encountered in the West. As a number of scholars have recently argued (Classen 2005; Pye 2007: 16–17), the Western museum has deprived visitors of almost all the non-visual sensory inputs that objects have possessed because of scopic regimes of late twentieth- and early twenty-first century Euro-American culture. Yet sometimes restrictions as to how objects may be experienced in museums through "do not touch" rules and barriers have been ignored, especially when religious experiences are possible (Roberts and Vogel 1994). In such instances, museum taboos have been subverted by faith and devotion.

In the paragraphs to follow, this chapter will demonstrate how African objects reflect intense experiences of touch through *visual tactility*. Consideration will be given to how Luba people of the DRC create objects that are touched for mnemonic purposes as well as spiritual mediation, validation, and empowerment. Then Sufi practices in Senegal will be glimpsed, as images are touched to obtain blessing. Touch and tactility participate in culturally specific sensory epistemologies, and people and spirits engage with, wield, and are affected by objects through ontological constructions of "thing-ness." Beliefs are materialized through objects meant to be touched, held, caressed, worn, or otherwise perceived haptically. Finally, examples of museum exhibitions that have defied "do not touch" taboos and resulting devotional engagement will be pondered.

Haptic visuality and visual tactility: knowledge based upon touch

An important literature on "haptic visuality" has emerged recently.[3] In her work on intercultural cinema, Laura Marks discusses how the act of watching a film may constitute a mode of touch, so that a viewer experiences multi-sensory dimensions of things and circumstances observed. In haptic visuality, the role of the viewer becomes intertwined with what is being viewed, and the barriers break down between observer and object. Furthermore, "the sense of touch may embody memories that are unavailable to vision." Marks posits an epistemology that "uses touch rather than vision as its model for knowledge, namely, mimesis" (2000: 22). Related analyses have been articulated, as when Christopher Pinney writes of experiences that South Asian devotees have before the images of Hindu gods. Pinney calls this embodied visuality "corpothetics," and develops the concept of *darshan* much further than an exchange of gaze between person and deity.[4] Corpothetics "entails a desire to fuse image and beholder, and the elevation of efficacy (as for example in *barkat*) as the central criterion of value" (2004: 194). At issue is a *performance* of perception through bodily engagement. Pinney also refers to Merleau-Ponty's concept of "double sensation," as touching and being touched, which the phenomenologist then applied to vision as necessarily reciprocal or doubled by another vision, because "he who sees cannot possess the visible unless he is possessed by it" (in ibid.: 194).

Haptic visuality is important to understanding the sensory impact of film as well as devotional experiences of "seeing" through which viewers do not touch the screen or the image of devotion, but are encouraged to place themselves "in" the screen and its images and so to become directly—even ontologically—engaged with them. The concept of haptic visuality is somewhat different from the experience of three-dimensional objects that are *actually* touched as mediators with the spirit world. With the objects and images to be discussed here, tangible touch contributes to meaning-making and the development of devotional practice, and leads to enhanced visuality and ultimately *insight*. Such a combination of seeing and touching produces particular outcomes, and the phrase "visual tactility" is contrasted with "haptic visuality" to explore the process whereby touch leads to engaged vision. In certain African contexts of spiritual mediation, vision before touch is superficial. Once tactility has intervened, *insight* becomes possible. Visual tactility suggests *embodiment*, as a way of using sight to lead to next levels of spiritual mediation. However, haptic visuality and corpothetics remain pertinent concepts, for it is in the intersubjectivity created by a tactile relationship that visuality is enabled and becomes insight. Outward vision is turned to inner vision through the materialization of contact. Furthermore, haptic visuality helps to theorize the process whereby spirits engage with objects without actual recourse to physical touch, but only through the kind of "seeing" that is mimetic by definition.

In a powerful invocation of materiality in the study of religion, Chidester discusses the way the sense of touch was discounted in earlier religious discourse as inferior to inner spirituality and doctrine. And contradictions are at work even within Christian experience, through which touch is denigrated and advocated, condemned and condoned. Chidester contends that this refusal to recognize the importance of touch in religious experience is a denial of a most important facet of religiosity: "Laying on hands, anointing with oils, washing feet, holy kissing, swearing oaths on the Bible, taking up snakes … are all forms of religious tactility that both signify and enact a direct, powerful, and even intimate contact with the sacred" (2005: 50). David Morgan further reinforces the interactive nature of devotional praxis: "Interacting with sacred images— dressing, praying to, speaking with, and studying before them, changing their appearance in accord with seasonal display—is a common and important way of making them part of daily life" (1998: 50). Touching in such contexts is the materialization of that which cannot be materialized. When a saint's bones are touched, the saint is present and absent simultaneously. When a hand is placed upon the Bible to swear an oath, God is present and absent. When a memory device is used for recollection, it works in defiance of obliviscence, no matter its inevitability. Reification of the sacred permits that which cannot be grasped to be apprehended nonetheless, while providing new subjectivities. Indeed, materialization of the sacred is always a process of becoming, as is suggested in a comparative case from India.

In his *Lives of Indian Images* (1997), Richard Davis discusses how Hindu icons serve as "point[s] of access (and ultimately transcendence) for human devotees." Such holy objects "are, in one sense, physical objects. They are material forms that can be seen and touched, and so allow the sensible contact with god that Visnu says humans crave and require" (ibid.: 30). In a detailed account, Davis traces a ritual program of "establishment" through which Indian temples and icons are brought to life. Such work "involves an elaborate sequence of rites that, through repeated imposition of mantras, powers, and substances, progressively constitutes the fabricated object as fully imbued with the attribute of divinity" (ibid.: 33–37). The process can include more than twenty constituent performances in a highly physical set of acts, often involving gestures of human touch and tactility with the object. "There is never a time when the image exists as an uncon-secrated object; its very coming into being is within ritual" (ibid.: 35).

To see so many works of African art in publications and museum galleries separated from their makers, owners, and users, and no longer connected to the consecrations and ritual transformations to which they were once integral, leads to a sterilization of the image and an elision of process. And yet, the mar-ket value of so many African objects is often determined, in part, by the quality of the "patina" or by the aesthetic effect of surface accretions dependent upon just such processual moments in the objects' lives. In her recent *Art of the Senses* (2004), Suzanne Blier addresses how patina and surface become regis-ters of biographies of objects, not only in their earlier phases in Africa, but once they enter Western contexts where they may be cleaned, oiled, stripped of accumulations, or "tidied up" in some other way to make them more appealing to collectors (ibid.: 22–3). Likewise, in museum contexts, objects may be fumigated, dusted, or conserved, subtly modifying their surfaces. And finally, each time works are exhibited, written about, and featured in auctions, they acquire new layers of "patina." Blier understands such processes as metaphorical patina, purposefully or inadvertently increasing the objects' commercial value through attention and authenticity so accorded (ibid.).

Touching to remember

Sometime in the eighteenth century, the Mbudye Association was created as a check and balance to the authority of Luba rulers. Mbudye members were custodians and transmitters of the past and the guardians of secret knowledge. The most prized possession of Mbudye was—and is, for the society still exists—a *lukasa*, a wooden mnemonic board covered with beads and other materials to encode the details of esoteric wisdom (Figure 4.2). Somewhat like a computer motherboard or a telephone switchboard, the multi-colored object stimulates memory as performed through recitation of historical narratives.[5]

While the *lukasa* is usually described in terms of its visual attributes, it is when an Mbudye official holds the object in his hand and uses his fingers to guide his thoughts through the loci of memory that the making of histories proceeds. But it is important to recognize that this can only happen once an official has entered a state of spirit possession: information is not simply waiting to be narrated. Rather, the Mbudye adept must be taken over by his spirit persona which he has acquired in the penultimate level in the association's initiations in order to acquire the "literacy" needed to "read" the board.[6] Hence, although information conveyed is historical (that is, the explanation of social relations over time that lead to the circumstances of a particular performance event), the process is one of spiritual engagement. And touch is the vehicle toward the acquisition of such insights.

A close parallel exists between the way an Mbudye member touches a *lukasa* memory board to organize knowledge and esoteric insight and the way that Luba people have described the tactility of women's scarification patterns to me. Scarification is a form of cosmetic beautification in which light incisions are cut into the skin in particular shapes and patterns, and then have herbal substances rubbed into them to create welts on the surface of the skin. Earlier Luba women created ample scarification patterns to perfect their bodies through esoteric communication, as is evidenced in sculptures from the nineteenth century and in early archival photographs from the colonial period (Figure 4.3). While the practice is no longer so popular, it is understood to have been a critically important means of personal and cultural identity in the past. A woman was simply not "Luba" without these "marks of civilization" (Rubin 1988).

Scarification patterns were also erotic. They were considered to be extremely beautiful to both sight and to touch, and as one Luba woman told me,

Figure 4.2   A *lukasa* memory board is held and "read" to recite
Luba history

Source: Collection of Susanne K. Bennet, Washington, D.C. Photo by
Jerry L. Thompson, 1996. Courtesy of The Museum for African Art, New York.

women would oil their skin at night so that their scarifications would glow
in the low light of the bedroom. "A man had only to rub his hands over the
scarification marks of his wife and he would be instantly excited." Without
overemphasizing this dimension of Luba scarification, an important message is to be discerned: the raised bumps across a woman's torso and back
ignited desire and sensual pleasure in much the same way that surface features of the *lukasa* provoke mnemonic recall. Both bespeak tactile engagement through embodiment.

A number of Luba interlocutors talked to me about how a *lukasa* has
"scarifications," as do almost all Luba royal emblems. Usually these are made
manifest through incised or embossed geometric patterns called *bizila* that
refer to the "secrets of Luba kingship." On a *lukasa*, these appear on the back

Figure 4.3   Scarifications were worn by women in southeastern Congo for cultural and cosmetic reasons, and valued for their beauty, tactility, and arcane meanings

Source: Photo by an unknown photographer, Kirungu, *c.* 1900.
Courtesy of Allen F. Roberts.

or "outside" of the board that rests upon the left hand holding it. But scarifications are also alluded to by the beads on the front or "inside" of the board, and Luba with whom I worked explicitly described a *lukasa* board as "the torso of a woman." In particular, the model for a lukasa is said to be the founding ancestress of the Mbudye Association—a woman who is also a tortoise. Such deeply mystical associations are rooted in place memory.

Memories are lodged in locales (*lieux de mémoire*), and one is reminded of how Classical orators are said to have composed their speeches by imagining features of and passages through memorized theaters (Yates 1966). It has been well documented that memory process is far more rooted in place than time.[7] A *lukasa* memory board is understood as a system of places of different scales and magnitudes, from the most microcosmic level of the features of a tortoise shell and the scarification patterns of a woman's body, to the mappings of royal compounds and other built environments, and finally to the vast expanses of Luba landscape. The board can be read with any of these implied and elaborated, either separately or through intellectual overlays reminiscent of the use of vellum or computerized models by Western architects. As a map of Luba landscape, spiritual associations can be reified. Luba landscape is dotted with sacred locales in which royal spirits reside. Such spiritual residences may be lakes and pools, forest groves, or striking peaks (see Allen Roberts's contribution to this volume). Priestesses who reside in such numinous locales are intermediaries (Roberts and Roberts 2007: 25).

More generally among Luba, women are conduits to spirits. Although men also serve such roles, very explicit statements suggest that women have a more direct association with the spirit world (see Nooter 1991: chap. 5). They can more readily serve as vessels for spirits and spiritual energy. Their ability to bear children provides the extra capacity necessary to embody the spirits of deceased rulers and Bavidye spirits of the Luba pantheon. For all these reasons, Luba royal authority is ambiguously gendered and "the king is a woman." That is, whereas men are overt rulers, women are their spiritual guides, keepers, and most ardent—and necessary—supporters. Mothers, daughters, sisters, and aunts play critically important roles in Luba royal life and often serve as advisors, ambassadors, and custodians of the secrets of Luba royalty which they hold within their breasts.

If emblems of Luba royalty depict women, it is because the spirits are more attracted to them and inhere in female forms, just as the spirit of a deceased king comes to reside in the body of a woman (see Roberts and Roberts 2007: 53–9). Such emblems are essential repositories for spiritual power, hence their perfection with women's marks of beauty and civilization. A *lukasa* memory board, then, "is" a woman, and the bumps and patterns across its surfaces are specifically intended to be *touched*. But this tactile relationship is by no means confined to sexualized readings, for scarifications are mnemonic. They encode information about a person's origins, marital status, and biography, as well as referring to natural phenomena and cultural precepts. Luba scarification patterns have names and make multi-referential symbolic allusions that *instigate* action, as Victor Turner (1970) wrote of the work of ritual more generally.

The association of scarifications with quotidian information and esoteric knowledge reinforces how a *lukasa* is a database, and that reading of its attributes is akin to reading the biography of a woman as worked into her skin (Roberts 2007: 55–9). Yet, the "woman" that is being read as a *lukasa* stands for Luba royal culture more generally, and feminine embodiment ensures mediation with the spirit world. A *lukasa*, then, is a material means to capture and convey knowledge, create ever-changing histories, and activate associations with spirits to effect necessary transformations in everyday life as well as at moments of social upheaval.

Memory is a matter of touch *and* vision in such circumstances. As one moves one's fingers across signifiers of the past, memory is stimulated and histories can be narrated. In their work on the relationships between art and memory, Susanne Küchler and Walter Mellion (1991) emphasize the importance of visual stimuli to mnemonic process; but I would add that a relationship between haptic visuality and visual tactility is engaged in the memory processes we have considered here. Signs of memory as beads and shells and metal shards or incised and raised geometric patterns carry knowledge that is generic until disposed on the surface of a female "body," be it that of the landscape, the royal court, or that of the Mbudye ancestress. Through the touch of the eyes and the eyes of touch, Luba keepers of memory and makers of history envision and enunciate that which is otherwise sacred and secret. Through their contact with the skin of the past, Mbudye members activate and embody memories for the present.

Touching for spiritual validation and spiritual mediation

Several sorts of Luba objects serve as vehicles for spiritual validation and mediation through tactility and the agency of the hand. One of the most common emblems of high-ranking persons is a staff of office (Figure 4.4). Such objects may belong to a king, chief, or titleholder, but they are equally important insignia for diviners, spirit mediums, and members of the Mbudye

Figure 4.4 Luba chiefs own and wield staffs as a sign of spiritual validation for their office and their royal pedigree

Source: Photo by Mary Nooter Roberts, DRC, 1989.

Association. Staffs of office are used in many other African societies to connote rank and status, while assisting healing and protection (A. Roberts 1994). Such staffs are gripped in the hand, leaned upon, or rested in the crook of an arm. They extend the body itself in metaphors about the reach of a ruler and the extent and nature of command (cf. Fraser and Cole 1972).

Among Luba, staffs of office are carved from wood and may incorporate iron and copper. They are not only held as emblems to be seen, but they may be touched as documents to be deciphered. Luba staffs of office are maps in three-dimensional sculptural form, diagramming a ruler's pedigree of family, clan, and lineage. They are literally loaded with meaning, given the medicinal charges they sometimes bear (cf. Jordán 1994); and they may be interpreted through oral performances in which the owner touches or caresses the places on the staff to which he refers as he recites his narrative (Roberts and Roberts 1996: Chapter V). Of all the photographs ever taken of Luba rulers and titleholders by missionaries and/or visitors to the region (including this author), it is difficult to find any that does not show the official holding his staff firmly. The tactile association with this object is not only prestige-based, for it also confers spiritual authority and historical legitimacy. Touching a staff is to witness the authenticity of power vested in an individual by the spirits of Luba royalty.

Perhaps the most tactile of all Luba objects are divination instruments. In their tactility, they have much in common with divination objects elsewhere in the world (see Mack 2007: 109–23). The very essence of the instrumentality of such things is in the hand of the diviner, as the vehicle activating the objects' arcane messages and transcendent powers. The two most commonly practiced forms of Luba divination emphasize touch and movement as processes through which spiritual insight is achieved. The first is *kashekeshe* and deploys a small wooden object carved as a female head surmounting a hollow rectangle.[8] The woman diviner grasps one side of the "body" of the figure with two fingers and her thumb, while the client takes hold of the other side (Figure 4.5). As she poses questions and a spirit responds, the figure swishes back and forth (hence the onomatopoetic name *kashekeskeke*) and makes circular motions of its own volition. The movements are codified and may be read for their meanings and messages, but only the diviner can provide their interpretation.

Whereas woman *kashekeshe* diviners have direct links to their divining spirits as established through dreams, male diviners using the same instrument must undergo *lusalo*. This involves cutting light incisions into defined locations of the hand and inserting medicinal/herbal substances. Once such ritual enhancement is established, a male diviner may activate the *kashekeshe* divining instrument through the touch of his hand as do his female counterparts.

A woman *kashekeshe* diviner with whom I worked rubbed her wooden figure with the pungent leaves of wild basil to awaken the spirit prior to her consultation with a client. Many early Luba *kashekeshe*

Figure 4.5   Luba *kashekesheke* divination is dependent on the hand
of the diviner, who holds one side of the instrument as the client
holds the other

Source: Photo by Mary Nooter Roberts, DRC, 1989.

instruments (sometimes called *katatora*) can be found in Western collections and few if any remain in local villages; nowadays, diviners often use
other kinds of objects for this same purpose—in one case a battered aluminum cup. What is critical is not so much what the object is made from
or what it looks like, but the fact that holding it with the hand activates
direct embodiment of the spirit by women practitioners, or with the
mediation of medicinal insertions in the hands of men. In either case,
touch proves the sensory threshold.

A second and more dramatic type of Luba divination is called Bulumbu,
and is practiced by male and female diviners through royal prerogative.
Bulumbu divination is also highly tactile, and its primary instruments are
object-filled gourds and carved human figures. The most important sort of
divination gourd is called an *mboko*, meaning a source of wellbeing,
wealth, good health, and truth, as a microcosm of social and physical universes. Within its hollow interior, an *mboko* contains myriad objects, some
manufactured and others derived from the natural world, each of which is
a cipher. When clients engage the diviner, they grasp an *mboko* and shake
it, creating a rhythmically percussive soundscape as the metal attachments
on the outside of the gourd and the many objects within are jostled about
and rearranged. When the lid of the gourd is lifted, a cloud of white chalk
dust is released as a blessing (white = light = enlightenment = grace). The

Figure 4.6   Bulumbu is a Luba divination practice that involves spirit possession
and the tactile manipulation of object-filled gourds

Source: Photo by Mary Nooter Roberts, DRC, 1988.

diviner peers inside the *mboko* to see the new contingencies of its jumbled
contents (Figure 4.6). Through gentle handling of discrete elements and
careful scrutiny of their relationships to each other, diviners and clients
locate meaning in the "little world" of the gourd (see Roberts and Roberts
1996: 206). With hand and eye as guided by spirit, the Bulumbu diviner
determines the sense of juxtapositions, interpreting their meanings for the
client seeking solution to a problem.

As when an Mbudye member "reads" a *lukasa* memory board, the diag-
nosis of Bulumbu gourd divination is possible because the adept is in trance.
Spirits are embodied during these ritual performances, enabling clairvoyance. But such critically important ability to define and address misfortune
requires the power of touch, for it is the sensory blending of tactility and
vision that leads to insight (Roberts 2000).

A blessing touch

A very different example of the way that touch can inform visual experience is found in practices of mystical Islam in West Africa. Devotees of the Mouride Way follow the writings and life lessons of Sheikh Amadou Bamba (1853–1927), a Senegalese Sufi saint (*wali Allah* in Arabic). Three major means provide miracles and blessing: the saint's tomb in the holy pilgrimage city of Touba, several hours east of Dakar; Bamba's sermons and poetry as a writer so prolific that it is said that only the ocean is sufficiently vast to hold the totality of his verse; and the saint's images, manifest in a stunning array of media but based upon a single photograph taken by French colonial authorities in 1913 as a surveillance instrument. Mouride artists produce Bamba's portrait in every imaginable medium, from plaster-of-Paris, painting, aluminum, cloth, wood, glass, and leather, to cuttlefish bone, coconut shell, and others as yet undetermined. The saint is to be seen in cities and towns throughout Senegal and around the world through an ever-expanding Mouride diaspora. The tactile relationship of viewers to Bamba's image will interest us here.[9]

It is very common to see Mourides approach images of Amadou Bamba and gently sweep their fingers across the saint's forehead and then bring these same fingers to their own foreheads. Once while I was examining a large painting of one of Bamba's sons (the Caliph at the time) at a street vendor's stand, a man crossed the boulevard to touch his own forehead to the painted Caliph's brow. On another occasion, during one of a great many interviews with the street artist known as "Papisto," a boy walking down the road took a detour to approach Papisto's wall-mural depiction of Fatou Guewel, a Mouride praise-singer especially famous for several deeply devotional—but infectiously popular—recordings (Figure 4.7). The young man kissed the diva's image before heading on up the road to fulfill his mother's errand. These and countless other instances constitute visual communion as mediated by touch.

When Mourides make these gestures, they obtain holy blessing energy called *baraka*, for portraits of Amadou Bamba are icons that possess and convey the saint's presence. By physically touching the image, Mourides seek to be protected and promoted. Shirts and sheets inscribed with talismanic letters and numbers may also be worn or wrapped about the body to impart *baraka*, and there are many other examples of touch-induced efficacy in the religions of Africa. For example, in Ethiopia, processional crosses of Coptic Christianity may be brought into contact with the skin of a sick person to effect healing. Many material manifestations of local African religions are used in similar ways, as when a Luba staff is rubbed over the skin of the critically ill. Such efficacious things—that Western collectors would consider works of art—mediate human and spiritual affairs through tactile acts of healing touch.

Figure 4.7   A portion of a painted wall by Papisto where passers-by
kiss and touch the images to obtain *baraka*, holy blessing energy

Source: Photo by Mary Nooter Roberts and Allen F. Roberts, Dakar, Senegal, 1999.

Touching the untouchable

Such wondrous African things are now found in many of the world's major
museums, yet tactile contact of the sort they once promoted is the first thing
denied to anyone wishing to engage them. "Do not touch" warnings mark
first and most memorable experiences of museums (with interactive displays
explicit exceptions). Who *hasn't* encountered a gruff guard whose responsibility to protect some painting overrides your innocent desire to look a little
closer or at the back of something? A code of conduct based upon practical-
ity and cultural construction warns visitors to keep their distance, with plexi
vitrines, motion-detector alarms, and video cameras for further enforcement
(Roberts and Vogel 1994). Indeed, a distinguishing feature of how one
beholds sacred things at their original sites versus how they may be presented

in museums is the prevention of physical engagement in the latter. A sacred icon in a St. Petersburg church may have a fervent line waiting to approach it and a cloth handy so that traces of kisses can be wiped away before leaving one's own kiss of hope and prayer upon the glass; yet in a museum, the same icon would never be so accessible to the blessings of touch. An ancestral figure from Mali created to receive layer upon layer of offerings as a touching testament to faith and purpose is placed behind glass.

Such determined avoidance is so ironclad a rule that exceptions through a few exhibitions of African materials are especially instructive. One such was *A Saint in the City: Sufi Arts of Urban Senegal* (2003–2008) that Allen Roberts and I curated for the Fowler Museum at UCLA. Given our awareness of how Mourides interact with images, we informed security staff that there might be devotees who would wish to touch images in the exhibition. We requested that they not stop them from doing so, since not only is this a common tactile practice in Senegal, but it would be a most powerful measure of the exhibition's success to so engage Mourides themselves.

Opening night at the Fowler was attended by many Mouride guests from the Senegalese community of Los Angeles, but others came from around the United States and a few directly from Senegal on their own initiative. The philosophy of the Saint informs and inspires Mouride travel about the globe for business, and helps them endure distance from their families. Perhaps the most moving place in the exhibition was the recreation of the prayer room of a holy man in Dakar that is covered with images, including ten larger-than-life photo-realist paintings by the devoted artist Assane Dione (Figure 4.8). Between these are many smaller images, some hand-made, others mass-produced, but all addressing aspects of the Amadou Bamba's life and miracles. Also in abundance are objects of Muslim material culture such as clocks in the form of mosques, prayer rugs, sacred books, tea-making instruments, prayer beads, calligraphic works, and glass-covered wall-pieces depicting the Kabbah of Mecca and other sacred locations. Included in the recreated room were two disco lights with colored facets upon which Assane Dione had inscribed the Ninety-Nine Names of God. As the lamps were illuminated, they turned in a dervish-like motion and mirage, caressing everyone in the room with the most holy of words.

Mourides gather in the hot afternoons of Dakar to drink tea and sing *khassaids* in the original room, as the saint's lyrical verses are put to melodic chants. The auditory effect joins the visual power of the dense visual landscape of Bamba's images. An important element of touch informs the overall experience of *baraka* blessings. Mouride visitors to the *Saint in the City* exhibition revealed this as they entered the recreated prayer room, for they circumambulated the place and gently touched their hands across the foreheads of the sainted persons in the paintings. Many non-Mouride visitors felt similar inspiration, and a Buddhist woman brought her circle to meditate in

Figure 4.8   Sufi visitors to the *Saint in the City* exhibition obtained
blessing from the paintings on display in this recreated prayer
room through touch

Source: Photo by Don Cole, 2003. Courtesy of the Fowler Museum at UCLA.

the room more than twenty times during the months the exhibition was on
view in Los Angeles.

One day an important *sheikh* from Senegal visited the exhibition,
accompanied by several of his followers from the San Francisco area. The
venerated man entered the prayer room, picked up a blank Koranic tablet
from the display, and inscribed a sacred poem on it with a pen from his
pocket. As he did so, each of his devotees approached in the lowest of
postures to demonstrate respect and transcendence as the holy man wrote
and sang the verses aloud. Another passage of the exhibition suggested the
visual impact typical of the streets of inner-city Dakar. A stand of the sort
selling tracts and images of Amadou Bamba drew the attention of a
Mouride gentleman who removed a booklet of Bamba's poetry, sat down,
and began to sing one of its *khassaids*. Mourides gathered around him to
sing together.

These are not the circumstances that one expects to encounter in museum
spaces. Visitors are not ordinarily allowed to touch, pick up, or write upon
objects. One can easily understand why this is—and often must be—the
case. Yet such things are by no means moribund, and are still capable of
touch. When interactions are permitted and do occur, they demonstrate an
authenticity that goes far beyond that of market value and connoisseurship.

Corporeal engagement is prompted by vision and demonstrates the enduring power of devotion.

Such sensory involvements have been especially evident in a number of exhibitions of African shrines created over the years by the Fowler Museum in Los Angeles and the Museum for African Art in New York. Two, in particular, have invited and witnessed tactile dimensions of devotional experience: *Face of the Gods: Art and Altars of Africa and the African Americas* (1993) curated by Robert Farris Thompson as assisted by Daniel Dawson at the Museum for African Art, and *Sacred Arts of Haitian Vodou* (1996), curated by Donald J. Cosentino and Marilyn Houlberg at the Fowler (see Roberts 2008). Both resulted in spontaneous interactions as visitors left money, flowers, photographs, and miscellaneous items of meaning and memory.

While the exhibited installations recreated actual altars, people nonetheless offered performances, consecrations, and blessing ceremonies before them. For example, on opening night of *Face of the Gods* in New York, a guest performed *capoera* before a Yoruba altar, and others prostrated themselves before shrines. In both this and *Sacred Arts*, so many gestures were enacted that the museum staff had to determine what to do with the resulting offerings (Roberts 1994: 52–54). Money left on altars was used to refurbish materials as the exhibitions traveled. Very particular responses were elicited in the different venue cities in the United States and the Caribbean, where diverse populations of African descent reside.

Notably, many of the individuals who engaged with all these displays are far from their homelands, or at least from the places of their heritage. As Laura Marks notes in the context of intercultural film, touching the "skin" of the film is a way for people to reconnect, to physically appropriate what may be otherwise lost in nostalgia (2000). Such experiences allow people to connect to memories, but also to the sacred. By defying any sense that the spiritual is out of reach, the devotee is able to bring the divine into human proximity and materialize the untouchable, reify the unknowable, and give form to the inchoate, even at the remove of a museum. In this moment, haptic visuality and visual tactility converge. Touch enables sight, and sight enables touch, as belief is felt and divinity embodied.

Notes

1 Research among Luba in southeastern Katanga Province (Democratic Republic of the Congo) from 1987 to 1989 was the basis for my dissertation, "Luba Art and Polity: Creating Power in a Central African Kingdom" (Art History, Columbia University, 1991). This same work led to a major NEH-funded traveling exhibition and book entitled *Memory: Luba Art and the Making of History* co-curated and co-authored with Allen F. Roberts whose research was among neighboring Tabwa, a Luba-related group (Roberts and Roberts 1996). The ethnographic present used in the sections of this article on Luba practices refers

to the late 1980s, a period of relative calm in the Congo before the horrific strife suffered ever since.

2   For detailed description and analysis of these object types, see Roberts and Roberts 1996 and 2007.

3   In addition to the writings of Marks on haptic visuality (2000, 2002), touch and multisensory experience have been addressed in recent publications by Blier (2004); Classen (2005); Miller (2005b); Mitchell (2005); Pink (2006); Pye (2007); and Stoller (1997) among others.

4   *Darshan* is:

> "seeing and being seen" by a deity, but which also connotes a whole range of ideas relating to "insight", "knowledge" and "philosophy" ... *Darshan's* mode of interaction ... mobilizes vision as part of a unified human sensorium, and visual interaction can be physically transformative.
>
> (Pinney 2004: 9)

Pinney goes on to discuss how seer and seen come into contact in such a way that one is "touched" by *darshan*.

5   For a detailed account of *lukasa* memory boards and the Mbudye association in Luba history, see Roberts and Roberts (1996) and Reefe (1977).

6   An expanded sense of the word "reading" is proposed in *Inscribing Meaning: Writing and Graphic Systems in African Art* (2007), an exhibition and edited volume jointly produced by the Smithsonian Institution and the Fowler Museum at UCLA. In the publication, which I co-edited and co-authored with Christine Mullen Kreamer, Elizabeth Harney, and Allyson Purpura, we argue that "writing" is not confined to narrow evolutionary-based models of alphabetic systems, and can manifest in a wide range of graphic systems of inscription, such as textile patterns, scarification and tattoos, and mystical gematria. The case studies explore alternative literacies, and demonstrate that "literacy" is culturally constructed and may be defined according to very particular prerogatives and erudition.

7   For more information about links between memory and place, see Casey (1987), Bachelard (1969), and Roberts and Roberts (1996: Introduction and Chapters IV and V).

8   *Kashekesheke* divination has been documented in early twentieth-century photography and text (Burton 1961: 65–67), and was performed during my research in late 1980s prior to the resurgence of civil war in the Congo (Roberts and Roberts 1996: 180–85).

9   Mouride visual culture is discussed in detail in *A Saint in the City: Sufi Arts of Urban Senegal* (Roberts and Roberts 2003), a book written to accompany a NEH-funded museum exhibition of the same title that visited five cities in the United States from 2003 to 2008. Such subtleties as the ways that images of the saint are produced rather than reproduced are considered there.

5

The feeling of Buddhahood, or guess who's coming to dinner?
Body, belief, and the practice of chod

Laura Harrington

The materialization of buddhist studies: the bigger picture
The *chod-pa* and the practice
Knowing with the body: a theoretical proposal
Closing thoughts

There is a well-known Tibetan tale about Milarepa, Tibet's most beloved Buddhist saint, giving a parting teaching to his star disciple, Gampopa (1079–1153 CE). Standing on a riverbank, Milarepa sings a half-dozen instructional verses to Gampopa, and grants him final blessings and initiations. "Now," Milarepa concludes, "I have only a single profound instruction left, but it is too valuable to give to you, so you better go now." Gampopa is across the river and almost out of earshot before Milarepa calls him back. "If I don't give this precious instruction to you," he told Gampopa, who returned to kneel at his feet, "to whom should I give it then? So I will teach it to you." Gampopa is elated: "Do I need a mandala to offer?" "No," replies Milarepa. "You don't need a mandala, but never waste this pith instruction! Here it is!" With that, Milarepa turns his back, lifts his cotton robe and flashes Gampopa a sight of his buttocks, rough and knobby with hard calluses. "There is nothing more profound than meditating on this pith instruction," he exclaims. "The qualities of my mind stream have arisen through my having meditated so persistently that my buttocks have become like this. You must also give rise to such heartfelt perseverance and meditate!" And with that, Tibet's most famous yogi-adept sends Gampopa on his way (Chang 1992: 492–96; Brunnholzl 2007: 33–41).

To those familiar with the broad contours of Tibetan Buddhist thought and literature, Milarepa's denouement is unsurprising. Milarepa is a Tantric *siddha*: a fully-realized master of an esoteric Buddhist tradition famous for its outrageous transgression of social norms, and for utilizing bodily sensation in the pursuit of enlightenment. Those of us trained by the Euro-American academy, however, fare differently. Conditioned by the dematerialized and disembodied understanding of religion that became prominent in the aftermath of the Protestant Reformation (see Asad 1993; Lopez 1998), Milarepa's apparently outrageous disrobing inevitably exposes our own presumption that "profound instructions" are necessarily heady affairs: abstruse concepts discrete from and beyond the materiality and subjectivity of bodily practice and physical sensation. And unlike Gampopa, we find ourselves brought down to earth. We are offended and disconcerted rather than delighted and illuminated.

But what if we were not content to stop with that? What if instead we asked ourselves why this tale insists on directing our attention so deliberately to the body? What insights are we being invited to grasp about the relationship between bodily experience and religious meaning? And if we want to know, then what assumptions of our own would we need first to unearth and perhaps rethink, so that in the end we too—like Gampopa—can appreciate Milarepa's "profound instructions" as a gift rather than a provocation?

In this essay, I aim to explore these questions through the disciplining lens of a Tibetan Buddhist meditation known as "*chod*" (literally "cutting"). *Chod* is a Tibetan Tantric ritual formalized in Milarepa's time by a female Tibetan saint named Machig Labdron. It is not a prayer but a multi-sensory drama. It is best performed, not in a monastery or temple but in a cemetery or charnel ground, buzzing with restless spirits and rank with the smell of decomposing flesh. Singing, dancing, and playing special bone instruments, the *chod* practitioner (*chod-pa*) summons an assembly of demons, spirits, and sentient beings to his side; visualizes the graphic dismemberment and cooking of his own body, and then, in the spirit of unconditional generosity and loving-kindness, offers it as a banquet to his honored guests.

Nevertheless (and here is another moment where we must be prepared to look beyond our own first reactions and assumptions), the *chod-pa* is prompted, not by scatology but soteriology. By imaginatively dismembering and sacrificing his carnal 'self,' the *chod-pa* actually seeks to "cut" his attachment to the false sense of self that keeps him trapped in the cycle of samsara. This conviction is the heart of Buddhism's foundational notion of *an-ātman*, "no-self." Who and what we are are neither essential nor fixed. Rather, we are empty of self-existence: we exist contingently, in dependence upon causes and conditions: a porous bundle of ever-changing dispositions, conceptions, and experiences. Empty of intrinsic identity, we are susceptible to modification and refashioning up to and including the ultimate transformation: buddhahood.

Unfortunately, our erroneous but deep-set conviction that we exist as fixed, autonomous entities ensures that our lives are controlled by desire and delusion, and marked by suffering. Only when we non-conceptually recognize people and things as empty can we attain liberation or enlightenment (Tib. *byang chub*; Skt. *bodhi*). This is the "profound teaching" the *chod-pa* seeks to realize through his dramatic synthesis of music, dance, and meditation. And no better illustration can be found of the ways in which Buddhist belief so often takes shape in the senses: in the material world of things, spaces, and practices.

The materialization of buddhist studies: the bigger picture

If this essay had been written even fifteen years ago, it is unlikely to have drawn such a conclusion about a ritual like this. Scholars would have asked questions about the origins, texts, and theoretical presumptions of *chod*, but few would have wondered about its affective dimensions. However, the 1990s saw a slow but significant movement within Buddhist Studies towards thinking about bodily experience and bodily practice that has now made it possible to rethink a lot of issues that used to feel settled. This new direction was informally inaugurated in 1991, when Gregory Schopen published his now canonical analysis of the impact of "Protestant presuppositions" on the academic study of Indian Buddhism (Schopen 1997).

The presupposition Schopen was most concerned with was the Protestant privileging of the text over the image as the location of "true religion"; or as Ulrich Zwingli so famously asserted in 1525: that "we ought to be taught by the word of God externally … and not by sculpture wrought by the artist's hands" (Schopen 1997: 13). Schopen argued that this theological valuation was uncritically replicated in the historical methodology of modern scholars, who likewise located "true Buddhism" in Buddhism's elite textual traditions, and rejected material remains as independent, critical sources for its history. By so doing, he argued, scholars obscured the histories and practices of actual Buddhists, for whom images, *stūpa*, and shrines were often the core of daily practice.

Today, most Buddhist scholars are highly sensitive to the ways in which the privileging of doctrine as the "essence" of religion has historically skewed the study of Buddhism. Many of its leading scholars call repeatedly for a new focus on the ways in which objects and their ritual uses act to channel and structure specific kinds of cognitive and emotional experiences, and do so in ways that require scholars to engage larger questions about social class, gender, and the dynamics of colonial interaction (see here Germano and Trainer 2004). College bookstores are now stocked with anthologies that explore the "practice" and "experience" of Buddhism—a sharp contrast to its predecessors, which were content to detail its "teachings" and "scriptures." Careful explorations of the ways in which relic veneration practices index power relations now complement text-based studies of after-death beliefs (Faure 2004); the consideration of the Buddhist book as a cultic object of devotion (Kieschnick 2003; Schopen 2005; Rambelli 2007) expands and challenges long-standing assumptions about the ways in which a text is meaningful.

As part of this larger trend, the last decades have also seen a burgeoning of works specifically on embodiment. These have ranged in focus from the ways in which bodies are created through monastic practice (Collins 1997), the intricacies of the gendered body (Gyatso 2003), to notions of ideal and virtuous bodies in Buddhist works (Ohnuma 2007; Mrozik 2007). Many efforts are interdisciplinary, drawing on insights from medical anthropology (Adams 2006), media studies (McLagan 2002), and the cognitive sciences (Varela 1992). At the far end of this literature, we even see the emergence of studies that attempt to probe the literal impact of meditative practice on brain function, and to correlate the practitioners' first-hand "felt" experience with more physiological data (Lutz *et al.* 2004, 2006).

Curiously, while a certain strand of Buddhist Studies has embraced the movement toward the material, students of *chod* have remained, for the large part, more conservative: focused on text and theoretical presumptions, or the biography of *chod*'s leading disseminator Machig Labdron (see Evens-Wentz 1967; Allione 1984; Gyatso 1985; Edou 1996; Orofino 2000; Harding 2003). There are understandable reasons for this: many of the core texts associated with this practice are still untranslated and there is a well-merited ethos in the field that sees translation as the foundational act of scholarship in Buddhist Studies. In addition, the complex fusion seen in this ritual of Indian Buddhist and indigenous Tibetan elements make it a compelling object of theoretical analysis. There is still a great deal to do and explore on these fronts, and other kinds of interdisciplinary, practice-oriented analyses, one might argue, can come later.

And yet, let us consider a particular fictional twelfth-century Tibetan *chod-pa* as he conducts his practice. Can we really do justice to him and all that matters in this ritual if we fail to address the complex ways in which the material mediates and organizes his understandings? To assist in the act of historical imagination, I have included two photographs of the modern *chod-pa* and his setting (Figures 5.1 and 5.2).

The *chod-pa* and the practice

The *chod-pa*

To answer this question, let us begin by looking more closely at the scene. Our hypothetical *chod-pa* resides in a village in twelfth-century Central Tibet called Tsomer, the birthplace of Machig Labdron, who had founded several lines of transmission before her death over a decade ago. Like most

Figure 5.1 Chod-pa in meditation, with thighbone horn and drum,
Derge, Eastern Tibet, 2005

Source: Photograph courtesy of Thomas Kelly.

of its residents, he is a Mahāyāna Buddhist. He wishes to become a buddha, not for his own sake but for the sake of helping others become free of suffering. Unlike his neighbors, he dedicates much of his energies to the formal cultivation of this motivation. He understands it to be necessary precondition for his own state of buddhahood.

But our *chod-pa* is not a "mainstream" Mahāyāna Buddhist. He practices Tantra: an esoteric form of Mahāyāna that has been transmitted from India since the eighth century. Tantra followed an emerging trend in medieval Indian Mahāyāna to reject all conventional conceptions of enlightenment that excluded "impure" activities or states of mind. Unenlightened beings mistakenly reify them, and so remain trapped in the hallucination of dualism. But for our *chod-pa*, the "impure" is fuel. Manure and menstrual blood, fear and fury—all can power his spiritual journey, for "pure" and "impure" are merely social conventions lacking ultimate ontological substance:

Figure 5.2 Chod-pa practitioner in Silwutsel charnel ground, Tarboche, Western Tibet, near Mt. Kailash, 2002

Source: Photograph courtesy of Bryan Phillips.

Although medicine and poison create contrary effects,
In their ultimate essence they are one;
Likewise, negative qualities and aids on the path,
One in essence, should not be differentiated.

(Dowman 1985: 272)

In other ritual contexts, our *chod-pa* sometimes generates sexual bliss as means of liberation from desire and attachment. The logic is homeopathic: "By using that very poison," states the *Hevajra Tantra*, "a tiny amount of which would kill any living being, the one who knows the nature of poisons dispels the poison utilizing that very poison" (Farrow 1992: 171, 173). In doing so, however, he is inverting foundational Buddhist "Hīnayāna" teachings such as the Four Noble Truths, which explicitly highlight sexual desire and ignorance as roots of suffering, and monastic celibacy as the royal road to freedom. Sensuality, warns the Buddha in the first-century *Cula-dhammasamadana Sutta*, can lead to "destitution, the realm of the hungry shades, hell in future lives." By contrast, the Buddha of the *Cakrasamvara Tantra* urges him to

"Worship the buddhas and bodhisattvas with one's own seminal drops, with sight and touch, and with hearing and thought. Have no doubt that one will thus be liberated from all sins" (Gray 2007: 58–9). Our *chod-pa* knows that his styles of spiritual transformation are controversial and partisan; in Tibetan Tantric literature, the term transformation (*sgyur*) is itself a critical term that marks the Tantric as distinctive from the so-called Hināyāna path.

He is acutely aware of how ambivalent a figure he is. His Tantric prowess gives him considerable stature in his community, yet it also antagonizes the monastics at the local *gompa*. The power these others derive from abstaining from "impure" practices is obviously inferior to the power he derives from his transgression of purity—or more specifically, from his ability to transmute the base metal of addictions into the gold of enlightenment.

And yet, why should he apologize for the practice that is capable of effecting such change? He and the monastics share a broader philosophical basis for their respective practices: namely, an understanding of *an-ātman*, selflessness. Indeed, it is because he is in fact "empty" of a fixed self that he can transform himself, including and up to the ultimate transformation: buddhahood. And it is to instantiate this understanding that he practices *chod*.

The practice[1]

It is nighttime, and the *chod-pa* sets off alone for his regular practice site. As usual, he is dressed in the unwashed clothing of a beggar—*chod* is a lifestyle, not merely a practice—and is carrying two musical instruments: a kangling (*rkang gling*) horn made from a human thighbone, and an hourglass-shaped pellet drum known as a "secret *chod* damaru" (*gsang gcod damaru*) (see Figure 5.1). He has carefully selected their materials in accordance with the instructions of his teacher Machig Labdron, who deemed it

> inappropriate to carry a [trumpet] bone that has the bad characteristic of being that of someone who was younger than sixteen or older than sixty … [or one belonging to] an infuriated man whose voracious rage at another had no chance to subside [before he died], who had no time for any other thought to arise in that voracious mind and who attacked and killed that person with a weapon.
>
> (Harding 2003: 143).

He knows that an inappropriate horn will be heard "as a perverted sound" and generate anger and violence in the listener, and that it should instead be made from:

> the bone of a qualified woman, or of a monastic whose sacred pledge is unbroken, or a man of sincere faith who has avoided sin … in particular, the right leg of someone who did in his or her prime with an unimpaired intellect is the instrument of heroes, and left leg is the instrument of heroines.
>
> (ibid.: 143)

He is also intimately familiar with some of their multiple symbolic associations. The skin of the drumhead as it rubs against his rags connotes for him "the unification of appearances and emptiness." As he glances at its waistband, ornamented with small shells, he is reminded of "the [Buddha's] Enjoyment body, ornamented with signs and marks." The two pellets dangling at either side are "the unification of skillful means and Wisdom" and as they reverberate against the head, he hears "the empty echo that describes the Self" (Dorje and Ellingson 1979: 78–81).

Now he is arriving at his "sacred power spot," and the smell of decomposing human flesh stings his nose. He is in a charnel ground, and as he glances at a skeletal hand lodged under a rock, and hears vultures flapping overhead, he is vividly aware of his own impermanence, and feels a deep dread (see Figure 5.2). Quickly, he recalls Machig's instruction:

> Think "Everything is the nature of death and impermanence!" Calculate both the virtue (that is to be practiced) and the vice (that is to be abandoned) in your actions. Look at the sufferings of cyclic existence in general and particular, especially those of the three bad existences. To always contemplate these … is the first obligation [of a *chod-pa*].
>
> (Harding 2003: 205)

With this in mind, he prepares the ground. Then, picking up the *damaru* in his right hand, and the thighbone trumpet with his left, he begins a sacred dance. The rattle of the *damaru* punctuates his stamping feet as he imaginatively stamps on his own ego; its union of wisdom and emptiness likewise grinds his delusions, fears, and dualistic conceptions into dust. The trumpeting of the thighbone signals his mastery over malignant forces. As he blows it strongly and hears its tone, he knows that he will be the victor of this battle of the ego.

Now the dance is done. He settles down on his seat and, still rhythmically turning the drum, generates *bodhicitta*: the resolution to achieve buddhahood for the sake of all sentient beings. This is a familiar practice, and as the feeling of unconditional altruism for all beings permeates his entire body, he moves on to take refuge in the Three Jewels: the Buddha, his teaching, and his community of followers. He meditates on the Four Immeasurables of love, compassion, joy, and equanimity. He pays homage to his teacher, to various buddha forms and protectors, and imaginatively gives them offerings. And throughout it all, he remembers their common underlying reality:

> The self who performs the offerings, the object of offering, and the essence of the offering, along with the specific rites of offering, are without any inherent real existence. To rest in the state of emptiness is the suchness of making offerings.
>
> (ibid.: 156)

Grounded in this understanding, he settles comfortably on his seat, and lifts the thighbone to his lips to summon his guests. He blows it three times and various forms of beings gather before him: demons, Dharma protectors, buddhas, and bodhisattvas. Each has palpable shape and form, and yet he remembers that each is also a projection of his own mind. Machig has taught him that the four kinds of demons he has summoned embody different aspects of his own fierce attachment to self. He understands the enlightened beings to represent his desires and wishes and positive motivations. And most important, he understands that all are empty and so ultimately not different from each other or from him.

> Now, the drumming speeds up. The *chod-pa* takes a deep breath:
> PHAT! [I see my] impure body, of habitual tendencies
> As big and fat and greasy.
> From within it, the pristine awareness
> In the form of [the wrathful buddha figure] Tromo,
> is separated by the sound PHAT.
> With one face and two arms, she holds a hooked knife and skull cup.
> She slices the skull from the body.
> Embracing the entire universe, this human head is placed on a hearth of three skulls.
> This body of elements is set out as the offering.
> With the light if the three syllables it blazes as nectar.
> OM AH HUNG [and] HA HO HRI
> OM AH HUNG [and] HA HO HRI.
>
> (see Liljenberg 2007: 16–17)

As his body simmers and bubbles over a low fire, the *chod-pa*, identifying himself as Tromo, experiences a profound awareness of the emptiness of all beings, and feels an unconditional generosity well up. He repeats OM AH HUNG [and] HA HO HRI as he offers his body as food to each group of guests in turn—a perfect gift. As the *chod-pa*/Tromo offers it to all the buddhas, he imagines his body is a subtle and delectable ambrosia. For the protectors of the Buddha's teaching, his body becomes a collection of riches and material things—garden, food clothing , medicine. When it is time to feed the demons, Tromo strips the skin off of the body and spreads it out over the three thousand worlds. It is a platter of cosmic proportions, and he piles on top of it heaps of bodies, flesh and blood. Finally, the *chod-pa*/ Tromo imagines that all the diseases, obstacles, and sins of the world dissolve into the heaps of bodies, which the demons devour. His body is now spent; he imagines it to be piece of charcoal:

> Today, I, the fearless yogin
> Offer this illusory body that distinguishes samsara from nirvana.

A magical display that fulfills all desires
I make this offering without grasping …
The drum of a supreme skull-cup beats brightly,
The great thighbone trumpet blows melodiously …
PHAT! …
May all who are associated with this feast gain enlightenment,
And be purified of all obligations and karmic debts.

(see Liljenberg 2007: 18–19, 26–27)

The *chod-pa* now meditates within a state of emptiness. As pangs of identification with his body arise, he reminds himself that it does not exist; it has been given to the demons. He shouts PHAT! and severs the demon of his self-grasping into the space of emptiness. This insight is his final offering to all beings—his psycho-physical embodiment of this most profound insight of the Buddhist path. He dedicates the merits of his practice to all sentient beings of the world, and reiterates his aspiration to become a buddha for their benefit. The drumming slows and ceases. The practice is complete.

Knowing with the body: a theoretical proposal

Music and meditation, demons and *damaru*—one would be hard pressed to separate the bodily, especially acoustic, dimensions of our *chod-pa*'s experience from the "profound teaching" he realizes through his practice. And why should we? We have at our disposal a growing body of interdisciplinary work that takes serious account of the way meaning, concepts, thought, and language are tied to bodily experience.

In the remainder of the chapter, I thus consider the ritual of *chod* in light of philosopher Mark Johnson's model of embodied aesthetics. In particular, I introduce here several of his key ideas and insights, and show some of the ways in which they may be applied to an analysis of the *chod* ritual: understood as a practice designed to enable a kind of embodied, visceral knowledge of the truth of *an-ātman*.

Metaphorically speaking

Mark Johnson's project of embodied knowing goes back to 1980, when he and linguist George Lakoff first drew on cognitive scientific insights to problematize the traditionalist Cartesian bifurcation of "body" and "reason." In their book, *Metaphors We Live By*, they famously demonstrated that the metaphors and metonymies of language actually derive from our embodied experience of the world. For example, our physical sensation of moving "up" and "down" came to serve as the starting point over time for a comparative cognitive category concerned with the relative experiences of happiness and sadness. When we are happy, we feel "up"; our spirits "rise"; we get a "lift." Our depression, however, brings us "low." We feel "down"; our spirits "sink."

In our own time, Lakoff and Johnson argue, these embodied metaphors and metonymies have become thoroughly second-nature. We think, make jokes, even philosophize through them, unaware of their bodily origins. Their omnipresence in both ordinary and philosophical language, however, necessarily problematizes any assumption we might have inherited from our Cartesian world-view that bodies and our experiences of them are properly distinct from minds and their proper functioning as organs of reason and logical thinking. Lakoff could be speaking to our own reaction to Milarepa's denouement when he subsequently asserts:

> On the traditional view, reason is abstract and disembodied. On the new view, reason has a bodily basis. The traditional view sees reason as literal, as primarily about propositions that can be objectively either true or false. The new view takes imaginative aspects of reason – metaphor, metonymy, and mental imagery – as central to reason, rather than as a peripheral and inconsequential adjunct to the literal.
>
> (Lakoff 1987: xi)

Significantly, Lakoff and Johnson go on to embed this insight into a broader hypothesis about the nature of religious ritual. Religious rituals are themselves, they say, metaphorical activities

> which usually involve metonymies – real world objects standing for entities in the world as defined by the conceptual system of the religion. The coherent structure of the ritual is commonly seen as paralleling some aspect of reality as seen through the religion. Everyday personal rituals are also experiential gestalts consisting of sequences of actions structured along the natural dimensions of experience – a part-whole structure, stages, causal relationships and a means of accomplishing goals.
>
> (Lakoff and Johnson 1980: 234)

Put differently, a religious ritual like *chod* "works" because it is itself a metaphorical and metonymous activity: it embeds culturally-specific religious truths at a deeply-intuitive, psycho-physical level, and this bodily dimension of the practice is why—exactly why—it is so profoundly transformative.

The art of bodily knowing

But that is not all. A further implication of this way of thinking is perhaps even more important: namely, if rituals are focused and disciplined ways of embodying religious truths, then if we want to understand what *chod* means—how it enables meaning-making for those who practice it—then we cannot confine our explorations to the domain of doctrine and ideas. We need the body.

Mark Johnson's latest work, *The Meaning in the Body* (2007), can help us better understand how this might be. Drawing on insights from cognitive science, linguistic theory, and aesthetics, Johnson took his earlier arguments, developed with Lakoff, a step further and insisted that the most fundamental loci of human meaning-making are actually found, not in our bodily interactions with our environment, but "on even more submerged dimensions of bodily understanding … the qualities, feelings, emotions and bodily processes that make meaning possible" (ibid.: x). It is in aesthetics and the meanings we derive from encounters with the arts, above all, that this becomes clear. Our ability to know and find meaning in art, Johnson argues, derives from our most primal psycho-physical experiences of embodied existence: a shiver down the spine, a flush of heat on the face, a quiver in the stomach, and so on. For this reason, Johnson concludes, it is impossible to theorize the aesthetic without discussing embodiment.

But there is yet more to say, because Johnson's argument here presumes what he calls an "experientialist" model of reality. The world as we know it does not exist "out there" waiting to be experienced, "consisting of middle-sized objects that possess objective properties … independent of beings" (ibid.: 46). For the experientialist, there are no mind-independent objects: we begin to learn about objects in the world by means of *affordances*: the particular ways in which they may or may not serve us in our specific embodied state. A blade of grass, for example, might afford climb-up-ability for a chigger, but not for a human. A slab of rotting meat might afford food for a maggot, but not for a person.

Now, let us take this insight further. If "objects" have no intrinsic qualities, but instead emerge through a dialogical process with various "subjects" (humans or maggots), then how do we come to know ourselves? The answer is by engaging with the experiential realities of our own bodies, as they present themselves to us. Deane Juhan makes this point eloquently in his discussion of tactile experience.

> Tactile experience tells me as much about myself as it tells me about anything I contact. I am constantly using the world to explore my reactions to assess the world. My sense of touch is very vague until I touch; at the moment of contact, two simultaneous streams of information begin to flow: information about an object, announced by my senses, and information about my body announced by the interaction with the object. Thus I learn I am more cohesive than water, softer than cotton balls, warmer than ice, smoother than tree bark, coarser than fine silk, more moist than flour, and so on …
>
> We can never touch just one thing; we always touch two at the same instant, an object and ourselves, and it is in the simultaneous interplay between these two contiguities than the internal sense of self … is encountered.
>
> (Juhan 1987: 34)

And so we learn that we are actually not autonomous pre-made "selves" interacting with the objects; rather, our processing of affordances is one way in which we define and produce the "self."

How might this insight help us think about Tantric practice? Through a so-called Johnsonian lens, the Tantric practitioner's counter-intuitive valorization of the "impure" emerges as a powerful strategy of self-transformation. When the *tantrika* substitutes "rotting fish guts" for "breakfast rice," and "rocky stinking graveyard" for "bedroom," he is deliberately re-orienting his affordances and so is necessarily "re-making" himself. Through a Buddhist lens, his ability to do so presumes the radically contingent nature of his self. As such, his self-conscious manipulation of affordances enacts for him the truth of *an-ātman*. It is, in short, an on-going meditation on emptiness.

Significantly, Johnson emphasizes that many of our affordances are intuited pre-verbally or sub-consciously. Before reflective thinking, the world comes forward aesthetically, from our senses. "Babies" he notes, "are not proposition crunchers. They do not lie in their cribs combing subjects and predicates into propositions by which they understand the world" (2007: 33). "Big Babies"— adults, that is—subsequently carry forward the many bodily ways in which infants make meaning into their mature acts of understanding, and reasoning. For our purposes, the implications of this are clear. If we want to understand the full anatomy of meaning-making in *chod*, we must now widen our analytical scope one last time to include non-propositional modes of knowing, including what is arguably the least "logical" kind of all: feelings.

Feelings

Let us remember our *chod-pa*, consumed with fear as he sits in a dark charnel ground, surrounded by piles of human bones and unseen spirits. The *chod-pa* deliberately evokes the feeling of fear to foreground his innate and mistaken sense of self. Once commentor observes:

> By summoning up what is most dreaded and openly offering what we usually most want to protect, the chod works to cut us out of the double bind of the ego and attachment to the body … the name chod means "to cut"; but it is the attachment, not the body itself, that is the problem to cut through.
>
> (Norbu and Shane 1986: 49)

Our *chod-pa*'s feeling of fear can be described as his conscious awareness of his pounding heart, his sweating palms, his shaking hands.

But if we look below the surface phenomenology here—and draw on some provocative insights from the new interdisciplinary fields of affective neuroscience—we see that its roots lie in the domain of pre-conscious, bodily-based meaning-making grounded on the organism's drive to survive. According to affective neuroscience, it would be because emotions are the starting point of all the meaning-making work we do as embodied humans. All of us continuously monitor our environment to respond to possible dangers or discover possible benefits: a masked gunman, for example, or an oasis in an arid desert. An emotional response is part of a hard-wired suite of tools for evaluation and appraisal that all of us possess. The distinctive range of chemical and neural responses that results in the body–mind, adapting in ways to ensure survival, directs us to move away from an aggressor or toward safety. An aggressive gesture comes to "mean" danger first and foremost on an emotional, bodily level; and to do so long before they are conceptually categorized as such.

And now finally we are in a position to understand—in neuroscientific terms—the centrality of fear as an emotion in the *chod* ritual , and why its transformation is such an effective catalyst to spiritual transformation. The *chod-pa* takes as his object of meditation the drive for self-preservation that lies at the base of human meaning-making. But he does not affirm it; he imaginatively negates it through the antidote of unconditional generosity:

> Today, I, the fearless yogin
> Offer this illusory body that distinguishes samsara from nirvana.
> A magical display that fulfills all desires
> I make this offering without grasping …

He completes this transformation at the psycho-physical level. His heart pounds, no longer in terror but from the exertion of the dance. His shaking hands grow steady and supple as they turn the *damaru* and trumpet the thighbone. Unconditional compassion for all beings becomes the new lens through which he views himself in relation to his environment. He is at the most primal, body-based level, re-wiring his understanding of what is meaningful. Self-preservation is replaced by self-lessness; meaningfulness grows out of the truth of *an-ātman*.

Music

Appreciating the embodied and affective roots of all human meaning-making also positions us now to better understand another central component of the *chod* ritual: music. Johnson notes that "music orders our experience using tone quality, pitch, meter, rhythm, and other processes that we feel in our body" (2007: 236). Everything in the *chod* ritual is designed to maximize that kind of ordering of experience. The *chod-pa*'s feeling for tempo, for example, has its basis in the involuntary movements of his nervous system and the body in the beating of his heart. His feeling for meter has its origins in the movements of breathing, with its alternation of up and down movements. The music so seamlessly interwoven into the liturgy and movement of the ritual facilitates changes in our *chod-pa*'s body–mind because it literally enacts his felt experience. Our *chod-pa* does not intellectually impute some intellectual meaning to the sounds of his *damaru* and trumpet. The sound of the *damaru* and trumpet *are* his insights. But they are filtered through his multiple layers of association he has learned over years of study, and so convey meaning that is simultaneously conceptual and bodily. The sound of the *damaru*'s two pellets reverberating against the head *is* the unification of "skillful means and Wisdom"; he hears in it "the empty echo that describes the Self" (text in Ellingson 1979: 78–81). These complex insights are carefully inscribed on the psycho-physical land-scape of the *chod-pa* as the music unfolds. The slowing drumbeats stabilize and support our *chod-pa*'s meditation on emptiness; the sharp bark of the trumpet signals his imaginative shift in subjectivity from *chod-pa* to Tromo.

Note my use of the landscape image above. This is not a casual allusion, but a very deliberate one because it allows me to transition to another important point: that we experience musical meaning through conceptual metaphors, metaphors that (as Johnson argued in his original work with Lakoff) derive originally from sensori-motor experience. Because music facilitates an experi-ence of moving our bodies in a rhythmic fashion from one place to another, we tacitly conceptualize a musical piece as an extended, three-dimensional, imagi-nary acoustic landscape, and ourselves as quasi-embodied travelers. As *observ-ers*, we may stand outside the music, making note of its structure, tempo or composition. As *participants*, we are fully engaged: our pulses quicken as we anticipate the crescendos and rests, and when we join in with our voices or instruments, we collapse the distinction between performer and the performed.

A piece of music thus produces a world and our experience of being mul-tiple, embodied travelers across an acoustic landscape. For a *chod-pa*, then, the orderly, unbroken experience of music and rhythmic change throughout the *chod* ritual metaphorically evokes the deeply-ingrained Buddhist image of spiritual development as a journey. The *chod-pa* "follows the Buddhist Path" and mediates "obstacles" in order to arrive at "the other shore." In Tantra, this metaphor is quite graphically employed: a visualization such as *chod* is understood to be a process of self-conscious world-making in which one performs a new enlightened "self" into being. Music and *chod* are domains in which one seamlessly morphs through multiple subjectivities. In Johnsonian terms, it is the metaphorical, body-based nature of music that makes this possible. For our *chod-pa*, it all leads to the truth of emptiness, made manifest in—and as—the music itself.

Closing thoughts

We are embodied, meaning-making creatures. The goal of a material approach to religion in general—and tantric studies perhaps in particular—must be to find new analytic approaches that do justice to the ways in which this is so. Certainly, it should be clear from this essay that text and doctrine take us only so far if we wish to make full sense of our *chod-pa* and his practice—not to speak of Milarepa's callused buttocks! In Tantra, the path to self-transformation begins in bodily practice and is facilitated through a series of bodily-based aesthetic experiences that direct the mind towards the all-important goal of emptiness.

Where can we go from here? Our next task, to which I can only gesture in these concluding thoughts, must be to find ways to integrate analyses like these back with both well-known and lesser-known scholarly literatures in the field that emphasize the centrality of the social and cultural. Our *chod-pa*, after all, is not just the sum of his psycho-physiological experiences; he is also a product of a millennia-old tradition whose values and goals are realized and advanced, not just by him, but by countless others around him, with whom he exists in a range of complex power relations. How do we make space in our thinking for all the levels of analysis essential for our work: the individual and the collective, the embodied and the social? A promising strategy comes to us from a tradition that is currently widely applied in American cultural anthropology, but has roots that go back to the Marxist Bakhtin circle from the 1920s, and found its mature working-out in the theorizing of the Frankfurt School after World War II. The basic claim is an apparently simple one, but profound in its implications. People and their social worlds co-produce each other in a dialectic process that can be rigorously described and analyzed (Zito 2008: 726–27).

This means that there is no contradiction between (1) insisting that we delve deeply into the embodied experiences of the actors of Tantric practice, (2) realizing that those experiences, one body at a time, act to create a new kind of collective social reality, and (3) appreciating that the social reality thus created further shapes ongoing experience. *Chod* may indeed be a deeply interior ritual practice, practiced in isolated charnel grounds, but it is likewise a potent form of social practice. From this starting point, we can begin to imagine the outline of a new kind of scholarship in which body, experience, practice, meaning, social structures, and power structures all find their proper place (see Meyer 2006: 11). It is hard to imagine a more enticing agenda for the future of the material study of religion.

Note

1 This narrative should be thought of as a hybrid and much simplified template for *chod* practice. It draws most heavily on the teachings attributed to Machig Labdron in *Gcod kyi chos skor*, Delhi: Tibet House, 1974, fols. 10–410. Readers are referred for translation to Harding (2003). It is also (anachronistically) informed by Jigme Lingpa's *gCod-yul mKha 'gro'i gad rgyangs* from the *Klong che snying thig* (1970). Readers are referred for translation to Liljenberg (2007). Tibetan Buddhist tradition requires that every practitioner be initiated before embarking on any Tantric practice.

Part III

THINGS

6

Tempering "the tyranny of *already*"
Re-signification and the migration of images

Allen F. Roberts

Stone doughnuts
Of cutting edges and monkey kings
Image sleuths
Moving on

Devotional images cannot sit still. To adapt an assertion of Denis Hollier (1992: 26), their meaning "exists only at risk. It is never fixed, never arrested. There are no guarantees. Meaning is uninsured. Not covered." Instead, religious images and, indeed, the material things that support, contribute to, and convey them, temper "the tyranny of already," in the evocative phrasing of Ivoirian art theorists Yacouba Konaté and Yaya Savané.[1] That is, images defy the arbitrariness of culturally constructed stasis, despite stifling ideological assertions that "we have always made or done or understood things this way." Indeed, we have not nor will we—with "we" of utmost inclusivity.

Images sometimes *float* or seem to possess an uncanny ability to get up and go, drifting off in startling new directions to fulfill astounding new purposes. In other instances, they "migrate endlessly, cutting back and forth across new times and contexts" (Pinney 2004: 206). Or they may follow established paths determined by economic, political, and other social motives and means.

Images and the visual practices they generate or accommodate may have been unimportant during their original careers, only to make the biggest of splashes in next stages of their "lives." The opposite may occur as well. Some images and other objects of visual interest have been lost over the generations and may be rediscovered; and even if they remain in the places where they were originally produced and used, they can assume radically different meanings and roles. Still other pictures travel, seemingly seeking to fulfill what *they* "want" (Mitchell 2005). The efficacy of images will be a theme that is not so much explored here as it has been elsewhere (e.g. Roberts and Roberts 2007), but that is nonetheless implicit in the discussion to follow as "not a history *of* art, but a history made *by* art" (Pinney 2004: 8, emphases added). In this, we shall ponder what Barbara Bolt understands as the "radical material performativity in [and of] the *work* of art" (2004: 10, emphasis added). Materiality itself makes things happen, in other words.

Images and their material supports always connote complex interactions, and creative processes are at play and available for contemplation in movements to be considered below. Let us consider the re-signification and migration of devotional images from several parts of the world, and then ask questions like the following: What creative processes may foster such wanderings, and how and why may on-the-move images prove so powerful in stimulating visual piety?[2] How and why may images have agency in any such transitions and transformations? A first case from the Democratic Republic of the Congo (DRC) illustrates how images and visual practices can migrate and morph across time.

Stone doughnuts

A few times within memory, farmers at Lubanda have made extraordinary discoveries while tilling their gardens: Their hoes have turned up flat stone disks that are four or five inches across and have large round holes bored through their middles (Figure 6.1).[3] Lubanda is a relatively large village lying just south of the Lufuko River delta on the southwestern shores of Lake Tanganyika in the DRC. The region marks the western extension of the Rift Valley along which Africa "comes unzipped" (Ballard 1983: 91) as the East African tectonic plate pulls away from the rest of the continent. Rugged mountains plunge directly into Lake Tanganyika, and only the smallest fishing

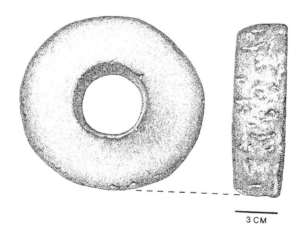

3 CM

Figure 6.1 Bored stone similar to that invested by the Earth spirit Kaomba; found in Lubanda, DRC

Source: Ink drawing by Margaret Van Bolt commissioned by the author, 1982, after an object in a private collection.

villages are possible along the narrow, rocky shores. At Lubanda, though, not only does the delta provide sufficient flat land to build a substantial village and surrounding hamlets, but the superb alluvial soil permits two annual crops rather than the single one possible elsewhere, thus supporting an unusual population density. It is in cultivating their fields that local people have unearthed the bored stones mentioned above. Their beautiful regularity is wondrous: What can one make of these fascinating things?

Archaeologists have their hypotheses. The manufacture of bored stones in central Africa may be a Late Stone Age industry dating back some centuries, but examples may be much older. Such artifacts were widespread in production and use in the Congo (Cabu 1938), and it is assumed that they were what are called *kwés* among people of the Kalahari in southern Africa: stone weights placed at the upper ends of long, pointed digging sticks to increase leverage as women pry edible roots from parched soil. Perhaps hunter–gatherers used *kwés* in the area before they moved southward long ago.

Such practical assertions are irrelevant to local understandings of bored stones found at Lubanda. Instead, the objects' material properties have led to very different associations as a visual piety has been created by and around them. In local reckoning, no human hand could shape such an impossibly hard substance with such evocative results. To paraphrase David Morgan in the Introduction to this volume, "materiality has *mediated* belief," and the formal perfection of the bored stones has led people to recognize their necessarily divine origins. Surely, they say, Earth spirits known as *ngulu* must be responsible for producing these remarkable objects.

Throughout this part of central Africa, Earth spirits have long been associated with dramatic peaks and startling breaks in the landscape, immense serpents that sometimes "sparkle like the stars," and alarming phenomena such as seismic activity, quicksand, waterspouts, and whirlpools. As an early Catholic missionary suggested, "from the heights of their mountains and the tops of their gigantic trees to the bottoms of their caverns and the depths of Lake Tanganyika, … [*ngulu*] direct the course of what is human" (Debeerst 1894: 2). Sublime places and events associated with such numinous spirits are understood as *lieux de mémoire* where people may supplicate *ngulu* regarding present concerns while recalling successful interventions in the past. Despite missionary efforts to eliminate any such practices, *ngulu* still may be offered what Wim van Binsbergen (1981: 111, 97–98) calls "ecological cults," as "an actional, symbolic and spatial counterpoint" to quotidian pursuits and dismaying misfortunes. At some point when a Lubanda farmer discovered a bored stone, the amazing object was deemed—undoubtedly through divination—to be a manifestation of a local *ngulu* named Kaomba.

Kaomba is responsible for the vast annual run of a five-inch-long catfish called *jagali* (*Chrysichthys sianenna*, Figure 6.2). Every September, a great many *jagali* leave Lake Tanganyika to mount the Lufuko and no other river,

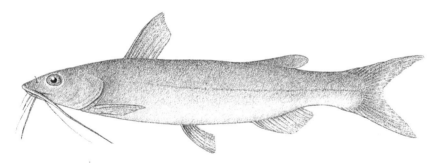

Figure 6.2 The catfish *Chrysichthys sianenna*, called *jagali* at Lubanda, DRC

Source: Ink drawing by Margaret Van Bolt commissioned by the author,
1982, after a specimen in the University of Michigan Museum of Zoology,
with permission of Professor Reeve M. Bailey, now Emeritus Curator of Fishes.

it would seem, spawning in the reedy meanders of its delta. In the 1890s, when four to five hundred traps were lodged in fishing dams in the Lufuko, over two hundred pounds (100kg) of *jagali* might be taken in a single trap, with a total catch in the tens of tons (Anonymous 1905: 209). Due to missionary insults to Kaomba, I was told, such vast numbers have not been caught for many years now. Yet although the little catfish no longer prove the pillar of local economy that they did in the nineteenth century, in the 1970s *jagali* were still trapped, smoked, and greatly prized at Lubanda. Of more interest here, however, is how the form and materiality of the rediscovered bored stone sustained these hugely important but localized practices.

When the very first gravid *jagali* left Lake Tanganyika to swim up the Lufuko River, it was caught in the hole of Kaomba's bored stone. This was the climax of a complex ritual process undertaken prior to the *jagali* season, when offerings of food would be made to Kaomba and locally brewed millet beer was sprayed by mouth upon the stone "as the custom bequeathed by the ancestors would have it" (White Fathers, 23 September 1890). Then the round stone propelled itself to the Lufuko to disappear beneath the waters and catch the first *jagali* venturing upstream. Chief Mpala's mother would display the *jagali* lodged in the stone's aperture, and fishing would begin. The first day's catch would be enjoyed in a village-wide feast of thanksgiving.

Catholic missionaries would have none of this. Believing that such practices were evil, they searched *jagali* traps for "diabolical devices" of local science meant to promote success in fishing (White Fathers, 26 August 1888). The priests mocked the possibility that Kaomba's stone could roll about of its own volition, and repeatedly tried to seize and destroy it. Local people said that Kaomba knew what the missionaries were about and went "wandering in the lake" to evade their efforts. African catechumens finally managed to apprehend Kaomba's bored stone, and several days before the opening of the *jagali* run of 1890, Brother Jérôme set the disk in a sill within the mission so that its central hole could serve as gudgeon for the pintle of a hingeless door.[4] The stone was later removed and sent to a White Fathers' museum in Belgium (Anonymous 1901), undoubtedly as "a symbolic apotheosis of the project of conquest," as the Burkinabé social theorist Jean-Bernard Ouédraogo (2008: 20) aptly writes of other colonial projects in Africa.

In the 1970s, local people told me a different story. When the missionaries caught Kaomba's stone, they thrust a stick through its hole, wrapped it in white cloths, bound it with a heavy chain, and sent it to Europe in a suitcase. Kaomba frustrated any such expropriation by escaping every time, yet the *ngulu* grew angry at such insults and finally abandoned Lubanda. It has not returned as a bored stone ever since, yet, as one man concluded, "Kaomba cannot die or disappear. Can a mountain die?" Indeed, some still encounter Kaomba through unusual circumstances of the spirit's devising, and a ritual was attempted to reestablish close contact with Kaomba during my years in Lubanda. Sadly, the effort was deemed a failure, not because of the impossibility of the task, but because those summoning the *ngulu* lacked ritual wherewithal. People bemoaned how the esoteric knowledge that had once sustained the community was lost to contemporary life amidst the travails occasioned by the increasingly vampiric government of Mobutu Sese Seko (see Nzongola-Ntalaja 1986).

Kaomba's bored stone both depicted and protected the fecundity of the Lufuko River. In this, it was like a *palladium*, a term that originally referred to a statue of Pallas Athena that assured the safety of Troy. As Hans Belting (2007: 90) explains, "from time immemorial, the presence of the protective divinity of a city or colony was guaranteed by his or her material image, in such a way that a 'face' was given to a place, distinguishing it from other places." In the case at hand, rather than portraying such a particular "face," the form and materiality of the bored stone provoked associations with more generalized sexuality and procreation as realized through the "ecological cult" offered to the Earth spirit identified with *jagali*-fishing in the Lufuko River.

That the "rape" of Kaomba was remembered through tales of missionaries thrusting a stick through the hole in its stone—and in this, suggesting an act not so different from Brother Jérôme's demeaning architectural joke—bespeaks colonial tragedies as well as acute anxieties about life in the Congo of the 1970s. Also vividly recalled was how the missionaries seized control of *jagali*-fishing at the same time they mistreated Kaomba, allocating the best sites for damming the Lufuko to their most favored followers. Religious change was matched by a hegemonic coup, in other words (see Roberts 1984, 1989).

This web of beliefs and practices of both Congolese and Europeans at Lubanda began with the formal, visual properties of a rediscovered Late Stone Age artifact. The meanings of bored stones were by no means "fixed" or "insured," as Hollier (1992: 26) would have it, for local people understood the unearthed object to be a manifestation of the Earth spirit Kaomba, while European priests and their followers took such propositions to be satanic. Such a contest of aesthetics possessed separate and converging political histories (cf. Rancière 2007: 17 and *passim*), yet in important ways both Africans and missionaries came to "a common appreciation that *the image of a god may be more immediately sacred than the god*" itself (Cosentino 2005: 243, original emphasis)—or at least more readily accessible for contemplation and application.

Let us now present two cases of image migration that follow distinctly different paths from that of Kaomba's bored stone. Rather than the compelling simplicity of the stone's form as endowed with subtle reasoning punctuated by esoteric practice, here we shall encounter images of astounding "visual and spiritual saturation" (Rush 1999: 62) and observe hermeneutics in the making. The first case provides visual links between Iberia and Haiti, the second between India and the Republic of Bénin.

Of cutting edges and monkey kings

As explained in *The Golden Legend* and other hagiographies elaborating New Testament stories, Christ's brother James was a favorite among His apostles, whom He nicknamed "Son of Thunder" because of James's impetuousness. Martyred by Herod, Saint James's remains were translated to Iberia in as miraculous a migration as one can imagine.[5] There they were discovered at Compostella in the ninth century CE, and this heavenly site has been a focus of fervent pilgrimage ever since (Turner and Turner 1978: 169–70 and *passim*). The most famous apparition of James was as the beloved Santiago, captured in images depicting the barefoot saint astride his rearing palomino (Figure 6.3), brandishing a sometimes-flaming sword and trampling Moors to inspire the Christian reconquest of Iberia (Cosentino 1995: 246, 424 FN 7).

In early 1492, the troops of Ferdinand II of Aragon and his spouse, Isabelle I of Castille, routed the last Muslim forces that had long occupied southern Iberia. Late the same year, their emissary, Christopher Columbus, "discovered" the fabled Caribbean isle of Hispaniola, and enslaved Africans were brought there in less than a decade to launch a plantation economy. The Pope decreed James the patron saint of Hispaniola as he was of Iberia, and enslaved Africans "embraced his cult with great enthusiasm," according to Church records (ibid.: 250). In the late seventeenth century, the French wrested the western third of Hispaniola from Spanish control and dubbed their new territory Saint-Domingue. As a sugar industry was developed, the colony became one of France's most lucrative. Saint Jacques (as James is known in French, or Sen Jak in Haitian Kréyol) remained the patron of these harsh circumstances, and his images would become far more broadly significant and deeply efficacious than the Pontiff could have possibly imagined (ibid.: 253).

Figure 6.3 Chromolithograph of Saint James (Saint Jacques, Sen Jak)
and Ogou, no date, paper

Source: UCLA Fowler Museum X94.74.5, photo by Don Cole, with permission.

Catholic priests forcibly baptized the enslaved Africans of Saint-Domingue, and for didactic purposes, they distributed inexpensive wood-cuts and lithographs depicting saints. These were "viewed with informed sympathy by the blacks," for "in such imagery they perceived ... truths they already knew" (Thompson 1983: 169). Theirs would be "a social act of looking" (Morgan 2005: 3), in other words, for these visual resources would be approached through collective hermeneutics.[6] Warrior saints like James, George, and the Archangel Michael drew special attention, and would inspire the Slave Revolt of 1791 and eventual triumph as Napoleon's forces were expelled from Saint-Domingue in 1804 and an independent Haiti was proclaimed.

Sen Jak gives courage and elation to Haitian Christians to this day, in large part because he is also Ogou. Brought to Haiti from what are now the West

African republics of Nigeria, Bénin, Togo, and Ghana, Ogou (Ogun, or Gu) is the Vodou deity of transformation achieved through metal tools and weapons.[7] "Lord of the Cutting Edge," as Robert Farris Thompson (1983: 53) suggests with the hot ideas and cold violence so implied, Ogou conveys means, strength, resolve, and potential, but always with lethal ambiguity a probable price. He is "King of Ire" according to Yoruba panegyric, and "blacksmith of all heaven" (ibid.: 52–53). The sword of Sen Jak is the saber of Ogou and "the central sign of war and smithing" (ibid.: 172). Such blades are the sort of heirloom still placed on shrines to Ogun in Bénin as maintained by taxi drivers and others depending upon the means of metal. And when, in his chromolithographic presence, Sen Jak casts his eyes heavenward while directing his trusty steed to tread upon the hapless enemies of so many centuries ago, he is also Ogou, "riding" the faithful whom he possesses in deeply performative healing and promotional trance (Cosentino 1995: 251).

The key to such multiplicity—that is, Saint Jacques and Ogou being both different and the same via a single image—is that the chromolithograph "inspires *narrative* about the deity and his relationships which constitute a living Vodou mythology. The chromo becomes a *revelatory* source, open to counter-analyses like rival Jewish, Christian, and Muslim hermeneutics of the same Old Testament text" (ibid.: 254, emphases added). As Donald Cosentino continues this line of reasoning, he cites the brilliant, sometimes surrealist anthropologist Michel Leiris:

> Plurality of attributes and of names for the same divinity or the same saint (between which a very extended and very complex play of corresponding elements of identification could be operative), extreme elasticity of possibilities of rapport ... variability of representations attached to the same divinity, and variability in the interpretations of forms, force one to ... pay attention to everything—for historic conjunctions and social conditions are of a kind that favor a syncretic process.
>
> (Leiris 1952: 204, cited in Cosentino 1995: 255)

That is, every detail, including those one has yet to notice, can and undoubtedly will be significant to someone at some point. Cosentino concludes that "given the breadth and fuzzy margins of the Catholic cult of the saint ... Vodouists do not lack for material upon which to work their hermeneutics .... The process is centripetal, pushing out into new forms like a jazz riff" (Cosentino 1995: 255). And as David Morgan might add, "the power of images is precisely their ambivalence" (2007: 250), which allows them to take such expressive voyages in several directions at once.

Narrated revelations achieved through images that have migrated from one set of circumstances to another are quickly *translated* (as were Saint Jacques' remains from the Holy Land to Iberia) to *performance*. Christopher

Pinney's assertions concerning popular visual devotions in India can be applied to Haiti: The "sensory immediacy" of popular, vividly colored images leads people to "speak of a depicted deity's efficacy, and link the origination of the image to *their own* biographies. The significance of images is expressed … through … a body praxis, a poetry of the body that helps give images what they want" (Pinney 2004: 21, emphasis added). And "what they want" is to assist those devoted to them. Yet Ogou does not ride his adepts lightly nor are his gifts frivolous. Instead, he and Sen Jak help people to cope with vicissitudes of contemporary Haiti that can be so terribly dire that they may make Job's afflictions pale in comparison.

The late Pierrot Barra, a devotional artist of Haitian Vodou who had few peers (Cosentino 1998), captured the necessary mobility of Sen Jak and Ogou in a remarkable sculpture made from recycled materials (Figure 6.4). An airplane is elegantly bejeweled, bedecked with stars, piped in gold, and hued the crimson and deep blue of the Haitian flag. Standing in the doorway, Jesus reveals his Sacred Heart while waiting to step forth as a "lwa [or Vodou god] who is pure and clean" (ibid.: 15). In the first window one glimpses Sen Jak, Christ's favorite "son of thunder," charging forth with the wrath and brilliance of Ogou to meet the most urgent of needs. Behind the airplane's wing is the Black Madonna of Częstochowa, peeking from her porthole as Ezili Dantò, "mother goddess of the Vodou pantheon" and rumored lover of Ogou, as the soap-operatic narratives of devotion inexorably play themselves out (ibid.: 9–10). The airplane is a *reposoire*—a place of rest and inherence for these great deities who, as Barra explained, move "like the wind" as they intervene on their postulants' behalf (ibid.: 15, and Donald Cosentino, pers. comm. 2009).

Figure 6.4 Pierrot Barra, "Ogou's Blue and Red Mystic Airplane," Port-au-Prince, Haiti, 1993; wood, velvet, glass, chromolithographs, ribbon, tin; length: 90 cm

Source: UCLA Fowler Museum, X94.76.9, photo by Don Cole, with permission.

Of equal alacrity are Vodun gods of the Republic of Bénin. Ogou as known to Haitians is descended from Gu (or Ogun), God of Iron and King of Ire in this small, coastal western African country. Creative use of images of Saint James in Haiti finds its parallel in Bénin, but here many pictures are of Hindu rather than Christian origin. The first of these were brought to West Africa early in the colonial period when British authorities encouraged South Asian shopkeepers to emigrate to cities such as Accra and Lagos so as to create a more formal (and so easier-to-control) commercial infrastructure than the thriving marketplaces that did and still do characterize coastal economies. Competition with local enterprise may have been meant to encourage African entrepreneurs, but as often as not, African initiative was hampered because local people lacked the credit and commodity supply enjoyed by expatriates. Nonetheless, as Henry Drewal (1988: 175–76) notes, local people closely observed privileged South Asian ways with fear and fascination, and paid special attention to Hindu devotions that seemed to hold the key to the shopkeepers' financial success. Attention was focused upon chromolithographs in the shrines that Hindu merchants composed in their shops and homes, and that they circulated through promotional calendars and similar publicity devices. To gain access to South Asian financial powers, religious practices were borrowed, adapted, and invented by Vodun adepts, with none more important than visual pieties constructed from Hindu images.

These same early colonial years were marked by the popularization of photography in West Africa, adapted to local needs and visual epistemologies (see Ouédraogo 2002). To this day, many practitioners of Vodun consider chromolithographs of Hindu deities to be "photographs" of the other world (Drewal 1988: 171). A locally defined indexicality is at play: The "truth" of the photograph is extended to the presumed authenticity of such wondrous pictures, understood to portray divine beings and to be efficacious as well (see Belting 2007: 74 and *passim*). Indeed, the chromos convey divine presence and blessing powers as do icons in many other religions of the world.[8]

Vivid details of these images envisioned what had long been known from the dreams, trances, and prophecies of Vodun, while adding new opportunities for narrative praxis. As Dana Rush (1999: 62) notes, such pictures presented—as they still do—"a vast conceptual assemblage of ideas, histories, legends, visions, and world belief systems contained in and stemming from a mass-produced print." Yet although at some point they must have been "newly seen, they have been approached in *Vodun* as something which was already known and understood, something already familiar within the *Vodun* pantheon" (ibid.), just as woodcuts and lithos were by enslaved Africans of old Saint Domingue (Thompson 1983: 169). Hans Belting (2005: 42) offers a means to understand such integration of newly migrated images with earlier ideas: "An image … often fluctuates between physical and mental existence. It may live in a work of art, but it does not coincide with it." That is, "images *happen* between we who look at them, and their media" (ibid.: 46, original emphasis). Such a sense of liminal separation between image as idea and the medium or media through which the event of recognition may be realized further explains how migration of images often occurs between and among different media (ibid.: 51). To return to Haiti for a moment, a line of visual translation may see Ogou as Santiago and vice versa, but then Ogou and Santiago may also be the hugely ripped Rambo character of Sylvester Stallone, as painted on the rear panel of a *tap-tap* passenger bus in Port-au-Prince (Cosentino 1995: 249).

Complementing such insights, Dana Rush holds that in Bénin, while devotional images in Vodun "are outwardly mobile in that they are easily transported, copied, and reproduced" across continents, they are also "*inwardly* mobile: their inherent forms and meanings do not remain stationary, and thus they accumulate multiple readings" in any given setting (Rush 1999: 62, emphasis added). An "unfinished aesthetic" results, for meanings continually morph and move (ibid.). "Similar images with different names appear in different *vodun*. In most cases the images are unrelated in every way except that they look alike" (ibid.: 62–63). Significantly, this is not an instance of *iconomachy*, as "images [may] engage in rivalry with one another, seeking to supplant or replace their competitors" (Morgan 2005: 12). Instead, a blending of visual and narrative practices is constantly *negotiated* among believers striving to maximize their own blessings for the most practical of reasons. Any seeming contradictions disappear in such an epistemology of intellectual and expressive exchange driven by necessity. The best way to comprehend such fluidity is through an example.

An artist named Kossivi Joseph Ahiator has painted a remarkable mural within a Vodun shrine in the port city of Cotonou, Bénin, that honors and assures the presence of a number of divinities. In Dana Rush's photograph of a portion of this dramatic painting (Figure 6.5), Gniblin Egu, Tohosu Amlina, Mami Dan, and Densu appear from left to right. That these might also be the Hindu deities Hanuman, Ganesh, Shiva, and Dattatreya to those familiar with South Asian devotional arts is largely irrelevant to Béninois engaged in devotional practices at the shrine (Rush 1999: 68–69).[9]

Gniblin Egu is a Vodun god whose name means "Cow-Person of Egu." The simian qualities some would recognize in the monkey-king Hanuman are understood as bovine, while Egu is the cognate of Gu or Ogun/Ogou in the Mina language of southwestern Bénin and southeastern Togo (ibid.: 66). Here is another King of Ire, in other words, ready to direct his aggressive means to the needs of the world. Chromolithographs sometimes show Gniblin Egu's tail aflame, and people fear he may burn entire villages if he becomes angry; but they still look to Gniblin Egu to beat witches with his blazing tail as he defends devotees from evil (ibid.). In the popular image from India that Ahiator has seen, Hanuman tears open his chest to reveal the great deities Rama and Sita, whom he carries within him at all times and to all places. From this visual prompt, Vodun adepts now tell of how Gniblin Egu once rent his own chest to

Figure 6.5 Portion of temple mural by Kossivi Joseph Ahiator portraying the Vodun gods (from left to right) Gniblin Egu, Tohosu, Mami Dan, and Densu. Cotonou, Republic of Bénin

Source: Photo by Dana Rush, 1996, with permission.

reveal his deceased parents, "thus proving his eternal respect for them" (ibid.). That he did so is proven by the chromolithograph.

A different, similarly well-known picture of Hanuman available in coastal West Africa portrays him bearing Rama and Rama's brother Lakshmana on his shoulders as he triumphs over Ravanna, the demon-king of Lanka. This image does not appear to depict Gniblin Egu, however, or at least not necessarily. For some the divinity is Attingali, a Muslim *vodun* to whom one turns for protection from witches like the one crushed beneath Attingali's foot (recognized as Ravanna in India).[10] For others, the deity is Foulani Agbokanli ("Fulani Cow-Animal") carrying the Ablewa "angels" on his shoulders that help him defeat witches (Rush 1999: 66). The name refers to the frictions farming people frequently feel as Fulani pastoralists, sometimes driven southward by drought, may encroach upon cultivated coastal lands. As Donald Cosentino (1995: 254) suggests with regard to the re-signification of Christian images in Haitian Vodou, so too in Bénin chromolithographs provide revelations that foster ongoing narratives, with no contradiction implied when differing stories are told, and no end in sight of such story-telling potential.

Tohosu Amlina is seated to the right of Gniblin Egu in Ahiator's wall painting. Tohosu is the *Vodun* of royalty, human deformities, and bodies of water, while Amlina means "strange" in Mina. The "deformities" associated with Tohosu such as hermaphrodism or being born with a caul are amplified in the "strange" nature of a being some might think of only or primarily or even as Ganesh (Rush 1999: 66, 69). The corpulence of the elephant-headed Hindu deity is "royal," as people in Bénin would expect of their opulent rulers, and his superhuman abilities could not be more evident than in his four arms and direct identification with the greatest of all beasts. Followers of Tohosu no longer kill rats because of the hallowed rodent seen at the foot of the extraordinary figure in widely distributed chromolithographs. So is visual piety born and so do narrative practices continue to evolve (ibid.: 69).

Beside Tohosu Amlina sits Mami Dan, also called Akpan. This deity is associated with Mami Wata, to be introduced below, for whom he "clears the path" in a Gu-like manner; and as Akpan—"the one with the bad temper" in Mina—he does so with distinct ambiguity, probably reinforced by the serpent draped around his neck (ibid.: 69). The trident behind the god refers to a tattoo pattern practiced on the bodies of Vodun adepts for protection and drawn on the ground in sacred powder as a cosmogram. Such devices are inscribed by many coastal West African devotional groups in open–ended and "valiant jousting contests of erudition" that cannot be "understood in any strict or linear Western way" (Thompson 1983: 244). The many other details of the image similarly provide exegetical opportunities. And for other devotees, this same picture may capture the altogether different divinity Ablewa Sika, who is associated with Vodun gods of Islam in this place of such astounding synaesthetics (Rush: 69–70).

The last character in the portion of Ahiator's painted pantheon depicted in figure five is the three-headed deity Densu. He is widely understood as the husband of Mami Wata, the pan-African goddess of capitalism to be discussed shortly. If one can imagine the way religious narrative grows and visual piety is constructed, the story might have gone something like this: Mami Wata has been with us for generations, and we are well aware of her wondrous abilities and gifts. Who better as the suitor and spouse of such a marvel than a being with three heads and six arms that the "photo" (or chromolithograph of the Hindu god Dattatreya) portrays? We did not know that Densu—or Papi Wata, as he is also known—would have so many appendages, but it certainly makes sense that he would, and now we know that he does!

Image sleuths

Two last cases of image migration add another dimension to visual culture-building. The first links chromos of a nineteenth-century Samoan woman snake-charmer who performed in a German circus, to visual pieties found throughout most of Africa and the African Americas. The second follows the trajectory of a picture of a Tunisian teenager taken around 1904 and published in *National Geographic* in 1914 that is now known as "a photograph of the Prophet Muhammad as a boy" in Iran, Senegal, and undoubtedly other Islamic countries.[11]

First, the story of Mami Wata or "Mother of Water." Mami, as she is known with a familiarity tinged with rank anxiety, hails from beneath the deepest waters and enjoys immense popularity (Drewal 2008b, 2008c). Water spirits are ancient beliefs along the stretching shores and in the lagoons, labyrinthine deltas, and boggy swamps of coastal Africa, as well as up the rivers and in great lakes of the interior. Fortunes come across the waters and from below them, yet as is inevitable in capitalism, some people benefit more than others. Is divine assistance available to them and not the rest of us? To be sure, and for a great many her name is Mami Wata. What Mami looks like, what her life must be like, and what sorts of Faustian promises one must make to garner her precious attentions differ much more than the reasons why people hope she will help *them* next.

The story of Mami Wata is as mystifying and mutable as water itself (Drewal 2008a: 28). In some manifestations, Mami is a mermaid, and her song seductive. She is vaingloriously attractive, as are the gains to be gotten from her help in business or politics. How else might former DRC president Mobutu Sese Seko have become the world's wealthiest dictator without her interventions? That many of Mobutu's kin perished in surprising ways and that he himself suffered an ignominious demise was part of the bargain: the "Guide" traded lives to Mami for power without limit, including his own (Jewsiewicki 2008a: 129). Mami is also mistress of serpents that, like the waters, have been of eternal interest throughout the world. Snakes are the subtlest of beasts and defy all definitions—"a straight line with one extremity lost in the infinity of the past and the other in the present," as one author has it (Gougaud 1973: 125). "They are as cold as eternity and as horizontal as we are vertical" (ibid.). How could Mami *not* be associated with such marvelous creatures?

A chromolithographic "photo" of Mami available since the late 1800s has settled any doubt and added details to marvel the more. A serene siren of brown beauty bears a cascade of lustrous black hair (Figure 6.6). Her gaze mesmerizes, and two huge serpents slithering about her form are at her complete command—as you will be too, as you inevitably fall under Mami's spell. A great many works of art and achievements of practice are associated with Mami Wata in this guise, many portraying her fateful ambiguities that may bring wealth and power yet will assuredly end in doom (Figure 6.7). Of interest here is Henry Drewal's remarkable detective work in tracing the snake charmer's peripatetic picture.

Carl Hagenbeck was an entrepreneur who created an animal sideshow in mid-nineteenth-century Hamburg. "Sensing the public's enormous appetite for the bizarre," Hagenbeck added exotic people to his growing circus, including Laplanders with reindeer and magicians from Ceylon (Drewal 2008a: 50). The wild success of these ventures led to Hagenbeck hiring a hunter of rare animals whom he dispatched to Southeast Asia. The fellow returned to Hamburg with wondrous beasts and a beautiful wife, perhaps from Samoa. She charmed

Figure 6.6 Chromolithograph of Mami Wata, from a late nineteenth-century poster portraying the German circus performer Maladamatjaute. Purchased *c.* 1970 in Lomé, Togo

Source: Ignacio A. Villareal Collection, with permission; photo by Don Cole, with permission.

snakes as well as hunters, and soon assumed the tongue-twisting stage name of Maladamatjaute for Hagenbeck's thrilling acts. A studio photograph from the late 1880s shows her boa-entwined, as does a circus poster (ibid.: 50–1). In some way and somehow, the image of Maladamatjaute found its way to a Bombay calendar company that translated it into a chromolithograph, and by the early 1900s the picture was in eager African hands (ibid.). A burst of local artistry followed, as this new glimpse of the divine Miss M inspired narratives that, like all hagiographies, were more about the trials, tribulations, and great expectations of her devotees than the goddess herself.

A no-less-astonishing trajectory has been traced by the image sleuths Pierre Centlivres and Micheline Centlivres-Demont (2005, 2006).[12] These intrepid Swiss anthropologists have collected popular Islamic arts for years, and became intrigued by posters depicting "the Prophet Muhammad as a boy" published in Iran beginning in the early 1990s (Figure 6.8). The image has wide appeal, and Oleg Grabar (2002: 1443) reports its availability "on paper or any sort of object" like the kitschy keychain he purchased in Teheran. In 2004 at a Parisian exhibition of the Orientalist photography of Rudolph

Figure 6.7 Mami Wata and soldier companion, Baule or Guro peoples,
Côte d'Ivoire, 1950s–1980s, wood, paint, 40 cm

Source: UCLA Fowler Museum × 95.43.2, gift of Philip Ravenhill and
Judith Timyan; photo by Don Cole, with permission.

Lehnert (1878–1948), the Centlivres happened upon a picture taken in
Tunisia around 1904 and widely circulated in the 1920s and 1930s as a
postcard printed in Germany and distributed from Cairo. An adolescent
Tunisian boy smiles "with parted lips, a turbaned head, and a jasmine
flower over the ear." The image bears the simple caption "Mohamed," and
it is the prototype for all subsequent images of "the Prophet as a boy"
(Centlivres and Centlivres-Demont 2006: 18–19).

A significant number of Lehnert's North African photographs portray
adolescent girls and boys in suggestive poses. "With their graceful look of
an age that hesitates between childhood and adolescence, between feminine
and masculine, these boys and girls as pictured by Lehnert corresponded to the
tastes of a European clientele, sensitive to Oriental phantasms and seduc-
tions" (ibid.: 18). In 1914, the Lehnert photograph of the Tunisian boy
accompanied Frank Johnson's long piece in *National Geographic* called
"Here and There in Northern Africa," accompanying his meandering just-
so stories of "How the Camel's Hump Gets Fat" and "How the Arabs
Drink Tea" (Johnson 1914: 35, 65, 106, and *passim*). While it is interesting
to speculate on how the photo was received by colonial audiences and
National Geographic readers (see Lutz and Collins 1993), how it has

Figure 6.8   "An Arab and his flower," photograph
by Rudolph Lehnert, Tunisia, *c.* 1904

Source: Published in *National Geographic* (vol. 25, 1914, p. 35),
public domain; photo by Seth Roberts, with permission.

migrated and why it has undergone such radical re-signification in Iran
deserves attention here.

Through patient research, the Centlivres have tracked down a number of
versions of the Lehnert photograph and what it has become as Iranian artists
have created paintings and posters based upon it, manipulating its content
to meet different—and, we would suggest, ever-evolving—hagiographical
needs.[13] As they note, "Iranian versions, touched up, keep something of the
seductiveness of the adolescent, but soften his excessively sensual expression
while trying to reconcile the sacred character of the Prophet to the disturbing
beauty of the young man" (ibid.: 19). In a poster dated 2001–2002, sacred
light emanates from the head of the future Prophet and the background is
enhanced to signal incidents of Muhammad's life to come (ibid.), suggesting
that the elaboration of the image has by no means ended. Indeed, in his book
Sayeh-I Aftab (*c.* 1991), Muhammad Hasan Rahimian illustrates a painting
derived from the Lehnert photograph and recalls that when it was brought to
the attention of the late Ayatollah Khomeini, to everyone's surprise the great
man had the picture placed in his study, opposite his favorite armchair. He

would pose questions about the painting to those approaching him, as a test of their mystical knowledge, and "it was heard" that one of the Ayatollah's lyrical poems was inspired by the painting.[14]

Most revealing, however, are captions of posters collected by the Centlivres in the late 1990s. One such from Teheran explains that this is:

> [a] blessed portrait of the Venerated Muhammad at the age of eighteen during a journey from Mecca to Damascus when he accompanied his venerated uncle on a trade expedition. Portrait due to the paintbrush of a Christian priest; the original painting is in a museum in Rum.[15]

The "Christian priest" was a Nestorian or Assyrian Christian monk named Bahira, whose encounter with the future prophet is recounted in reflections upon the Prophet's life from the eighth and ninth centuries CE.[16] This miraculous encounter is complex and compelling, and has been debated—often hotly—for well over a millennium, for it reveals an ancient will to image made manifest in mystically produced portraits of deities that include Christ and the Virgin Mary (see Belting 2007). That the story of Bahira has provided sufficient structure for yet another apparition, this time of "a photo of the Prophet as a boy," underscores the vitality and plasticity of the narrative. Anything one might say about the Orientalist purposes of Rudolph Lehnert, Frank Johnson, or those who enjoyed their productions is irrelevant, for according to the visual pieties constructed from the "photograph of the Prophet as a boy," miracles are at work that transcend any such fruitlessly mundane considerations.

Moving on

Through five case studies, we have glanced at visual epistemologies and practices that could be—and thankfully are being—performed and studied for lifetimes. A great deal more could be said, but a sense of visual process emerges nonetheless. Devotional images not only permit but *provoke* re–signification, as they pop up out of the "nowhere" of a Congolese garden, "migrate" along routes predetermined by histories of trade and politics, or float off in less decided directions to end up in Iran. "Image migration" can refer to temporal, cultural, and/or geographical distances, but it may also denote shifts between and among media: Pierrot Barra's Vodou spirit airplane is made from recycled materials (cardboard, cloth, golden piping, and the like), including the images that began and continue as modes of divine presence for Christians but that also serve as *reposoire* "resting places" for the ever-evolving gods of Vodou.

In each of our cases, *already* is tempered, however tyrannical its stases may be, especially as innovative artists like the late Monsieur Barra find new ways to enliven old ideas. Furthermore, "the 'rhizomatic' global patterns of image circulation" such as the ones considered here tend to "elude the West" (Pinney

2004: 164) and its linear logic of hegemonic control of visual and other realities. If we who do not consider ourselves within these image-scapes are to grasp the dynamism of such expression—and especially if we wish to participate in it—then different parameters of and for visual praxis will be required, as the artists and authors whose works inform this chapter make abundantly clear.

Notes

1 Konaté and Savané (1994: 75), emphasis added, from a discussion of recycling in Africa. My title also echoes de Tocqueville's ([1835] 2003: 335) reflection on how, in early America, municipal institutions "temper[ed] the tyranny of the majority," thus "maintain[ing] a democratic republic." When devotional images temper "the tyranny of *already*," democratic meaning-making is fostered.

2 Images may actively structure as well as or rather than passively illustrating devotion; on "visual piety," see Morgan (1998).

3 See Roberts (1984, 1986, 1989). The "ethnographic present" employed here refers to the mid-1970s when I conducted forty-five months of anthropological research among Tabwa people at Lubanda, the important village of Chief Mpala. Sadly, because of more than thirty years of devastating civil strife in the area, I do not know which practices among those I studied are still observed today.

4 White Fathers, 23 September 1890. A gudgeon is a "socket of a hinge into which the pin fits" so that an axle or door may turn, whereas a pintle is the "upright pin or bolt" of a door, rudder, gun carriage, or trailer hitch, as derived from a term for "penis" in Middle and Old English, early French, and Old German (AHDEL 1969: 584, 996). We cannot know if Brother Jérôme knew any such etymology or usage, but one can presume that his ingenious use of the bored stone was informed by such obvious sexual allusions.

5 William Caxton translated (in the more usual sense of the word) the influential "Golden Legend" of Jacopo da Varagine (*c.* 1260 CE) from Latin to English in 1483; see www.fordham.edu/halsall/basis/goldenlegend. "Translation" of relics is explained in Brown (1982: 86–105).

6 As Morgan (2005: 74) further notes, "Vision is a complex assemblage of seeing what is there, seeing by virtue of habit what one expects to see there, seeing what one desires to be there, and seeing what one is told to see there."

7 "Vodou," as the term is pronounced in Haiti and written in French orthography, is "Vodun" in Bénin and adjacent lands of coastal West Africa. Vodou may refer to a particular deity or to the religion through which such divinities are recognized and supplicated. Haitian devotees of Vodou are sometimes called "Vodouists."

8 "Indexicality," as a term coined by the semiotician Charles Sanders Peirce, has been widely applied by theorists and historians of photography to refer to the ways that a photographic image is "taken to participate in the reality of the object depicted" (Sontag 1977: 155). Such an understanding of chromolithographs is not foreign to many Hindus: see Pinney's "*Photos of the Gods*" (2004: 18 and *passim*).

9 There is a difference here, then, between the either–or/both understanding that Haitians bring to Christian chromos, since they are Christians even as they are

Vodouists; and the seeming obliviousness of people in Bénin to a Hindu faith that they do not share.

10   As Dana Rush (1999: 95, n. 6) suggests, "'Islamic *Vodun*' may seem to be a contradiction in terms, [but] it is not. *Vodun*, as a religious system, incorporates and embraces foreign elements which may appear, at first, antithetical in nature. *Vodun* thrives on apparent contradictions." Furthermore, some Muslims in Bénin may also practice Vodun, and there may be such overlap between the talismanic practices of mystical Islam and those of Vodun that distinguishing them is pointless.

11   "Culture-building" is a useful phrase developed by Robert Blauner as discussed in Caulfield (1972: 202) and further elucidated in Roberts (1996). Elisabeth Edwards and Janice Hart (2004: 4–5) consider the "trajectory of a photograph" and its "two forms of social biography," the one concerning content and a history of meanings, the other the history of a photograph as a particular material object.

12   This case study is considered in greater detail in Roberts and Roberts (2008), where Senegalese use of the same image is discussed. The fraught issues of Islamic visual culture are too complex to address here; see Roberts and Roberts (2003).

13   Hagiography causes and/or permits the reader, listener, or viewer to become swept up by biographical narratives in such a way that his/her life is understood as an extension of a saint's; see Roberts and Roberts (2003: 84–107).

14   Thanks to Andrew Lane (pers. comm. 2005) for forwarding an undated posting by Mahdi Tourage from the *IslamAAR* listserve (that is, of the American Academy of Religion) upon which these lines are based.

15   Centlivres and Centlivres-Demont (2006: 19). The Centlivres (ibid.) suggest that Muhammad is more commonly understood as having been twelve years old when these incidents occurred. "Rum" refers to Christians locales and perhaps more specifically to Byzantium (Grabar 2002: 1434, 1436).

16   See entries on Ibd Sa'd and Ibn Hisham in the *Encyclopedia of Islam* (1999).

7

Out of this world
The materiality of the beyond

Jeremy Biles

Out of this world and into the *mysterium*
Paramediation and the religious uncanny
Ecstasies: bodies of proof
Apparitions: authentic hoaxes
Invasions: uncanny evidences

Out of this world and into the *mysterium*

In April 2005, in the shadowy interval of a freeway underpass on Chicago's Northwest Side, the Blessed Virgin Mary made an unlikely appearance (Figure 7.1). She seeped from a crack in the concrete wall in the form of salty runoff, the radiating stain limning her robed figure. A Catholic woman passing in a car spotted her first, during evening rush hour; by midnight, the area's pious were gathering to behold the otherworldly apparition. During my visit to the site, I observed candles, crosses, and bouquets of flowers accumulating at the foot of the Virgin, while pictures and scribbled prayers were fixed to the wall around her, all mounting in a makeshift altar at which believers genuflected, kneeled, whispered prayers, and even wept. Nearly all the believers crossed themselves. Many also caressed the image.

While the pious hailed the miraculous origins of Our Lady of the Underpass, as the stain was dubbed, others doubted its divine origin, perceiving merely a nebulous blotch on a gritty viaduct wall upon which deluded religionists could project personal wishes and subjective meanings. Whether an authentic apparition or a chance likeness, Our Lady of the Underpass was particularly interesting for the role that digital technology played in enhancing and reproducing the Marian image. Cell phones "were being held aloft like candles in a vigil," as one journalist put it, "the eyes of the enraptured tilted toward a constellation" of tiny screens transmitting glowing images of the suggestive stain (Schmich 2005: 1). Thus, while its origins were in dispute, all seemed to agree that the stain's resemblance to a prayerful Mary was enhanced when seen on the interface of a digital screen.

Some who thought the blotch to be nothing more than runoff nonetheless admitted that the photographed stain bore a curious resemblance to the popular icon depicting "The Virgin of Guadalupe," who, according to tradition,

Figure 7.1   Our Lady of the Underpass, Kennedy Expressway, Chicago, 2005

Source: Courtesy Nataline Viray-Fung.

appeared through the humble medium of a Mexican peasant's cloak in 1531. For many Catholics, particularly from Chicago's Latino community, this was more than a fortuitous likeness; it constituted a miraculous iteration of a historical image of the Virgin that has become a symbol for Catholic Mexicans. Some members of Chicago's prominent Polish population, meanwhile, embraced the notion that the Virgin's appearance was a communication from the then recently deceased Pope John Paul II; the Virgin appeared while the papal conclave was convening to determine John Paul's successor. The uncertainty of that moment was palpable amidst the general reverence. A pervasive attitude of expectation, solemnity, and awe were evident, as expressed in the gestures and words of the pilgrims. "Everything is strange," one said, capturing the numinous atmosphere within the busy underpass. A sense of shock registered among the solemn congregation, so unexpected and unusual was the apparition: "You see [believers'] faces when they walk away and it gives you chills" (Schmich 2005: 7).

While specific cultural, social, and historical contexts shaped varying interpretations of Our Lady of the Underpass, digital photography provided a common and conspicuous means for believers to practice their faith. The clicking of cameras and the devoted attention to their digital images were as integral to the reverence as the genuflections and murmured prayers—for countless photos of Our Lady of the Underpass were destined for assimilation within the homes and lives of believers. Indeed, the photos were instant icons that in some sense improved upon the "real" thing; the rather nebulous salt stain came into sharper focus through miniaturization on cell phones, while also being enhanced by the alluring aura emanating from the digital screen. The interface of the screen doubled as an interface with the transcendent, perhaps even partaking of its otherworldly power (Morgan 2009).

The details in this brief description of a paranormal occurrence—understood in the present context as an object or experience held to derive from a religious or supernatural "beyond"—and its varying receptions gesture toward a wide range of questions that confront scholars of religion seeking to investigate the materiality and material effects of "otherworldly" phenomena: How do physical materials embody and mediate the supernatural, the immaterial, the transcendent? What role does personal experience play in determining and evaluating that which does not originate in the familiar world? How do such occurrences both shape and re-shape religious beliefs? Such questions arise when studying the multifarious forms of the otherworldly or paranormal in religions across times, places, and cultures—from spirit possession in Japanese Shinto to the trances of Haitian voodoun practitioners; from the relics that mediated communication with the world of the dead in the medieval cult of saints to the angels and demons that populated Christendom in the Middle Ages; from the ecstatic visions of Hindu mystics to UFO cults in alliance with extraterrestrials; and from ghosts and spirits to the monsters, miracles, and other extraordinary phenomena that haunt the cultural imaginations of peoples across the globe.

Paramediation and the religious uncanny

Attempting, in the following pages, to sketch an approach to the kind of questions these strange and often intractable phenomena provoke, I delineate and investigate three broad categories of otherworldly experience: ecstasies, apparitions, and extraterrestrial invasions. Given the enormous variety of paranormal experience comprised under these rubrics, I want to adapt a concept that has broad applicability for understanding the unsettling effects of the otherworldly: the uncanny. The uncanny has enjoyed great currency in literary and art criticism since Sigmund Freud penned his classic essay on the subject in 1919, but it has found relatively little purchase in the field of religious studies.[1]

In "Das Unheimlich," Freud claims that the uncanny is "that class of the frightening which leads back to what is known of old and long familiar." It is "nothing new or alien" but rather something "familiar … in the mind and which has become alienated from it through the process of repression" (Freud 1995: 121, 142). The uncanny betokens a return of the repressed, and does so in ambivalent and fearful fashion, for when the repressed returns, it does so in disguised, distorted, or monstrous forms—doubles, ghosts, revenants, or mirror-others that embody a felt tension between the familiar, everyday, or homely

(*Heimlich*) and the paranormal, strange, or unhomely (*Unheimlich*). "Anything that obscures or echoes the real," as one commentator writes, "including reversals of the mirror-world, is related to our experience of the uncanny" (Rabinovitch 2004: 20). Such doubles, Freud writes, have a morbid aspect; they are "harbingers of death" (Freud 1995: 136). Living bodies taking on the mechanical aspect of an automaton, acting as if under the sway of a power beyond itself, is a further instigator of the uncanny, which is "often and easily produced when the distinction between imagination and reality is effaced" (ibid.: 145).

In elaborating his theory, Freud rejects Ernst Jentsch's earlier notion that uncanny effects derive from "intellectual uncertainty; so that the uncanny would always … be something one does not know one's way about in" (ibid.: 122). Jentsch specifically postulated that fearful sensations emerge where there is "uncertainty" as to whether a figure is a human or an automaton, animate or inanimate. The *ambivalence* of an object or figure at once living and lifeless, alive and dead, gives rise to an intractable uncertainty to which Jentsch finds attached the effects of the uncanny. And Freud makes no mention of Rudolf Otto's widely read book *The Idea of the Holy*, which first appeared in German in 1917, two years before "Das Unheimlich." In this book, Otto develops a phenomenological account of religious experience defined by the unique, irreducibly mysterious, and non-rational quality of the "numinous." The numinous arises through encounters with the fascinating and awe-ful *mysterium*—the ambivalent "wholly other" before which we "recoil in a wonder that strikes us chill and dumb" (Otto 1958: 28). He characterizes such experiences as "uncanny," though in a register that differs markedly from Freud's: for Otto, the wholly other is "quite beyond the sphere of the usual, the intelligible and the familiar, which therefore falls quite outside the limits of the 'canny,' and is contrasted with it, filling the mind with blank wonder and astonishment" (ibid.: 26). For Otto, the uncanny is resolutely unfamiliar, unusual, nonrational, and beyond conceptualization.

While Freud's may be the most widely consulted work on the uncanny, all three understandings of the uncanny—as the effect of repression, automation, or estranged familiarity; as intellectual uncertainty; and as that which is "wholly other," beyond intellection—return in encounters with the otherworldly. According to all three understandings, the uncanny is a feeling, an affective response to those objects and experiences that appear to derive from beyond the familiar world. More than that, it marks a disturbance, a moment that gestures beyond rational limits, when lived feelings and experiences upset everyday order. When the derivation of such experiences is taken to be supernatural or divine, we might thus speak of the *religious* uncanny. And indeed, the ambivalence of the uncanny exhibited in these three models distinctly recalls the ambivalence often attributed to the "sacred."

Classic conceptions of the sacred in Emile Durkheim, Rudolf Otto, and Mircea Eliade all emphasize the fundamentally ambiguous and ambivalent

nature of the sacred.² In ways that recall the etymology of the "holy" as simultaneously divine and accursed, high and low, pure and polluted, such thinkers
characterize the sacred in terms that evoke tension, contradiction, and ambivalence. According to Durkheim, for religionists, the world can be divided
according to the strict distinction between the sacred and its opposite, the profane (Durkheim 1965: 52). He further renders the sacred internally divided,
distinguishing between what are often termed the "right" and "left" aspects of
the sacred—the beneficent, purifying, vital sacred and the dangerous, polluted,
morbid sacred, respectively. Otto similarly casts the sacred in dualistic or
ambivalent terms, calling attention to the simultaneously overwhelming, powerful, and fearful aspects of the sacred, and the seductive, compelling, enchanting aspects. "These two qualities … combine in a strange harmony of contrasts:
mysterium and *fascinans*," accounting for "the resultant dual character of the
numinous consciousness" (Otto 1958: 31). Eliade, in some respects synthesiz-
ing Durkheim and Otto, claims the holy manifests itself in "hierophanies,"
those occasions in which a divine power erupts within the everyday, invading
profane, quotidian materials with sacred force. The numinous state of mind
and affective quality in the believer that attends the sacred is "something of a
wholly different order"—in other words, paranormal (Eliade 1959: 11).

This curious accord of the uncanny and the sacred, captured and con-
tracted in the concept of the "religious uncanny," is one preoccupation of this
chapter. But in attempting to come to terms with subject matter so haunted
by the ambivalences, contradictions, and tensions of the otherworldly, I want
to train attention upon the concrete, the material, and the this-worldly. In
particular, I want to examine how the religious uncanny arises in relation to
what I call "paramediation"—occasions in which those material mediums
and objects in which the paranormal appears provoke intellectual uncertainty, taking on aspects at once "long familiar" and/or "wholly other." The
prefix "para-" keys this term to the religious uncanny, while also signaling
how these mediums—be they dreams, images, bodies, technologies, or other
objects—appear in ways that recall the dual, ambivalent, or uncertain nature
of the religious uncanny. Paramediation thus refers to those modes of materiality through which believers take themselves to be in the presence of something heterogeneous, paranormal, or deriving from the beyond.

Indeed, "para-," according to its etymology, means alongside, beyond,
altered, or against. Each of these meanings points to the uncanny ability of
everyday mediums not only to transmit or represent the paranormal, but
also to saliently *embody* attributes classically associated with the sacred:
contradiction, ambivalence, undecidablity, or otherness. As such, paramediation also refers to that inexplicable residue, that surplus of felt meaning,
which purely rational accounts of the heterogeneous and paranormal
struggle to explain. It is a term that acknowledges the interpenetration of
the material with the otherworldly or immaterial in the lived experiences
of believers. In some cases, like that of the digitally enhanced Marian

apparition, paramediation may even call forth a kind of "technospiritualism," a piety achieved specifically in relation to some aspect of technology.

In this way, the phenomenon of paramediation marks an inversion of the ideas forwarded in Walter Benjamin's famous essay on "The Work of Art in the Age of Technological Reproduction." Benjamin argues that reproductions undercut the presence, or here-and-now-ness, of the original work of art, consequently degrading or "withering" its aura and disenchanting the work (Benjamin 1968: 221). Today, however, we find something quite different; no longer agents of demystification, technologies and, I hope to show, other mediums not only promote or even create an auratic presence of the image (even as they sometimes replicate it); in many cases the media themselves take on an auratic appeal, embodying that quality of numinous otherness and incomprehensibility connected with mysterious, otherworldly powers. In this connection, paramediation is a way of talking about the enchantment of the material medium—how it not only solicits and informs "religious sensations" such as awe, wonder, and fear, but also how those affective responses charge perception of the medium itself.[3]

This dialectic of matter and affect thus creates a sort of positive feedback loop; the medium embodies the numinous, even as the aura of the "otherness" is conferred upon the medium, each bolstering the other. As we shall see, discerning this uncanny dynamic reveals that "immediate" religious experience, even at its most acute, is in fact mediated—and is all the more intense for being so. To put it another way, "immediate" religious experience is *experience of the medium*. Paradoxes such as this give rise to further tensions and contradictions when considered in relation to paranormal experience, where thought and object frequently interpenetrate to a dizzying degree.[4] For example, as Jentsch suggests, the confusion of material and immaterial, worldly and otherworldly, provokes uncanny sensations. And yet, the resultant uncertainty can, paradoxically, serve as a (shifting) ground for the most deeply felt beliefs.

The strange relation between intellectual uncertainty and passionate belief also raises questions concerning the "authenticity" of otherworldly experiences. Indeed, issues of authenticity haunt the more speculative moments of this essay, just as they pervade so much of the discourse surrounding the paranormal—a discourse fraught with speculation. Authenticity, we will find, appears in various guises, from questions of certainty, proof, and evidence to the vicissitudes of human desire. It emerges, time and again, amidst the controversies, conundrums, and contradictions that lend ecstasies, apparitions, and alien invasions the enchanting and troubling air of the *mysterium*.

Ecstasies: bodies of proof

Considered according to its etymological roots, "ecstasy"—from the Greek *ek-stasis*, meaning to stand outside of oneself—characterizes diverse groups of phenomena. Dream journeys, out-of-body experiences, trances, spirit posses-sions, visionary apprehensions, drug-induced raptures, and "divine" madness all exhibit ecstatic elements. Such transports feature prominently in the history of religions. To take but one example, Tibetan Buddhism adapted yogic prac-tices in construing itineraries for otherworldly journeys by the deceased. The experience of the *bardo*, or the intermediate state between this world and rebirth in the next, includes an array of numinous phenomena, such as "sounds, colored lights and rays of light," that cause "terror and bewilderment" in the traveler seeking to leave behind his body (Couliano 1991: 94).

While religions throughout history and across cultures are rife with accounts of otherworldly transports, one of the most prominent forms of ecstasy occurs within the context of mysticism. Exhibiting, in its most ostensive forms, that quintessential aspect of ecstasy—being transported outside of oneself—mystical experiences are often predicated upon a sepa-ration of spirit from body, the immaterial from the physical—sometimes even to the extent of disavowing the body. And yet, as the examples below reveal, far from affirming some form of Cartesian dualism, mystical rap-tures dramatically exhibit the ultimate inseparability of mind, spirit, and body, for such experiences are shot through with imagery and grounded in bodies practiced in "techniques of ecstasy."[5] Whether the body is ostensibly reviled, relinquished, or reveled in, it remains the very basis of ecstatic expe-rience, often taking on an otherworldly quality of its own.

Bodily violence, illness, and death haunt the history of mysticism, where techniques of ecstasy include ascetic bodily disciplines ranging from flagel-lation and fasting to mutilation and other mortifications. Observing mys-tics' egregious bodily exercises led Marcel Mauss to comment that "underlying all our mystic states are corporeal techniques, biological meth-ods of entering into communication with God" (Mauss 1973: 86–87). For example, medieval German mystic Henry Suso (1300–1366) devised an astonishingly inventive array of means for chastising his body, including fastening a barbed cross to his back and opening fleshly wounds by the use of nails.[6] In modern India, Ramakrishna (1836–1886), a devotee of the violent (and violently sexual) goddess Kali, was less sanguinary but no less excessive in his bodily practices. As portrayed in Jeffrey Kripal's compelling account, Ramakrishna's mystical ecstasies culminated by at once summon-ing and disavowing erotic energies, resulting in a self-shattering rapture, an experience of union with the object of his devotion (Kripal 1995).

The most pronounced mystical raptures—in which the subject experiences a union with the immediate presence of god—are thus traumatic, evoking both psychical and bodily wounding or death. While some mystics in the Christian tradition have reviled the body, seeing it as an emblem of humani-ty's sinful nature, the body is nonetheless integral to their raptures, which sometimes take on erotic overtones. The sixteenth-century Carmelite nun

Teresa of Avila exemplifies this mingling of sensuality and death.[7] Teresa's early life was fraught with "serious illness." In addition to fainting spells, a "dreadful distress" left her feeling as if "every bone in [her] body" had been "wrenched asunder."[8] She was "worse than dead" (Teresa 1957: 45).

Teresa's striking morbidity is, however, part and parcel of a "favour" from God, for the patient endurance of her illness coincides with her spiritual practices of solitude and prayer. In describing the vicissitudes of the body—"indispositions" as well as the "alteration of the humours"—Teresa both distinguishes body from soul while also affirming their mutual influences. Though the body is an "evil guest" that "imprisons" the soul, the soul should "serve the body" so that "the body may serve the soul" (ibid.: 82). This mingling of the mortal body and the immortal soul is nowhere so pronounced as in the well-known passage, rendered by Bernini (Figure 7.2), in which Teresa is seized by an ecstasy that brings her to the brink of death. She describes a vision of an angel holding a "great golden spear" tipped by a "point of fire." The angel thrusts the spear into her "so that it penetrate[s] to [her] entrails." Upon being wounded, she is "utterly consumed by the

Figure 7.2 Gianlorenzo Bernini, *The Ecstasy of St. Theresa of Avila*, Cornaro Chapel, Rome

Source: Courtesy Scala/Art Resource, NY.

great love of God" while being overwhelmed by a pain "so severe that it [makes her] utter several moans" (ibid.: 210).

The palpable eroticism of this passage becomes increasingly pronounced: "The sweetness caused by this intense pain is so extreme that one cannot possibly wish it to cease … This is not a physical, but a spiritual pain, though the body has some share in it—even a considerable share" (ibid.: 210). Though Teresa's spasms might readily be interpreted as orgasmic—a convulsive unleashing of repressed sexual energies—it is the tension embedded in her description that grants insight into the traumatic dynamic that produces her experience of the divine. Teresa insists that the shattering pain is spiritual, not physical. Yet it is precisely the "considerable share" of physicality—from the vision of the angel with face aflame to the visceral lancing which she rapturously suffers—that is the substance of her experience. Teresa's spiritual experience is (also) corporeal; the "immediate" presence of God is an experience of the paramedium of her body.

Teresa's rapture thus affirms the uncanny logic of "sensible ecstasy," in which one is beside oneself precisely by experiencing the body as altered, as other—and as subject to a transcendent power.[9] In this mystical paradox, the dispossessed, ecstatic body is the body experienced as traumatized and even dead: a felt coincidence of life and death. In a single convulsion, this mystic's body is separated from the soul and coincident with it, experiencing a wounding that comes as if from a power of wholly different order. It might be said that this spiritual experience does not so much transcend the body as it engages the body *as other*, as unfamiliar in a mixture of pleasure and pain—a tormented bliss that affirms the matter of the spirit and the soul of the body.

This felt interpenetration of body and soul, as well as matter and mind, conveys its effects beyond the momentary ecstasy itself. Considered within their historical context, Teresa's mystical raptures are politicized, forming the center of a controversy over their putative authenticity. For Christians in the sixteenth century, religious life was fraught with anxiety over how to discern demonic influences. Adjudicating claims to immediate religious experience and negotiating the fear of demonic deception was symptomatic of that "craving for certainty that haunted every aspect of early modern thought." Teresa's insistent attempts to confirm the authenticity of her experiences, and thus her authority to instruct others, discloses an "anxiety about the apparent 'instability of truth'" (Schreiner 2003: 118, 120). While Teresa made rational appeals to ecclesial hierarchy and proffered theological claims to the Holy Spirit in attempting to stabilize the truth, discriminating between divine inspiration and its demonic counterfeit, as Susan Schreiner has argued, ultimately comes down to a personal experience or *feeling* of certitude.

In an era in Spanish history pervaded by a fear of mysticism, the "overarching problem was the preoccupation with experience, principally the authority being vested in personal or individual experience" (Schreiner 2003: 123–24).

Though Teresa sought to "formulate objective and external standards" by which to authenticate claims to mystical union with God, such methods for testing the spirit proved insufficient, for the devil can replicate the very evidence that would authenticate experience; the work of reason and intellect are insufficient to the task legitimating such claims (ibid.: 126). Teresa therefore relies on "experiential effects" to authenticate her raptures. Demonic flights leave the soul agitated, while those of divine origin produce a sense of equanimity, clarity, and assurance. Authentic spiritual experience is adjudicated according to those "feelings within the soul that the devil cannot counterfeit" (ibid.: 130).

And yet, as Teresa knew, the devil *can* replicate those feelings, "creat[ing] a false quiet, consolation, and vision." She therefore resorted to the very experience of certainty as proof of the authenticity of her spiritual exploits, specifying the feeling of "certainty itself as the ultimate test" of authenticity. As she wrote, genuine mystical experience produces "a certitude so strong that an assurance is left that cannot be overcome." The circularity here is obvious: certainty grants and guarantees certitude (ibid.: 130–32). There is a paradoxical turn, then, in the decisive role that *feelings* play in adjudicating authenticity. Rational, theologically grounded attempts to prove the genuinely divine origins of rapture are epistemologically insupportable. Uncertainty is ultimately rectified by that suspicious medium of religious experience, the "evil guest" of the body, locus of the self-authenticating sense of certitude.

Such certitude thus derives from the traumatic nature of the mystical convulsions: the experience of the otherness of the dispossessed body ratifies the authenticity of the experience itself. This sense of being possessed by an otherness so profound as to be intolerable is also a feeling so intense in its heterogeneity as to be indubitable. And this conveys the uncanny aspect of mystical certainty. It is not the certainty of ratiocinative thought, but a compelling surety grounded in the experience of the body as a paramedium. Belief deriving from this experience is best conveyed in paradoxical terms, such as those Teresa wrote from that liminal state in which life and death mingle: "I die because I cannot die."

Apparitions: authentic hoaxes

Death comes to life again in a paranormal byway in the history of religions, the story of modern Spiritualism and spirit photography. In 1848, in the hamlet of Hydesville in upstate New York, two sisters—Kate and Margaretta Fox, ages 11 and 15, respectively—claimed to have established contact with the beyond. For months, the sisters and their parents had endured nights interrupted by odd "rappings" in their cottage. The source of these acoustic disturbances remained unexplained until the sisters discovered that their own clapping solicited responses in kind, leading them to attribute the knockings to an invisible interloper—the spirit of a murdered peddler haunting their house. The girls' older sister, Leah, and the Fox parents joined in the exchanges, establishing communication with the spirit world (Sconce 2000: 22).

Eventually it came to light that these putatively supernatural rappings were in fact of mundane origins: one of the younger sisters had cultivated the odd talent of cracking her toe joints loudly and at will. But this admission did not surface until the very real reverberations of the hoax had spread far beyond their native New York. While the "haunted" house in which the Foxes lived became a destination for those seeking firsthand acquaintance with the beyond, the Fox girls also went on tour, displaying occult powers that garnered international attention, and instigating a global movement (as well as a church) known as Spiritualism. But if Spiritualism was a fake, it was, in David Chidester's formulation, an "authentic fake," for as we will see, it accomplished the "authentic religious work" of "forging a community, focusing desire, and facilitating exchange in ways that look just like religion" (Chidester 2005: viii–viii).

Based on a belief that communication with the dead was possible through human mediums who could channel the spirit world, Spiritualism coincided with the atmosphere of "utopian technophilia" that characterized mid-nineteenth-century America and Europe. The tapping of Samuel Morse's first electromagnetic telegraph message occurred in 1844, marking an astonishing achievement of disembodied exchange whose near instantaneity "must have truly tested the limits of credulity." And yet, thanks to the incredible nature of this new technological medium, many were led to predict—or fantasize—a paradise that would establish the "practical unity of the human race; of which we have never yet had a foreshadowing, except in the gospel of Christ." Just as Morse's telegraph realized the seemingly supernatural possibilities of discorporate communication, so did the Fox girls and subsequent mediums open "a 'telegraph line' to another world" (Sconce 2000: 22). Eventually this telegraph line to the dead became a system of communication comprising conventionalized symbols reminiscent of Morse code. But first it was a paramedium in which the bodies of the Fox girls and other mediums acted as ontological connections between this world and the next.

This strange coincidence of technology and the occult evinces the mid-nineteenth century's collective fascination with the paranormal (séances, Ouija boards, clairvoyance, and such were in fashion), as well as its faith in the promises of the new and numinous frontier of electronic communications. Occult enthusiasts sought to connect their practices with the "similarly fantastic" innovations of electromagnetic telegraphy (Sconce 2000: 24). This quest for concord between the technological and the spiritual was linked to a wider cultural obsession with adducing proof in the form of material evidence of the spirit world, and thus the afterlife—evidence that would meet the standards of scientific inquiry. But while telegraphy dramatically displayed the possibility of separating consciousness, and by extension the immortal spirit, from its material substrate, no technological medium was more central to the quest for empirical proof of the afterlife than photography.

Spiritualists eagerly incorporated photography into their séances, exploiting its powers of reduplication to generate "evidence" of their spectral interlocutors. Just as the predominantly female mediums were believed able to channel the beyond thanks to their spiritual sensitivity (a "feminine" quality), so could cameras render visible on their photosensitive plates those spirits imperceptible to the human eye (Gunning 2004: 11). Spirit photographs executed by mediums from the latter half of the nineteenth century frequently picture a subject who has posed for a portrait; upon developing the plate, the subject appears accompanied by "extras" hovering in his vicinity—images of the dearly departed. Some photos portray spirit "materializations" during séances (Figure 7.3); specters garbed in conventional ghostly attire—veils or sheets—"assume a visible and often palpable body" (ibid.: 12) available to the touch of the séance participants (often men were tacitly encouraged to grope the veiled bodies of the female spirits, adding an erotic frisson to the otherworldly experience). Other images are at once more luminous and less

Figure 7.3 Enrico Imoda, Materialization of a Young Woman, produced by the Medium Linda Gazzera, photograph, 1909

Source: Courtesy The Metropolitan Museum of Art, Gilman Collection, Gift of The Howard Gilman Foundation, 2005 (2005.100.385.1). © The Metropolitan Museum of Art.

legible, containing auratic streaks or glowing blobs and smears. Still others capture ectoplasm, that otherworldly substance "situated ... ambiguously between the realms of spirits and the material universe" which was exuded from the bodily orifices of the channeling medium (ibid.: 13).

Today, such photos appear patently fraudulent, and belief in them seems laughably naïve. The "extras" were created through processes of composite printing or double exposure; "materializations" were nothing more than tricked out women complicit with dissembling mediums; the luminous auras were the result of manipulation or fortuitous printing flaws. Even the ectoplasmic effluvia ostensibly purged from the mediums' bodies in convulsive trances were merely theatrical props of mundane materials, chiefly cheesecloth or netting. And yet, however tawdry these photos might appear to our eyes, they possessed a power that had quite real effects in their original context.

In an era desiring scientific proof of the afterlife (perhaps especially among those mourning loved ones lost to the war), photography was embraced as an ideal means for perceiving otherwise invisible spirits in their material form. Because it "acted mechanically, objectively, and independently of the mind of its user" (Warner 2006: 223), the camera, it was believed, "could not lie"; it would thus supply unassailable evidence of the spirit world. As Tom Gunning has argued, the Spiritualists' desire to provide empirical proof of the existence of spirits thus looked to photography's "dual identity as an icon, a bearer of resemblance, and as an index, a trace left by a past event." That photography could capture traces of a presence—person, place, or thing—afforded photography "a key role as evidence, in some sense apodictic" (Gunning 1995: 42). If spirits could be captured in documentary images, they must exist, and they must also enjoy material dimensions.

But while the photographic medium was a tool of scientific positivism, it was no less uncanny for that. As Gunning emphasizes, Freud related the experience of the uncanny to the theme of the double, and indeed the camera's ability to produce doubles of its subject would have engendered an unsettling sense of the uncanny in its nineteenth-century audience. Exposed to this new mode of paramediation, sensitive to spirits and capable of producing doubles, "the first generations to view photographs endowed the new technology with a supernatural dimension as much as an apodictic clarity" (Schoonover 2003: 35). The technological apparatus itself partakes of a numinous power beyond even the grasp of its users.

> Neither the images, nor their producers, nor their proponents offered any explanation of how ghosts ended up in pictures. Therefore, to have accepted these images as real was to grant photography a supernatural agency since the ghosts only appeared via the mysteries of its technology.
>
> (ibid.: 33)

It is this ambivalent status of the enchanted medium of photography—the camera as both a tool of empirical certainty as well as a kind of supernaturally attuned technology—that make it, like its telegraphic counterpart, a curiously apt medium for a dialectic of belief and desire. For the story of spirit photography is the story of "the *desire* to believe, the *desire* for evidence of immortality and contact with the dead" (Gunning 2004: 14). While believing Spiritualists relied on the objective powers of the camera for proof of the afterlife, their longings for such proof likely led to rationalizing in the face of increasingly obvious fraud.[10] Over time, as the critiques of skeptical investigators intensified along with increasing understanding of the camera's mechanism and their operators' dissimulations, spirit photographs failed to hold up as authentic proof of the afterlife.

What they do evidence, however, is the profound manner in which human desire and the scientific impulse can inflect and refract each other: the otherworldly powers of the camera were "evidenced" by the spirits it allegedly captured and multiplied, while its positivistic capacities were confirmed by the very real "uncanny sensations" the camera solicited in producing its doubles. In other words, belief in spirits and the afterlife was held so tenaciously by many Spiritualists not despite uncertainty but because of it. The intellectual uncertainty concerning not only spirits but the medium of photography in which those spirits were conveyed formed unstable but fertile ground for beliefs that focused desire for an afterlife and hope for communion with the dearly departed.

Invasions: uncanny evidences

Conjuring up and communicating with the deceased were the desire of the Spiritualists of the nineteenth and early twentieth centuries. But contemporary North American Spiritualism engages a different beyond: extraterrestrial beings believed to herald a techno-spiritual utopia. Such latter-day Spiritualists are hardly the first or only religionists to relate to life on other planets. Swedish scientist, theologian, and mystic Emanuel Swedenborg (1688–1772), for example, not only enjoyed visions of angels and demons; he also claimed contact with interplanetary beings encountered on his disembodied galactic sojourns. But Spiritualism, along with Theosophy and Christianity, constitute the three main strands of an astonishing array of UFO religions that have arisen since 1947, when American businessman Kenneth Arnold sighted ten luminous discs above the Cascade Mountains while piloting his private plane.[11] It was just a few weeks later that the infamous incident at Roswell, New Mexico, occurred: an alleged alien spacecraft crashed to earth, its debris quickly cleaned up (and covered up?) by the US Air Force. Roswell was to become a "key ufological 'sacred site'," inspiring all manner of "religious attitudes and actions," including "pilgrimages" to the place. Such "sacralisation of the extraterrestrial" has pervaded subsequent UFO culture (Partridge 2003: 6–7).

UFO religions are characterized by "the belief that one or several individuals are in touch with beings in flying saucers and regularly fulfill the role of mediums who transmit prophetic messages, religious teaching, and moral instruction" (Saliba 1995: 27). Those religions deriving from the Theosophical tradition tend to adapt Theosophy founder Madame Blavatsky's key tenets and ideas concerning "cosmic wisdom" and "cosmic masters" to an extraterrestrial context. The contactees—those with whom extraterrestrials communicate directly—act as mediums or channelers, conveying otherworldly wisdom from their space brethren (chiefly Masters of the Theosophical Society who descend to Earth in flying saucers). Movements more squarely within the Spiritualist tradition place less emphasis on space-crafts, and rely on telepathic human mediums to receive messages from distant extraterrestrial Masters. Like their Spiritualist and Theosophical counterparts, Christian UFO religions believe in the existence of intelligent extraterrestrial life, but these cults emerge when the extraterrestrials' activities "are accepted as central to the Christian message, which is interpreted anew by prophetic leaders who claim some connection with ... space creatures" (ibid.: 31).

Each of these strands of UFO spirituality encompasses an enormous range of beliefs, practices, and participants. There is, for instance, the flying saucer cult of Unarius, formerly led by the theatrically garbed Uriel, who heralded the advent of the "electronic body." In the Raelien movement, meanwhile, a guide or channeler transmits a "cellular code" through a ceremony resembling baptism, while the movement's erotic philosophy encourages exploration of sex through "sensual meditation" aimed at achieving a "cosmic orgasm" (Palmer 1995: 107–10). And there are, of course, varieties of UFO spirituality that remain outside these broad categories, including the personal religious beliefs of those who have had firsthand contact with alien life, engendering a spiritual "awakening."

Whatever form the encounter takes, however, aliens tend to invade everyday life through already-available cultural outlets. Religious traditions, as we have seen, supply one channel, but there are many other outlets through which belief in extraterrestrial intelligence takes shape. In America, popular culture—literature, cinema, television, and the like—has embraced the image of the flying saucer, while the iconic visage of the alien—capacious bald head featuring preternaturally large, dark eyes—can be found on everything from key chains and lunchboxes to T-shirts and bumper stickers (Whitmore 1995: 80). Similarly, descriptions of alien technology deriving from contactees tend to evolve over time, reflecting current popular science on earth. All this is to suggest that alien invasions occur in dialectical relation to the American collective imagination, spreading like a cultural contagion. As the culture embraces and reproduces UFO-related images inspired by contact accounts, such abduction stories increase, taking on the features of the pervasive cultural artifacts; visionary experiences are "cast in a framework of space age technology" and popular scientific imagery (Melton 1995: 10).

And yet, while the channels in which aliens manifest themselves are familiar, they also take on aspects of inexorable otherness—the uncanniness of the familiar under a strange aspect. The "sacralisation of the extraterrestrial" is stimulated by encounters of a wholly different order; there is a "direct experience with ... extraordinary occurrences" (ibid.: 10) that gives rise to the numinous consciousness to which Otto refers. To be sure, extraterrestrial encounters, whether in the form of UFO sightings, contact with aliens, or abductions, take on hierophanic qualities for those who experience them; aliens and their technologies are living metaphors for otherness. This alterity can be attributed to the way in which UFO phenomena—saucers, aliens, and abductions—evoke various dimensions of the uncanny.

Materializing and dematerializing, fleeting and evasive, flying saucers seem to exist in that "twilight zone between dream and reality" (Grosso 1989: 92). This quality has led some ufologists to speculate that flying saucers are psychic phenomena existing in that uncanny space in which, as Freud put it, the "distinction between reality and imagination is erased." This idea is literalized in the preponderance of photographs of UFOs. Photographs capturing UFOs are typically grainy or out of focus, with unidentified objects appearing as ambiguous specks, blobs, or streaks (Figure 7.4). In their underdetermined nature they resemble Rorschach blots, taking the

Figure 7.4 Photograph of an aerial phenomenon considered by some to be an unidentified flying object, taken on October 20, 1960, in Minneapolis, Minnesota

Source: Photo courtesy of UFO Casebook, www.ufocasebook.com

form, as some claim, of preconceived expectations. Others suggest that these ambiguous spots are alien objects "in transition between being in a solid state and being in a pure energy state" (Rojcewicz 1989: 77). In either case, the very qualities that make these photos highly questionable as "evidence" make them potent agents in the shaping of belief.

Extraterrestrial beings likewise stimulate uncanny sensations. While they come in a wide variety of shapes and sizes, aliens described by abductees tend to be roughly humanoid in shape but "other" in their attributes and accoutrements. Their large foreheads suggest superior intelligence, while shimmering garments enhance their strangeness. Extraterrestrials often fly, are able to communicate telepathically, and can materialize and dematerialize at will, passing through walls or popping into existence at one's bedside. Abductees report further registers of otherness, as well: in the course of abduction scenarios, abductees are inserted into an unfamiliar temporal mode; taken aboard spacecrafts or exposed to other extraordinary technologies; subjected to terrifying bodily probing; inspired by unusual feelings of love and arousal; and spiritually awakened into higher moral being. Ontologically uncertain and ethically ambiguous, aliens are at once frightening and comforting, ferocious and loving, clinical and caring. Such ambivalences and ambiguities make of alien experiences the "very condensation of the strange and unfamiliar" (Whitmore 1995: 79).

But the uncertain nature of UFOs is most patent in their ambiguous relationship to modes of rational, scientific inquiry. If, to speak generally, scientific thought emerges in part on the basis of the law of non-contradiction, UFOs remain—to some extent, at least—beyond its purview; the uncanny interpenetration of thought and thing, dream and reality, spirit and substance, renders UFO phenomena unsusceptible to the usual modes of rational inquiry based upon binary logic: either material or immaterial, physical or spiritual.[12]

The mingling of matter and spirit is part of what defines paramediation, from Marian apparitions and ghosts to mystical ecstasies and alien invasions. But UFO phenomena are not only rendered through paramediation— the dreams, hallucinations, or uncanny photographs in which the physical and spiritual mingle. These also *thematize* the problem of paramediation itself, raising the question of how to think about those things that are not really *things* in the usual sense. UFOs are "partially no-*things*, meaningful nothings … possessing multiple natures" that cannot be perceived in their totality by a strictly rational perspective (Rojcewicz 1989: 78).

While the empirical mode of inquiry may be able to account for things that derive from and remain firmly grounded in the material world, a scientistic world-view—in which the supernatural is rejected under the assumption that *all* phenomena are ultimately explainable by natural causes—curtails those approaches that admit the existence of the paranormal, those phenomena that, as "dynamic composites of consciousness and matter" (ibid.: 78), simultaneously spiritual and material, dramatically refuse the logic of the either/or. Such ambiguous phenomena are the uncanny matters of parame-diation, where the medium is both itself and something more or *other* than itself—material and spiritual. And while the objects and experiences deriv-ing from beyond the familiar world may be insubstantial, unstable, ephem-eral, or ambiguous, the uncertainty they evoke is, for those attuned to them, the very basis of belief.

Notes

1 This is, of course, undoubtedly due in part to Freud's assessment of religion as a form of mass neurosis. For a consideration of Freud's concept of the uncanny in the context of religion, see Dawson (1989) and Rabinovitch (2004).
2 These three concepts of the sacred have each met with criticism, but remain helpful starting points in examining the religious uncanny.
3 See Meyer (2006) for a discussion of "religious sensations."
4 Michael Taussig (1992: 126) discusses the manner in which "thought and object interpenetrate" in the context of a discussion of Durkheim's concept of fetishism.
5 I am adapting Eliade's term for shamanistic practice. See Eliade (1992).
6 For a discussion of "the spirituality of imaging Christ" in relation to Henry Suso's practice, see Morgan (1998: 61–3). See also Hamburger (1989).
7 See Bataille (1986) for a discussion of the relation of death and sensuality in Teresa.
8 Teresa (1957: 33).
9 See Hollywood (2002) for a discussion of the relationship between trauma and mystical ecstasies.
10 See Gunning (1995: 65), where he speaks of the "base rationalizations trying to cover up clear examples of fraud."
11 See Saliba (1995: 26–31) for an overview of types of UFO cults.
12 Partridge (2003: 35) discusses abductees' "strident critique of the reductionist methodology utilized by much Western science," citing J. L. Mack, who claims that:

> The difficulty for our society and for our mentality is, we have a kind of either/or mentality. It's either ... physical or it's in the spiritual other realm, the unseen realm. What we seem to have no place for ... are phenomena that can begin in the unseen realm, and cross over and manifest ... in our ... physical world.

8

"Dolls are scary"
The locus of the spiritual in contemporary Japanese homes

Inge Daniels

Belief and religious activity within anthropology
Dolls and domestic concerns
"Dolls (and other things with faces) are scary"
The second life of dolls?
Conclusion: material culture and religion

Belief and religious activity within anthropology

During the nineteenth and much of the twentieth century most anthropologists have uncritically used belief as a universal, analytical category to conceptualize and compare cultures (often described as systems of beliefs). Moreover, within ongoing debates about modernity and the rationalization of society, belief was defined as a subjective, inner quality opposed to objective knowledge at the base of science.[1] It is only since the 1950s, with the growing awareness of the dialectical relation between religious ideas and practices within any cultural context, that questions began to be raised about the usefulness of universals such as "belief" (see, for example, Leach 1954).

In a widely cited publication from 1972, Needham, for example, draws on philosophical and psychological accounts, to question 'whether 'I believe in' is the definite feature of a religious attitude' (Needham 1972: 74). He disputes the use of the difficult to translate English language term "belief" because it is so firmly embedded in a Christian tradition that distinguishes between belief-statements and experiences; the latter in turn being understood as either cognitive or affective depending on whether one studies "advanced" or "primitive" people (ibid.: 189).[2] In a subsequently historical, cross-cultural exploration of the ambiguity surrounding the concept of belief, Malcolm Ruel (1982), similarly, concludes that the anthropological study of religion has been compromised by the Christian tradition with its respect for belief and supernatural beings. He, then, identifies the following four, persistent fallacies in the study of religion: (1) belief is central to all religion; (2) belief is fundamental to a person's behavior; (3) belief is an inward, psychological condition; (4) determining belief is more important than its content (Ruel 1982: 19–21). Hence, "the dangers of excessive historical universalization," also pointed out by Tambiah in a seminal article in which he debunks the supposed analogy between "primitive"magic and "modern" science (Tambiah 1985: 77), have been at the forefront of anthropological discussions about religion.

In the 1990s, Asad (1993) made an important contribution to the debate by challenging Geertz's universal definition of religion that prioritizes a modern, privatized Christian notion of belief as "a state of mind rather than a constituting activity in the world" or "a sense of conviction, not a corpus of practical knowledge" (Asad 1993: 47). Second, and even more important for the Japanese case study that I will discuss below, he criticizes Geertz's distinction between religious and non-religious experiences. In his view,

> religious symbols – whether one thinks of them in terms of communication or of cognition, of guiding action or of expressing emotion – cannot be understood independently of their historical relation with non religious symbols or of their articulation in and of social life.
>
> (ibid.: 53)

Rappaport takes this latter debate a step further by suggesting not only that ritual is at the core of all social life, but also that belief "is an inward state, knowable subjectively if at all, and it would be entirely unwarranted either for us or for participants or witnesses to assume that participation in a ritual necessary indicates such a state" (Rappaport 1999: 120).

This latter statement echoes insights from a number of ethnographies carried out by anthropologists working in Japan (Reader 1991; Reader and Tanabe 1998; Traphagen 2004). These studies have inspired my own research by providing strong evidence in support of the view that "human understanding is not a prerequisite for ritual to have power or effect [as] … practical and rational technologies supplement each other in the production of good results" (Reader and Tanabe 1998). John Traphagen has argued that in the case of Japan "rather than being organized around doctrine or institutional affiliation, religious activity is centered on the idea of concern" (Traphagen 2004: 81). Although he draws on Tillich's well-known definition of religion as "ultimate concern that determines our being or not being," his approach places less stress on the individual. Indeed, in the Japanese context, the personal and collective are considered complementary, and the notion of concern is integrated in the everyday lives of people through the enactment of rituals that recognize and maintain connections with others; whether with other people, dead or alive, with deities or with the inanimate world.

In this chapter, I will explore this "emic" notion of religion as "intimate" concern through an ethnographic investigation of how beneficial connections are ritually enacted by families in contemporary, urban Japanese homes. By drawing attention to the domestic arena as a space embroiled in religious activity, I hope to extend a number of recent ethnographies, grounded in material culture studies (Miller 2001) and phenomenology (Helliwell 1996), that have demonstrated that the home is a continuously changing, dynamic space, (re)produced through a series of social and material practices. The specific data presented were collected during a one-year ethnography (2003) carried out in thirty, middle-class homes in the Kansai region (Osaka, Kobe, Kyoto).[3]

Dolls and domestic concerns

Those participating in my study habitually expressed concern for all those living under the same roof by sharing food inside the home and exchanging gifts with the outside world in order to create, consolidate and renew connections among people, ancestors and deities. Moreover, at specific times of the year they performed a series of prescribed rituals that help to deflect malevolent influences from the home and ensure the happiness and wellbeing of its occupants. Japanese ethnologists have argued that these rituals, called "annual events" (*nenjû gyôji*), cleanse pollution through "offerings made to the deities that are afterwards consumed among the community" (Yanagita 1951: 449). In 2003, celebrations for Shinto deities (*kami*) such as the New Year and Buddhist commemorations of ancestors such as Obon (August) were held in all the homes studied. In the former case, the Shinto shelf (*kamidana*), which houses protective deities, and in the latter case the Buddhist altar, where the ancestors are enshrined, are the focus of attention. However, concern is also expressed on a daily basis in front of both domestic altars. Although individual practices differ considerably, even among members of the same family, in most homes offerings of food and drink were made and both personal greetings and petitions for the wellbeing of the family were addressed to the ancestors and guardian spirits. Importantly, concern can also be enacted without reference to these two loci as other parts of the home may be transformed into ritual space (Ito 1995: 131).[4] During the days leading up to the auspicious Girls' (March 3) and Boys' Day (May 5), popular "annual events" that focus on the health and happiness of children, for example, seasonal dolls are displayed in Japanese-style rooms. (I will discuss these displays in detail below.[5])

In all the homes studied, multiple beneficial connections were created with religious institutions. Every Buddhist altar, for example, is linked with a family grave and by extension a Buddhist temple where the cemetery is located. Descendants' obligations towards their ancestors entail caring for both the altar and the grave. Neglecting these duties may have dire consequences as ancestors can become wandering spirits (*mu-en botoke*, literally *buddhas* without attachments) that cause misfortune (Smith 1974: 41–42). I will return to the idea that harm may befall those who neglect to maintain or break connections as it elucidates why dolls that have been inside the home for a long period of time need to be treated with special care. Connections with religious centers are, second, embodied by a myriad of lucky objects that are motivating devices that affirm divine help from a specific deity located in a particular temple or shrine. Charms are not venerated, but strategically placed in hallways, kitchens, and Japanese-style rooms.[6] As there are no parameters for areas of concern, temples and shrines market themselves as being useful for a multitude of benefits ranging from recovering from illness and passing exams to safety in travel and finding a love match.[7] In times of need, one person, usually an elderly or middle-aged married woman, takes on the responsibility as a representative of the family group of visiting a religious center to perform a series of ritual actions (including washing hands, rubbing statues, writing petitions, donating money, and eventually bringing home charms). I have discussed the circulation and domestic consumption of the material culture of luck in detail elsewhere (Daniels 2003); here I would like to focus on some similarities between lucky charms and dolls, the focus of this chapter. Both are mass-produced objects that belong to a category of domestic goods that cannot easily be disposed off because they embody connections with others but also because their shape is imbued with special powers. The majority are gifts that embody connections between people and they flow into the home in large quantities whether or not the inhabitants actually want them (Daniels 2009a).

Dolls in glass boxes, whether displayed or stored away, were a common feature in all the homes studied.[8] Several dolls were business gifts or souvenirs from trips, but rites of passage are the main occasions when dolls are given. Some received dolls for their weddings or sixty-first birthdays, but most were gifts for births. In the Kansai region it is common for grandparents, but sometimes also other family members and intimate friends, to present infants for their first Girls (March 3) or Boys festival (May 5) (*hatsuzekku*) with display dolls. Although boys also receive dolls, the correlation between girls and dolls is stronger, so I will focus on two types of dolls given at the birth of daughters.

First, Ichimatsu dolls are realistic representations of female (or male) children dressed in kimono (Figure 8.1).[9] These are effigies that absorb any evil that may befall the child to whom they are given. They can be traced back to two dolls employed to protect infants since the Muromachi period (1392–1573). The "heavenly child" (*amagatsu*) was a stick figure that was placed next to newborn babies, mainly boys, to absorb illness and ward off evil (Baten 2000: 13). The "lowly child" (*hôko*) was an X-shaped textile doll associated with girls, and was considered to capture evil spirits who mistook the doll for the baby (ibid.: 37).[10] A second type of doll, given to first-born daughters by maternal grandparents of the newborn, are a set of miniatures that depict a royal wedding party from the Heian period (794–1192), called Hina dolls (*hina ningyô* or *o-hina-san*; Figure 8.2).[11] These dolls are considered to be temporary embodiments of the deities (*katashiro*) and are displayed during the weeks leading up to the Dolls' Festival (*hina matsuri*) on the third of March, when people eat auspicious foods and pray for the health, happiness, and the reproductive capabilities of girls. It is significant that the

Figure 8.1 Two Ichimatsu dolls that belong to Yasuko and Yuko Takahashi, who are both in their late twenties and are still living in their family home in Nara. The dolls are placed in the decorative alcove of a Japanese-style room on the second floor that also functions as the girls' bedroom

Source: Photo by Susan Andrews, 2006.

Figure 8.2 Mrs. Kadonaga, a single lawyer in her mid-fifties, continues to display this treasured pair of Hina dolls in the home she shares with her aging mother on the outskirts of Kobe

Source: Photo by Susan Andrews, 2006.

dolls depict a wedding because marriage was—and often still is—considered to be the desired path for Japanese girls. Interestingly, Hina dolls may also be employed as effigies since, during the Doll's Festival, many religious centers hold ceremonies in which a pair of paper Hina doll is rubbed against the body or breathed on before being set adrift on a river to take any bad luck away with them (Kawasaki and Moteki 2002: 58–61).

Although both Ichimatsu and Hina dolls might once have been toys (Baten 2000: 107), these days they are primarily put on display.[12] Both types of dolls are produced and distributed through commercial channels, which supports the view that economic activities are not thought to decrease the power of the spiritual in Japan. Ichimatsu dolls are expensive crafts made by specialists. In May 2003, I attended an exhibition and sale of these dolls at the Maruzen bookstore in Kyoto. Prices for standard size dolls started at 40,000 yen (£200), but many cost more than 100,000 yen (£500).[13] Dolls are preferably displayed in Japanese-style rooms. Those in my sample who possessed a decorative alcove preferred to display their Ichimatsu dolls (as well as other dolls) in glass boxes in there (Figure 8.3), while others placed them on top of chests and wardrobes

Figure 8.3 Three dolls in glass boxes surrounded by other decorative objects in the decorative alcove in the Sakai's two-storied house in the south of Osaka

Source: Photo by Susan Andrews, 2006.

kept inside tatami rooms that also functioned as bedrooms.[14] However, more than half of the participants also kept display dolls in storage.

Whereas Ichimatsu dolls are supposed to be displayed throughout the year, Hina dolls are seasonal objects. From mid-February until early March, participants in my study with unmarried daughters displayed sets of miniature dolls. Hina dolls come in a variety of configurations and prices, and may be acquired at specialty shops and department stores, but also at convenient stores and other small, local shops. Some families in my sample such as the Matsuis, the Kuwaharas, and the Takahashis erected a large, tiered platform (*hina-dana*) covered with a velvet cloth on which they arranged an elaborate display of dolls depicting a noble wedding from the Heian period. The married couple is placed prominently on the top shelf, while the other shelves present their entourage of court ladies, pages, soldiers, and musicians, each with his or her appropriate accoutrements. Also displayed is a miniature version of a "traditional" bride's trousseau.

Advertising for dolls reveals that prices for elaborate Hina sets range between 180,000 and 380,000 yen (£900 and £1,900). Ornate sets are not only expensive but they also take up a lot of space, and during my fieldwork displays consisting of only of the married couple of Hina dolls were common.[15] As girls grew older, some families with ornate sets felt less inclined to go through the trouble of presenting them. However, many feared that if they did not display any dolls (or if they forgot to take the display down at the end of the festival,) their daughters might remain single. As a precaution, they elected to display a single pair of miniature Hina dolls with some flowers and sweets. The preferred spot for this arrangement was the top of shoe closets in hallways.

In Japan, as in many other cultural contexts, dolls have a long history of being employed as substitutes for people. The Japanese characters that comprise the word for doll, 人形, can also be read as *hitogata*, which literally means "human shape." Both dolls under discussion are used as effigies that protect children, whether they absorb bad luck in lieu of the child or increase good fortune, for example, in bringing about a prosperous future marriage. Moreover, as both Law (1997) and Gerbert (2001) point out, dolls also have a long history of acting as mediators between worlds.[16] They are

> not simply metaphors for the human, but actually compose a world of their own, a parallel world bridging the domains of the humans and the divine ... as an intersection of these worlds, [the doll] is powerful and frightening, eliciting both fear and fascination.
>
> (Gerbert 2001: 62)

"Dolls (and other things with faces) are scary"

Many participants found dolls frightening (*kowaii*). A minority focused on their hair. Thirty-year old Shigeko Kagemori, a PhD student living in Osaka, for example, told me that dolls are scary because in the past they had real hair, and there were some whose hair seemed to keep growing.

Inge:	Have you come across this kind of dolls?
Shigeko:	In the summer you often hear these stories on TV. But *Okiku* dolls (*okiku-san ningyo*) existed before as well, isn't it, mam? Mam quite likes these kind of stories.
Mrs. Kagemori:	Yes, *Okiku* dolls are quite famous. They existed already during the Edo-period and the hair started to grow and even if the hair was cut it kept on growing and, well, the face of those dolls was very scary, and cold.

As the conversation above indicates, negative attitudes towards dolls are influenced by their depiction as malicious creatures that intend to harm people in the media; whether on TV, in anime or in literature (Gerbert 2001).

However, most people highlighted the particular scary facial features of dolls. According to Yoshiko, the youngest Kuwahara daughter in Osaka, for example, contemporary Hina dolls with small faces and big eyes "that look a bit like foreigners are considered cute," while "the faces of dolls from the Edo period are really big and their eyes look scary, a bit like a fox."[17] By contrast, her older sister, Keiko, thought that French dolls with their large, blue eyes were much creepier. This prompted Mrs. Kuwahara to narrate the story of a friend's daughter who stayed in their guestroom and woke up in the middle of the night scared of a French doll that she thought was watching her in the dark. Similarly, other people worried about dolls' eyes, saying: "they always watch you" or "their eyes may turn red." These ideas concerning the special powers of dolls may be extended to a broad category of doll-like objects. Kageyama-san, a single girl in her early twenties who recently split up with her boyfriend, wanted to dispose of a stuffed Koala bear she had received as a souvenir from him from a trip to China. However, during my visits the bear continued to lie disregarded, face down on a pile of magazines in her room because she thought that "it is scary to throw away dolls and other things with a face."

The majority of stories about wicked dolls concern dolls that belong to other people. Indeed, most women I talked to were not scared of their own dolls. The two Takahashi daughters in Nara, for instance, have always slept in the tatami room where their Ichimatsu dolls in glass boxes are on display. They are really fond of them, think they are cute, and have given them personal names. Moreover, I was repeatedly told that over time, as the bond between a doll and child intensifies, the face of the doll may come to resemble the child's. Schattschneider (2004) discusses this mimetic quality of the face of dolls in detail in her stunning ethnography of spirit marriages in northern Japan. In these ceremonies a bride doll, imbued with the spirit of the deity Jizo in a consecration rite, is given (married) to a dead child of the opposite sex represented in a photograph. Over time, through proxy, the initially generic face of the mass-produced doll comes to resemble the dead child and eventually both enter the world of the dead together (ibid.: 150). Similarly, Ichimatsu dolls are mass-produced objects that are generic representations of little girls. Initially these 'new' commodities are associated with the giver (the grandparents) as they embody intimate (maternal) family connections across the generations. Indeed, the dolls are often dressed in kimono made from fabric that was previously worn by the child's grandmother. However, as time passes by, and doll and child age, they become inalienably linked. This association is achieved through mimesis of the face of the doll and the child. Thus, both types of dolls are simultaneously representations and embodiments with "a dynamic, active presence" (ibid.: 143).

Interestingly, many people took special care to protect the face of their dolls when storing them away. Mrs. Kadonaga, for example, claimed that one has to made sure that "dolls are not in distress (*kurushii*)" by protecting their face with a cloth and storing them facing upwards. After Shigeko Kagemori showed me her pair of expensive wooden Hina dolls, she wrapped them in paper turning each doll round and round, while saying: "bottom, top, bottom, top." She explained that "if the dolls are placed face down they will feel uncomfortable. Well, lying face down for a whole year is probably distressing, don't you think. And, you know, then they might call for me: 'SHI-GE-KO' (laughs)." Again, Schattschneider offers convincing evidence for the strong relationship between face and personhood in Japan, drawing on a range of examples such as miraculous religious images, the power of masks used in rituals, and the manipulation of the face to reconstitute the person in folk tales, films and anime (2004: 151–52). A doll that is withering away, alone, deep inside a closet is considered powerful because it is prevented from forming a strong bond with those to whom it was given. By covering the face of dolls that are stored away, one can temporarily deactivate or freeze a particular relationship. A final, rather unusual example of covering the face (and eyes) of dolls further illustrates this practice. In August 2003, Ms. Kema, a single woman in her forties and a long-term friend of mine, presented me with a doll that she found in her parents' home after her mother passed away. She was convinced that, because I had become interested in dolls through my work, I would take good care of the doll, and she stressed that I need not worry since it was a 'new' doll that had been stored away with its eyes covered. In other words, the dolls had been prevented from forming a connection with humans and therefore from becoming imbued with their spirit.

The second life of dolls?

Dolls given at important phases in a woman's life cycle are expected to act as companions who may ease the transition into a new role or identity. The bride dolls, discussed above, for example, were presented by the incoming bride to the mother in-law. According to Schattschneider, these dolls function as "mediating operators, establishing a gradual projective identification between daughter-in-law and mother-in-law," facilitating the daughter-in-law's progression from in-coming outsider to powerful insider (Schattschneider 2004: 151). Ichimatsu and Hina dolls, on the other hand, evoke the passing of childhood. They are given at birth to mediate a girl's safe transition from child to mature woman. However, this raises the question what to do with these dolls once they have fulfilled their purpose and a woman leaves home to marry into her husband's family. During my fieldwork many people expressed anxiety about the future of these dolls after a child has left home, declaring that they are "things that one would like to dispose of, but are difficult to throw away."

Marriage is a major ritual of separation for women, and one explanation for the ambivalence surrounding the dispersal and disposal of dolls is that it reflects a more general unease about breaking attachments and the potential misfortune that this may cause. However, as the next example illustrates, although marriage will loosen maternal family relationships, it is uncommon for these ties to be completely severed. Many married women told me that they stayed in touch with their own families and made sporadic visits home. Moreover, it remains common for pregnant women to return to their parents' home before the baby is due and enjoy a few weeks of care among their close kin after the delivery. As we have seen above, maternal grandparents also present their new-born grandchildren with dolls. Finally, a number of married women in my sample, especially single children, stressed that in the future they would like to take care of not only their husbands, but for their own parents (Daniels 2010).

Considering the above, it comes as no surprise that some Hina dolls accompany brides into their new home. A detailed examination of some of the Hina displays revealed that they consisted of a mixture of new and old dolls and accessories that had belonged to a child's mother or even her grandmother. Mrs. Matsui, an only child, for example, displayed her own Hina set for her daughter's Doll's Festival, but some of the accessories such as a lacquered miniature dowry set had been part of her mother's display. Mrs.Kuwahara clarified that first-born daughters are expected to take the display with them in order to use it for their own daughters, while when a second daughter gives birth to a girl, her parents will buy their granddaughter a new set.

Moreover, the fact that growing numbers of Japanese women remain single is another reason why dolls may remain connected with a particular woman throughout her lifetime. Ms. Kadonaga, a 55-year-old unmarried lawyer in Kobe, for example, considered her dolls to be among her most treasured possessions that she stored away very carefully. She is particularly fond of a pair of Hina dolls and an Ichimatsu doll, which belonged to her mother, and whose kimono was made by her grandmother. Similarly four other single women in my sample treasured their dolls, and some even went as far as to refer to them as their children.

As I have demonstrated elsewhere, because of the small size of the average urban home when moving house difficult decisions have to be made about what to keep and what to throw away, and it is not uncommon for married children to continue using their parents' home as extra storage space (Daniels 2010). Dolls are large ornamental items that take up a lot of space whether in everyday living space or storage, and for some woman in my sample, marriage had offered an opportunity to conveniently 'forget' their dolls in their parental home. Some of the younger women such as the Kuwaharas daughters took a practical approach to the future of their dolls. Yoshiko who collects dolls and displays them in her bedroom as well as a Japanese style-room on the first floor, told me that she hoped to "be able to take at least her favorite dolls when she leaves home." Keiko thought that it really depends on the size of the future house that one will live in, saying: "If it was a house like a castle we would take everything."

Passing "old" dolls on to others is problematic as they, first, may end up in a home where they are not wanted and as a consequence are unable to create new connections that in turn may lead to misfortune. By the same logic, it is fine to give dolls to someone who "will treat them with affection" (*kawaigatte morareru*). Over the past fifteen years of visiting Japan I have been given numerous dolls since many Japanese assume that "foreigners particularly like dolls."[18] In Spring 1999, for example, one of the women who participated in my PhD fieldwork on Miyajima, a small island south-west of Hiroshima, gave me a doll she had made in a local hobby club as a farewell present. I did not want to travel home with this doll because I am not particularly found of dolls and I had already been given several on previous occasions, but more importantly I had no space in my luggage. I assumed my home-stay family would not mind adding another doll to their already large collection, but to my surprise they fiercely opposed the idea. They found this doll scary and they castigated the women for giving me such a present. Thus, the next day one of the daughters marched me to the local temple where we left the doll, carefully wrapped in paper and placed in a shopping bag, in a special bin for ritual garbage.

Participants in my study also pointed out that "old," unwanted, and damaged dolls could be taken to religious institutions where they are ritually disposed of in special ceremonies (*kuyô*) (Kretschmer 2000). Yoshiko Kuwahara brought a damaged doll dressed in a white kimono, "like those worn by dead people," to a local shrine where the doll was ritually burned along with an mixture of other goods that need to be treated with special care. In March of 2003, a Kyoto newspaper noted the continuing popularity of the ritual disposal of dolls, reporting that the Awajishima Shrine in Wakayama, south of Osaka, disposed of more then 20,000 dolls for the Doll's Festival.[19] This particular shrine belongs to a list of forty-six temples and shrines across Japan that specialize in memorial services for dolls.[20] In order to adapt to people's busy life styles and changing family make-up, all these institutions also allow for dolls to be sent by post for ritual disposal. Moreover, today most religious centers make efficient use of the Internet and have created impressive websites with detailed information about all aspects of ritual disposal.

Finally, "old" dolls may be re-circulated through commercial channels. The fact that people are willing to pay money for their purchases suggests that they will value them. The two main sites where second-hand dolls are sold primarily target foreigners. First, the Internet has become the leader in the international trade in antique Japanese dolls, which are sold on specialty sites for doll collectors as well as on eBay. A second site where many "old" dolls start a new life (whether or not they are antiques) is the temple market (Figures 8.4, 8.5, and 8.6). During monthly visits to two temple markets in Kyoto dolls in a multitude of sizes and shapes were on sale. According to stall owners, and in compliance with my own observations, these dolls are almost exclusively bought by foreigners who take them home as "exotic" souvenirs.

Figure 8.4 Two Ichimatsu dolls, girl and boy, await a possible journey abroad at the Todaiji Temple Market in Kyoto, May 2006

Source: Photo by author.

Figure 8.5 An Ichimatsu doll and a French doll share a box at the Todaiji Temple Market, May 2006

Source: Photo by author.

Figure 8.6 A pair of "old" Hina dolls in search of a new connection at the Tôji Temple Market, May 2006

Source: Photo by author.

Conclusion: material culture and religion

Two recent developments within the anthropology of religion risk polarizing the discipline between those who stress the universality of cognitive processes and those who accent the specific efficacy of material practices. First, cognitive anthropologists have developed a number of influential, 'grand' theories of religion that reveal laws and patterns of mental functioning at the base of complex rituals by using a combination of neuroscience models and psychological rhetoric (Boyer 2001; Whitehouse 2002).[21] Second, social anthropologists interested in material culture, working at the intersection of the anthropology of art, consumption, globalization, visual media, and everyday life, have drawn on detailed ethnographies from around the world to highlight the significance of material practices within specific religious activities (Morphy 1991; Starrett 1995; Spyer 1998; Meyer 1998; Daniels 2003).[22] Although the work I have presented in this chapter is firmly embedded in this latter research tradition, through an examination of Japanese religious practices concerning dolls I have attempted to engage with both mental and material processes in order to transcend persistent dichotomies such as the spiritual and the material, the scared and the profane, and belief and practice.

In my view, important insights may be gained were material culture be given more primacy in the anthropological study of religion. Because most anthropologists tend to emphasize the intentionality and control of subjects within a supposedly ordered world, the focus tends to be on an "inner belief" considered to exist prior to any religious activity. My Japanese case study refutes this proposition by demonstrating the effectiveness of material, ritual practices embedded in an all-encompassing, relational ontology, irrespective of the specific state of mind of those involved. By enacting rituals that aim to forge and maintain beneficial, reciprocal connections with others (people, ancestors, deities, and objects), Japanese people are able to guard their homes and all those within from harm. This relational power of ritual cannot be reduced to social facts in the Durkheimean tradition since in practice social reality and material and spiritual efficacy intertwine.

Dolls belong to a category of domestic things that initially embody efficacious connections among people (they are often gifts), while over time they may become intimately linked with a particular person whom they protect through a particular phase of the person's life. Importantly, the people closely connected to the recipients of dolls, those who share the same environment (i.e. the family group inside their home) will also be affected by both the spiritual benefits and risks associated with dolls. In other words, things such as dolls (and people) do not float in some kind of virtual reality, they are part of a particular material environment, in this case the home. Thus, whether a doll stands in a decorative alcove in a Japanese-style room or in a hallway, or is "indefinitely" stored in a box in a closet determines its efficacy. In this regard, my ethnography of the domestic practices surrounding dolls also exposes a weakness underlying many studies of materiality; namely, the failure to situate people and things in space.

Those participating in my study did not dismiss the impact of the non-human world on their lives, and extended the notion of ultimate concern to things. Many entertained the possibility that if certain things are not treated with respect, they might act against humans and cause malevolent effects. Thus, when dolls have fulfilled their purpose, they should be treated with care and disposed of respectfully. During my fieldwork, stories about scary dolls were ubiquitous but this does not necessary mean that people "believed in" their power. As a matter of fact, many were skeptical and some joked about their homes being haunted by dolls. Still, all took care of their dolls because, in the words of 45-year-old Mrs. Kubota, "one never knows ... and it doesn't hurt." This concern with the wellbeing of objects and with one's obligation to provide care is grounded in an awareness of the interrelatedness and mutual dependence of human and non-human entities (Daniels 2003).

This chapter, therefore, challenges Euro-centric assumptions both about the relationship between belief and action, and people and things. Japan offers such an interesting ethnographic example because it is a modern capitalist society where everyday rituals are the base of all social life, and where people and things are experienced as intermingled agencies. Importantly, this specific sensibility towards the inanimate world should not be understood as a timeless, essential component of Japanese culture, but as a dynamic, changing attitude grounded in a blurring of the boundary between people and things. In this view, things are not understood to be mere representations or objectifications that people manipulate to create and negotiate meanings in their lives. Instead, the material world (things and their environment) may also be understood to be dynamic and changing, and to influence or—dare one suggest—direct human actions.

Notes

1 These ideas need to be contextualized within evolutionary ideas that were popular within anthropology until the 1940s. As a result, cultures were ranked based on degrees of rationality (e.g. Frazer), and progressive rationalization was thought to inevitably lead to "disenchantment" (e.g. Weber).

2 Although as early as 1873, Tylor defined religion as "beliefs in spiritual beings" (Tylor 1891: 424), generally distinctions were made between church-based, institutionalized practices defined as "religion," and animism and other "primitive" forms of spirituality defined as "magic."

3 I will not be able to discuss my fieldwork in detail here, but the data were collected in 2003 inside the homes of twenty-three families and seven single people

living in the Kansai region. The main outcome of this research is a richly illustrated monograph entitled *The Japanese House: Material Culture in the Modern Home* to be published by Berg in 2010. The research was made possible thanks to the generous support of the Japanese Society for the Promotion of Science (2002–2003). Moreover, in 2006 I was awarded a British Academy Small Grant for a collaborative project with the professional photographer Susan Andrews, who has kindly given me permission to include three of her images in this chapter. Finally, I would like to thank all those who opened up their homes for me, but especially Kema-san and the Yano, the Kagemori, Kadonaga, Kuwahara, Matsui, Nakao, Nishiki, Sakai, and Takahashi families.

4   Only 60 percent of Japanese possess a Buddhist altar (generally purchased after a close relative has passed away) and Shinto shelves are even less common.

5   Smith argues that both the Buddhist altar and the Shinto God shelf are of recent origin and that the spirits can be invoked anywhere by setting up an altar and summoning them (Smith 1974: 86).

6   Japanese-style rooms with decorative alcoves, present in about one-third of the homes studied, are spaces that are generally associated with ritual. Moreover, this is also the area where Buddhist altars tend to be kept. The entrance of the homes I studied generally faces eastward and is therefore considered inauspicious.

7   Because the efficacy of lucky objects is linked with their shape independent of their connection with religious centers, they may also be distributed through commercial channels.

8   Because institutional affiliation is not linked with commitment to faith, people tend to mention multi-affiliations when asked about their religion. Moreover, Buddhist, Shinto, Taoist, and Confucianist thought have a long history of amalgamation. Historical and ethnographic data further reveal that deities which have fallen out of fashion are easily replaced with new ones that might deal better with current circumstances such as the recently established deity for dementia (Traphagen 2004).

9   Yamada traces "dolls in glass display cases" (*keisu ire ningyô*) back to "dolls in a box" (*hako ire ningyô*), which are display dolls put in wooden boxes with a glass lid. They appear in Japanese interiors from the 1910s onwards. Another type of display doll from the same period that could also be seen as a predecessor are "dolls in glass globes" (*galusu hoya ire ningyô*; Yamada, 1991: 77). Some participants used the term "Yamato doll" (*yamato ningyô*) or "Japanese doll" (*nihon ningyô*) to refer to these dolls.

10 The head of these dolls consists of a mixture of sawdust and glue with a special coating, while the body is made of papier-mâché or wood with textile joints. The hair is either real human hair or silk and the eyes are made of glass. The dolls wear kimonos since they are realistic representations of children dressed in the outfits they traditionally wear to visit religious centers to celebrate their third, fifth, and seventh birthdays. Schattschneider points out that Ichimatsu dolls, first produced during the eighteenth century, were modeled after the famous Kabuki actor Sanokawa Ichimatsu, known for his portrayal of young women (Schattschneider 2004: 151).

11 Law, who offers a rare overview in English of the use of Japanese dolls in ritual practices, argues that both dolls were spirit substitutes that were offered at shrines to pray for the health and longevity of children (Law 1997: 32–8). Miniature *hôko*-type textile dolls are still common charms and two women in their twenties in my sample received them as souvenirs. Yu Ebara hung one from the mirror in her car, while Noriko Kageyama attached a similar doll to a key holder.

12 The word *hina* originates in *hiina*, which refers to miniature objects such as dolls made of paper or clay that were used as embodiments of the deities during religious ceremonies (Mingu jiten 1997: 477).

13 During the Doll Festival 2003, 4-year-old Nao Matsui was allowed to play with her Ichimatsu doll, temporarily removed from her glass box. Moreover, in most homes children had not been able to resist the temptation to play with their miniature dolls and many sets had either been damaged or become incomplete. However, doll sets that were permanently stored away were not safe from damage either, although in this case the cause was moths or mice.

14 Ichimatsu dolls have been produced since the eighteenth century, but Kawasai and Moteki argue that until fairly recently the majority of Japanese would only be able to present children with paper dolls (Kawasaki and Moteki 2002: 60–1). Their widespread use as gifts during the second half of the twentieth century is probably linked with the fact that they finally became affordable for the majority of the population.

15 Suzuki (2002) argues that Japanese dolls belong to a group of Japanese-style *wafû* objects that fit best into a "traditional" aesthetic scheme associated with tatami rooms.

16 During the 1920s, so-called Friendship Dolls were also used as mediators to improve relations between the United States and Japan. In return for more than 12,000 blue-eyed dolls from the US, the Japanese sent 58 Ichimatsu dolls, each representing one prefecture.

17 An antique dealer in Kyoto, by contrast, claimed that generally these kinds of round faces are liked because the Japanese term for this kind of shape, *fuku-yoka*, also means good luck.

18 Japanese dolls are strongly associated with "Japaneseness" and they have always been popular souvenirs for international travelers. Some, such as the Bride dolls, were initially created for the tourist market, while Geisha dolls were popular souvenirs brought home by US soldiers stationed in Japan after World War II (Schattschneider 2004: 151).

19 The dolls were stacked high onto several boats that were set afloat on the river (Kyoto Shinbun, April 3, 2003). I was unable to find out what happens with the boats and their potent cargo once they are sent off, and whether people are at all concerned about the dolls polluting the river. However, some participants told me that in recent years some temples have refused to accept dolls because of environmental reasons.

20 These religious institutions are listed on a national survey of annual events (*zenkoku kakuchi no gyôji annai*), which I consulted online on March 3, 2009 (www.kougetsu.co.p/kuyou). Ten of these sites accept donations of dolls

throughout the year, but the majority only collect dolls on the day of the memorial service or a few days beforehand. Fees to conduct memorial services for dolls are calculated according to the size of the box they are sent in, ranging from 1,300 yen (£7) for a box of 80 cm (length × width × depth), to 12,000 yen (£60) for a 180 cm box.

21 Carrette (2005) offers an interesting critique of cognitive theories of religion. In short, he argues for the need to contextualize these ideas within their socio-economic and political context, and to acknowledge the research of previous thinkers.

22 Tambiah's 1984 ethnography of Buddhist Saints in Thailand should be seen as a forerunner for these studies, as it includes a detailed account of material practices surrounding sacred amulets invested with the charisma of mountain saints. These anthropologists have published the bulk of their work within the context of inter-disciplinary research collaborations with historians, religious studies and area specialists; see, for example, Babb and Wadley (1995), and Meyer and Pels (2003).

Part IV

SPACES

9

Staging Baroque worship in Brazil

Jens Baumgarten

Neo-Baroque staging of the Baroque
Staging and the public in the seventeenth and eighteenth centuries
Visual rhetorics
Vision–body–sensation
Conclusion

Staging appears to be inherent to the Baroque. Baroque religiosity, worship, and the material side of religion are the visible face of the Baroque that captures the admiration of latter-day audiences. This is true even more so in the case of Latin American and especially Brazilian colonial art. Given the intrinsic role of theatricality in the Baroque style, I propose that the staging of Baroque worship may be fruitfully analyzed by reflecting on a modernist, Neo-Baroque (re-)staging of the Brazilian colonial Baroque (Calabrese 1992; Moser 2001; Ndalianis 2004). Therefore, the first part of the chapter will focus on the architecture, decoration, and other visual materials of a twentieth-century church, *Nossa Senhora do Brasil*, one of the best-known and impressive churches in São Paulo, which can be classified as "Neo-Baroque." The church combines different elements that reflect a political, religious, and aesthetic project of Brazilian culture and history. It shows also the configurations of the discourse about an historical Baroque and a transcultural and historical Neo-Baroque. Built for the upper class, this church is situated in an upmarket area of São Paulo and is famous for its wedding celebrations, which sometimes can be watched on national television. The architecture, as well as the decoration, clearly reflects a relationship between Brazilian and European art history, especially with regard to a concept of one common Baroque. The visual discourse of the church, as I will show, aims to establish a political, religious, and aesthetic position for the city with respect to its many and varied immigrant groups, which must also be seen as part of the Brazilian "national project." Scrutinizing the nature of staging will lead to consideration of the function of visual, bodily or sensorial experience within the stage setting of the Brazilian colonial churches. My examples will draw mainly from northeastern Brazil, though I will include one sculpture from São Paulo.

It is also important to ask what religious space and visual representation mean in the Brazilian colonial context. Additional inquiry about space and visuality arises from the lack of indigenous image worship in Brazil, which prevented Jesuit and Franciscan missionaries from replacing local cultic images with their own visual representations. Therefore, I will examine the construction of space in the religious, aesthetic, and social dimensions of church architecture and their decoration in Portuguese South America, focusing on iconographical superimpositions, the establishment of parallel visual systems, and their meaning and consequences for religious space.

Neo-Baroque staging of the Baroque

The church *Nossa Senhora do Brasil* was inaugurated in 1940; the first mass was held on 23 September 1954 (Figure 9.1). The church's decoration consists mainly of mural paintings by Antônio Paim Vieira, produced during the 1950s, tiles in different colors executed through the present day by different artists, and panel paintings of the late 1980s and early 1990s. Recently, a contract was signed to construct a new crypt, a type of grotto that will be carried out in the next several years. This latter is also a hint that this Neo-Baroque project can be understood as an open one with a continuing visual use, re-use and re-re-use of the Baroque—or in other terms, a re-staging of Baroque worship. Its eclectic architecture, designed by Bruno Simões Magro, combines stylistic elements of churches in Minas Gerais and other Brazilian states, as well as a "small copy" of Bernini's colonnades from St. Peter's Cathedral in Rome (Figure 9.2). The sculptures that decorate the entrance make a stylistic reference to Alejadinho's Prophets in Congonhas, one of the most important Brazilian artifacts of colonial times and, as to be explained later, the founding myth of a national Brazilian art. The main altar, which was transferred to the new church, belonged originally to the Church Sant'Ana of Mogi de Cruzes and, as the description by the French scholar Germain Bazin in one of the most recognized books on Brazilian "Baroque" emphasizes, was made in 1740 (Bazin 1955).

The Sacred Heart of Mary was chosen to serve as patron saint of the missionary efforts of the Capuchins in Northeastern Brazil, in Pernambuco, in 1725 (Figure 9.3). Traditionally, the image is attributed to the Jesuits, even to José de Anchieta, a famous and beatified missionary in Brazil. The original image was transferred to Italy in the nineteenth century where it was given the name "Madonna del Brasile" by the population of Naples. In 1924, when the Brazilian bishop Frederico Benício de Souza Costa heard of the image, he asked for a copy, which was later installed in Nossa Senhora do Brazil.

During the inauguration in 1958, the sermon pointed out the importance of the *mestizagem* as national project: "You are neither Italian, nor French, nor Greek. You are Brazilian. Truly Brazilian, just like your dark child," referring to the mestizo Christ child of the cult image.[1] Thus, the visual discourse of the church aims to establish a political, religious, and aesthetic position for the city with regard to its multiethnic immigrants.

Figure 9.1 Façade, Nossa Senhora do Brasil, São Paulo, Brazil

Source: Photo courtesy of Adilson Fernando Ferreira.

Figure 9.2 External Gallery, Nossa Senhora do Brasil, São Paulo, Brazil

Source: Photo courtesy of Adilson Fernando Ferreira.

Figure 9.3 Interior, Nossa Senhora do Brasil, São Paulo, Brazil

Source: Photo courtesy of Adilson Fernando Ferreira.

But there remains a very interesting aspect to mention: the cult image we find in the Brazilian church does not correspond to the description. It refers to its "original" in Italy, which originally had been in Brazil and, according to legend, was made there. The aspect of "mestizagem" appears only in the paintings of Antônio Vieira.

It was important for the modernist movement to analyze and re-appropriate the Baroque and install a Neo-Baroque. Also, the authentic altar and the cult image condensed the main ideas of a trans-historical and -cultural Neo-Baroque. They reflect also an internal and an external transfer. The altar was transferred from Mogi das Cruzes to the newly erected church. The city in the interior represents the "heroic" history of the Bandeirantes and their efforts in promoting the myth of a civilizing Baroque.

The cult image itself is not present, but only the copy of the Italian original. It represents also this mutual exchange and therefore evokes the question of the image itself, which was one of the crucial questions of the Baroque. The original one is in Italy, which is originally an image that survived in Brazil to be recognized as a miraculous image in Italy. In Brazil, we are able only to find a copy of the image that does not resemble the original, but which is represented in the decoration of the apse.

The church's main decoration consists of an original series of tiles (*azulejos*), which combines important events from the history of Catholicism, as well as Brazilian and church history. Furthermore, the series depicts the main sanctuaries in Brazil and Latin America, including Guadalupe, and also in Jerusalem and Rome. However, there are also "new" profane sanctuaries included like the building of the United Nations in New York. The paintings of the ceiling were made during the past fifteen years and consist mainly of copies of Michelangelo's frescoes in the Sistine Chapel, combined with other European artists who belong to the Western art historical canon such as Raphael, Zurbarán, and Caravaggio. The European Baroque canon is represented in a Baroque form and decorative pattern of the Brazilian Baroque architectural structure, which will be explained in the second part of this chapter.

What do these Neo-Baroque visual art histories of the Baroque mean for staging Baroque worship? In my view, the term Baroque may be seen in this context from both a historiographical and a theoretical or conceptual perspective. This leads to the question whether there are different, culturally-defined "Baroques" and different—or conflicting, even contradictory—inscriptions in local discourses. This includes a distinct meaning of the term itself and its cultural meanings and categories. The discourse of the Baroque in the Latin American and especially Brazilian contexts reflects these shifting, flickering "Baroques." So, in the case of Brazil, we become aware of the connection of the Baroque and the Neo-Baroque to other terms that are similarly amorphous, such as "modernity" or "national art." The style of worship combines European models within a previously defined Brazilian framework, where a European aesthetic and Brazilian art developed in parallel fashion.

Staging and the public in the seventeenth and eighteenth centuries

Neo-Baroque staging is not a mere recapitulation, but involves complex visual and sensorial systems, which combine and juxtapose various models of representation and visualization from the European and colonial past. In the colonial context it is important to remember that the explicit social distinctions manifested in particular spaces intended (respectively) for the colonial elite, free citizens, and slaves. In particular, the so-called "third orders," which were lay associations, played an extraordinary role in social organization, institutionalization, missionary practice, and hence in the spatial organization of Portuguese South America. For example, the church of the Franciscan Tertiaries was central to the constitution of the elite in Salvador, the capital of Bahia. Similarly, churches consecrated to Our Lady of the Rosary (Nossa Senhora do Rosário) were reserved for slaves or descendants of freed Africans.

It is impossible to treat northern and northeastern Brazilian churches in general or address every methodological implication of the approaches to visual and spatial studies defined by Martina Löw (Löw 2001: 158–72; Woydack 2005: 41–43, 192–204). Thus, I will confine myself to one example that formed part of a larger project of visual systems in colonial Brazil: the Franciscan convent of Santo Antônio in João Pessoa (at Paraíba). Based on Löw's sociological theories, I define space as a variable construct in a particular location. Church spaces, including their decoration, can be described as institutionalized places of a political, social, aesthetic, and theological nature. Within a space organized along these lines, actors who participate in the space put (or move) themselves in certain locations and therefore change the space by the use of language or speech (such as sermons) as well as through visual representations or images. I will investigate the institutionalization, social norms, aspects of synthesis, and the "spacing" of individuals within colonial churches and their spatial configurations.

The first Franciscan convent in Paraíba was erected in 1589 and survived until the Dutch conquest of northeastern Brazil in 1634.[2] After the Portuguese return in the second half of the seventeenth century, the Franciscans began to rebuild what became one of the most splendid examples of seventeenth- and eighteenth-century colonial architecture.

Entering it, we see not only the typical structure of early modern Portuguese convents—a court centered on a main façade decorated with iconographical elements of the Franciscan order and framed by lateral walls depicting a cycle of Azulejos' Passion of Christ[3]—but also three Chinese sculptures, probably from Macau. Two lions and a masque as apotropaic figures suggest how, in an apparently European visual system, parallel systems were established via superimpositions. Traditional historiography interprets colonial Brazilian artistic production as derivative and of lesser value than its European models. In the wake of predominantly stylistic analysis, even the concept of "hybridity," formulated in particular by Serge Gruzinski, fails to yield convincing results—at least for Brazil.[4] In this particular case, we can detect a construction and constitution of the "other": the Chinese sculptures are included or, rather, incorporated into the dominant spatial and visual system. How do the forms of such superimpositions constitute parallel systems and organize social space? To answer this question, I will briefly discuss two different spatial contexts in the convent—the painting of Saint Francis in the main church and that of Elijah in the Tertiaries' church.

Visual rhetorics

Visual representations create virtual spaces that may be considered in terms developed in recent spatial theory. Illusionist decorations establish spaces of virtual experiences, encounters, and transitions, and in religious contexts invoke the categories of worship. Encounters and transitions take place between spectators, between representations, and between representations and spectators in a network of visual systems configured within church space. In order to elaborate on the aspect of superimposition, the analysis now turns to ceiling paintings on wood in the churches of the first and third orders. The artist is unknown, but stylistic similarities suggest Joaquim de Rocha, who executed other ceiling paintings in the capital, Salvador de Bahia. In the centre of the nave of the first order church, an illusionistic painting follows the rules of the *quadratura* (Figure 9.4). In the main cartouche on the altar side we find the

Figure 9.4 Saint Francis and Nossa Senhora da Conceição, ceiling painting, Franciscan Convent Santo Antônio, First Order's Church, João Pessoa, Paraíba, Brazil

Source: Photo courtesy of Adilson Fernando Ferreira.

Immaculate Conception together with the Trinity. Angels hold an inscription referring to the birth of Saint Francis and his role as "alter" Christ: "*Stigmata Dei Jesu in corpore meo porto*—I carry the wounds of Christ in my body" (Burity 1988: 79). The second inscription—"The earth in which the religion continues is a holy earth"—refers to the other side of the altar, with rays of light emanating from Francis to illuminate four continents, represented by Franciscan missionaries. These are most likely Anthony, as allegory for Europe, on the right side; on the opposite side, one of the Moroccan martyr saints as Africa; on the bottom, Francis Solano as America, represented by an indigenous figure; and one of the martyrs from Japan converting Asia. The missionaries to Africa and America look down on the continents to be converted, as if to observe and control, while the allegories of Europe and Asia are presented to the Virgin. Rather than following Salvadorian iconographic conventions for the continents, the artist transferred and emulated the Jesuit tradition of depictions of Ignatius, in which divine rays reflecting from his heart illuminate the whole, as Pozzo depicted him in San Ignazio in Rome (Figure 9.5).

Figure 9.5 Andrea Pozzo, Saint Ignatius, ceiling painting, Jesuit Church, San Ignazio, Rome, Italy

Source: Photo courtesy Anthony Majanlahti.

Therefore, it seems necessary to discuss post-Tridentine theory for the staging of worship, which converged with the views of the Jesuit Andrea Pozzo (1642–1709). Il Gesù was the second most important building in Rome, and named after the founder of the order. Consequently, it possessed an importance beyond Italian borders. In his treatise on perspective, which was published in two parts in 1693 and 1703, Pozzo wanted to analyze the possibilities of the art of perspective to produce optical illusions (compare Pozzo 1693 and 1700). The heavens open within a painted, illusionistic architecture. In the center stands the Trinity surrounded by saints and angels. At the head, the founder of the Jesuit order, Ignatius of Loyola. All heavenly light streams from Christ and hits Ignatius in his heart. From there it splits fivefold. Four rays strike the allegories of the four known continents, which were thereby to be made free of heretics. Important for further argumentation is the composition of the entire illusionistic dome. This fresco means a development in the discourse of the creation of affects for the viewer—which seems to have been developed by Pozzo before he authored his treatise. The whole fresco over the main nave has been constructed from the ideal point of view. From this point one is unable to distinguish between painted and actual architecture. From all other points the architecture seems to "tilt," but there exist different states of it: "It is this blurring between reality and fiction that produces a feeling of uncertainty, which could be real or simulated. But this feeling is very important for the creation of illusion" (Burda-Stengel 2001: 97). Burda-Stengel explains in his analysis, that this fresco needs a moving viewer, one who can only receive the whole composition by movement within the space. Following Lione Pascoli (Pascoli 1933:

256–60), he distinguishes between the "external" (eyes of the body) and the "internal" (eyes of the spirit). While striding through the church, the viewer can decode the fresco like an anamorph (Burda-Stengel 2001: 101). Only from the ideal point of view can the figure of Christ be "read" correctly. At this point, real space converges with the fictional space. The internal and the external eyes correspond. Here, as Burda-Stengel stresses, in my opinion correctly, the observer takes over the Jesuit post-Tridentine perspective:

> From the view-point of the Jesuits, the building of the world is sensible and correct. If you depart from this one point of view, the whole construction is made to fall down or to sway, until the building of the world is going to collapse.
>
> (ibid.: 103, 105)

Furthermore, one may stress a certain form of individuality, because in one moment only a single person can have this ideal point of view. In my opinion, this point of view reflects the attitude of Gabriele Paleotti (1522–1597), papal representative at the Council of Trent and author of an important treatise on images. Paleotti states that the individual effects should be reached corresponding to each person's capacities. By this means the corporate and collective fundaments of a visible Catholic church may be visualized. Only this visualization makes possible the acceptance of discipline according to individual and corporate needs.

In the case of the Franciscan colonial church there is a continuity of this visual staging. But the iconography is not the only simplified aspect; the illusionistic form of the central painting also seems far less developed than in the painted architecture that serves as a theatrical stage for the composition of the Immaculate Conception and Francis. The perspective of the lateral parts, in which popes connect the real space of the church with the illusionistic one, is more accurately painted in comparison with the flat appearance of the central medallion. The Franciscans thus inscribed themselves in a Jesuit tradition and superimposed two distinct European models. Furthermore, the stylistic simplification of the central medallion merged the reception of Francis not only iconographically in allusions to Ignatius, but presented the central image less as narrative and more as a cult image. The religious and aesthetic construction of the space focuses on the individual missionary efforts of the Franciscan elite in Paraíba and stabilizes the order's communitarian aspects and self-confidence in contrast to the Jesuits.

In order to understand the configuration of the visual and spatial patterns it is necessary to deepen the iconographical analysis of Saint Francis. The nave's central figure in the Tertiaries' church, which shows a similarly painted architectural decoration, includes an even more unusual iconographic depiction. In a fiery chariot, a figure in a Franciscan habit ascends to heaven (Figure 9.6). The chariot and ascension allude to the prophet Elijah, a harbinger of Christ, whereas the habit with the knotted cord refers to Francis himself—and so a depiction of the

Figure 9.6 Saint Francis and the Chariot, ceiling painting, Franciscan Convent
Santo Antônio, Third Order's Church, João Pessoa, Paraíba, Brazil

Source: Photo courtesy of Adilson Fernando Ferreira.

saint could be intended. The following analysis intends to present the visual
transfer of different iconographic models between Europe and the Americas as
constitutive for the understanding of the visual spaces in colonial Brazil.

The representation of the central figure in the painting relies on
Bonaventure's *Legenda Minor S. Francisci*, In relation to the theme here, in
which Franciscan friars are overwhelmed with a vision, Bonaventure writes:

> A fiery chariot of wonderful brilliance came through the little door of the
> brothers' dwelling. Over this chariot ... there rested a bright ball of light,
> which resembled the sun. Those who were awake were stunned at this
> remarkable, brilliant sight ... They experienced a brightness with their
> hearts as much as with their bodies, while the conscience of each was laid
> bare to the others by the power of that marvelous light.

(Bonaventure 2000: 691)

The iconographic analysis shows a very dense relation of models between
Europe and Latin America—a strong relation between the internal and
external missionary efforts of the Catholic Church.

The examples of St. Francis cycles presented in the analysis include the
episode of the fiery chariot. The solution presented in colonial Brazil,

however, was completely different in execution, focusing instead on the figure of Francis. In the Paraíba Tertiaries' church we find the isolation and dramatization of the scene at the central point of the virtual space. Regarding the missing Franciscan friars, we can imagine the convent's friars as active spectators in the actual church and therefore as witnesses to the event. The Tertiaries thus stand in for the 'original' friars, transferring the vision of the saint through time and space to the temporality and locality of its observers.

In an iconological appropriation, the political, religious, and cultural aspects of the spatial construction of the church can be understood and interpreted along three analytical axes which enlarge the interpretation of these images: first, superimposition of different models directed against Protestants; second, indigenous missions; and third, millenarian and eschatological concepts. I will take these up in order.

Superimposition is the most obvious interpretation and it has been already pointed out: the representation of Francis as Ignatius. We must add the factor of missionary competition with a Carmelite convent which, like the Jesuit institution, was situated nearby: the prophet Elijah was the legendary founder of the Carmelite order. We can analyze these representations of Francis—as both Elijah and Ignatius—not merely as a stylistic transfer of Pozzo's Italian model, but additionally as an iconographic superimposition of the traditions of different orders. Furthermore, after the Portuguese re-conquest of Pernambuco and Paraíba in 1655, reasons for the choice of figures like Ignatius and Elijah are obvious. Ignatius fulfills the function of an anti-Protestant saint, while Elijah also plays a role in Dutch Protestant theology. In this context it would seem desirable to "re-conquer" the Dutch prophet, to re-Catholicize and re-appropriate him as the Catholic Saint Francis.[5]

Second, in indigenous missions, especially in Pernambuco and Paraíba, prophecy and prophets held enormous relevance. This matter relates to the status of the image itself and to its spacing. As Jesuit and Franciscan missionaries, in contrast to the situation found in Mexico or in Peru, had not confronted indigenous image worship on any scale, typical methods did not work. Substitution of "right images" for "false idols," realized by the fusion and superimposition of indigenous and European models, was not practicable. Instead, as Nóbrega related to Rome, missionaries encountered "Caraíbas," who were called sorcerers by the European invaders. They functioned as prophets or shamans and thus reproduced the same dichotomy already encountered between image and idol. In their efforts for spiritual conquest, then, missionaries had to replace "false prophets" with real ones. Cristina Pompa has analyzed this dynamic, showing how European symbols were re-elaborated by indigenous cultures. It functioned in a way that led to the development of a discourse on false and true prophets that negotiated the differing cultural systems (Pompa 2001: 27–44; 2002: 49–51; Andrade 2002: 77–124). In this context we can interpret Elijah, the only Old Testament figure to become a Catholic saint, as an Anti-Caraíba. The true prophet replaces the false one. As promoters of his cult, Franciscans demonstrate this process in the pictorial representation of this saint as an alter-Elijah in their proper holy space, the church of the third order of Saint Francis.[6]

Finally, the eschatological element of representations of Francis as Elijah is immediately evident in the ascension episode, which prefigures that of Christ and his transfiguration flanked by Moses and Elijah. But in order to clarify its significance in the colonial Brazilian spatial context, we must consider Portuguese and Brazilian millenarianism, which is a singular eschatological form. Missionaries to Mexico defined themselves as new apostles and sought to found a millenarian kingdom to justify the conquest theologically (Rubial García 1996: 101–86). Although the situation in Portugal was completely different, it fits the Habsburg pattern. Following the death of King Sebastian in 1578 at the battle of El-Ksar el Kbir during a crusade against the Islamic kingdoms of North Africa, not only was a significant part of the Portuguese elite killed or enslaved, but shortly afterwards, Portugal lost its independence to Spain. Sebastianism, a myth and associated movement, fed hopes that the king would return to save Portugal, expel the Spanish, and found a millennial kingdom (Hermann 1998, 2000; Megiani 2003, 2004). Until then, he was to live as a hidden king. Popular sympathy for Sebastianism served as fertile ground for utopian thinking in Brazil, as well as leading the Portuguese elite nationalist movement, which used it to justify the House of Bragança's struggle for independence. In the Latin American context, moreover, Franciscan and Jesuit concepts were associated with millenarian and eschatological ideas.

What do these strands tell us about the Paraíba paintings, representations of Saint Francis as Elijah, and social spacing? The representation of Francis as Elijah fits into an eschatological scenario in which it enjoys various possible meanings from popular Sebastianism to Vieira's elite tone (Pécora 1994; Cohen 1998: 150–92; Andrade 2003: 53–70; Lima 2004: 91–112). In the Franciscan convent, the figure both extended its signification in the narrative of alter-Elijah and alter-Christ. Also, in another location, it re-conquered the position of the Jesuit Saint Ignatius. Taken together, the paintings in the churches of the first and third orders allow us to analyze the transformation of the theological and textual discourse into a pictorial one.

Vision–body–sensation

The figure of St. Francis plays also another important role within the discourse about the bodily experience of belief in the Brazilian colonial context with the spatial and visual staging analyzed above. The visual systems that constitute the convent's space consist of simplifications, on the one hand, and a complex intervening network of visual superimpositions, on the other. Moving to the physical perceptions of the individuals who experience church space, this chapter has so far focused on visuality. However, other senses must be addressed as well. On the basis of another example, a sculpture from the second half of the seventeenth century, found today in the Museu de Arte Sacra in São Paulo, which shows the stigmatization of St. Francis, it is possible to discuss the relation of the visual and the body in the discourse of colonial Brazil religious culture. The sculpture "S. Francisco the Chagas" (St. Francis with the stigmata) was made of burned clay and painted polychrome with the proportions of 99 cm in height and 56 cm in circumference (Figure 9.7). Originally the sculpture was commissioned for the Capela de Nossa Senhora dos Aflitos and found in the church San Francisco in São Paulo.

Like the other Franciscan example, its iconographic model refers to the main events essentially narrated and thus traditionalized by Bonaventura and Tomaso de Celano: The Miracle of Monte Alverne from the year 1224 served in order to illustrate foremost the "imitatio," the succession of Christ by Saint Francis exemplified by the stigmata on his body. According to this legend, St. Francis was able to recognize Christ flanked by the wings of a Seraph as the crucified one on account of the wounds on his hands, feet and the right side of his body.[7]

Figure 9.7 Saint Francis with stigmata and Christ, clay, 99 × 56 cm, Museu de Arte Sacra, São Paulo, Brazil

Source: Photo courtesy of Adilson Fernando Ferreira.

In seventeenth-century Portuguese South America, there existed an immense production in the medium of sculpture and only few examples in the medium of painting. It is possible to state that the iconographic models of Rubens and Bernini, which later proliferated through prints, served as a basis for the translation of history in the medium of sculpture and conclusively in the body itself. In the example from São Paulo, the different traditions were synthesized in order to achieve, as in the paintings, an apparent simplification, accompanied by an "embodiment" and/ or "theatralization," which also refers to the same complex visual systems.

One model for the sculpture can be found in the most impressive example portraying a saint in an embrace with Christ is found in the work of Ribalta. A painting of 1625 shows the life-sized figures of St. Bernard and Christ on the cross in embrace. Christ leans his head towards Bernard and embraces him with both arms while the later responds to the embrace with an ecstatic attitude and expression as he appears to rest his face on the right arm of Christ. The gentle character of the physical contact would appear to be important for iconographic analysis (Stoichita 1997: 154). In Ribalta's work, the physical contact is particularly emphasized. With this in mind, the portrayal of a dialogue of eye contact that would normally be found in the iconography of visions is avoided. In actuality, Ribalta inverts the hierarchy of eye contact. In this instance, Christ directs his gaze down to Bernard who closes his eyes in order to enjoy the sacred embrace more fully and be viewed by the deity. However, this pleasure is again an internal and external experience manifested in the body. The body itself becomes the medium of witness. In earlier examples the visual witnesses—either the sacred one himself or persons in close proximity—were essential. However, the closed eyes and relaxed body in Ribalta's work prove the equivalence if not the superiority of the experience of the physical-bodily contact (ibid.: 161).

From the above, we can additionally constitute the nexus of the iconographic model of St. Bernard's Ecstasy with that of St. Francis. In the painting "Saint Francis Embraces the Crucified," also from Ribalta in the year 1620 and found today in the Museum of Valencia, Francis holds Christ around his abdomen as Christ releases his hand from the cross to caress Francis. As in the example of St. Bernard, here too, the eyes of the saint are closed and the act of the embrace occurs at the level of Christ's abdomen. In the opinion of Stoichita, these paintings show a condition of ecstatic trance as well as the internal personal experience as felt by Francis or Bernard. However, in distinction thereof Stoichita prefers to refer to an internalized experience as opposed to that of one which is internal. But at least in the case of Ribalta, the ecstasy occurs not only *in spiritu* but also *in carne*. Ribalta emphasizes the later variation involving the observer in the event as well. In my opinion, the physical-bodily experience provides the essential key to the interpretation. Thus, the body must be understood at all levels of interpretation: the body as illustrative location, as illustration itself, the body in respect to the individual physical experience, and as medium of *communicatio* (ibid.: 163).[8] The body functions here as representation of an internal and internalized experience: or with respect to the theory of communication, the body takes on the role of the transmitter, recipient, and medium of the message. This potential confusion is even more enhanced by the theme itself: the mystical union, which actually designates the symbiosis of god and man and is expressed in a spiritual as well as physical experience.

With this in mind, the São Paulo sculpture provides an unusual example following Ribalta's representational forms, on the one hand, and engages traditional iconography, on the other. The sculpture can be identified as selective interpretation of the different iconographic models. How is it possible to explain the symbiosis of the iconographies of Bernard and Francis in the colonial context? We find in the São Paulo sculpture the attempt to visualize, through means of the body, the dogma over the soul and the relationship between body and soul. As a result, a quasi-inversion of the roles of activity and passivity takes place: Francis receives the stigmata, however, he appears to show resistance and in this way is no longer passive, or at least he portrays a different form of activity; and Christ's behavior shows yet another form of activity as in the previous example in that he embraces Francis with both arms as well as with the wings. This love is decidedly not an act of the invisible soul but rather an act translated by means of the body and thus visible as well as attainable and touchable and moreover perceptible in a tactile sense.

In colonial Brazil during the second half of the seventeenth century, a specific interpretation of mysticism existed as well as the theology associated with it. This translated the symbiosis into a physical-body experience. I would like, therefore, to approach the central source more closely with a second interpretation: a sermon by the most famous author in the Portuguese language, Antônio Vieira, from the year 1643, entitled "On the Stigmata of St. Francis". Just a few years after its presentation, the sermon was published and became available throughout Portugal and especially its South American colonies. Following the post-Tridentine tradition, Vieira emphasized the importance of visual perception above all other human capacities (Vieira 2001: 410). In Gabriele Paleotti's 1582 treatise on images (*Discorso intorno alle imagine sacre e profane*), as well as in the theories of other post-Tridentine theologians, the image possessed a special significance in that it had the ability to evoke an internal image (Vieira 2001: 411).[9] In relation to the colonial period and especially in sacred rhetoric this concept won a particularly significant place.

The basis of Vieira's concepts can be found in post-Tridentine theology and especially in its visual theory. Italians like Paleotti and Robert Bellarmine used the relation of word and image to focus on the concept of perception and to attempt to explore the relationship between internal and external images. These post-Tridentine theologians took into account the specific qualities and capacities of images. Not only did they try to discipline external images, they also believed in the need to control internal images (Baumgarten 2004: 127–38). They were well aware of the impossibility of scrutinizing and controlling non-collective images. Therefore, they sought to influence internal images via pictorial propaganda.

A sophisticated acceptance of these Italian concepts can be found in Vieira`s texts. The sermon on the tears of Saint Peter from 1669 shows the value he accorded to the visual sense and the role of emotions, and the sermon, preached on the 22nd Day after Pentecost exposes his use of the image metaphor to describe the objectives and limits of good government. In the first sermon, the image was connected with visual perception and the in the second with pictorial metaphor, political aesthetics, and, implicitly, with the role of the visual arts. In his classic study of the origins of Brazil, Sergio Buarque de Holanda has also emphasized the importance of vision in the colonial context by referring to Vieira (Holanda 1996: 230).[10] In his sermon on Peter's tears, Vieira declared the unique value of the eyes, which were also perils that theologians faced in controlling the visual sense. He followed the usual seventeenth-century topoi in literature and the visual arts, as, for example, in a 1643 painting by Carlo Dolci depicting the penitent saint, and a marble mask of unknown authorship in Belém, Pará (Imorde 2004: 113–20). Vieira explained the connection between the visual sense and the translation of emotions in the following description of the capacities of the eyes:

> [Only] the eyes have two objectives: to see and to cry … Seeing is the happier action, crying the sadder. Without seeing … there is no joy, because the taste of all joys is seeing; in contrast, crying is the drop of pain, the blood of the soul, the ink of the heart, the gall of life, the liquid of sentiment.

He continued: "And these are our eyes: they cry because they see, and see to cry. Crying is the lamentable aim of seeing; and seeing is the sad principle of crying" (Vieira 1959: vol. 5, 98). Vieira illustrated the concept of internal images and their relation to the emotions with the biblical history of the Fall of Man: "our eyes are two sources, each with two channels and two registers: one channel that runs inside, and that opens the register of seeing: the other channel that runs outside, and opens with the register of crying" (ibid.: 103). The predominant role of the eyes for all psychological and rational evil occurrences was also mentioned in his description of the function of tears: "Yes; it is just that the eyes pay for all, for they are the reason or instrument for all sins … The soul has sinned, the eyes are guilty … The body has sinned, the eyes are delinquents" (ibid.: 100).[11] As in the examples concerning eyes and visual perception, the image and therefore the visual arts were also implicitly evoked. Within this context of sin, Vieira also related the importance of the word and the image, again, with negative argumentation: "Even if the tongue … pronounced [the negation of Christ], the eyes had already been guilty before: the tongue was the instrument, the eyes gave the reason" (ibid.: 104). In conclusion, Vieira rehabilitated human eyes by revealing the potential grace of the gaze of Christ and its ability to illuminate the eyes of mankind: "Let us close our eyes so that we don't see the vanity and madness of the world. Let us open the eyes so they can undo, with tears, that which you have negated and offended" (ibid.: 116). Thus, Vieira related the control of internal images, the effects entailed by the act of seeing itself, to the propositions of post-Tridentine Italian authors.

But Vieira serves as the testimony concerning the inclusion of the bodily experience in the visual discourse. He used metaphors taken from the relationship of sculpture and prints (Vieira 2001: 412–13), which refer to the body of Francis as the true image of Christ: "Only Francis was a natural image of the stigmatized Christ; ... Francis was immediate; the others followed" (ibid.: 419). This quotation proves the existence of an even higher form of witness than the eyes, namely, the body. Vieira chose a most impressive metaphor to describe the physicality of stigmatization. In the following example he utilizes the medium of sculpture, which, in my opinion, plays a dominant role in the arts of Portuguese South America:

And as the stigmata, which once opened and sculpted themselves on Mount Calvary, so would they open and sculpt again on Mount Alverne. Therefore, the angel declares that not only would happen the stone to open and sculpt itself but rather it would happen to open by themselves the same openings, and would happen to sculpt by themselves the same sculptures: once opened and sculpted in Christ, and again opened and sculpted in Francis. In Christ opened and sculpted the stone; in Francis opened and sculpted the sculptures.

(ibid.: 421)

In this context, Vieira connected the discourses of the body with others in solving an apparent paradox: "However, if Christ promised never to give his glory to another, how could he give it to St. Francis?" (ibid.: 416). Vieira answers:

St. Francis made it thus. He negated himself in such a way that he was no longer that which he had been before. Thus, if Francis were not Francis, who was he? He was Christ ... Christ says that he could not give the glory of his passion to anyone; meanwhile he gives it to Francis; because of Francis' resolve of self-denial he ceased to be Francis and through the strength of the unification, became Christ; although Christ gave his glory to Francis, he gave it to no other.

(ibid.: 416–17)

Thereupon, Vieira described the five degrees of the ecstatic union, which were likewise expressed through the body: "Extermination, conformity, transformation, identity and sanctification" (ibid.: 417).

As a central theme of the sermon, Vieira explained the relationship between soul and body by quoting St. Bernard. Proceeding from this example, we can explain the symbiosis of the iconography of St. Francis and St. Bernard in the São Paulo sculpture.

> For insight into this unusual thinking we must accept two things: first of all, I accept that just as the humanity of Christ is made up of soul and body, so are the stigmata of the soul. This credence comes from St. Bernard ... The wound marks of the feet, of the hands, and the side of Christ have been caused by hatred from the Jews; however, they were already caused by the love of humans. The hatred caused them in the body; the love caused them in the soul. Bernard proved this same new thought in the Song of Songs.
>
> (ibid.: 419)

In the colonial context with its missionary requirements it appeared necessary—returning now to the São Paulo example—to translate the medium of painting, in which the most integral examples of Iberian and Italian iconography were accomplished, into the medium of sculpture by means of the medium of the theater. In this way, among others, the body became the central focus of the artists. Therefore, the Iberian concepts and especially those where the body, with it the physical-individual experience, was essential, were used as references for the artists. The sculpture, as in the example of São Paulo, specifically stresses the performed act itself. Colonial theologians as well as the sermons of Vieira evidence an interpretation that refers to individual physical experience.

Conclusion

The architecture and the decoration of the church of Nossa Senhora do Brazil present different art histories: aesthetic, religious, and political. They narrate and present visually in a Neo-Baroque manner the art history of the Baroque. They re-negotiate the national and modernist impact, and fashion the Baroque discourse as a relation between Europe and Latin America. Accordingly, we can speak of a return to and a return of the Baroque.

Staging Baroque worship reveals several layers in the analysis of religious material culture. The spatial organization of the staging itself and the intricacies of borrowing and re-deploying European paradigms require a careful historiography of motifs in the colonial period. These aspects affect the study of religious material culture in a broader sense. The superimpositions of a religiously, socially, and aesthetically defined space engage worship, the saints, and divine revelation with interests that integrate the church into its surrounding social worlds—in colonial Portuguese South America no less than in twentieth-century Brazil. Furthermore, the setting of the imagery can be analyzed by iconographical method, but the scholar should also consider more recent approaches to the study of the body and gender in order to take sensation very seriously as the Baroque medium of the bodily revelation of the sacred, as we saw in the case of St. Francis. This interweaving of factors suggests that material culture is not objects alone, but also the conceptual framework that a cultural setting relies on to organize experience. The staging considered here is not simply a material object for scrutiny, but is also the conceptual apparatus of space, body, stage, and performance that constructs the Baroque and Neo-Baroque worship settings. Realizing this makes it possible to investigate the ideas that can be said to stage the staging of the sacred. Material culture is object *and* idea— not a dualism, but a single cultural unity.

Notes

1 Found in the official material published not officially by the parish. Some part of it can be found under http://www.nossasenhoradobrasil.com.br/ (accessed May 2007). The analysis of the architecture and decoration of the church is part of a larger project on religious and polical visual culture and the reception of colonial art. About the decoration it is also written that "each of the paintings represents one race and one epoch."

2 It is not possible to analyze the full range of interlocking relationships between the different architectural spaces within the Paraiban convent. For a general history of the convent, see Burity (1988) and Oliveira (2003: 81–84). The most important source about the church and its inventory is Willeke (1966: 173–207). In general, regarding the Franciscans in Brazil, see Röwer (1947 and 1941); Primeiro (1940); Miranda (1969).

3 On the importance of the Azulejos' cycles in Northeastern Brazil and the religious iconography, see Barata (1955: 137–56).

4 See Gruzinski and Bernand (1988); Gruzinski (1988, 1990, 1991, 2004). I am aware of the problems with the term "hybridity," which was recently criticized by Dean and Leibsohn (2003: 5–35); and treated in some different methodological aspects by Farago (1995).

5 Elijah is also one of the most common figures evoked in and associated with posthumous portrayals of Martin Luther in German painting, so it is potentially an even larger re-appropriation. Concerning the visual construction of Luther's memory, see Warnke (1984); Hofmann (1983); Brückner (2006: 36–57); Coupe (1998: 187–96).

6 The importance of the lack of cult images in the Brazilian context becomes particularly apparent when we compare it with the situation in Peru, for example, Mills (1997); Dean (1999); Mills and Grafton (2003).

7 On the first traditions of the legend, see Trexler (2002: 463–97); on the stigmata, see Menke and Vinken (2004) and Frugoni (2004: 109–12).

8   See also Teuber (2004: 164–79); on the noteworthy relation to Teresa von Ávila, see Bal (2003: 1–30).
9   On these aesthetic and political discourses, see Baumgarten (2004) and Krüger (2001).
10   For the relation between sermons and visual arts for the colonial context, see Ávila (2001/2004: 43–70).
11   For further discussion of the psychological discourses in Vieira's sermons, see Massimi (2001: 17–34, 2005: 205–18, 233–44).

10

Form, function, and failure in postwar Protestant Christian education buildings

Gretchen T. Buggeln

I have one particularly vivid memory of my early Sunday School days at Walnut Creek Presbyterian Church in northern California. It was the early 1970s. I was sitting in a metal folding chair in a large, cool, common room with light green walls on the second floor of our postwar-era education building. We primary-grade children, arranged in neat rows, faced a middle-aged woman who announced the leaders in the memory verse competition. Over the course of my childhood, I spent hours and hours in that building. I am certain that it shaped my understanding of Christianity and Christian community in important ways. While I remember those days with a certain nostalgic fondness, I don't remember the classrooms as particularly warm, child-centered, colorful, or cheerful. Rather, my memories of those postwar Protestant Sunday school spaces are akin to my memories of modern public school classrooms of the same era: bland, institutional, hardly beautiful.

Thus, I was somewhat astonished as I read through the ecumenical prescriptive literature written by church education leaders and architects of the era and discovered, the careful deliberation postwar Americans brought to designing church education buildings. They knew, beyond a doubt, that the setting for Christian education would have an enormous impact on what was to be learned. The most common quotation in period books, conference reports, and journal articles is Winston Churchill's famous remark regarding the rebuilding of the British House of Commons, destroyed by the German Luftwaffe in 1941: "we shape our buildings, and afterwards our buildings shape us." These writers were acutely aware of the importance of architecture in contributing to our understanding of the world and our relationships with others. For instance, Lois Blankenship, a Christian education specialist speaking to architects and church leaders at a 1959 conference in Los Angeles, insisted on the importance of proper space for Christian education.[1] "Children, in particular," she argued, "are susceptible to their environment for they are unable to separate themselves from it and therefore absorb much of the emotional tone of the place set up for their learning" (Blankenship 1959: D3).

American Protestants of the postwar era were deeply concerned with shaping both the content and context of Christian education. They sought to clarify the lessons of modern Christianity and to introduce fresh and relevant truths to young Christians in up-to-date, welcoming spaces that served their developing bodies and psyches. In the prewar decades, there had been considerable tension over the goals, content, and methods of Sunday Schools between the professional religious educators (who tended to be theologically liberal) and the most successful, at least in terms of numbers, practitioners (old-school evangelicals). In the two decades following the war there was less cause for tension; mainline professionals were often theologically neo-orthodox, while practitioners were more receptive to new educational methods. Across the board, it was a time of innovation and renewed vigor in Sunday schools (Lynn and Wright 1980: 133–35). In other words, in many ways, mainline Christian education professionals and local practitioners were on the same page in these postwar decades. How does one explain, then, the evident gap between prescription and material reality, between theory and practice? Some of these education buildings were successful, rising to the level promised in the literature. Many others, however, served the basic practical needs of church education simply as undistinguished containers for instruction and social events.

These postwar education buildings are rich terrain for studying the material experience of American Christians in the two decades following World War II, particularly in the booming suburban communities where they proliferated. In the introduction to this volume, David Morgan suggests that by looking at how belief is transmitted to the next generation, "*how, when,* and *where*" people instruct their children, we might be able to understand religion, as practiced, in fundamental ways. As the youngest members of a religious community are taught how to practice their beliefs, joining into a "community of feeling" that is "public and verifiable," the material circumstances of that transfer of belief matters considerably. Buildings fall into what Morgan calls "the conditions that shape the feeling, emotions, senses, spaces, and performances of belief." Undoubtedly, Protestant Christian education buildings of the postwar era—their stature on the land, their relationship to worship spaces, the textures, contours and colors of the classrooms, the way sounds echoed down their halls—inflected the religious experiences of literally millions of young minds, week after week.

A careful reading of the remaining material evidence should help us understand the complexity of that religious experience. But here is a case where, in order to understand that historical experience, it is vitally important to consider intention along with outcome. Postwar Christian education buildings, in many of their features (and in their very existence) certainly do tell tales about the Protestant culture of that era. Both conscious and unconscious meaning is embodied in these structures, and both are relevant for our understanding of postwar Protestantism. It would be wrong, however, to read them only as the self-satisfied expression of an eagerly expanding Protestantism when the buildings were fraught with ambiguity even at the time of their construction. These buildings were, above all, compromises. In their awkwardness and insufficiency, they are instructive of a relationship between material and belief that can be marked with considerable failure—a tension between what the material world "ought" to be and do, in the service of religion, and what in fact it is and does. In the case of architecture, especially, a group of believers is left with a material envelope for a long time. The congregation celebrates, denigrates, embraces, and adapts the space over many years. We need to ask three things, then, as we approach these buildings: What were they meant to be? How did those ideas take material form? And, in what conscious and unconscious ways did they contribute to the formation of the learners who encountered Christianity in their spaces?

The first part of this chapter engages the postwar conversation among architects, theologians, and educators about what Christian education **should** be and "how, when, and where" it should take place. While hardly naïve about the realities of contemporary building projects, these leaders nonetheless remained hopeful about the potential of this architecture to nurture faith intentionally and successfully. The second part of the chapter will examine five Midwestern postwar education buildings in light of these aims. The examples illustrate how, at the local level, the physical realities of architecture often emerge as compromises between well-intentioned ideals and practical considerations such as budgets and pressing needs for space. Finally, the chapter considers what the buildings did in fact achieve in the service of religious instruction. Although they rarely reached the height of the rhetoric, that rhetoric came to fruition at least on this point: for better or worse, these buildings have shaped two generations of American Protestants.

Prescriptions for church education buildings

Postwar Protestants, in the middle of a church building surge of a magnitude not witnessed before or since in America, knew they had a rare chance to reshape the American religious landscape. American demographics put pressure on educators and builders. Thirty-two million children were born in the 1940s, and over forty million in the 1950s. These children populated the Sunday schools of expanding congregations, many of which were starting from scratch in rapidly expanding suburbs, where Sunday school programs were the primary reason many families gravitated towards church involvement in the first place. In both 1957 and 1958 over \$860 million was spent nationally on church architecture, roughly 50 per cent of that on the education buildings that often preceded sanctuaries in construction (Atkinson 1956; Blankenship 1959). Perceived moral decline also contributed to the builders' sense of urgency. The forces working against American Christian values appeared to be gathering steam. "Modern means of communication project vividly into our homes," the pundits warned. And, while media did usher in a few good things, it also introduced and accentuated "fears, uncertainties, prejudices, distorted values, moral laxities ... and those subtle perversions which make evil glamorous and socially acceptable" (Atkinson 1956: 6). Christian education bore the burden of moral development as well as evangelism.

In the midst of energetic building campaigns, Protestants reaffirmed that the church was people, not architecture, and not an institution that existed for its own sake but one that had a responsibility to serve a deeply troubled society. Pastor and church historian Martin Marty, speaking to an audience of church leaders and architects in Seattle in 1963, cited Dietrich Bonheoffer's plea for a church that would be:

> her true self only when she exists for humanity ... she must take part in the social life of the world, not lording over men, but helping and serving them. She must tell men, whatever their calling, what it means to live in Christ, to exist for others.
>
> (Marty 1963: 11–12)

Marty urged his audience to develop this message into a vision for church buildings, for "the single most visible concrete example which the parish churches give to the world ... is the church building."

Edward A. Sovik, one of the most articulate church architects of the day, shared Marty's belief that true religious building must have a clear relationship to vision. The only structures justifiably called "religious architecture," he argued, possessed "a quality in the architecture itself which makes it a reflection, an expression, an echo, an evocation, a communicator of the religious understanding or vision" (Sovik 1967: 8). A desire to make church architecture a "reflection" and "expression" of contemporary Christianity appears frequently in the writings of church leaders and church architects of the period. Most commonly this was understood not in terms of doctrine but of general principles for Christian living, such as honesty, integrity, humility, and service. Church buildings were not to be grand monuments or sacred enclaves, but generous, open spaces that represented the nature of Christian community and its relationship with the broader world—comfortable and welcoming places where "the undisciplined possibilities of human personalities" would come into contact with "the transforming influence of the person of Jesus Christ" (Atkinson 1956: 6). Architecture, understood this way, was a humble site for dramatic spiritual transformation.

The development of a coherent vision for church architecture was at the heart of ongoing conversations between church leaders and church architects, conversations that took place locally, within denominational bodies, and also within and among national organizations such as the Church Architecture Guild (later renamed the Guild of Religious Architecture) and the Department of Church Building and Architecture of the National Council of Churches. These bodies provided ample advice to congregations and architects in the form of local and national conferences, and easily available print publications, visual media, and consultants. Their leaders insisted that the style and form of the architecture needed to keep pace with the modern world. According to Edward Frey, Director of the Commission on Architecture for the Lutheran Church in America, "it is less and less possible for anachronistic architecture to penetrate the inner life of contemporary man" (1959: 6). Frey and others objected to the continued use of historic styles of architecture—Gothic and Colonial in particular—for buildings that were supposed to speak to the contemporary community.

By the early 1960s, architects and church leaders believed that the modern style of architecture had emerged victorious, a 1950s modernism that was, at least by definition, committed to principles of "honesty" and "authenticity"— conveniently, the same principles espoused by the contemporary church (Wagoner 1961). The triumph of the modern style in church architecture (in the new suburbs of the West and Midwest, in particular) is evident on the landscape: boxy or experimental geometric forms; unadorned, sleek surfaces; and the use of new materials such as aluminum and glass walls, enamel panels, and poured concrete predominated. Good architecture, however, was as much about functionality as style. Church buildings had to accommodate two equally important purposes, worship and education. These two were hardly mutually exclusive, but intertwined in practice in the Sunday and weekday activities of the church; congregants were taught in the worship setting, and worship was a part of the regular teaching activities of the church. Nonetheless, the two functions required different sorts of spaces: sanctuaries for worship and purpose-built education facilities for small-group instruction. While Sunday school and other classroom instruction often drove the need for and the design of education buildings, congregations conceptualized these buildings as spaces for most of the non-worship needs of the congregation; they included, as well as classrooms, fellowship halls (often with a stage), kitchens, youth recreation areas, restrooms, choir rooms, and storage areas. A particular challenge of this two-pronged mission was to keep the functions separate enough to prevent one from impeding the other (ensuring noise barriers, for example) while integrating space enough so as not to isolate one function or one group of people from the whole.

By the mid-twentieth century, the scope of educational activities for the average congregation, led by an increasingly professionalized cadre of directors of Christian education, had expanded considerably. Reverend J. Gordon Chamberlain, professor of Christian Education at Pittsburgh Theological Seminary, claimed that in recent decades:

the educational program of the church has proliferated with weekday schools, released-time classes,[2] extended sessions of Sunday morning church school from two to three hours, Sunday evening programs for young adults, new weekday programs of religious education, and the growth of religious libraries.

(Chamberlain 1961: 51)

Defining program was important, for denominational leaders and architects insisted that congregations had to be clear about what programs they wanted the building to facilitate before they could expect an architect to do his work; function had to determine form. Scott Turner Rittenour, Chairman of the 1954 Conference on Christian Education and Church Building, was gratified that Christian educators were getting better at conveying "principles of Christian education in terms of program," thus enabling architects and build-ers "to translate them into terms of building needs" (Atkinson 1956: 3).

In developing educational programs, church planners enthusiastically embraced the newest thought about how children learn as well as cutting edge ideas about public school buildings. Although some skeptics voiced concern, the pervasive thought throughout this period was that the churches needed to keep up with the schools. Harold Atkinson, the executive director of the National Council of Churches Bureau of Church Building and Architecture, wrote in his widely circulated 1956 book, *Building and Equipping for Christian Education*,

the attractive surroundings with which our children are environed while in public school, and the great variety of interesting activities which make up the curricula of these institutions, lend further incentives to the church to provide facilities and procedures which do not suffer by comparison. Failure to meet this challenge puts religious teaching at a serious disadvantage.

(Atkinson 1956: 6–7)

The relevant hallmarks of the new public education were its emphasis on flexibility, informality, and comfort—a cheerful, student-centered approach to instruction (an "enclosed little world managed by teachers but designed, built, and operated for the child") and a curriculum and environment that recognized that children learn by doing (Caudill 1954: 3). The material result was the age-specific "self-contained" classroom: a larger room with movable furniture, zones for creative discovery and quiet reflection, individual student storage areas, and a sink/restroom facility. Lessons from physics and psychol-ogy contributed to a richer understanding of how light, color, and the move-ment of air affected learners, and building manuals uniformly covered topics such as the practical arrangement of space, the use of color according to age group, the appropriate height of windows and width of hallways, planning for convenient circulation of air and people, and effective sanitation.

Much of this educational innovation found its way to discussions about the Sunday school, where it was given a religious spin. Church leaders turned to secular experts but insisted that "sound psychological, educational, and sociological principles must be combined with our theological base to determine our Christian education philosophy and the methods which derive from it" (Blankenship 1959: D2–3). Ideal classrooms were to be larger and informal, with more freedom leading to greater student engagement. This approach promised to convey a more holistic understanding of Christian faith, conduct, and community. Atkinson claimed that, by employing adaptable space and curricula, "the group learns to live the Christian life by living and working together within the classroom" (1956: 8). Educators geared the program to the development of the whole child—body, mind, and spirit (Lynn and Wright 1980).

The self-contained classroom idea dominated thinking about church school. Experts recommended that "large self-contained classrooms where groups remain for the entire learning period (in contrast to assembly rooms and adjoining tiny cubbyhole classrooms) furnish a setting for almost unlimited flexibility in the program" (Blankenship 1962: 60). Staffed by instructional teams, these classrooms would enable teachers to experiment with new teaching techniques and respond to the needs of students rather than herding them into rigid patterns of teacher-centered instruction. The antithesis of this new thought was the nineteenth-century "Akron Plan" which organized small classrooms radially around a large central gathering area with a dominant superintendent. The idea of gathering children together for a "children's church" version of worship also fell out of favor. Many previous Sunday school areas had a special altar and liturgical objects for use in children's worship, and professional educators increasingly deemed this practice inappropriate and false. Children's worship, church educators believed, "is more meaningful when it takes place in the classroom to 'celebrate' the fact that the Holy Spirit can make himself real through the learning experience" (Blankenship 1962: 61).

Church educators advocated addressing the specific spiritual, psychological, and physical needs of learners at each stage of development. This led to detailed material recommendations for the spaces of every age group: "each room must express the feelings, needs and interests of the age group that will use it" (Wagoner *et al.* 1960, D4–2). In discussions of these spaces, one can see how church leaders adapted public education conversations for Christian purposes. For instance, Atkinson informed his readers that "Kindergarten children grow spiritually in an environment which carries intimations of God." His suggested floor plan included a number of "interest stations [that would] stimulate attention, moments of worship, and conversation between teacher and child" (Figure 10.1). This plan called for two classrooms, one for fours and one for fives, joined by a common "reception room." The labeled

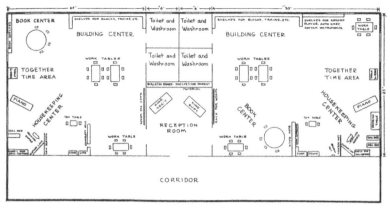

A Plan for a Complete Kindergarten Department

When it is possible to provide two rooms, one for the fours and one for the fives, together with a common reception room, this is a practical plan and is highly recommended. Each room is adequate for twenty kindergarten children.

Figure 10.1 Plan for Kindergarten Room

Source: Harry Atkinson, *Building and Equipping for Christian Education*, 1956, p. 33.

furnishings indicate possible activities: "book center" with tables for reading, "housekeeping center" with "doll beds," a play kitchen area, and a "tea table," music areas, and "together time area with a "table for Bible." Rooms such as these anticipated that "spontaneous worship arising under guidance out of situations meaningful to the child will make God more real than a so called 'worship period' imposed upon him as a routine procedure" (Atkinson 1956: 31–2). These prescriptions for rooms convey the idea of open, flexible spaces that are responsive to the needs of individual learners without prescribing a rigid program of activity; they define a multivalent architecture where ideas of God were to be *discovered* by active learners, never forced.

Designers of teen spaces were similarly careful to integrate social and spiritual needs. Teens were believed to be especially susceptible to attractive elements of the wayward culture, and the church needed to present a compelling alternative. The need for seriousness and contemporary attractiveness in the teen spaces was emphasized:

> Rooms for older young people should be conducive to group study, discussion, and related activities … it is psychologically important that the rooms be fresh and modern in their colors, furnishings, uses of light, and arrangements. Nothing inhibits the use of a room more than an impression of overall unimaginative dullness.
>
> (Morse 1969: 115)

Throughout the literature, whether discussing youth rooms or kitchens, several themes predominate. First, architecture should be contemporary, lacking nothing of the attractiveness and functionality of other modern spaces. Second, rooms should be flexible, allowing for multiple uses. Finally, and closer to the idea of "vision" articulated by Marty and Sovik, religious architecture should facilitate the work of Christians in the world and demonstrate to the wider community the power and relevance of a counter-cultural message of transformation. The creation of church architecture that could be both familiarly contemporary and transformative at the same time was perhaps more challenging than it seemed.

Examples of church education buildings

These earnest and rich conversations about Christian education and its architecture took place in the midst of the frenetic pace of church planting, church building, and a busy calendar of church-related activities. Congregations eager to build and expand after the lean times of the war years had big plans, and they were impatient to start building. Today so many of these structures are run-down, nearly empty, and in other ways obsolete that it is hard to recover their original use patterns and meanings, and especially difficult to reconstruct an honest sense of the vitality they once embodied. The fabric of the buildings, however, taken in tandem with the rhetoric of the day, suggests the shape of a vital yet imperfect system of bringing children into the full life of the church.

The 1950s church education buildings of Park Forest, Illinois, illustrate the most rapid and intensive type of suburban church growth. Park Forest, 30 miles south of Chicago, was a Midwestern suburb on the model of Long Island's Levittown, a total creation by a team of developers offering affordable housing to GIs and their families. In 1948, the first families moved into court apartments on land that had been farms and a golf course just a few years earlier. By 1956, over 26,000 people lived in Park Forest, many of them children. There were no churches waiting to absorb these young families—houses, churches, schools, all had to be created from the ground up. Believing in the importance of religious organizations for sound community (and recognizing moral stability as a selling point for their new town), the developers of Park Forest actively encouraged the formation of churches and synagogues and provided land for religious buildings. In an effort to mobilize assorted Protestants to form viable congregations, the builders supported a town chaplain and encouraged the formation of United Protestant churches, umbrella organizations designed to work like military chaplaincies, with Protestants coming together for worship, education, and fellowship while not abandoning individual denominational affiliations. Four of these congregations eventually formed in Park Forest. Jews and liturgically distinctive Catholics, Episcopalians, and Lutherans, plus a few other groups, preferred to organize separately (Whyte 1956; Randall 2003).

In Park Forest, springing up at virtually one moment in time under the oversight of a developer, the architecture of houses, churches, schools, and shopping centers followed a coherent, uniformly modern, suburban style. Park Forest's architects, the firm of Loebl, Schlossman and Bennett of Chicago, designed its houses, central shopping area, and some of the schools and churches. Other architects who designed buildings in Park Forest kept the modern and progressive spirit of the place and their designs were subject to review by community planners. While hardly the factory of conformity immortalized in William Whyte's *Organization Man* (1956), overall architectural uniformity prevailed. This was deliberate and valued, and church building committees often expressed their desire to build structures that fit into their surroundings.

Trinity Lutheran, a congregation formed in the early months of Park Forest's history, built the first Protestant church and parsonage in town, a small building on Western Avenue, the main north–south thoroughfare (Figure 10.2). It was a simple, $35,000 California redwood-framed and clad structure designed by Richard M. Bennett (of Loebl, Schlossman and Bennett) as the "first unit" building of the congregation. "First unit" structures were a common tool of these builders, functional buildings raised in a hurry at low cost until a larger sanctuary and more extensive church plant could be erected. Trinity was an adaptable, two-story building (the first story was half basement with natural light), housing classrooms and offices, with a chapel area on the southern end of the second floor. The architect, Bennett, was invested in creating spaces that were human-scale, employed new technologies and materials, and reflected his

Figure 10.2 Trinity Lutheran Church, Park Forest, Illinois. First Unit, Richard M. Bennett, architect, 1950

Source: Photo by author.

vision of community. His firm also designed Park Forest elementary, the community's first school, in the same modern, functional, no-nonsense style, and his houses, while often conservatively "colonial" on the outside, favored open-plan interiors, picture windows, and modern décor. The congregation converted this original building to Sunday school space when the new sanctuary (also by Bennett) was built in 1959–60 (at a cost of $180,000). The lower level of the new sanctuary contained more classrooms and a community hall with kitchen and stage. This building housed many activities beyond the Sunday morning program: preschool, scouts, Vacation Bible School, Kiwanis, Luther League, Women's and Men's clubs, banquets and bazaars. The dedication book for the second sanctuary claimed the building provided a space for "translating the Christian faith into a compelling seven-day-a-week outreach into the common life" (Trinity Lutheran 1960: n.p.).

The history of this congregation is typical for Park Forest. A small group of Lutherans began worshipping together in early 1950 in one of the Park Forest apartment rentals. At that time as many as fifty-five people crammed into this compact space for worship, with Sunday school classes for as many as sixty-three held in three upstairs bedrooms and the basement, itself divided into three rooms by hanging burlap curtains. The pace of growth in Park Forest's churches is illustrated in the rapid increase of Trinity's membership. The 1950 sanctuary could seat 168; in 1954–55 alone, 167 new members joined by letter of transfer. Despite bursting at the seams, the congregation was strapped for funds, and in 1954 voted to save money by trying to best utilize the first building while paying down the debt. This involved considerable juggling of space and schedules. For instance, Marge Roeder remembered her Wednesday woman's Bible study coinciding with church school for the 3- and 4-year-olds because there was no room for them on Sunday mornings (Roeder 2007). At Hope Lutheran, the Missouri Synod congregation in Park Forest, the church grew so rapidly that soon after the construction of the first unit building there were three sessions of Sunday school, and some classes had to meet in school buses in the parking lot (Boie 2007).

The first and largest of the United Protestant churches, Faith, had similar urgent needs for Sunday school space. Approximately five hundred charter members representing thirty-five denominations organized the congregation in 1950. By 1953, Sunday school enrollment exceeded one thousand, and church membership reached 1200. In those early years, the Sunday school program alone required 120 volunteers. The congregation dedicated its new Christian education building in 1953 and it was immediately filled to capacity, serving both church and community needs (Figure 10.3). (In fact, the first social event held in the building was the bar mitzvah of the son of the chief developer, Philip Klutznik.) The well-known Chicago firm of Schweikher and Elting designed this building, and also, several years later, the 1957 sanctuary. By this time the Sunday school enrolled a staggering 1,500 children (Faith United Protestant Church 1991).

Figure 10.3 Faith United Protestant Church, Park Forest, Illinois.
Education building, Schweikher and Elting, architects, 1953

Source: Photo by author.

The 14,600 square foot education building, which cost $155,000 furnished, housed twenty-three classrooms that two Sunday shifts of church school filled to capacity. Demonstrating the primacy of economic concerns, the building committee remarked that the newly completed structure "compares favorably in unit cost with any building in this area" (Faith United Protestant Church 1953: n.p.). The committee also reported that inexpensive "wood as a skeletal construction has been used in a manner characteristic of the best modern architecture" (ibid.). Massive stone and concrete end walls supported a frame filled with glass and wood curtain walls. "We now have a modern, functional building," the congregation was pleased to note, "that embodies simplicity, utility, integrity, and dignity; one that is designed to meet our needs, scaled to fit our community" (ibid.).

Park Forest's Holy Family Episcopal Church, a much smaller congregation, built a utilitarian parish hall in 1954 that served for worship services, church school, and social events. By 1957, plans were begun for a larger church, primarily because of the growth of the school and the high cost of renting classrooms for that purpose. Edward Dart of Chicago, himself an Episcopalian, designed the new church with an undercroft rather than creating a separate education building. By December of 1957, the primary grades were meeting in that large, open, multi-purpose space, using dividers to separate the classes. This building reflects very little of the advice of church leaders regarding education buildings: Sunday school children were placed in a multi-purpose, leaky, and dark basement. Yet this was nonetheless a considerable improvement over the previous, crowded arrangement.

A final example of Park Forest's 1950s education buildings is the two-story structure that the resident American Baptists erected in 1958 (Figure 10.4). This

Figure 10.4 First Baptist Church, Park Forest, Illinois. Education wing, Taylor and West, architects, 1958

Source: Photo by author.

congregation, organized separately in 1954 for reasons of identity and doctrine, resisting the United Protestant movement. As a consequence they faced some difficulty acquiring land from the developer (Sang 2008). Architects Robert Taylor and Derald West of Oak Park, Illinois, designed this $110,000 first unit as a strictly functional building housing six classrooms upstairs, and two classrooms, kitchen, and "assembly area" downstairs (Figure 10.5). This building type is a typical representative of the extremely common rectangular, unadorned, inexpensive education wings of the era (Figure 10.6). The large downstairs room, which could hold two hundred worshippers, served as the worship space until the separate church was built (1964). The education wing was expected to hold 600 persons for classes. Today, movable screens divide this large basement room. Here again, construction was bare bones: face brick, concrete floors, laminated wood beams, and acoustical tile ceilings in the classrooms, with "color schemes specifically designed for each age group" and "movable partitions ... to permit flexible use of various rooms" (*Park Forest Star* 1958: n.p.).

In contrast to these economical suburban structures is Eero Saarinen's education wing (1962) for Christ Church Lutheran, Minneapolis (Figure 10.7). Christ Church (1949), designed by Eero's father Eliel, was and continues to be one of the most heralded American churches of the postwar period. Unlike the new congregations of Park Forest, Christ Church, in an older Minneapolis neighborhood, had a history dating back to the nineteenth century and a cluster of functioning but outdated buildings. Using a basic rectangular form and modern materials, Saarinen created an intimate, numinous, acoustically perfect sanctuary. The Sunday school met in the old parish hall on the property next door for a decade until the congregation determined it could afford to build the

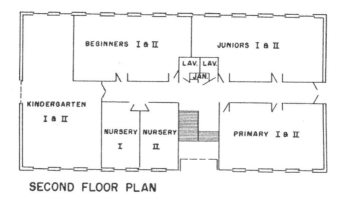

SECOND FLOOR PLAN

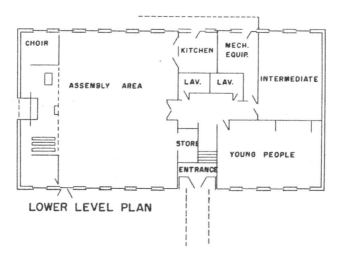

LOWER LEVEL PLAN

Figure 10.5 First Baptist Church, Park Forest, Illinois. Education wing plan, 1958

Source: Courtesy, Park Forest Public Library. Photo by author.

planned education wing. By 1959, with 1,196 communicant members and 517 registered for church school plus 152 on the cradle roll, the need for space was becoming acute. Saarinen's equally famous son Eero and his busy firm agreed to take on the design for the new wing, undoubtedly to protect the integrity of his father's famous building (Christ Church 1962).

   This education wing has many high-quality features that answer directly the rhetoric of the prescriptive literature and set it apart, at least in terms of style and finish, from the previous examples. From the street, the passerby sees a low roofed (14' maximum above grade) structure with a glass and aluminum curtain wall to the left and a solid masonry wall to the right. Between the church and education wing is a landscaped courtyard with a connecting arcade and a fountain; an office corridor to the rear joins the two buildings. Despite a general distaste for church basements by this time, the

Figure 10.6 Classroom, First Baptist Church, Park Forest, Illinois

Source: Photo by author.

Figure 10.7 Christ Church Lutheran, Minneapolis. Education
wing, Eero Saarinen and Associates, 1962

Source: Photo by author.

wing included an extensive underground story, joined by tunnels to the basement of the 1949 church. In this settled area, land for a sprawling one-story structure was unavailable, so the church burrowed in.[3]

The congregation originally anticipated spending about $400,000 on the addition; in the end the building cost over $730,000 (Christ Church 1960). This expense is most apparent in the fine qualities of the details. For instance, the "Adult Lounge" with its three walls of teak paneling, elegant fireplace, and original Knoll furnishings, could hold its own with any corporate boardroom of the era. The upstairs, finished in bright colors, is capacious and light-filled (Figure 10.8). Six roomy classrooms with clear glass corridor walls, and a kindergarten room (24 x 57 feet, designed to fit over 80 children), were all equipped with the recommended blackboards and tack boards, sinks, built-in storage, and worship centers. These rooms, finished in vinyl floor and acoustic ceiling tile, line up on wide, sky-lit hallways.

The basement today is a rabbit warren of dark spaces, but, again in the details, one can sense some of its earlier glory. A full-size gymnasium/theater with a professional quality stage covers nearly half of the footprint of the building. Lockers and showers, a library, large meeting room, offices and a huge, well-equipped kitchen testify to the original social aims of the building and the desire of the congregation to create a building that might in the future be used as a Christian day school. At the time, the congregation felt that the 30×42 feet

Figure 10.8 Christ Church Lutheran, Minneapolis. Education wing interior

Source: Photo by author.

"youth lounge" was the "exclusive domain of young people" and "perhaps one of the most interesting rooms in the building" (Christ Lutheran Church 1962: n.p.). Amenities included cabinets with built in hi-fi and worship center, a snack bar with a stove, sink, and refrigerator. The casual mood of the room was enhanced by concealed floodlights, with cushions and informal seating surrounding a fireplace. Many youth rooms of this era share these features—the fireplace nook, snack bar, contemporary design, and an overall emphasis on crafting a space where teens would feel in their element. Christ Church's education building, busy and noisy in its heyday, was used intensively and creatively for diverse social and educational functions. Like the buildings of Park Forest, however, today this building is far too large and complex for the congregation's current needs and is fraught with expensive maintenance issues.

Experience and meaning in church education buildings

The ubiquity of church education buildings from this era proves how purposefully postwar Protestants approached Christian education. Often equal in size to the sanctuary, they signal that many institutional activities accompanied ritual worship, and offer a picture of busy and businesslike congregations. It is clear today, however, that in the eyes of thoughtful contemporaries the majority of postwar education buildings failed to achieve the potential promised by the rhetoric of the day. Like the structures at Faith United Protestant or First Baptist in Park Forest, they are collections of mostly uniform classrooms organized around interior hallways, uninspired buildings that feel overwhelmingly institutional. There is enough in the language of building dedications and newspaper accounts to indicate that the builders of these structures, both elaborate buildings like Christ Church and its poorer relations, certainly *were* aware of broader theological and architectural conversations about education buildings. They wanted the structures to serve their mission in the community not simply through providing space but by giving attention to aesthetic effect and by incorporating the latest thought about how children learn. So why the dramatic disparity between claim and reality?

The sheer cost of these buildings goes a long way toward explaining why they were so often pedestrian efforts that demonstrate little of the creativity one finds in the rhetoric. In the press of the urgent need for space, and given their very limited resources, many congregations felt compelled to cut corners in order to be able to build *something*, quickly, to house the educational and social activities of the congregation. A convenient aspect of the modern style in church architecture is that it was relatively cheap to build, much cheaper, in fact, than the Gothic masonry structures it often replaced. And there was excitement in creating a community landscape that was overall fresh and new. The young adults who moved into places like Park Forest built their own vision of a coherent suburban paradise, with their social spaces—churches, schools, malls—central in location, easily accessible, and uniform in scale and style. Church builders frequently used the language of the "modern"—modern materials, modern methods, and modern style—and were very intentional about creating buildings that would "fit in." Modern design features that contributed to a sense of contemporary openness included large windows, lighter structural framing, and often (especially in the Midwest), light, buff-colored building materials.

But modernism is a style that can easily be achieved poorly and unimaginatively, and indeed it often was. Perceptive contemporaries suspected that architects and building committees gave little thought to these spaces, considering them secondary to the sanctuary and of lesser spiritual importance. Architects willing to endure the aggravation of working with church building committees, while being poorly compensated for their efforts, often did so for the challenges of sanctuary design, not education buildings. Spaces with classrooms, kitchens, and fellowship halls could be inexpensive boxes removed from the spiritual center of the architecture. The "education wing" concept itself was of concern to some critics. This type of plan, they argued, "can cause young people and older ones as well, to think of education as divorced from the main life and principal activity of the church. Young people especially begin to think of 'their place' as opposed to adult areas" (Morse 1969: 115–16). The workaday, detached, institutional character of some of these education structures was another concern. "What view of the church does a child have," questioned one church leader,

> if he is dropped off at the parking lot and makes his way on a campus plan to a rabbit hutch cubicle in a hallway where he meets three other children and a well-meaning teacher; talks and reads and sings with them; turns out and follows the map to the parking lot?
>
> (Marty 1963: 13)

By advocating educational spaces that were flexible and open, and by resisting the idea that architecture would rigidly direct religious practice, church leaders handed architects a difficult task: convey a religious ethos and create spaces of transformation, but in architecture that "fits in" with the architectural idiom of the day and avoids historical references. It is no wonder that architects resorted to thinking along the lines of new public school buildings, collections of classrooms intended to sort and organize learners. In many cases, practical function seems to have eclipsed spiritual function. Religious leaders were of course aware that Sunday school had to be something more than a facsimile of weekday public school. Some educators suggested that Christian art and symbol would distinguish these spaces, promoting, for example, the "use of appropriate symbols in corridors and on entrances" (Blankenship 1962: 59). Others advocated displaying evidence of God's handiwork in the form of plants or large open windows. But it was more often the spirit of the place and the skills of the teachers, rather than any distinctive material difference, that was emphasized:

How can Christian education building help create a climate of expectancy of the Holy Spirit? Not by the use of children's chapels or stained glass windows in mysteriously darkened rooms. If the building facilitates a creative program, the teachers and learners can establish the climate of freedom and openness.

(ibid.: 60)

Despite the rhetoric of individuality and exploration, these buildings still speak of institutional conformity. In large part, this is because it was job of the furnishings, the art, and above all the teachers to make distinctions and recognize difference. The building fabric rarely gives clues that the structures were intended for religious purposes. Worship "centers," if they did exist in individual classrooms, were temporary and undistinguished. And, although a desire to make a church "homelike," appears throughout much of the rhetoric, no child could miss the point that these were not homes, but schools. In fact, material distinctions were made even more blurry by the fact that the same rhetoric of comfort and character formation was applied to public schools, with similar promotion of "homey" features like carpets and plants. Without distinctive markers, how would children know that these spaces were *not* schools, and that the activities within called for a response to "the transforming influence of the person of Jesus Christ?" "The unimaginative sterility of most of the Sunday School rooms in our new educational wings," lamented Rev. Hugo Leinberger, the former chaplain of Park Forest, "make them very poor copies of the public schools. Is it any wonder that many of the children who attend such classes regularly hardly realize that they have been to church?" (Leinberger 1969: 86).

By relying on secular examples, the buildings might also have communicated unintended messages. Although they do not embody the rigid hierarchical discipline of former, monumental Sunday school buildings, they nonetheless display an order that allowed for the efficient management of hundreds and even thousands of lively young people within the church setting. The structures communicated order not only by their separation of children by grade, but in the sequence of classrooms within the building. For instance, the movement of rooms in the Park Forest Baptist Church building (see Figure 10.5) starts on the second floor with nursery classroom, progresses down the hall through the age groups until moving to the lower story for the teen rooms (echoing the basement "recreation rooms" of many houses of the period). Teen areas were most frequently placed far away from sanctuaries—not the best message, perhaps, if congregations wanted to integrate these rising adults into full participation in the church. In the ordering of spaces, many of these buildings do, as some critics warned, suggest a progression from nursery to primary to high school and on out of the building; one graduated, as it were, from Christian education and church at the same time.

These criticisms suggest why the structures look and feel so bland today: practical imperatives, combined with a lack of critical thought by building committees and architects, compromised vision for the sake of expediency. It was not that builders consciously exchanged a message of transformation and openness for institutional conformity. That might have been the result, but it was not the intention. And it must not be forgotten that other, positive meanings and associations certainly obtained, based on personal or community history and perhaps bearing little relation to the material details of the building at hand. As anyone knows who has moved into a dreary, empty apartment, with a few weeks and some personal touches, the place does, indeed, become "home." Charles Sang, a charter member of Park Forest's Baptist Church, echoes the experience of many when he says that "our life was more or less built around the church" (Sang 2008). Sang speaks fondly of the church's education building, despite the fact that its cheap construction led to maintenance issues from day one; the building's meaning came not from its material fabric as much as the role it played in the daily life of Sang's family. It is also clear from my conversations with former church members, and this is not surprising, that having played a part in a construction project makes one, on the whole, more enduringly sympathetic to the outcome; though children did not necessarily share this fondness for the buildings. One can imagine a tension between several forces in the experiences of those whose religious identities were being formed and practiced in these structures: a comfort level bred by familiarity and positive affective associations with the practices of a church community, a rhetoric of inclusion and openness, yet combined with a building that suggested conformity, ordinariness, and a progression through an educational system.

I am often struck by simple details when I walk through these buildings, such as small, gray bathroom tile that reminds me of the restrooms in my own elementary school, or linoleum floors that are nothing if not common institutional fare. Modern after the fashion of public schools, no longer monumental, and often cheaply built and unimaginatively designed—what were the lessons taught by these buildings? Did they represent the apotheosis of the Sunday school, or rather its dissolution into the ordinary? Scholars of American religion chart a decline in church affiliation that began with the adult children of the postwar generation. The reasons for that decline are numerous and complex, but it would be indeed ironic if these educational structures played some role in the exodus from the church, when the intention of their builders was so clearly to draw young people into permanent fellowship.

Notes

1   Annual conferences were an important venue for opening conversation between architects, church leaders, and interested lay people, and included not just panel discussions but church tours and juried exhibitions of religious architecture and

art. In general, the conferences supported a panel or two on issues of Christian education. The 1959 Los Angeles conference, on the theme of "Building for Christian Community" was unusually focused on this topic. The detailed, printed reports of these conferences have been a major, comprehensive, ecumenical source for this research.

2 Public school release time for religious education was a real possibility and certainly on the minds of church builders as they envisioned the tasks that education buildings would have to perform. A Supreme Court ruling in 1948 declared unconstitutional the practice of released time classes held in the public schools. Another Supreme Court decision in 1952 made it legal to hold such programs off school property (logically, in church buildings). Although the practice still exists in some more remote corners of the US, it never became common practice and church education buildings were rarely used for this purpose. On the other hand, Kindergarten classes often began in the churches before becoming a standard part of the public schools (Lynn and Wright 1980: 4).

3 Another reason for the basement and low profile was to avoid visual competition with the elder Saarinen's sanctuary building.

11

Materializing ancestor spirits
Name tablets, portraits, and tombs in Korea

Insoo Cho

Shrine: a place where name tablets dwell
Portrait: sacred effigy of an ancestor
Tomb: an eternal place for ancestor spirits
Conclusion

Confucianism values self-cultivation through art as a method for becoming a revered sage. Confucian scholars over the ages have contemplated nature and pursued the state in which the self unites with the external world. They developed an aesthetic view of art that became the fundamental philosophy for the creation and appreciation of art works and promoted distinctive arts such as calligraphy and literati paintings in East Asia (Cahill 1960). Confucian visual culture, however, includes not only art works categorized as fine art but also various objects used in daily life. It is the world of functional, ritual, and material things.

The rules and rituals emphasized in Confucianism are revealed visually as they are embedded in the forms, decorations, and uses of various objects ranging from architectural structures to bronze vessels. Compared to practical goods used in everyday life, ceremonial objects are distinguished in terms of material, size, shape, and function, and possess special symbolic meanings. During the pre-modern period, these ritual objects were not solely for aesthetic appreciation like ordinary art works. On the contrary, things that were neither useful nor fine art often occupied an important position in rituals and recalled the powerful presence of Confucian ethics. However, this does not mean that Confucian material culture merely reflected ritual protocols. Things forming visual or material culture represent Confucian beliefs concretely and, at the same time, lead them to be practiced in a proper way. The important place that material objects occupied in the diverse cultures of Confucian scholars is due to the many ways in which Confucian scholars utilized them in performing the Confucian rites.

While studying portraits in the Joseon Dynasty (1392–1910) in Korea, I took note of their ritual functions and attempted to reinterpret them from the viewpoint of material culture (Cho 2007). In addition, as portraits are examined in connection to funerals and ancestor worship, tombs as artificial monuments also need to be investigated in tandem with funerary and devotional practices. However, what were valued most in Confucian ancestor rites were neither portraits nor tombs. Rather, name tablets, which are merely small pieces of wood (Figure 11.1), were most highly esteemed. Until now, portraits have been studied as painting in art history, and tombs have been covered in archaeology or anthropology. Name tablets have been discussed by ethnographers once in a while. However, the three things are closely interrelated with one another in Confucian ancestral worship and were often used together in specific places like shrines. As the three objects embody the social relation between the living and the dead through different material forms and media, they need to be considered in connection to one another. It is difficult to understand the rich and multi-faceted meaning and function of portraits, tombs, and name tablets through traditional art historical approaches. Consequently, it is helpful to see them from the common ground of material culture.

It is still uncertain whether material culture study and art history are interchangeable with each other (Prown 1982; Westermann 2005). What is obvious is that traditional art history does not overlap much with material culture study.

Figure 11.1 Name tablet of Choe Ikhyeon in Modeok Shrine, twentieth century

Source: Photo by author.

Material culture study, which stands in close relation to anthropology, criticizes the narrow definition of art and the interpretive practice of keeping an "aesthetic" distance (see Morgan, Introduction in this volume). Art history has tended to focus on art itself rather than on human society. This is related to the tradition of Kantian aesthetics that emphasizes contemplative beauty and aesthetic autonomy characterized by disinterest. However, material culture study abandons Kantian aesthetics. It believes that the unequal dichotomy of mind and matter should be overcome and that the creation of art should not be separated from the consumption of art (Miller 1987). For this reason, when art is concerned in material culture study, it cannot help being criticized by the definition of art coined by other disciplines, namely art history and aesthetics. What is discussed in material culture study is not fine art in terms of the stance of traditional art history. To solve the difficulty, Alfred Gell asserted that anything can be regarded as art from the anthropological viewpoint (Gell 1998: 1–11). Paradoxically, he is saying that it is wrong to conclude definitely what art is. A thing arouses various responses in different cultural areas. Accordingly, in order to perceive art works correctly, which are a kind of thing, we should disregard the aesthetics of romantic and transcendental indifference advocated by Kant, and pay attention to actual responses to art works. Gell maintains that anthropology of art is "not being anthropological enough," because it is not free from the attitude of the aesthetic approach to art (Rampley 2005: 529). According to him, the concept of art defined from the viewpoint of Western modern aesthetics has been applied one-sidedly and wrongly to other cultures. This is a limitation inherent in anthropology. That is, anthropology, which is a byproduct of military colonization and economic expansionism, made the mistake of defining central and marginal areas and regarding non-Western and pre-modern arts as primitive and uncivilized from the beginning. A good example is that Western art works are displayed in art museums but non-Western ones are often exhibited in ethnographic or folk art museums (Mrazek and Pitelka 2007). When objects are considered in the social and cultural contexts in which they were produced, cultural artifacts exhibit their own unique value. Recognizing that each culture has self-consistent and distinctive patterns, we are able to avoid the mistake of asserting that a particular culture is superior to others.

The modern Western view of art, which has driven the study of art history, has prized contemplative beauty over all other forms of visual experience, resulting in the exclusion of rival emotional responses such as fear, awe, attachment, anxiety, rage, and indignation. However, portraits used in ancestral worship in East Asia emphasized more the expression of personality than the resemblance to the figure. Rather than forms such as line, color, and composition, the character of the sitter expressed by such formal elements are more important. The main point was to describe the sitter's disposition on the premise of the fictitiousness of reproduction. Accordingly, it is difficult to understand properly the nature of such portraits in art history based on Western modern aesthetics. If art history assumes the viewpoint of material culture study, it may be able to expand its domain easily to common material culture by comprehending various things including craftworks. With this widened perspective, tombs and name tablets can be equally treated together with portrait images. This is giving priority to outward images and things rather than emphasizing inner nature specific to each object as Kant did. For example, when religious art works are used by a worshipper, relief from the worshipper's agony supersedes aesthetic contemplation. At the same time, it is important to give attention to visuality and materiality rather than reading what one already knows into images or things, as historians often do. In this sense, portraits, name tablets, and tombs used in ancestral worship were considered important objects by means of which descendants communicated with ancestors and expressed their filial piety.

Shrine: a place where name tablets dwell

Confucianism regarded filial piety as the foundation of all virtues and the principle ruling the world. It was filial piety that connected dead ancestors and living descendants. Ancestors and parents were to be rewarded for giving of life to their descendants, and the fulfillment of this duty sustained the family. Parental love was to be repaid wholly not only during this lifetime but also after death, and in this sense it was the common duty for all human beings from king to commoners to establish a shrine and to enshrine their ancestors in the form of name tablets or portraits.

Ancestor worship has been one of the most important cultural elements in Korea and exhibits multiple levels of meanings, including religious, cultural, and political. The religious and political aspects did not significantly change during the Joseon Dynasty. The issue of ancestor worship takes on an interesting complexity when put in the context of material culture since ancestor rites and material objects are deeply entwined. Various objects were created in connection to ancestral worship and memorial service, and the commitment of filial piety was expressed effectively through such objects. The architecture of the house as the place of daily life also reflects an order based on filial piety. The shrine as a ritual space was included within the residential space so that ancestors and descendants coexisted spiritually (Kim 2007: 188–91). Confucianism taught that when one dies, the soul ascends to heaven and the body returns to the ground. Family members built a shrine for the ancestor's spirit, and a tomb for the body. In the shrine—an architectural space for ancestral worship—were enshrined name tablets or portraits, which were regarded as representations of the spirits of the dead. Memorial services were conducted there. The shrine was the most sacred place in houses and their spiritual center. It ritualized the space of daily by observing regular services.

Neither tomb nor shrine occupied significant space in the Goryeo Dynasty (918–1392), which followed the Buddhist rule of the funeral. But the

Confucian scholars who founded the Joseon Dynasty made efforts to spread Confucian-style funeral practices and forcefully promoted the establishment of the shrine as a governmental policy. In upper-class homes, the shrine was a sacred place banning access without permission, so it was usually positioned in the deepest, northeastern part of the grounds, furthest from the gate (Figure 11.2). Although it was in the rear side of the house, it was sometimes erected on a higher ground or was fenced and gated. Accordingly, its position reveals hierarchically the private and sacred nature of the shrine (ibid.: 289–90). The shrine, in which memorial services were held, was a place upon which ancestral spirits descended. Thus, the shrine and its interior were decorated simply in order to arouse reverence in those participating in the memorial service. A name tablet was seated on a chair, and the sacrificial table was placed in front of it. These pieces of furniture were austere in shape and decorated minimally, maintaining the natural color of wood unpainted or painted in black.

A shrine was a sacred and solemn closed space, even producing a mystical atmosphere. It was sequestered from people's approach, and accessible only to the select few. Paradoxically, the isolation and secrecy strengthened the symbolism and solemnity of the shrine. Confucian elites in the Joseon Dynasty cherished reverence and memory in their daily life by setting up a shrine in their homes for their deceased ancestors.

From ancient times, Confucian doctrines have insisted on the enshrinement of a name tablet, a mortuary marker made of wood, for ancestor worship. With a deceased person's name on it, such a tablet is a virtual body representing the

Figure 11.2 Modeok shrine for Choe Ikhyeon (1833–1906), Cheongyang, early twentieth century

Source: Photo by author.

spirit of a deceased ancestor who left his body. In ancient times, a grandson substituting for the grandfather was seated on the altar in memorial services. The practice was to avoid the emptiness and desolation felt from the absence of the deceased. This custom gradually changed, and a name tablet inscribed with the dead person's official title and name came to be used instead. A name tablet is completed by writing the name of the dead on a prepared wood plate immediately following the burial ceremony at the tomb site. In so doing, the spirit of the dead was transmitted from the body to the tablet. As the deceased was usually believed to reach the status of an ancestor god after the burial, the tablet was respected as an embodiment of the spirit. Therefore, people deified it in a shrine and paid their respects every morning and night, and held memorial services and reported important domestic matters to the name tablet/ancestor.

Name tablets were always considered the most important objects in the house. They were kept in the shrine for services of worship to family ancestors on the anniversary of their deaths and seasonal occasions. Since at least the sixteenth century, the use of name tablets has been the orthodox way to serve ancestor spirits in Korea. An ancestor tablet was attended for four generations, or about one hundred years. The newly made tablet of the deceased parent was put together with previous ancestors' name tablets in the shrine. The name tablets of ancestors who had passed five generations were buried in the ground near the shrine or beside their tombs. The spirits of ancestors were not believed to exist eternally, but to disappear after a period of time. In many ancestor shrines for Confucian scholars, instead of life-size pictorial images, small wooden tablets became the focal point of ancestor worship. There was no iconic image, no realistic representation of the human figure, and no colorful picture, but only a simple and humble tablet with several characters. Confucian classics and ritual manuals mention name tablets frequently, and record detailed illustrations and specifications for their manufacture (Choi 2001). According to *Five Rites of State*, a name tablet is made of chestnut wood, around 24 cm high, 6 cm wide and 2.4 cm thick, cut with the head round. Name tablets were sometimes covered with *do* made of silk, and kept in a wooden box called *judok*. If a family could not afford to build a shrine, a small tablet cabinet was stored in a room. The small furniture for containing name tablets was sometimes shaped like a miniature shrine. Even in commoners' humble houses, name tablets were preserved in the corner of a room and used for ancestor worship. Lower classes often used disposable paper tablets in simplified services. As a result, various ways of enshrining were developed out of a pious mindset toward name tablets.

In terms of Confucian doctrines, ancestor worship with name tablets was ritually correct. Although a name tablet is a small wooden piece, it is a sacred item incorporating an ancestor's spirit. Name tablets were treated like living beings, being seated on a chair and offered food and drink. This suggests that the name tablet was essential to ancestral worship. Thus, it was to be handled and kept most carefully in the home. When the house was evacuated for a fire or a war, the name tablets were removed first and, if the tablets needed to be discarded inevitably, they were to be buried in the ground. Those who had protected the name tablet safely in a time of trouble, were praised and rewarded. Those who failed to secure the tablets could not escape reproach.

The importance of name tablets in ancestral worship is demonstrated well by the case of Yun Jichung (1759–1792) in the late Joseon period. This Confucian scholar converted to Christianity and, obeying the Pope's authority and the bishop's order to prohibit memorial services for ancestor worship, he burned his parents' name tablets and abolished memorial services according to his new religious belief (Jeong 1996). It was a grave misdeed that challenged Confucianism as the governing ideology of the state and social ethics. In the end, Yun Jichung was convicted of a wicked crime, an act "as bad as patricide," and was executed under the condemnation, "He should not be allowed to live between heaven and earth even a day" (ibid.: 145). Is it because he neglected the tremendous materiality of a name tablet or because he knew it too well?

It is clear that interest in name tablets as *objets d'art* was not tolerated from the beginning because they were sacred things. The ritual manuals specified the material, size, and format to be followed in the production of tablets, and it was unthinkable to make any changes. Creativity or innovation was not an option. Furthermore, names of tablet makers were not disclosed, and the quality of tablets was never discussed. Among several name tablets for Yi Yi (1536–1584), the celebrated scholar enshrined in more than twenty shrines in various private schools, no distinction was made between originals and replicas. As a result, it is hard to find an instance in which name tablets were collected and displayed as beautiful artworks or profitable commodities like other artifacts. Only recently have they begun to be exhibited in ethnographic museums. Until now, discourses on name tablets have been conducted in a religious context rather than artistic, and their evidence as material culture has not been spotlighted.

Buddhism lost its prestigious status and declined in Korea in the fifteenth century. However, it became much more popular and even secularized during the Joseon dynasty. Interestingly, the Confucian idea of name tablets influenced Buddhist commemoration practice. Name tablets were originally used in Confucianism, but later on they were widely adopted by Buddhism. The Confucian custom of ancestor worship was mixed with Buddhist practice. In order to save the souls of dead ancestors and guide them to paradise, descendants offered name tablets in Buddhist monasteries (Figure 11.3). The Ghost festival was the most popular practice related to filial piety. In order to save relatives who became hungry ghosts in hell, people donated to the festival by offering food and prepared paper tablets. These indicate the amalgamation of the Buddhist idea of hell and Confucian filial piety.

Figure 11.3 Installation of paper tablets in Bongjeong Buddhist temple, Andong

Source: Photo by author.

Portrait: sacred effigy of an ancestor

The portrait has been widely used in the history of art for purposes of commemoration and edification, but in Confucian ancestral worship its ritual function has been given priority.[1] In order to understand the unique character of East Asian portraits, we need to know how they were connected to memorial services associated with Confucian ancestral worship. According to Confucian beliefs, when a dead person was buried, the spirit moved to a name tablet. With the spread of the Buddhist custom of making human images for religious worship, however, ancestor portrait sculptures and paintings were introduced in East Asia. Because of their strong impression, portraits, which were more concrete and realistic than abstract and imaginative name tablets, could play an important role in memorial services for ancestors. As people recognized the effectiveness of more visually compelling image as an object of worshipping, portraits often replaced name tablets and enshrined at shrines.

In China, the custom of hanging portraits in the shrine spread in the Tang Dynasty (618–907) under the influence of Buddhism and Taoism that made many statues and offered services to them (Omura 1931: 612–13). There are records showing that portraits were drawn before the introduction of Buddhism and the walls of an ancient tomb were decorated with the tomb occupant's portrait, yet they were not for worshiping but more for illustrating the afterlife of the deceased. After sealing tombs, these pictures disappeared from the sight of descendants. Contrary to this earlier and indigenous custom, iconic portraits created as visual representations of transcendental beings under the influence of Buddhist art mediated between the living and the dead in a more powerful and direct way in grandiose and pious rituals.

In Confucian classics, however, it is uncertain whether portraits could be used instead of name tablets. In China, Song Dynasty scholars Sima Guang (1019–1086) and Cheng Yi (1033–1107) discussed the irrelevance of using portraits in ancestor worship (Sima 1725: chap. 5; Zhu 1725: chap. 22). Sima Guang admitted the use of portraits partially in consideration of the extant custom of enshrining portraits, although it was contrary to the Confucian doctrine. Cheong Yi mentioned the inappropriateness of the use of portraits in funerals, saying, "It is not the person if even a strand of hair is different from the deceased" (Zhu 1725: chap. 22–14b, 15a). Based on these commentaries, the use of portraits in funerals and memorial services was sometimes criticized by Confucian scholars (Sommer 1994).

Confucian elites in the Joseon Dynasty were also well aware of this problem. In the beginning of the dynasty, kings' and their queens' portraits were kept in shrines, but with the deeper understanding of Confucianism, many royal portrait halls that originated in Buddhist funerary custom were abolished, or transformed into Confucian-style shrines with name tablets. Yet with the settlement of Confucianism and the spread of the custom enshrining name tablets, ironically the trend of using portraits in ancestral worship revived. The premise of this revival was that portraits could be allowed only as secondary objects to tablets. During the Joseon Dynasty a structure called *Yeongdang,* or portrait hall, was even built for the purpose of enshrining portraits. During their lifetime, Confucian elites reflected on themselves through observing their own portraits, and after they passed away, their portraits were enshrined so that their descendants might learn their virtue. In this way, a ritual function was added to portraits.

Because it was extremely important to draw a figure with verisimilitude, portraits in the Joseon Dynasty were almost hyperrealistic (Figure 11.4). Furthermore, based on the painting theory that not only outward appearance but also the inner spirit should be conveyed, the face of a self-disciplined scholar was reproduced with a pale but rigid look. Although few of Confucian scholars drew their own self-portraits, they were involved actively in the process of portrait painting by supervising professional painters.

In the portraits of Confucian scholars during the Joseon Dynasty, the figure is usually seated in a cap and official uniform and with hands concealed in the sleeves. Portraits described the figure's face with meticulous refinement, but simplified the body and background. The background was treated as an empty space and the floor covered with a carpet. In other words, figures were portrayed in a highly typical form with difference only in their face. Clearly distinguished from Western portraits exhibiting diverse styles since the Renaissance, East Asian portraits were patterned in a similar style. In a Western portrait, the figure's natural pose might be expressed realistically and the background filled with various props related to the person's profession or social station. By contrast, East Asian portraits consistently rely on a stiff pose and empty background.

Figure 11.4 Chae Yongsin, Portrait of Choe Ikhyeon,
ink and color on silk, 1909, Modeok Shrine

Source: Photo by author.

This difference is closely related to the visual culture of ancestral worship in Confucianism. While Western portraits capture scenes of daily life and are exhibited in open places, East Asian portraits, portrayed with the solemnity of a deity, are displayed in the limited access of shrines. Thus, it is rare to pay attention to the figure's secular look or painting technique as in Western portraits. Accordingly, an ancestral portrait was an object of private reverence and worship rather than an occasion for public viewing, appreciation, and enjoyment. Although realism and appropriate style were important in painting an ancestor's portrait, once it was finished, the portrait was not meant to be seen but to be worshipped. When it left the painter's hand and was installed in a shrine, the portrait became the very dignity of the ancestor. The portrait ascended from the material to the cerebral, and then to the spiritual by the worshippers was not so much a symbol as a sacred relic (Freedberg 1989: 161–81). An ancestor portrait mediates the dead person's absence and his viewer's presence. A portrait, which resembles the almost exact look of the figure during lifetime, incorporates the soul of the person in the medium of a painting on a hanging scroll, which replaces the lost body. Therefore, an ancestor portrait is a more sacred thing than a work of art. Because the portrait holds the soul of the actual person, because it is the ancestor himself who returns the viewer's gaze, the attitude of viewers toward the image is quite different from their attitude toward works of art. Clearly, there in no case is a figure made in the form of painting or sculpture to be confused with the real person. But an ancestor portrait was considered to host a spiritual power, and was treated with deference toward and faith in that power. Sometimes, portraits were rejected as idol worship, and iconoclasm was practiced repeatedly. Portrait images went through many trials such as the destruction of Confucius' portrait sculptures and the burning of traitors' portraits. These incidents usually came from the fear of transcendental or divinity believed to dwell mystically in the portraits. The ritual meaning of portraits has been lost today beneath the exercise of totally different visual practices. Displayed and exposed nakedly under bright spotlights in a tidy exhibition hall, portraits are separated from the ritual context and deprived of their mystical aura. They are counted in the same category as landscape paintings or flower-bird paintings and exposed to the indifferent viewer's eye.

In light of the history of iconoclasm committed both against and by Confucians, what may be said regarding the relation between name tablets, whose destruction took Yun Jichung's life, and portraits, which were destroyed by Confucian authorities? The art historian Hans Belting has understood art works by dividing them into image, body, and medium (Belting 2005). In portraits, the medium of painting is like an artificial body, and in the situation that the body composed of flesh and blood no longer exists, the medium is a dwelling place of an image like the body. The extinct body is replaced by the virtual body of a painting or sculpture, and the image becomes the new body. In ancient arts, we can see that portrait sculpture is created using the skull, and a statue is made of the bones. Through the visible object, image, body and medium cross the boundary of death. In addition, the image is activated by eyes responding to the object. People are able to distinguish between the extinct body and its medium. As shown by masks, although the limitation of the medium is obvious, people see the portrait based on the implicit agreement that the image is more important than the medium. Accordingly, attachment to resemblance and insisting "Even a strand of hair should not be different" seems to emphasize the ceremonial use of portraits but, at the same time, it considers the formal aspect of painting. If we accept Belting's viewpoint, portraits and name tablets mediate the deceased in different ways using image and text, respectively. That is, instead of the extinct body, they incorporate the image in the media of a hanging scroll and a wooden tablet by means of image and text. The two sometimes confront each other exclusively, but sometimes fuse supplementarily to one another.

In memorial services, both portraits and spirit tablets are often enshrined together. In such cases, we may raise the question of whether the different media of planar paintings and three-dimensional tablets suggest the same image or different, and whether an image can be represented by multiple media like self-replication. The complex relation between name tablets and portraits can be examined in many other cases. The situation has changed since photography was introduced to make portrait images in the early twentieth century. Now people can easily have a photographic portrait at a cheap price. Even Confucian scholars prefer photographs to name tablets. Relying on computer technology, people can easily make a name tablet. In order to make it simple and efficient, descendants can put in names and design ancestor name tablets using computer software. Surprisingly, computer technology has already combined portraits and tablets by attaching an image to a name tablet. With the introduction of photography and computer technologies, images in the two different media are often juxtaposed with each other for funeral and ritual functions. Ancestor portraits and name tablets have finally been conflated and used together, or have become interchangeable. The conflict between portraits and tablets is resolved in the new visual culture of the computer-generated photo tablet. The relation between portraits and name tablets continues to change.

Tomb: an eternal place for ancestor spirits

According to Confucian ancestral worship, a dead person's spirit dwells in the name tablet, and his body is buried in the tomb. As discussed above, a name tablet is handled with much care but is enshrined only temporarily. On the other hand, a tomb, if protected properly, is a place that preserves the ancestor's body permanently. People believed that if a service were offered to the tomb, the spirit would descend upon it. In the long run, the center of ancestral worship may be the tomb keeping the body rather than the shrine with the name tablet. In a sense, the tomb of a parent or family member who died recently may arouse filial piety more than the shrine keeping the simple name tablets of remote unknown ancestors. The careful maintenance of and frequent visit to the tomb were not only ceremonial acts but also behavior motivated by personal emotion. Furthermore, in regard to memorial service, the tomb is the dead person's resting place and, at the same time, a center of social activities where many people gather and conduct memorial services periodically.

A tomb in the Joseon Dynasty differed in size according to the person's social status. It took the form of a hemispheric mound of earth under which the coffin was buried (Figure 11.5). Around the tomb were erected various stone statues and accessory buildings. In this way, the shape of a tomb was simple in appearance but an artificial mound clearly distinguished itself from the surrounding natural environment. What was important was the buried body in the tomb, which would have an eternal rest without being forgotten. The tomb of a great figure who had brought honor to his family became a sacred place, a pilgrimage site for descendants, and a permanent anchor for the honor of memory to be display by generations of descendants. To this end, the memory was materialized by the addition of stone objects.

Figure 11.5 Choe Ikhyeon's tomb, re-buried 1910, Yesan

Source: Photo by author.

In the tombs of Confucian elites during the Joseon Dynasty, various stone objects were deployed to visualize the dead person's social status. The tomb of a respectable and influential figure contained funerary objects together with the body, and a tomb stele inscribed with brief records of the deceased was erected beside the mound. In front of the stele was placed a rectangular stone table, which was regarded as a site for the soul to loiter around and for the descendants to offer sacrifices in memorial services. In some space ahead of the table, stone lanterns were erected to light up the graveyard. A pair of stone pillars and a pair of statues were located on the left and right sides. The pillars made the tomb recognizable from a long distance, and the statues, depicting civil and military officials, watch over the tomb.

The erection of statues at the tomb is a venerable tradition dating to ancient times. In Korea, stone images were built around tombs from the Unified Shilla period (668–935). During the Joseon Dynasty many civil and official statues were set up. *Five Rites of the State,* compiled in the early Joseon period, specifies the size of stone objects for royal tombs. According to the specification, civil official statues were around 250 cm high and military official statues around 270 cm high. Statues of officials during the Joseon Dynasty usually have a round and flat face and stand straight on their feet in a stiff posture with somewhat shrunken shoulders and slightly bent waist. The heavy feeling of rock is unmistakable, and organic features of the body

Figure 11.6 Royal tomb of King Myeongjong and Queen Insun
(Gangneung), late sixteenth century, Seoul

Source: Photo by author.

are not emphasized (Figure 11.6). The whole body, except the head and the hands, are covered with thick clothes, and this hides the natural bodyline and gives a blunt feeling to the figure like a square pillar. Body proportion is also unrealistic with a large head and hands and short legs. After all, they are stone objects necessary at the tomb as a space of a dead person, creating a solemn and pious atmosphere, rather than showing a daily scene through the realistic portrayal of the beauty of the human body. Stone objects represented by official statues suggest that the man buried in the tomb had been in a high position or had a noble spirit. In addition, they show the descendants' commendable filial piety who paid the heavy expense of the stone objects. Contrary to a plain earth mound, large stone objects laboriously made from hard granite commemorate the dead person permanently.

In their original religious, ceremonial, and social contexts, stone objects at tombs are not just decorative and static formal objects. They maintain social order by emphasizing rituals and norms through visible objects, and the material of stone embodies stability and eternity. Consequently, these formal objects refresh collective memory among the corresponding group members, and induce them to perceive the immortality and durability of traditions and customs, and to accept them as necessities.

Conclusion

According to Confucian teachings, when we observe rules and etiquette in treating people and things in the world, we have strength to maintain the order and harmony of society. Confucian scholars led a smooth and peaceful life through observing decorum in even small matters. In such a life, various objects were created, courteous human relations were defined, and unique Confucian visual and material culture was cultivated. Among Confucian ideologies, ancestral worship was most important, and portraits and name tablets for worship were regarded as extremely precious. After all, portrait, name tablet, and tomb mediated the same cultural principle in different forms and media in the process of ancestral worship. In addition, it is noteworthy that all the three are material objects.

Interpreted from the viewpoint of traditional art history alone, we cannot understand the rich, multilayered, and fluid nature of portraits, name tablets, and tombs. Since they are different material images and media representing the social relation between the dead and the living, when the three are considered in connection to one another, we may be able to change prevailing ideas about art. Various phenomena surrounding portraits, name tablets and tombs do not originate just from the aesthetic properties of art works. In order to understand them, we need to regard them as things rather than as aesthetic objects. In other words, we may approach them from the viewpoint of anthropology and material culture. Proceeding in this fashion, we may expect to achieve a fuller understanding of ritual objects related to funerals, of the nature of things used in commemoration, and of the human relations mediated by cultural and religious performances using such objects.

Note

1 For the ritual function of Chinese portraits, see Vinograd (1992); Hornby (2000); and Siggstedt (1991).

Part V

PERFORMANCE

12

Clothing as embodied experience of belief

Anna-Karina Hermkens

Clothing, belief, and performance
"Maisin is tapa"
Tapacloth, ancestors, and women
Tapacloth and the containment of women's bodies
Mourning rituals: removing the cloth/clothing the body
Marking the end of mourning: emergence
Clothing and the embodied performance of belief

Clothing, belief, and performance

All over the world, clothing, which often involves the decoration of the entire body—wrapping it in cloth, but also oiling, painting and decorating it with animal furs, flowers, feathers, necklaces and other objects, tattoos, and piercings—is intimately intertwined with the spiritual and the social. According to Jane Schneider, the spiritual properties of cloth and clothing "render these materials ideal media for connecting humans with the world of spirits and divinities, and with one another" (Schneider 2006: 204). The property of cloth to mediate ancestral and spiritual forces is known in many places. As eloquently explored by Gillian Feeley-Harnik (1989) for Madagascar, cloth connects the living with the ancestors and with spirits. While ancestors are wrapped in cloth, spirits are clothed or clothe themselves, thereby making them speak. Elisha Renne (1991) shows that among the Bunu people in Africa, white cloth is crucial in mediating relations between humans and spirits. It protects people against illnesses and evil spirits, while women might also attract spirits by wearing a set of white cloths. In some instances, for example among the Dayak in Kalimantan, cloth itself serves as a medium for facilitating such connection, enabling spirits to enter the human world via strings of cloth. In other instances, human mediums wear particular types of clothing (such as Marian blue dresses) in order to facilitate communication with ancestors, spirits, or saints like Mary. Moreover, cloth and clothing are important items in life-cycle rituals, guiding people from birth to death through means of wrapping, clothing and enshrouding (Schneider 2006: 204). In these performances, cloth and clothing have the ability to intensify social relations (ibid.), but also on global levels, cloth mediates social relations (Niessen and Brydon 1998: xi). As clothing is intertwined with gender, social, and ethnic identity (Barnes and Eicher 1992; Eicher 1995; Hendrickson 1995; Hermkens 2005), it actually gives material form to social categories and hierarchies (Weiner 1989; Keane 2006: 198).

This chapter elaborates on the spiritual and social properties of cloth that come together in daily and ritual performances. It reveals how cloth engages beliefs about the creation of the world and of humanity, including social relations between people. Such beliefs, combined in the term cosmology, tend to be classified as superstitious, or as being opposed to religion and or science. However, cosmologies are actually forms of knowledge that encompass both religion and science (Barth 1990; Herzfeld 2001: 192).

Often, cosmologies are studied by focusing on myths and rituals, but they are also embodied in and mediated through things like cloth. In particular, it is shown that cloth not only signifies or communicates cosmologies, but actually embodies belief as something that a person does or performs as the body that cloth bestows. Belief is not simply a set of ideas, but the performance of body practices. Clothing materializes values, ideas, relationships, and identities that are internalized and mediated both within and on the surface of the body. For example, among indigenous groups in Latin America, weaving has specific cosmological associations and is related to notions about reproduction, childbirth, and creation, which are important in defining womanhood (Schneider 1987: 413; Hendrickson 1995). Similar associations can be found in the Pacific (Teilhet 1983; Colchester 2003: 9; Young Leslie and Addo 2007: 19). These examples show that cosmology and cloth are closely related, and that clothing is more than a mere symbol that touches the outer skin. The case study of this chapter concerns the Maisin people of Papua New Guinea. Their manufacturing, and the wearing of particular types of cloth, reveal cosmological beliefs about creation, and the power of clothing to transform the individual and the social body as they embody or mediate the reproduction and orderings of social relations.

The properties of cloth and clothing that embody belief are activated and expanded by performance. The performance of cloth and the clothed body brings about an experiential dimension to both viewer and wearer (Hansen 2004: 373). For example, in Papua New Guinea, Kaluli ceremonial dancers clothed with paint, feathers, ornaments, cloth and leafs, evoke emotional outbursts from their hosts. The dancers transcend time and place as they address in dances and songs their hosts' deceased relatives and land. In revenge for experiencing grief, the hosts burn the dancers' shoulders. By means of their clothing, the dancers themselves have transformed from ordinary men into withdrawn figures of splendor, beauty and pathos (Schieffelin 1976: 21–25). Among the Maisin, such experiential dimensions to both viewer and wearer come to the fore in life-cycle rituals and church festivals. In the context of the latter, religiosity, ancestral descent, gender and sexuality are expressed through people's clothing (Hermkens 2007a). At church festivals, male and female dancers dressed in their traditional clan regalia communicate their affiliation with and dedication to the Anglican Church. At the same time, the dancers not only enact their clan ancestors at the time of creation, they become the ancestors through the particular clothing they wear. Moreover, the ways male and female bodies move and interact reveal that notions of gender behavior, aesthetics and sexuality are equally expressed and embodied (ibid.). These examples show how mystery, religiosity, spiritual motivation, emotions—such as anger, grief, joy—and sensuality are integral to clothing (Schneider 2006: 205).

While on the one hand clothing is so malleable that it can be shaped to construct appearance and transform identity, one's lived experience with cloth and clothing is also dependent upon how others evaluate the performance of the clothed body (Hansen 2004: 373). In fact, clothing infuses the human body with meaning and determines its behavior, often beyond personal preference. It may be controlled by others, or, as Bolton (2003: 122) argues for clothing in Vanuatu, by "systems of rights and privileges and by ritual proscribtions of various kinds." Moreover, clothing may not only change our skin and transform our physiology, it may actually define it by controlling our body movements. In these cases, the body is shaped by cultural order, interweaving cloth, cosmology and physiology in, what David Morgan coins in his Introduction to this volume, "an embodied experience of belief." In the next sections, these various properties and aspects of cloth and performance come to the fore by focusing on the ways cosmological beliefs take shape in the daily and ritual performance of tapa cloth among the Maisin.

"Maisin is tapa"

Among the Maisin, loincloths made from beaten strips of tree bark (barkcloth), or "tapa," as it is locally called in English, are important in various ways. As an object of wealth that is both "alienable" and "inalienable" (Weiner 1992), tapa cloth features in Maisin economic, political, social, and spiritual life. Sold at national and international markets as an object of indigenous art, it contributes significantly to Maisin livelihood. This alienable tapacloth is also used in barter and ceremonial exchanges. At the same time, tapa decorated with particular designs features as inalienable clan property. It may not be given away outside the clan, or sold. This inalienable cloth is often used as festive and ceremonial dress, playing an important role in church festivals and life-cycle rituals, such as marriages and mourning rituals. Moreover, tapa constitutes beliefs and values about gender relations and identity, mediating relations between the individual and the social. At the same time, tapa connects the living with the ancestors, God, and the Church. In short, tapacloth is intertwined with all aspects of life.

Maisin people, who define themselves on the basis of a shared language, belong to thirty-six patrilineal clans that are dispersed over ten villages situated along the southern and central shores of Collingwood Bay in Oro province, Papua New Guinea (Figure 12.1). They live in sago-leaf roof thatched houses

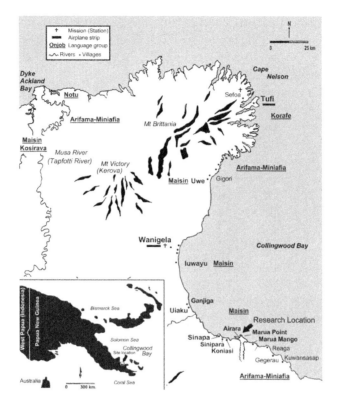

Figure 12.1 Map showing Maisin villages in Collingwood Bay

Source: Drawing on paper by Anna-Karina Hermkens.

built on small stretches of beach between the Owen Stanley Range and the Solomon Sea. Today, about 1200 Maisin people live in Collingwood Bay, although local populations rise and fall due to the movement of people between the villages and towns like Port Moresby. People's livelihood is mainly based upon subsistence farming, fishing, and hunting. Additional goods such as cloths, rice, batteries (for radios and torches), and money mainly derive from relatives living in towns, and from recent attempts at selling locally grown vanilla and the sale of decorated barkcloth.

Around 1900, Anglican missionaries ventured into Collingwood Bay. Conversion to Christianity was in many areas put into practice by clothing local bodies. Often viewed as indecent and associated with indigenous ritual practices, traditional clothing was in many colonial and missionary enterprises replaced by western-style dress, thereby believing civil, moral and spiritual transformation to be accomplished (Eves 1996: 86; Colchester 2003: 1–5; Bolton 2003: 127; Küchler and Were 2005; Hermkens 2007b). However, although some Anglican missionaries preferred western dress, in general those stationed in Collingwood Bay seemed not much concerned with dressing local bodies. Only local people living on the Mission Station and having married into the Mission wore western types of clothing. Only in particular instances did missionaries remove tapa cloths and decorations, mainly from women's bodies. Missionaries strongly related belief, moral behaviour and outward performance, to clothing and gender (Hermkens 2005: 276–79).

As a result of Anglican proselytizing,[1] Maisin cosmology becomes a complex and dynamic mixture of belief in ancestors, spirits, ghosts, sorcery, witchcraft and magic, and (Anglican) Christian beliefs and practices.[2] The synthesis is a spiritual landscape where humans live among a host of spiritual beings and deities who act upon the human world (Barker 2008: 120). God is often classified as the creator of Maisin ancestors. Like spirits, both are considered somewhat equal in force (ibid.: 131). Importantly, Maisin believe humans have but limited influence over these spiritual forces. While people can try to connect with God, Mary and other Christian saints through prayer, only sorcerors and healers can connect with spiritual forces residing in the bush or those dwelling among the living. Maisin fear sorcery, which they tend to classify as evil, and have repeatedly tried to ban, however without much success (ibid.: 133–35). The presence of malignant spiritual forces, which might be influenced by sorcerors or act upon their own, infests Maisin daily life with potential dangers, such as misfortune, sickness and death. Maisin conceptualize sorcery and other spiritual attacks on humans as punishment for the latter's lack of sociality and immoral behavior. However, what is regarded as immoral conduct can vary from committing adultery to refusing to share wealth with others.

Part of Maisin cosmology is expressed in the myth dealing with how Maisin came on this earth. It describes how each clan ancestor emerged from a pit located in the Lower Musa River area, each bringing specific attributes, ornaments, abilities, and powers:

> Maisin people were inside a hole in the ground. Suddenly, through a very small opening, light came from above. People were wondering where this light came from. So some of them climbed all the way up, outside the hole. As soon as they came out, they cut a cane and lowered it inside the hole, pulling the people up who were still down there. But not everybody was pulled up. One by one they came and each person took something with him, an ability or power to for instance heal, or to make people's enemies sick. So each clan brought *"ari kawo"*, his clan emblems. But only those who had good things were allowed to come up. People with the power to instantly kill were not allowed to come out as the others cut the cane before they had a chance to climb up.
>
> (Maisin elders, Airara village 2001)

The Maisin ancestors emerging to the surface symbolize the beginning of space and time. From this moment onwards, Maisin ancestors are identified by their names and emblems, as well as by their subsequent settlement and travels in which they produced space by naming the landscape around them. Time is created by the ancestor's alternating episodes of travel and settlement that characterize Maisin clan history. In addition to specific hierarchical relations between clans, the division of labor between men and women, their social and moral behavior and the way they should be clothed are related to ancestral origins and recalled in mythical narratives. The significance of clothing becomes apparent when one considers that in both daily and ritual life, Maisin cosmological order, and in particular people's relationship with the ancestors, God, and with each other, are mediated and regenerated in tapa cloth. In the next section, the role of cosmological beliefs in the creation and reproduction, and the orderings of clan and gender relations through the manufacturing and the wearing of tapa cloth in daily life are explored.

Tapacloth, ancestors, and women

All clans are different from each other: their way of dressing up, gardening, building houses, fishing, canoeing, or making tapa designs. For example, some will wear rattles, others small white shells ... So, this is our tradition. It is ours alone. No one will use it, or take something that belongs to other clans. They all have different things that others don't have. That's why I am telling you; this is how we are living.

(Raymond, Airara village)

As indicated above, Maisin believe that when emerging from the hole, each clan ancestor brought his clan emblems, his *kawo*. Clan emblems can vary from types of magic, social conduct, and fire, to drums, dancing gear, and tapa designs (*evovi*). Tapa clan designs are named and often figurative, visualizing mountains, animals, or specific artifacts that relate to the clan ancestor's travels and his claims on land, animals and artifacts.

Women are traditionally responsible for manufacturing the tapa, designing the decorative motifs, and painting it (Figure 12.2). This is true for the alienable tapa decorated with imaginairy designs, which may be sold and exchanged, but especially for tapa decorated with clan designs. In fact, women are the caretakers of these inalienable designs and at the same time responsible for the creation of new ones. The knowledge of designing clan designs is transferred from one female generation to another within a patrilineal clan. In addition, some women claim to receive new clan designs in their dreams, constituting a spiritual link between women, the ancestors, and the continuation of the patrilineal clan.

In addition to women's responsibility as caretakers of ancestral designs and creators of new clan designs, women are connected with clan tapa through the ritual manufacturing of the red pigment that is used to color tapa designs. In most

Figure 12.2 Applying the red dye, Airara village, 2001. Today, this is performed in public and children are allowed to sit with their mothers when painting the cloth. But while some men have started to design tapa, making and applying the dye is still a woman's task

Source: Photo by Anna-Karina Hermkens.

Oceanic cultures the manufacturing of pigment is "a magico-symbolic process" (Teilhet 1983: 49; see also Hoskins 1989). Among the Maisin, this was equally the case as in the past the manufacturing of the red pigment (*dun*), as well as the painting with *dun*, was bounded by rules and taboos. The red dye was mixed and boiled inside the house in a separate clay pot, which was not to be used for cooking food. Small children and men were not allowed to look at it or come near. Also, they were not allowed to make any noise. The view was that their presence would "spoil" the paint by making it "less red" or "dry up." As a consequence, men and children had to be excluded from its production and use, which therefore took place in secret or in seclusion. While working with the dye, women were not allowed to eat and drink, or to have sexual intercourse (Barker 2008: 114). They also had to speak quietly, and out of respect and fear of "spoiling" the paint, they would refer to the dye as *tambuta* or *taabuta*, meaning "red blood."[3] Since the ingredients of the dye have to be boiled and the resulting *dun* has to be applied when it is still warm, the association with living blood becomes more apparent. But whose blood is it we are talking about, and how come especially men are regarded as potentially dangerous in "spoiling" this blood?

Various symbolic connections between the red dye and women suggest that the pigment was regarded as female blood. The association between *dun* or *taabuta* and female blood becomes clear when we consider the use of a particular type of cloth in female initiation rituals, which were last performed in the 1990s. In these rituals, young girls received a facial tattoo after which they were clothed in a loincloth soaked in red dye, leaving only a white fringe on the bottom, and shown to the public. Both facial tattoos and red loincloth marked the girls' transition from young and non-sexually active adolescents (*momorobi* or *ififi*) to sexually active and marriageable girls (*momorobi susuki*). According to Barker and Tietjen (1990: 224), the red cloths refered to "the blood let during the initiation," and to the advent of the girl's (menstrual) blood, and, as such, to the girl's fertility and maturity. The connection between red dye and female blood, or rather, with women's reproduction capacities, also transpires in the belief that a foetus is created out of a mixture of semen (*voto*) and female blood (*taa*). Both are essential for the conception of a child. So, while the ancestral clan designs depicted on tapa cloth can be seen as representing the male part in the conception of clan tapa, the red dye refers to the female blood that is necessary to complete it, and make the design (and cloth) alive. Through the designing and painting process, a woman thus gives birth to an entity of cloth, thereby reproducing the patrilineal clan and its ancestral origins. This symbolized production of new life connects the ability to design and paint tapa with the character of womanhood. Only strong women were believed to be able to handle the paint, referring to initiated, and thus mature and sexually active women.

Men, and especially their external bodily substances, were dangerous for the dye/blood because these are regarded as "matters out of place" (Douglas 2004: 50). Maisin believe that both male and female external substances can be harmful when brought in contact with the opposite sex. For example, lactating women are prohibited from having sexual intercourse, as it is believed that the newborn baby might get sick from the semen entering the child via the mother's milk. In a similar way, male substances were believed to harm the red dye/female blood by making it weak. In the following section, it is shown that female substances are regarded as "matters out of place" that need to be controlled and contained by tapa-cloth.

Tapacloth and the containment of women's bodies

As women, our bodies are different. We do not step over them [men]. We hold on to our *embobi* [tapa or cotton skirts], bend down and walk past them.

(Louisa, Airara village)

Figure 12.3 Maisin woman and men dressed up in their traditional tapa loincloths while performing a dance during a Church festival in Sefoa village

Source: Photo by Anna-Karina Hermkens.

While women are responsible for its manufacturing, both Maisin men and women have a tradition of wearing tapa loincloths. The female garment, called *embobi*, is rectangular in shape and wrapped around the hips with a girdle, covering the thighs and the knees. The male garment, *koefi*, is a long and narrow piece of barkcloth worn between the legs and wrapped around the hips, one end covering the genitals and the other pendant over the buttocks (Figure 12.3). While *embobi* (either made from tapa or cotton) are rather tightly wrapped around women's hips, thereby limiting and even directing their bodymovement, the male garment poses no bodily restrictions. This containment of women's physiology reflects the belief that female sexuality is dangerous and that female bodily movements and fluids need to be contained and controlled by wearing tapa cloths or skirts that cover the locus of female sexuality: their thighs and upper legs.

Although to a lesser extent than in the past, women's bodies are still covered up and restricted in their movements. Whereas men can walk in shorts with bare chests or swim nude, women always have to hold their skirt close to their body, even if they are among other women. Whether they are bathing, canoeing, working in the garden or sitting, their skirts will always cover their private parts and legs. When getting up, they have to make sure their legs and especially their thighs are not visible. When leaving a group of people, they cannot tower over men and walk over their legs. This is considered disrespectful, but also dangerous, since touching a man with one's *embobi* might make him weak and even sick. In the past, it was believed that a man would not be able to outrun enemy spears after having been in contact with women's skirts. So, women's *embobi* not just represent femaleness, they actually embody female sexuality and substances. Next to making a man weak, touching a woman's skirt, or seeing her upper legs and thighs may also result in adultery. As Christobel (circa 80 years, Airara village) related:

> It is a custom that women must always cover their thighs. If she does not hide them, men might see them and get attracted to her, they get aroused and want to sleep with her. Other men may therefore not see a woman's thighs, only the husband. They could get interested in her and this is not good: the wife may commit adultery.

The shielding of female sexuality, by sometimes several layers of skirts that cover a large part of women's legs, also creates a discourse of imagination and sexual attention, as well as play. Although the general morality prescribes that women "are ashamed and also scared to show other men their legs," as one informant stated, women can also play with their sexuality. For instance, by wearing only one layer of cloth, which shows the body's contours, or casually lifting up the skirt, thereby revealing one's thigh.

The intimate physical and symbolic relationship between tapa, red dye, and gender elucidates how clothing can be regarded as an embodied performance of belief. For Maisin, these beliefs concern the cosmological order between the ancestors and the living, between men and women, and between the individual and the social. As such, clothing embodies a whole set of beliefs that are part of what constitutes and forms Maisin social and cosmological lives. These beliefs are not only expressed and regenerated in daily practices, but also in ceremonial performances, such as initiation rituals.

Mourning rituals: removing the cloth/clothing the body

Especially in the past, Maisin used to perform several rituals that marked a change of status in a person's life. Today, mainly marriages and death and mourning rituals are performed. Especially in the latter, the significance of clothing as an embodied performance of belief comes to the fore. In mourning rituals, performances with cloth exemplify how clothing and the removal of clothing changes the body, integrates and re-socializes it into various social settings, and mediates relations among social actors and among the living and the death.

When someone dies, Maisin adhere to the three days of public mourning, after which the partner of the deceased, and his or her close relatives, take an individual mourning period into account. This individual mourning (called *ro-waro*) involves several transitions of the widow or widower's identity. It is characterized by two phases; a period of seclusion, which in the past could take up till several months, followed by a lengthy period of re-socialization. Although both men and women must adhere to this isolation and the following re-initiation into society, these ritual practices were (and are) especially harsh for women.

In the past, when going out during the first phase, widows had to cover themselves with a large undecorated piece of tapa and follow, crawling on hands and knees, an in-law, who would drag a stick in the sand to form a trail for them to follow. After having spent at least one month in isolation, the mourner would enter her or his second phase of mourning. During this phase, she or he is re-introduced into all facets of life, such as food, work, and places to visit. The re-entering into society is performed by the widow's in-laws, and today may take from several weeks up to several years. The time of re-socialization depends on the unexpectedness of death, but also on the relationship between mourner and in-laws, as the latter decide when the mourning period ends.

Today, widows and widowers wear black, or old clothes during both the first and second phase of mourning, but in the past, each phase was visualized by particular clothing. After the first period of isolation, widows would wear heavy barkcloth shirts and little barkcloth caps, both decorated with coix-seeds. Widowers wore a piece of folded barkcloth over their heads, which was painted and/or decorated with coix-seeds. At various points during the mourning phases these regalia were removed from the body, until the mourning period had ended and the person in mourning was clothed with a new tapa and new ornaments, signalling his or her mourning period had ended.

Elements of seclusion, punishment, nurture (by both widow and in-laws), and re-socialization are combined in the *ro-waro*. During this period, especially the widow is under control and nurture of her in-laws. She is restricted from joyful contacts with other people, and by means of hard labor for her in-laws, re-socialized in Maisin relationships, practices, and places. As Julie, who lost her husband at a fairly young age, remembers:

When my husband died, I stayed with his parents for one year. I could only stay by myself inside the house. The first two weeks, if I wanted to go to the toilet, I had to wear a piece of cloth over my head. After this period, my husband's cousins, both men and women, introduced me to things and showed me around. Wherever they wanted me to go, they would take me. They would take me to the gardens and show me how to do the work. They showed me how to cut pandanus for making mats, so I could make mats for all my in-laws. I made heaps of mats! Chopping firewood was a bit less straining. It only took me two days of work, chopping and giving the firewood to the in-laws. But making all those mats took me a couple of weeks. Also, when I would see an in-law walking with a pot, I had to get it and fetch water for her. My everyday job was to take care of all my in-laws. The children were staying with me. I was very strong this time! I was not allowed to sit in a group where people were sitting and joking, it was hard work! I was not allowed to shout or call out, until they gave me permission to do so. In a similar way, I could not read a book until they gave me one to read.

In addition to the hard labor widows have to perform, chances are that the gardens, and all the other properties (house, clothing, utensils, etc.), belonging to her and her deceased husband, are destroyed, or confiscated by her in-laws. This practice, where close relatives of the deceased claim their "brother's" or "sister's" "work," is referred to as *dauvan*.[4] *Dauvan* is related to the ceremony that ends the mourning period, thereby completing the series of transitions from death (seclusion), to childhood (re-socialization) into, finally, maturity. This ceremony is called *ro-babassi*. It signals the returning, or rather renewed initiation, of the mature individual. During this ceremony, the widower or widow receives an amount of return gifts from his or her in-laws that should ideally compensate the *dauvan* taken earlier.[5]

Marking the end of mourning: emergence

The *ro-babassi* ceremony, in which the mourner is washed and made beautiful again, signals the end of the *ro-waro* period in which the mourner was subjected to several bodily, social, and emotional observances. The in-laws, who are responsible for the organization of this ritual, decide when the *ro-waro* period ends by performing the *ro-babassi*. Julie described her *ro-babassi* as follows:

> That morning, they [Julie's female in-laws] took me out in the salt water where I had my wash. They gave me tapa with my husband's clan design to wear, and took me to sit on the mat and on some tapa. There they trimmed my hair and decorated me with necklaces and rubbed my skin with coconut. They gave me my hairclippings, which was folded in a small piece of tapa that also had their clan design on it. [See also Figures 12.4 and 12.5.]

To summarize, by taking *dauvan* and secluding Julie for two weeks, thereby prohibiting visual and verbal contacts with other people than her in-laws, she was symbolically and socially killed. It was not only her identity as a married woman that was stripped off, her self was denied, leaving only her body to be molded into a new social form. This molding took place during her second phase of mourning, in which the transition from child to adult took place.

Figure 12.4 Airara village, 2001. Abraham undergoing his *ro-babassi*, one year after his wife died. His in-laws decided he was ready to be initiated, and took him in the morning out for a wash, clothed him in new clothes (traditionally a tapa loincloth) and started trimming his hair and beard

Source: Photo by Anna-Karina Hermkens.

Figure 12.5 Airara village, 2001. Abraham is seated on several layers of cotton cloth and a piece of tapa that were given to him to compensate the *dauvan* they took one year earlier

Source: Photo by Anna-Karina Hermkens.

Through re-socialization by her in-laws, nurturing, guiding her and making her work for them, she still did not have an acknowledged self and identity. Julie's new identity as an unmarried, or, rather, marriageable woman, was socially and materially inscribed on her body during her *ro-babassi*. During this ceremony, both Julie's in-laws and her father's family cooked food in clay-pots, which were exchanged, and Julie was given a tapa to wear that featured her husband's clan design. By giving Julie this tapa, her deceased's husband's clan-members emphasized Julie's identity as still being part of their clan, although her status had now changed from being the wife and subsequent widow of their relative, to that of a marriageable woman.

The previous description of Maisin mourning rituals shows the importance of clothing in life cycle rituals. Through the removal and susbsequent applying of clothing, the body is transformed, but, more importantly also the person's social status and identity are altered. Julie's identity changed from a widow into that of a marriageable woman. At the same time, the rituals guided her through her personal grieving and allowed her to adjust to her new status within her deceased's husband's clan. As such, this performance of cloth and the clothed body does not just communicate, but actually helps people to embody a new identity. This was especially strong in the past when each mourning phase entailed a specific type of clothing, but also today, the ritual performance of the clothed body both facilitates and internalizes integration and re-socialization into new social settings. In addition to these social and personal relations among the living, mourning rituals entail a spiritual component. By taking *dauvan* and giving the widower or widow his or her *ro-babassi*, the social relations between the living and the deceased are redefined and, eventually, closed.

Clothing and the embodied performance of belief

In this chapter, the relationship between belief, things, and performance has been pursued through the materiality of tapa among the Maisin. It is in daily and ritual performances of the clothed body that the "embodied epistemology" (Morgan, Introduction, this volume) of Maisin—of self, community, cosmos and the transcendent—becomes visible.

The manufacturing and use of clan tapa show how Maisin invest cloth and clothing with "their beliefs regarding the mediation of divine or ancestral agency" (Colchester 2003: 16). Tapa cloth and, in particular, clan designs have an ancestral origin and by making and wearing these cloths, the ancestors and their particular claims on land and status are brought back to life. People feel not only spiritually and emotionally connected with their ancestors, they embody their ancestors through the clothes they wear and the gendered movements of their bodies (Hermkens 2007a). In addition to belief, clothing thus also expresses powerful claims, (ancestral) connections, and experiences.

In daily performances, the making and wearing of tapa are related to "a complex of practices and rituals involving food taboos, birthing and infant care practices and gender etiquette" (Barker 2008: 114). Maisin values regarding gender identity and gender relations as embodied in cloth and clothing signify how Maisin conceptualize the order and hierarchical nature of the relationships between men and women. Each time women make and wear loincloths, these beliefs and values are regenerated, as well as internalized and embodied. At the same time, these performances allow for interaction and reinterpretation, which actually constitutes cosmologies as being "in the making" (Barth 1990). This dynamic chararcter of belief transpires in the fact that nowadays children are allowed to sit with their mothers making red dye and applying the paint, and men are able to witness this whole process. In the past, this was believed to have grave spiritual consequences, causing misfortune or sickness to those who transgressed the sacred rules and boundaries.

The embodied performance of belief is especially salient in life-cycle rituals. Birth, puberty, marriage, mourning, and death are considered as crises and major transformations in a person's life-cycle. Life-cycle rituals guide people through these often difficult transitions and inform them about the cause and direction of their lives (Grimes 2000: 5–6). By being performed, life-cycle rituals transform self and experience in a regenerative manner and reproduce, as well as reinterpret the existing social and cosmological order. Among Maisin, the ritual undressing, neglect, mutilation, isolation, and physical labor of the body strips it from its previous identity, while the subsequent clothing of the body gives it a new social identity. At the same time, this individual transition is part of the life-cycle of society itself in which social relations and relations between the living and the dead need to be established due to birth and marriage and closed due to death (Hermkens 2005: 178). In this ritual process, it is in particular the exchange and wearing of tapa cloth that intensifies sociality, and, in the end, terminates it. So the skin-like properties of cloth have a dual quality (Hansen 2004: 372) in being able to enhance, deepen, and transform both individual and collective identities, as well as relationships.

Importantly, cosmological beliefs, as expressed in and through clothing, deconstruct the scholarly boundaries between the sacred and the profane, nature and culture, material and immaterial and between the individual and the social.[6] The Maisin case shows that clothing incorporates a whole set of meanings, values, and beliefs about the human and the spiritual world that transgress such dichotomies. These beliefs are often difficult to translate into words. Instead, they are visualized, experienced, and communicated through things. As argued by John Barker for the Maisin (2008: 115), people "experience the spiritual world much more than they rationalize it." The manufacturing and use of tapacloth in both daily and ritual performances elucidate that this experience is not superficial, or restricted to the outer skin. They work "deeply into the bone," as stated by Grimes (2000) for life-cycle rituals. The ability of cloth and clothing to transform people's identity and their social relations, as well as determining their physiology, as, for example, shown with regard to the loincloths worn by Maisin women, reveals that these things have agency. For Daniel Miller (2005: 2), this powerful property is only logical, as cloth and clothing are part of "what constitutes and forms lives, cosmologies, reasons, causes and effects." Maisin people agree with him when stating: "Maisin is tapa."

Notes

1 In addition to the Anglican Church, which is still the main denomination, Seventh Day Adventists (SDA), Jehova Witnesses and Pentecostal Churches have gained hold in Collingwood Bay. While the Anglican Church does not interfere with notions about spirits and many other customary beliefs, the SDA in particular reject these, including traditional dressing, singing, and dancing.

2 By making this distinction between local and biblical teachings, I am not suggesting a hierarchical or any other value-based distinction between indigenous religion and Christianity. On the contrary, both are forms of knowledge that deal with our place in the universe and the relationship between nature and culture (Herzfeld 2001: 192).

3 *Taa* means blood, and *buta* is another word for *mu*, which means red or ripe. Today, the manufacturing of the red dye may be performed in public and children are allowed to sit with their mothers when applying it on the tapa cloth. But while some men have started to design tapa, making and applying the dye are still a woman's task.

4 The only objects that may not be taken from the deceased's house and remain clan property, are ancestral objects and clan tapa. All other objects may be confiscated or destroyed.

5 The amount of return gifts during the *ro-babassi* does not always match the amount of objects taken at *dauvan*. The growing inflow of consumer goods and inequality produced by people who benefit from having working relatives in town, created situations whereby people suffered severe material losses that were not compensated for. This imbalance, but also the destruction of gardens, have led to comments and objections by a few people. Because of this, some in-laws do not take *dauvan*, but the *ro-babassi* they have to organize becomes problematic as well in the sense that they have to give what they did not take.

6 See also Herzfeld's chapter on cosmologies (2001: 192–216), in which he deconstructs the boundaries between cosmology, belief, and science while describing how various anthropological sholars have addressed these themes.

13

Dressing the Ka'ba from Cairo
The aesthetics of pilgrimage to Mecca

Richard McGregor

To both visitors and indigenous chroniclers of Egyptian life, many of the most noteworthy and colorful events were public processions. The disorderly, bustling streets of Cairo seemed to be frequently the site of variegated and noisy parades. The occasions were many: an imperial entrance by a victorious sultan, the celebration of a marriage, the circumcision of a first son, the birthday of the Prophet, or the saint-day of a beloved holy person whose grave had become an important hub for devotional traffic. The city of Cairo also saw great public celebrations upon the yearly Opening of the Canal, a ritual cutting of a dam that not only filled the city's canals, but also marked the inundation of the Nile—something that all of Egypt's agriculture depended upon each year. Here processions included the nobles, the religious class, and the military elite. But likely the most engaging and complex processions were those associated with the Hajj pilgrimage to Mecca. In contrast to the various occasions of purely local significance, this event, which traveled the major arteries of the city, was part of the immense wider web of bodies, objects, and terrain that stretched across the Muslim world. Yet despite its universality as a religious obligation upon all Muslims, in important ways the Hajj was deeply grounded in the visual and material life of all Cairenes. The pilgrimage procession, along with its attendant escorts, texts, fabrics, images, palanquin, mounts, itineraries, and audiences, embodied this central duty and belief. The Hajj was not simply something that was done out in the desert wastes of Egypt and the Hijaz. It did not begin with the departure from Cairo, nor did it end in Mecca by simply reaching the Ka'ba. The pilgrimage routes, the Great Mosque, the Black Stone, are of course essential components—ground to be crossed, stone to be kissed, prayers to be said, shrine to be decorated—but as the following discussion will endeavor to show, the Hajj also remained very much in Cairo.

The two central objects in these parades were the *kiswa* covering, a large elaborately inscribed covering destined to hang from the Ka'ba (Figure 13.1), and the *mahmal*, a special decorated empty palanquin or litter (Figures 13.2 and 13.3), which would accompany the *kiswa* on its journey to Mecca. A new *kiswa*, bearing various Qur'anic passages, was sewn and dispatched every year on the Hajj, while the *mahmal* made the return journey and its decoration would normally change only when its royal patron was replaced with his successor. The origins of the practice of covering the Ka'ba predate the Islamic period, and the practice continues today, but its accompanying *mahmal* has a clearly demarcated start and end point in Islamic history. As we shall see below, although *mahmals* could originate from just about any capital within the Islamic world, in practice, the vast majority came from Cairo. From its first appearance in 1277 to its ultimate demise in 1953, the *mahmal* tradition was associated with Egypt. These objects were the focal point of the Cairo processions, with the *mahmal* making a striking impression on the vast crowds who would turn out to see, and, if possible, touch it. One visitor to the city in the mid-nineteenth century describes the intensity of this interaction. At one procession he reports,

> Many of the people in the streets pressed violently towards it [the *mahmal*], to touch it with their hands, which, having done so, they kissed; and many of the women who witnessed the spectacle from the latticed windows of the houses let down their shawls or head-veils, in order to touch with them the sacred object.

(Lane 1989: 480)

Figure 13.1 Ka'ba wearing modern *kiswa*

Source: Courtesy S. M. Amin/Saudi Aramco World/PADIA.

Figure 13.2, an image from the late nineteenth century, captures the intensity of the crowds and the visual prominence of the *mahmal* in particular.

An essential but problematic component of this dramaturgy is the identifying features of the *kiswa* and *mahmal*. We shall return to these in detail below, but as a preliminary it will be noted that these objects display an ambiguity when conceived according to the traditional distinction we make between temporal authority and religion. Arabic historiography and social history has often set this binary in the terms *din* (religion) and *dawla* (dynasty/empire). Interestingly, both are represented in the identifying features of the *mahmal* and *kiswa*. The former seems to have always displayed prominently the emblem of its patron, the current ruler of Egypt. At the same time the *mahmal* bore explicit reference to its religious function, by displaying Qur'anic passages, pious phrases, and most obviously a pictorial representation of the Ka'ba and its immediate holy precinct. For example, Figure 13.3 shows the Ottoman sultan's cipher in the round panel at the top of the front panel, just above a square panel rendering of the Ka'ba. Likewise the *kiswa*, from earliest accounts, also bore the name of the reigning Egyptian sovereign alongside its more prominent scriptural components.

The wider question as to the nature of these objects needs to be considered. It is perhaps puzzling at first to find that they barely register in the survey literature on Islamic religion. Textbooks such as those by David Waines (2001)

Figure 13.2 Procession of the *mahmal* and *kiswa*—Egypt

Source: Courtesy Travelers in the Middle East Archive (TIMEA).

Figure 13.3 The *mahmal*—Egypt 1834

Source: Courtesy Travelers in the Middle East Archive (TIMEA)

or Daniel Brown (2004) pass over the *mahmal* and *kiswa* in silence. This would not be a surprise to us if we were to attribute such an omission to the common academic blind spot for visual culture as a register for religious phenomena. However, this problem likely has deeper roots, specifically in the universalizing tendency of our comparative discourses on religion. The methodological problem is how to conceive of, and then describe, religion—with the unavoidable but unanswerable question of how wide to spread our descriptive nets, and how much we should rely on abstract categories or models. The problem with descriptive approaches is that at some point we are faced with a zero sum gain, in which more data lead only to a more complex description, not a clearer definition. One way to address (but not resolve) the problem is to abstract religious phenomena, to leave the historical and cultural particulars aside. The quest is then for an abstracted core of the religious tradition under scrutiny, something that is supposed to be representative for all time and in all instances. However, this quest is unlikely ever to yield the universally valid description it assumes is out there. Recently, scholars have sought a way out of this problem not by utterly rejecting the abstraction of structures and systems, but rather by counterbalancing them with historical and cultural particulars. William Paden has recently proposed such an approach, while Donald Wiebe claims there are precedents for such a balanced method among the earliest proponents of modern comparative religion (Paden 1996: 5–7; Wiebe 1996: 22–28).

It is this tendency towards abstracting an essential "Islam" that pushes phenomena like our *mahmal* and *kiswa* off of the survey (course) maps. Traditional approaches to Islamic studies fail to register this type of religiosity because of its deep roots in the local and the historical. The *kiswa* is inextricable from its immediate context of patronage—it is always local in the sense that it has a patron donor whose authority over holy sites is literally recorded upon the object itself. Thus, all careful treatments of the *kiswa* will inevitably pull any universalizing descriptions down into the particular. Even more so with the *mahmal*, which has circulated only within a limited period of the history of the Hajj. Abstracted descriptions of the Hajj would not surprisingly prefer to steer clear of any part of the pilgrimage that seems to be impermanent, and thus supposedly not essential. Here we are faced with a methodological dilemma. If we were to have taken up this question any time before the demise of the practice in 1953, we would be hard pressed to ignore such a striking practice that after all had been in effect for almost seven hundred years. Clearly, many other central phenomena of the Islamic tradition also have identifiable beginnings, a fact that does not lead to their dismissal as peripheral. The advent of the major schools of law (*madhahib*) in the ninth century, or the birth of the madrasa in the tenth, come to mind as easy examples.

This universalizing impulse is also typically dependent on the doctrinal and legal discourses relating to Islamic practice, an approach that leads to normative rather than descriptive accounts. The assumption here is that describing what Muslims "should do," positions us to make sound deductions about what is actually happening. This impulse has been challenged by scholars such as Carl Ernst, who has recently traced the Protestant Orientalist projection of the "scripturalist fallacy" onto Islamic religious culture (Ernst 2003: 55). This critique is helpful in that it illuminates the underlying and unstated principles behind the search for essential descriptions. A similar point has been raised by William Graham, who argues that relying too heavily on "high" literate expressions of religious traditions will distort our perspective, and blind us to parallel arenas of religiosity (Graham 1987: 47). This is certainly a helpful observation, however, Graham continues to hold out hope for the retrieval of a normative Islam; for him, the essence might be less abstract, but it's still out there somewhere.

Another approach that has had some currency among anthropologists of religion proposes a universal and ahistorical model based on the theme of "center and periphery." We are told:

> The concept of centre is important in understanding motives and interests because of the appeal the centre, as sacred space, has for Muslims. Proximity to the centre is assumed to invest persons or institutions with greater sanctity and thus, religious or political legitimacy. Muslims pray towards Mecca, and if possible culminate their lives by making pilgrimage to it.
>
> (Eickelman and Piscatori 1990: 12)

The claim here is that we may read the center as categorically superior to the periphery, since that is apparently how (in our case) Egyptian Muslims see it. This certainly does have some resonance with Islamic sacred topologies and cosmologies, but we would do well to recall Jonathan Smith's critique of the academic search for origins, which he claims all too easily finds resonance in theological language. Smith's point is that the centers or origins of religious systems are unreliable and offer no real footing for the historian (Smith 1993: 289, 307). In this same spirit, our exploration of the *kiswa* and *mahmal* will decenter such a simple binary of center and periphery. Egypt did not replace one center with another—it did not vie to be the goal of pilgrimage for example—but rather I will argue that the *kiswa* and *mahmal* when fully grounded in their performative and material cultures are better thought of as "scattering" the location of the Ka'ba and Hajj.

We might consider an approach that seeks to interpret the symbols of the Hajj. Such a strategy would promise to make the unarticulated meaning of the visible actions, objects, and utterances of pilgrims explicit. The problem with decoding symbols, however, lies in the predeterminations inherent in every interpreter's lens; that is, despite our best intentions, we cannot escape the determinative role the reader plays in interpretation. This critical insight was established long ago, and constitutes one of the central concerns of the study of hermeneutics. If an interpretation is skewed by the person applying it, the reading of religious symbols clearly becomes problematic.

One proposed solution has been to move beyond the vagaries of the individual, and to recognize entire communities as interpreters. The assumption here is that a coherent and predictable lens, or series of lenses, encompasses the range of possible individual readings—all within an identifiable cohort. Fred Denny proposes just such an approach to decoding the symbols of the Hajj. Denny wants to move away from a normative reading, towards a descriptive one—something that should steer us away from simply repeating the standard rationales, and get us toward the data itself. In the face of religious symbols at play, Denny proposes a decoding not of universal categories, but a reading from within an Islamic world-view. More specifically, for him this would free us from the temptation to apply our pre-established markers of "religion" generally. He claims, "What is needed is attention to the spatial-temporal dimensions and orientations of Islam for purposes of better understanding Islamic symbolism as it is understood from within" (Denny 1985: 71).

An approach that responds to and recognizes the value of an Islamic perspective seems promising, but claiming that we are then reading from an Islamic viewpoint is a problematic assertion. The first objection to this would be that in reality we have simply changed the location of our problem, and that in fact there is no single self-apparent reading possible, only a series of conflicting (now "Islamic") interpretations. Stanley Fish might be evoked here, in the hope of defending the viability of the conception of reading communities. Fish recognized the plurality of readings possible within a single community, but he anchored them within the limits of the existing institutional realities (Fish 1980: 306). In other words, returning to our Islamic interpretive community, there could be a variety of possible readings for a given symbol, but this variety would be limited by existing interpretive discourses, e.g. schools of interpretation, theological paradigms, philosophical or cultural traditions. But here we are quickly slipping into an unwieldy historical reconstruction, the scope of which makes the project impossible. Again we are faced with the unpleasant reality that ever widening description does not clarify, but rather obfuscates. A second objection to Denny's proposal is that, having presumably left the interpretive choices to others, we are now standing outside of the interpretive equation. This pretense to dispassionate observation can hardly be sustained in light of the modern critiques of Orientalist comparative religion. Standing outside of that equation is an illusion that would only allow default categories—typically Protestant Christian—to insert themselves into the supposedly passive reception of data. The many choices we would be required to make in our reconstruction of an Islamic world-view would remain our own, but only now they will be obscured with the trappings of Islamic discourse.

Another critique of Denny's symbol reading in relation to the practice of religious ritual has been posed by Talal Asad. The issue is raised not as to what the proper readings of symbols are, but instead whether ritual is necessarily symbolic at all. Through a study of Medieval Christian monastic discipline, he argues that the understanding of ritual has moved from one of physical discipline and the practice of virtue, to one that reads the ritual symbols as articulations of a modern Christian world-view (Asad 1993: 76–79). The methodological implications are significant. We must first note that Asad is pushing us to consider that the understanding of ritual may relate much more directly to its material and visual substance than we might have supposed. In his medieval example, these substances have become the medium for the exercise of piety. This observation resonates well with Morgan's theory of "belief" as we shall make clear shortly. But beyond Asad's shift to the material, his critique also illustrates another problem with symbolic reading. As we noted above, Denny has proposed the reconstruction of an Islamic reading community in which we might ground our interpretation of symbols. However, in so doing, we would be siding with one Islamic approach among many, and we would be assigning descriptive authority to one perspective at the expense of another. This is not only a failure in our descriptive efforts, but the implications for normative accounts follow close behind. Asad notes that in his examples the symbolist reading can be situated in the modern period, with its peculiar social institutions and assumptions about the individual, and thus if we were to insist on symbolic reading we would be endorsing a modern Christian version of that religious tradition. If one were to do the same following Denny, one would inadvertently be setting up symbol reading as the normative approach to the Muslim experience of religious ritual.

Our concern above was to understand why the *kiswa* and *mahmal* processions have normally failed to register in discussions and descriptions of Islamic religious practice. The most pressing challenges were those raised by universal discourses on religion, and the problems associated with the symbolic reading of ritual. We might turn to a more promising approach that seeks neither the abstracted categories nor the retrieved meanings of religious practice. Here the recent rethinking of religion in light of visual culture is promising. David Morgan among others has presented detailed reflections on the study of religion through visual culture. Briefly, he wants to locate the practice of religion within the set of visual and physical practices that constitute the lived environment of believers. Thus, we may refocus our view, away from doctrinal propositions and state-ments of faith, towards visual practice—a field that includes images as well as all the practices and habits that rely on them (Morgan 2005: 3–6). Here the practice of religion and the exercise of "belief" are constituted within the visual cultures through which people construct the worlds they live in (ibid.: 2). I am arguing that it is just this shift that will bring our *kiswa* and *mahmal* examples into focus. Morgan is anchoring "belief" in shared spaces and visual fields: "Belief should not be understood as coming only before [images and acts] but as being consti-tuted by them" (Morgan, Introduction, p. 11). This approach not only allows us a much better take on the real significance of the *mahmal* and *kiswa* for Egyptian Muslims, but it will also serve us in our reconsideration of the nature of the Hajj in that same environment.

The rite of Hajj is an obligation for all Muslims to be completed at least once, assuming travel is safe, and that one has the financial means. Visiting the Prophet's mosque and tomb in Medina has also long been part of the typical pilgrim's itinerary, however, this pious detour is not, strictly speaking, part of the Hajj. As the daily salat prayers are oriented towards Mecca, so too the trek of each pilgrim leads to the Sacred Mosque (*al-masjid al-haram*) and the Ka'ba. The pilgrimage consists of a series of rituals: the circumambulation of the Ka'ba, kissing or pointing to the Black Stone embedded in the south-east corner of the Ka'ba, drinking from the nearby Zamzam well, running back and forth between the hillocks of Safa and Marwa, traveling out to Mount Arafat, and the symbolic stoning of Satan on the return road to Mecca.

Although essentially an empty structure—and entering it does not constitute part of the Hajj rite—the Ka'ba makes a dramatic impression on pilgrims as they enter the complex. In its current form it rises almost 13 meters from the ground, with a length at about 12m and a width about 10m. The overall form is roughly that of a cube (Arabic: *ka'ba*; see Figure 13.1). Three of the four corners are named according to their geographic orientation—the northern corner is the Iraqi, the eastern the Syrian, and the southern the Yemeni. The eastern corner holds the Black Stone, embedded about 1.5 m off of the ground, in a silver frame. The eastern wall of the structure holds the single access point, a door raised 2m from the floor. In its immediate context within the Great Mosque, it dwarfs the series of lesser objects that occupy the sanctuary court-yard with it. Of these the most important are the well of Zamzam, the Station of Abraham (*maqam Ibrahim*), and the Enclosure (*hijr*) of Ismail, a low fence-like structure forming a semi-circle across the northwestern face of the Ka'ba.

There have been variations in the structure of the Ka'ba, for example in the first century of the Islamic era it was rebuilt to temporarily include a second door, and lengthened to include the *hijr* (Gaudefroy-Demombynes 1977: 28, 38; Azraqi 1858: 115; see Figure 13.1 for a partial view of the modern *hijr*).

The Ka'ba and the Hajj in the pre-Islamic period are well attested to in the Islamic sources, having been key to a series of different pilgrimages, and hosting a variety of deities and idols (Al-Jarim 1923: 127–67). A highpoint of Muhammad's prophetic career was his cleansing of the idols from the sacred precinct of Mecca. This foundational act of iconoclasm marked the reconfiguration of the shrine, aligning it with the new Islamic expression of worship. One account of the prophet Solomon recounts his passing by a saddened Ka'ba, which bemoaned its condition as a site for polytheistic devotions. When traveling through Mecca,

> He saw idols around the House (i.e. Ka'ba) which were worshipped instead of God. So he went by the House, and when he had passed on, the House wept. And God, revealing Himself to the House, said: "What makes you weep?" It said: "Lord, this is one of your prophets and party of Your saints, and they have passed me by, and did not alight by me, and did not pray in me, and did not mention You in my presence, while these idols are worshipped around me instead of You." The story continues that God revealed to it: "Do not weep, for verily I will fill you with faces worshipping Me ... I will impose upon My worshippers a religious duty which shall hasten their walk to you with a gait as hurried as the swift flight of eagles to their nests, and they shall yearn for you with the yearning of the female camel for her young, and the pigeon for her eggs. And I will purify you from idols and from devil-worship."
>
> (Tha'labi 2002: 496)

In the biography of Muhammad the "breaking of the idols" is commemorated by a poet thus: "Had you seen Muhammad and this troops / The day the idols were smashed when he entered / You would have seen God's light become manifest / And darkness covering the face of idolatry" (Ibn Ishaq 1967: 552).

The Ka'ba is also woven into the earliest narrative of human history through its association with Adam and Eve. By the third century of the Islamic era the Ka'ba had been clearly identified as the earthly parallel to God's throne, the center of the earth, and the point in creation nearest to heaven. Upon their fall from the Garden, Adam and Eve are informed that their exile is not absolute.

> God sent down one of the sapphires of the Garden, and set it down at the place of the House in the size of the Ka'ba ... Then God inspired Adam: "I have a Sanctuary located directly under My Throne; so go to it and circumambulate it, as (the angels) circumambulate My Throne, and pray there, as they pray at My Throne, for there I shall answer your prayer."
>
> (Tha'labi 2002: 60)

This Ka'ba of heavenly origin was to remain in place until the Flood, at which time it was raised up to Mount Abu Qubays, saving it from destruction (ibid. 2002: 148). Its location remained empty, although not completely lost, since the Ark during its travels across the vast expanses of the watery globe stopped for one week to piously circle the site from above (ibid.: 99).

The history of the Ka'ba is restarted with new foundation narratives identifying it with the prophet Abraham. Here the site is restored, and the origin of some of the related Hajj rituals is established through the figure of Hagar. To guide Abraham as he worked to build a "House on Earth" for God, one account describes a gale (*sakina*) with two heads, another relates a cloud "in the form of the Ka'ba," being sent down to indicate the required location and dimensions of the structure (ibid.: 149). In the same story Hagar is sorely tested in the desert, running between the hills of Safa and Marwa in search of water—an act recreated in the Hajj ritual of *sa'y*. Likewise she is at the origin of the well of Zamzam, with Gabriel revealing it to save her and Ishmael from thirst (ibid.: 140). Another important component of the Ka'ba complex is the Station of Abraham, a stone bearing his footprints marking the moment at which he positioned the final stone into the structure (Bukhari 1994: vol. 4, 141).

Throughout its life as a ritual object, the Ka'ba has been animated by its *kiswa* coverings, with the most common interpretation being to personify the Ka'ba as a woman dressed in her finery. The tradition of covering extends back beyond the historical record. The earliest record of Ka'ba veiling is likely the report found in Ibn Kathir's Qur'an commentary, in which a fifth-century CE Yemeni king who threatened to destroy the Ka'ba is convinced by two Jews of its religious significance. He then not only converts to Judaism, but also "circumambulated the Ka'ba, and dressed it in a fine seamless Yemeni cloth, with striped fabrics and colorful paint for decoration" (Ibn Kathir 2002: vol. 4, 164; Wheeler 2006: 26). The earliest leaders of the Muslim community are recorded as adorning the Ka'ba with brocade and white cotton coverings (Azraqi 1858: 178–80). A variety of styles and material are attested to in the sources: a white veil in the summer, a "shirt" (*qamis*) in the winter, red brocade, green or black silk. In the early twentieth century one pilgrim notes that just before the opening of the Hajj, the Ka'ba is stripped and dressed in its seamless white undercloth, in imitation of its visitors' dressing in ritually pure *ihram* (Batanuni 1911: 108). In the nineteenth century one traveler reports that when the Ka'ba is between coverings, it is referred to as "naked" (Burton 1906: 211–14).

In what may be considered an embodiment of the sanctuary status of the site—from pre-Islamic times violence in the vicinity of the Ka'ba was prohibited—the *kiswa* is understood to offer safety to all afflicted pilgrims. This asylum, however, did not protect the many who died in the Qarmatian rebel attack of 930 CE, and whose bodies were unceremoniously dumped into the Zamzam well. These victims are recorded as having sought shelter by grasping onto the *kiswa* (Gaudefroy-Demombynes 1977: 50). The section of the Kaʿba between the Black Stone and the door—the *multazam*—is identified as the most efficacious point to seek asylum. This protective function of the Kaʿba and its *kiswa* is even extended to the drama of spiritual salvation. In one medieval account of the virtues of the Dome of the Rock in Jerusalem, we are told that at the end of time the Kaʿba will be presented to the Rock as a bride, with every person who ever came to her on Hajj, clinging to her garment, rising to heaven (Ulaymi: n.d. 209).

Although the term "*mahmal*" can refer to a variety of litters and palanquins, the shape of the Hajj *mahmal* is quite consistent. The object is made of two components, a lower section, almost cubic, and an upper section in a tent or pyramid shape. The *mahmal* sent by sultan al-Ghuri (d. 1516) is preserved in the Topkapi museum in Istanbul. Both its lower section (1.5m high, 1.6m long, 1.1m wide) and upper (1.75m high) are adorned with calligraphic text (Jomier 1972: 184–86). The lower and upper sections repeat the sultan's name along with various honorifics, while a horizontal band joining the two on all four sides displays devotional text expressing the pilgrims desire to see the Kaʿba, to be rewarded in this world and the afterlife for completing the pilgrimage, all thanks to the intercession of the Prophet (*bi-jah al-mustafa*). Later *mahmals* similarly displayed a combination of texts identifying the royal patron, along with pious and devotional messages. In the second half of the nineteenth century however, one *mahmal* also displayed the pilgrim's longing for the Kaʿba as an image (see Figure 13.3).

Also part of the *mahmal* are the five silver balls, topped with finials, rising from the four corners and apex of the pyramid shaped section. These are attested to in photographs of various *mahmals*, but their use in earlier periods can only be surmised. The background fabric could be a variety of colors; in Egypt, examples are yellow, red, and green.

Mahmals were mounted from several capitals other than Cairo, including Baghdad, Damascus, and in the Ottoman period Istanbul. Regardless of the wider diplomatic and political realities, in which Egypt's status variously rose and fell over the centuries, the Egyptian *mahmal* aggressively asserted its superiority over competitors, regardless of origin. Between the thirteenth and fifteenth centuries, on the few occasions the Syrian *mahmal* was sent to Mecca, it seems to have been humiliated each time by its Egyptian counterpart (Jomier 1953: 47; Peters 1994: 348). Accounts are also preserved of Yemeni officials being beaten and arrested by Egyptian authorities for overstepping the ritual boundaries of *mahmal* pilgrimage—boundaries that invariably required ritual deference to the *mahmal* from Cairo.

In 1807, with the Wahhabis in control of Mecca, the *mahmal* itself was attacked and burned (Jomier 1953: 144). Nevertheless, in the following year another was sent. In the nineteenth century ship and rail travel become the most reliable means of travel in the region, and from this period on the *mahmal* is only borne by a camel when it parades within urban centers (Cairo, Suez, Jedda, Mecca, and to Medina; Figure 13.4).

Records indicate that Egyptian rulers made elaborate coverings for the Ka'ba from at least the tenth century. As became the case later with the *mahmal*, the decorations on the *kiswa* were primarily in calligraphy, recording the name of the patron along with pious phrases and Qur'anic text (Gaudefroy-Demombynes 1954: 13–17). One historian records the Fatimid Egyptian caliph's elaborate offering for the year 973 CE, which displayed twelve outward spans (*shamsa*) from a center of circular Arabic text (Ibn Muyassir 1981: 161–62). The fabric for the *kiswa* background typically consisted of eight vertical bands, two for each face of the Ka'ba, with a band (*hizam*) running around the entire structure near the top (see Figure 13.1). This band displays several verses and even entire chapters of Qur'anic text. There is no agreed upon format for *kiswa* calligraphy, nor is Qur'an material fixed—many descriptions of both have been preserved (Batanuni 1911: 134–37; Burton 1906: vol. 2, 215).

Within the Egyptian capital the *mahmal* and the *kiswa* were usually paraded three times a year. The first occasion was mid-Rajab, the seventh month of the Islamic calendar. The second was just before the departure of the Hajj caravan, and the third as part of the return parade of the pilgrims. The earliest record of parading the *kiswa* is from the year 1263, which saw the covering processed on mules, accompanied by judges, jurists, Qur'an reciters, Sufis, and preachers. This preceded the advent of the *mahmal*, which only joined the rituals in 1277 (Jomier 1953: 35, 36).

Figure 13.4 The *mahmal* and *kiswa* arrive at the port of Suez by train. Railcar adapted to accommodate height of *mahmal*.

Source: Courtesy Travelers in the Middle East Archive (TIMEA).

In the mid-fourteenth century one visitor reports a mid-Rajab procession of judges, jurists, heads of guilds, and officers of the state, forming up at the Citadel, where they are greeted by the amir of the Hajj, designated for that year, and the *mahmal*. Joined by detachments of soldiers and water-carriers on camels, the entire group processes around the city. We have no record of the crowds gathered, but we are told that, "resolves [for the Hajj] are inflamed, desires are excited, and impulses are stirred up" (Ibn Battuta 1958: 59). This procession became a major event in the city's life. In the fifteenth century we are told of the great crowds that gathered in front of the citadel to celebrate and take in the martial games of Mamluk soldiers, the fireworks, the bonfires, and the music. These festivities kept up all night (Jomier 1953: 37; Maloy 2006: 412). Soldiers' displays included mock battles, tossing and catching lances, and equestrian tricks. They also dressed in frightening costumes, becoming known as the "demons (*'afarit*) of the *mahmal*." They colored their faces, and some wore false beards and teeth (Maloy 2006: 419). By 1467, after several instances of excess—including abduction of women and boys, and the looting of local shops—the "demons" were suppressed by the Sultan.

From the sixteenth century the Rajab procession was delayed, taking place later, only two or three weeks before the Hajj departure. We have a report from 1679 of the *kiswa* circulating in pieces, mounted on wooden frames, and being touched by the crowds as a source of blessing (*baraka*) (Jomier 1953: 63). Partially recorded in Figure 13.5 (1908), another account describes the

Figure 13.5 The *mahmal* and *kiswa* process below the Citadel of Cairo, *c*. 1908

Source: Courtesy Travelers in the Middle East Archive (TIMEA).

ceremony before the Citadel, in which the *kiswa* and *mahmal* circle three times around the square, and the Egyptian Khedive is then presented with a decorated bag containing the key to the Ka'ba. The *kiswa*, along with a decorated covering for the Station of Abraham (see above), are further displayed by men on foot carrying them in view of the crowds (Gaudefroy-Demombynes 1954: 18). Another report of this ceremony seven years earlier includes the ritual details of seven rather than three circles (evoking the number of circumambulations the pilgrims will make of the Ka'ba), and of the amir of the Hajj kissing the reins of the *mahmal* camel after having received them from the Khedive. The procession then moved off across the city to the shrine-mosque of Husayn, where it deposited the *kiswa* (Jomier 1953: 66). Here it was displayed for two weeks, hung up on the walls—where people could come to visit and touch the *kiswa*, even cutting small pieces from it for the *baraka*—before leaving by train for the port of Suez (Gaudefroy-Demombynes 1954: 18; see Figure 13.4).

In the 1920s and 1930s conflicts with the Wahhabi rulers of Arabia led to the Egyptian *mahmal* and *kiswa* being stopped. The Hajj continued for pilgrims, but the *mahmal* would subsequently parade only in a limited fashion, and primarily as part of the welcoming home of hajjis. These limited processions within Egypt, however, continued until 1953, with reports from 1945 on the continued reverence for the *mahmal* among the crowds that continued to gather for it (Jomier 1953: 71). In a peculiar end, the processions were halted and the *mahmal* was relegated to Cairo's museum of Islamic Art, effectively neutralizing it as a devotional object. The *kiswa* continued to be sewn in Egypt until the 1960s, when fabrication was taken over by the Sa'udi state.

In the modern period, Egyptian critics of *mahmal* parading and *kiswa* displays objected to what they took to be substitutions for "proper" Hajj rites. I shall leave these criticisms aside, since they warrant attention beyond what can be provided here. The academic positions on the nature of the *mahmal* and *kiswa* parades can, however, be characterized in light of our comments at the beginning of this chapter on the problems of essentialized categories for religion and the problem with symbolist readings of ritual. The prevailing position argues that the *mahmal* and *kiswa* are at heart statements of political authority and that their significance as religious practices is negligible (Maloy 2006: 408; Schimmel 1965: 365; Jomier 1953: 68–70; Gaudefroy-Demombynes 1977: 158). These conclusions are striking in their one-sidedness, turning exclusively to the symbols of political authority despite the copious examples of religious behavior described in these same studies. This is clearly a methodological failure, one that I argue is due to the impasse of a symbolist approach. These scholars have been confronted with objects, rituals, texts, and performances, which have within them both religious and political dimensions. If one is committed to identifying and tracing symbols back to a system of reference (be it political or religious), one will need to decide which system is at play. By their very nature, symbolic systems have clear boundaries, one cannot jump from one to another. Reading symbols requires a commitment to one symbolic system, a reality that forces the hand of our scholars, and leads them to choose one and to reject the other.

A second criticism to be advanced here revisits the problem of the essentialist impulse in the treatment of "religion." The absence of the *mahmal* and *kiswa* practices in typical descriptions of Islamic religious practice and belief is striking in light of the ample evidence, presented in the pages above, of significant religious ritual, experience, and sensibility. I argue that this curious fate may be explained by the religionist's urge to isolate an essential and unchanging core of a religious tradition, and that such a move quickly excludes the Egyptian *mahmal* and *kiswa* practices of faith. They are easily pushed aside once their local and historical identities emerge. If we commit to such a view of "religion," then the *mahmal* and the Egyptian *kiswa* will quickly be marginalized.

However, such conclusions are unsustainable, and seem incomplete before the evidence. Building on the notions of visual and material culture, as described earlier, a more convincing take on these phenomena will begin with the people, objects, and performances themselves—building out from those points towards meaning and experience in religious life. I mentioned earlier the "scattering" of the Ka'ba as a way to escape the one-way model of the pilgrim in pursuit of a distant goal. This seems to resonate with the *mahmal* and *kiswa* practices as religious impulses. Through such belief the Hajj is not neglected by all those who do not reach the Ka'ba to perform the required rites. The Ka'ba is not a distant idealized and imagined goal that few will ever reach, but rather it is attained in a real way by its completion in Cairo through the seeing, touching, parading, and viewing, undertaken by the pious. These gestures thus constitute the very object that they finally target. After all, we are told that when the well-dressed Ka'ba ascends to heaven, with the pious multitudes clinging to her dress, she will be told, "Welcome O you who are both pilgrim and the goal of pilgrimage!" (Ulaymi n.d.: 209).

14

Performing statues

Jon P. Mitchell

The presence and power of Catholic saints
Performing with statues
Invisible performances
Statues that perform
Conclusion

Today, 16th February, 2009, at about 12.55 p.m., Catherine Caruana (wife of Angelik) noticed that the statue of the Immaculate Conception they have at home had once again wept tears of blood. These tears had issued from the left eye of the statue. Also materializing on the said statue are salt (a sign that the Christian is to be the salt of the earth) and oil (a sign of healing).

(Posted by Theotokos at 10:18 PM)[1]

Angelik Caruana is a seer, and at the center of a small but growing devotional movement in the Mediterranean island state of Malta. On 23 January 2006 he noticed that the statue his wife had bought a few days earlier, of the Immaculate Conception of the Blessed Virgin Mary, was weeping tears of blood (Figure 14.1). On 21 April of the same year, Angelik began to receive messages and see visions of the Virgin Mary, initially in his house, and at prayer meetings, then at the hill-top neolithic temple site of Borg-in-Nadur. Mary had instructed him to go to Borg-in-Nadur, as she wished it to become a place of prayer, pilgrimage, and conversion. Since then, and until March 2009, when this chapter was written, weekly prayer meetings have been organized at the site, with Angelik frequently attending to receive messages and see visions of the Virgin. The statue has continued to weep blood—which has been confirmed by DNA testing to be Angelik's own blood—and secrete other substances, including oil and salt.

Angelik is a member of the prayer group *Mir*, at whose meetings his early communications from and visions of Mary took place. *Mir*—the Croatian for "peace"—was established after a group of Maltese pilgrims returned from Medjugorje, the town in Bosnia and Herzegovina where visions of the Virgin have been reported since 1981. Despite the Church's unwillingness to acknowledge the authenticity of the claims to visions in Medjugorje, it has grown into an affluent and influential pilgrimage site for European and

Figure 14.1 The Statue of Our Lady of the Immaculate Conception (Marija Immakulata) during her annual *festa* in the Maltese town of Bormla. The feast is celebrated on 8 December

Source: Photo courtesy of Jon P. Mitchell.

American Catholics (Bax 1995). Zimdars-Swartz sees direct links between the visions at Medjugorje and those at the Irish village of Melleray in 1985, which had, like Angelik's visions, been preceded by a pilgrimage to Medjugorje (1991: 16–19). After the Maltese pilgrims had returned home, they asked their spiritual director, a Capuchin Priest, to hold prayer meetings, and *Mir* meetings were soon to attract up to 500 participants. The emphasis at the *Mir* meetings is "conversion"—a strong theme of the Medjugorje Virgin's messages. The theme is also central to the messages received by Angelik:

> *Jiena s-Sultana tal-Paci u tal-Familja! Konverzjoni! Konverzjoni fil-familji!*
> "I am the Queen of Peace and the Family! Conversion! Conversion in the families!"
> (second message, received on 11 May 2006, prior to a *Mir* meeting)
>
> *Jiena s-Sultana tal-Paci u l-Familja! Konverzjoni fl-Iran, fl-Awstralja, fic-Cina, fir-Russja u fl-Amerka!*
> "I am the Queen of Peace and the Family! Conversion in Iran, Australia, China, Russia and America!"[2]

A number of explanations have been proposed by scholars of religion, for the emergence of movements such as the one that has developed around Angelik and Borg-in-Nadur. Visions are often linked to periods of religious and social uncertainty. For both believers and analysts, the appearance of saintly figures— and particularly the Virgin Mary—is evidence of broader socio-religious concern, about the state of the world or the authority of the Catholic Church (Christian 1992: 7–8; Zimdars-Swartz 1991: 17; Kaufman 2005: 6). The Virgin's call for conversion in the family, and her choice of Iran, China, Russia, and America seem to confirm this. In contemporary Malta, there are deep-seated anxieties about the potential erosion of family values and disintegration of the family as an institution by processes of Europeanization and modernization (see Mitchell 2002a: 89–91, 2002b). The list of countries reveals concern over international geopolitical stability, with the superpowers targeted alongside Iran, which came to occupy a particular position in US President George W. Bush's "Axis of Evil," and Australia, which has a particular place in the Maltese imagination, as a prominent destination for Maltese emigrants. The call to convert these areas may stem not only from a wish to spread peace, but also from a more millennial concern to prepare the way for Christ's Second Coming—a theme that is common to many Virgin visions (Zimdars-Swartz 1991: 17). Mart Bax (1995) links the emergence and development of Medjugorje to inter-ordernary conflict within the Catholic Church, and the politics of local administrative autonomy and authority. Christian, in a series of books on Spanish visions (1989a, 1989b, 1992, 1996), has developed a similar argument, exploring the subtle intersection of local, national and transnational interests that feed into competing interpretations and attributions of vision phenomena—from conflict between holy orders, politics of local anti-clericalism, and relations between local church and the Vatican.

This chapter is less concerned with these sociological explanations of vision phenomena than with their phenomenology–what is going on when people have experiences of the supernatural? Likewise, I am less concerned with the visions and locutions—inner voices—than with the related, and, in Angelik's case, preceding phenomenon of moving statues. Statues in popular Catholicism link the material world and the immaterial—the natural and the supernatural— in ways that resolve inherent tensions within Catholic theology, between immanence and transcendence, or the closeness and distance of God and the saints (Daly 1980). Saints are close to people because they can intervene in everyday life, and involve themselves in people's lives, helping to solve personal, social, even military problems.[3] They can also intercede, petitioning God on behalf of a particular person or group. They are distant because the possibility of such intervention and intercession is unpredictable, and although "lurking" (Perniola 2003: 313) in everyday space–time ready to intervene, they simultaneously occupy the eternal space–time of heaven. This dual temporality is a central feature of saint-hood. After all, saints are not merely supernatural entities, derived from mythology, but also historical figures whose lives can be empirically confirmed. They are hybrids: part historical, part mythological; part everyday, part transcendental; part natural, part supernatural (see Mitchell 2002c). Statues of saints both communicate and resolve this duality.

The presence and power of Catholic saints

Material culture has been at the center of Catholic understandings of the saints since the emergence of saints' cults in late antiquity (Brown 1981; Primiano 1999; Kaufman 2005). From the third and fourth centuries of the Common Era, pilgrimage centers developed around living saints, often hermit "holy men," and at the sites of the tombs of Christian martyrs (Brown 1981; Frank 2000). Such sites were places where the religious could experience the power—or *potentia*—of the saints through a spiritual engagement with their presence—or *praesentia* (Brown 1981: 88). The notion of *praesentia* mediated the duality of distance and proximity inherent in sainthood:

> The carefully maintained tension between distance and proximity ... [at pilgrimage sites] ... ensured one thing: *praesentia*, the physical presence of the holy, whether in the midst of a particular community or in the possession of particular individuals, was the greatest blessing that a late-antique Christian could enjoy ... the *praesentia* on which such heady enthusiasm focused was the presence of an invisible person.
>
> (ibid.: 88)

Praesentia, however, was not limited to the pilgrimage site. Saints could also be present in the smallest relic of their lives. These could be "particles of clothing or objects associated with ... [the saint] ... during their lives, particles of dust or vials of oil collected at the site of their tombs, or actual portions of their bodies" (Geary 1986: 174). Relics permitted a portable *praesentia* that by the early mediaeval period—roughly 750–1150 CE—had fuelled a pan-European circulation of relics. Based on the principal that every church altar should contain the relic of a saint, relics were exchanged as gifts, stolen, and sold in an intense period of sacred commerce (ibid.: 176ff.). Saints were also present in statues. As three-dimensional depictions of saints' bodies, their significance was not merely symbolic, or representational. They did not "stand for" or symbolize the saint, nor "communicate" saintliness. Rather, they brought saints into being, generating a presence—*praesentia*—and a power—*potentia*—of their own, and of the saint. To this extent, they achieved the same combination of presence and power as the pilgrimage site or relic, and indeed they later became objects of pilgrimage in and of themselves. As James has argued of Byzantine Constantinople, "statues were perceived on both the popular and the intellectual level as animated, dangerous and talismanic" (James 1996: 15)—animated by the presence of the saint; dangerous because they had the power to protect themselves against attack, as in the image of the Virgin that retaliated against a man who threw a stone at her by crushing his head; and talismanic because they also had the power to protect those devoted to them.

Although I do not wish to suggest that nothing has changed in Catholic thought since Byzantine times, the significance of saints' statues as manifestations of power and presence has endured. In contemporary Malta, statues are an important feature of popular religiosity. They adorn the insides of houses and churches, are carried in procession around villages and towns during the frequent religious feasts—*festi* (singular, *festa*)—and are in some cases thought to have miraculous curative properties. Statues are not merely objects, they are objects that are engaged with, and interacted with, particularly on ritual occasions, and it is through the performance of ritual that their power and presence are confirmed.

If statues have the power to influence the world–through miraculous curative properties, for example—this suggests that they have agency: the capacity to act. Alfred Gell explored the agency of objects and artifacts in his posthumously-published *Art and Agency* (1998). The book rejects semiological, or symbolic, approaches to art, and those rooted in "comparative aesthetics," which seek to locate the meaning of a particular artifact within a given cultural system of meaning and value (ibid.: 5–6). Rather, he locates the power of art—and here his argument goes beyond art *stricto facto* to encompass broader material culture—in its ability to act upon the person, or the patient, as he calls them. Using the relatively trivial example of the anthropomorphizing of motor cars— what he wryly calls "vehicular animism"—Gell demonstrates artifacts' possession of intentional capacities to initiate causal events (by breaking down, for example) (ibid.: 18). This capacity is projected onto objects through a cognitive module of "theory of mind," which attributes psychological intentionality to social persons (ibid.: 125–29). The "theory of mind" is central to human social life. Where an object or artifact is also considered a "social person"—as in the case of the saints' statues—this understanding of intentionality is extended to the artifact. The thrust of Gell's argument is that it is perfectly normal for a person to do this. Attributing agency to objects is a perfectly routine part of people's everyday encounters with the material world around them. It is particularly so when artifacts incorporate the human figure (Looper 2003).

If the *potentia* of the saints' statues can be attributed to their agency, their *praesentia* is achieved through performance. Statues are not merely looked upon, but also engaged with. This engagement is accentuated during *festa*, when statues are removed from their daily position in a glass-fronted niche of the church, and processed around the parish. During this time, statues become animated. They are spoken to directly, touched, and made to "dance" along the streets—they are performed with, generating presence. As Schieffelin has argued:

Performance is … concerned with something … [analysts] … have always found hard to characterize theoretically: the creation of presence. Performances, whether ritual or dramatic, create and make present realities vivid enough to beguile, amuse or terrify. And through these presences, they alter moods, social relations, bodily dispositions and states of mind.

(Schieffelin 1998: 194)

Performing with statues

The feast of St Paul—*festa San Pawl*—takes place every February in the parish of St. Paul's Shipwreck, in Malta's capital city, Valletta. *San Pawl* is not only the celebration of the local parish patron saint, but also that of the national patron. St. Paul is thought to have converted the Maltese to Christianity in 60 CE, when the ship that was taking him to Rome to stand trial for preaching the gospel was shipwrecked on the island.[4] The *festa* begins on a weekend two weeks before the feast day of 10 February. The first function is the *Hrug tal-Vara*—the "taking out of the statue"—in which the statue is removed from its year-long place in a glass-fronted niche and carried shoulder-high to the main altar of the church (Figure 14.2), where it is rested

Figure 14.2 The Statue of St. Paul during his *festa* in Valletta. After it is taken out of its niche, the statue sits in the decorated church, where it is the focus of devotion, in advance of *festa* day (February 10), and the procession

Source: Photo courtesy of Jon P. Mitchell.

for a few minutes. A prayer is said by the parish archpriest and the congregation sing the hymn of St. Paul. The *Hrug* is well attended and a moment of great emotion. As the towering figure emerges from its niche, the shouts begin: *Viva San Pawl, Viva L-Ghaxqa ta'Malta* (Long Live St. Paul, Long Live Malta's delight). It is the first opportunity for a year for people to have a proximate engagement with their saint. As the huge—probably 10-feet tall—solid wood statue is walked down the central aisle of the church, faces look up in awe and tears begin to well up. The statue is then placed on an ornate wooden pedestal in a side apse of the church, where it will rest until the final day of *festa*.

The *Hrug* is important in that it makes the statue, and the saint, available to everybody for a more totalized experiential engagement than is possible throughout the year. It can be walked around, and touched: experiences of the saint that cannot be gained at any other time of the year, while the saint is behind glass in his niche. When in his niche, contact with the saint is mediated through prayer and offerings of money and candles, placed respectively in the small metal box and rack that sit in front of the niche. After the *Hrug*, people change their way of relating to the statue. It becomes animated, as somebody to whom one can talk directly. When he is sitting in the church, people avoid turning their backs on the saint, and when they do, they will apologize: *Sorry Pawlu*. These are days when special prayers can be offered to the saint, with the physical proximity signaling also a spiritual proximity—or presence—that assures, or assumes, an increased possibility of intercession.

Central to the animation of the statue are a series of "framing" mechanisms, through which it is set aside as special. Framing is discussed by Daniel Miller (1987) as part of the process whereby artifacts of material culture acquire value. Framing may involve particular activities associated with an object, or just as often other objects, the sole purpose of which is to "frame" the main object or artifact. As in the ornate frames given to works of art, their function is to draw attention to the work itself, while nevertheless constituting valuable artifacts in their own right (Miller 1987: 100–01). Such "humble objects" sacrifice their own value to that of the main artifact, and abound in *festa*. Throughout the year the statue is literally framed by the prominent niche in which it is housed. At the end of the *Hrug* it is placed on an ornate wooden pedestal, and the space in front of it is decorated with flowers and candles, forming a space in which people congregate to chat, pray or simply sit and stare in wonder at the presence of "The Apostle of Malta"—*L-Apostlu ta'Malta*.

The framing of the statue is a prelude to its performance on *festa* day itself. This is the culmination of a fortnight's activities, both inside and outside the church, involving solemn mass celebrations and lively brass band marches; veneration of St. Paul's relic (his right radius) and elaborate fireworks displays; panegyric addresses by well-placed clerics and performances by local rock bands and DJs.[5] *Festa* day begins with the pontifical mass in the church, then the exuberant "one-o'clock march" which sees hundreds of rowdy, and often drunken, revelers escort the band of La Valette—the "house" band of *festa San Pawl*—around the streets of Valletta. This begins and ends outside the parish church, and when it ends, the climax of festivities begins—*Il-Purcissjoni tal-Vara,* "The Procession of the Statue."

The *Purcissjoni* leaves the church just after dusk. Crowds congregate both inside and outside the church, to watch the statue—the saint—on his way. As he is lifted from the pedestal, there is more shouting and clapping: *Magnus*— "Magnificent One." As he leaves the church, there is a long volley of airborne fireworks, some of which light up the sky with colorful flourishes, while others simply explode as powerful petards. Firecrackers are set off on the roof of the church, and the saint begins his journey around the parish.[6]

St. Paul is carried by a group of twelve men—*reffiegha*—who are specially chosen for the occasion, as both strong enough and worthy enough for this important task (Figure 14.3). Performing the task gives public recognition of their trustworthiness, reliability, and strength, conveying a certain masculine status (Mitchell 1998b). The *reffiegha* take it in turns. Only eight are required at any one time, with the other four walking alongside carrying *forcina*—the elaborate forked poles that are used to support

Figure 14.3 The Statue of St. Paul as it leaves the parish church of St. Paul's Shipwreck, Valletta. This is the climax of *festa* San Pawl, which ensures the presence and power of the saint within Malta

Source: Photo courtesy of Jon P. Mitchell.

the statue when it rests at street corners. Care is taken to walk in time to the brass band music that accompanies the *Purcissjoni*, making the statue sway from side to side as though St. Paul himself were dancing. The procession stops at each street corner, and on certain corners, the *reffiegha* turn the statue around to "look" down the streets through which it will not pass, to demonstrate that the saint is still maintaining his patronage over the whole parish, even though he might not walk down every street during the *festa*. Every effort is made to animate the statue—to generate presence through performance. The procession, and the *reffiegha* at the center of it, are subject to rigorous scrutiny, and numerous "post-mortems" are held in the parish and elsewhere, in the weeks and months following *festa*. Video recordings are scrutinized in houses, cafés, and bars to judge the success or failure of the performance in its invocation of saintly presence.

Towards the end of the procession, the *reffiegha* leave the statue, to give ordinary men an opportunity to carry the figure. It is a chance for those who are not official *reffiegha* to show commitment to the saint through physical engagement with his image. Men crowd round the *vara*, jostling to get a position on one of the long poles on which it is carried. Each pole ends up with two or three temporary *reffiegha*, who "take a piece"—*jiehdu bicca*—before returning to their families and friends with stories of how heavy it is. Many— both official and ad hoc *reffiegha*—describe carrying the statue as a kind of penance, or *weghda*, given out of gratitude or hope for intercession. The physical and symbolic subjection of the body to the trauma of being underneath the heavy statue is a literal and figurative subjection of the person to the power of the saint (Scarry 1985). This produces a kind of euphoria that many find it difficult to explain. It is described as *tal-ostja*—"of the host," a rather blasphemous but common phrase for "amazing." One man, a regular *reffiegh*, commented to me: "It's incredible … the biggest 'high' you could possibly get. You get taken over by it—it's amazing. Like [St.] Paul is with you." For regular *reffiegha* these experiences are inscribed on the body, in the form of a large callous on the shoulder—referred to as a *hobza*, or "bread bun"—an index of the presence and power of the saint: his *praesentia* and *potentia*. Not only is the statue performed with, but also through this he himself performs.

The power of the saint flows directly from his presence, established through performance. It is a felt power, experienced by those who physically engage with the statue, either by carrying it—which is perhaps the "pinnacle" of engagement—or by interacting with it in other ways: talking, praying, touching, or simply gazing. If his performance is done badly, when *reffiegha* forget to make him look down parish streets, for example, his presence comes into doubt, and his power is diminished. This is particularly acute when bad weather prevents the procession from taking place. Each year, there is a tense build-up to the *festa*, with a keen eye kept on the unpredictable February weather. On a number of occasions over the last fifteen years I have witnessed, heavy rain "miraculously" clear in time for the procession, which locals attribute to the power of the saint. On the rare years when the procession has to be postponed, there is a general atmosphere of gloominess—almost depression—among devotees of St. Paul, until it can be successfully expedited. Without performing the procession, the presence of the saint is in doubt, and with that his patronage over the parish and the nation.

Invisible performances

St. Paul is not the only powerful presence in the parish of St. Paul's Shipwreck. Many of the devotees of and *reffiegha* for *San Pawl* also perform in the annual Good Friday procession, and the pilgrimage of Our Lady of Sorrows, held the previous Friday. The Good Friday procession—*Il-Gimgha L-Kbira*—is a large-scale pageant and pilgrimage involving hundreds of participants, many of whom dress up as Roman soldiers or other Biblical characters. Members of the confraternity[7] responsible for the organization of the procession walk with the procession, often hooded and barefoot, as a penance. These pilgrims accompany statues that depict the various stages of Christ's Passion: Christ in the garden of Gethsemane, Christ bound, the Ecce Homo,[8] Veronica, Christ redeemed, Christ crucified, Our Lady of Sorrows, and Christ's tomb. The procession is an emotional counterpoint to the enthusiastic and joyful atmosphere of *festa*. It is a slow pilgrimage with funereal music and an atmosphere of solemnity. The statues do not dance, but gently sway, as they make their way through the streets. The pilgrimage of Our Lady of Sorrows is, if anything, even more solemn. On this day, thousands of penitents follow the statue of Our Lady of Sorrows on its route around Valletta, barefoot or in stocking feet, reciting the rosary over and over.

The Good Friday procession begins and ends from the Franciscan convent church of Our Lady of Jesus—known locally as *Ta'Giezu*, "of Jesus." Like the church of St. Paul's Shipwreck, this dates from the late sixteenth century, in the early years of the building of Valletta. Its dedication to the union of Mary and Jesus–accomplished through the dedication of side chapels to Our Lady of Sorrows and the Holy Crucifix—earned it the title "Della Passione"—of the Passion (Aquilina 1986: 1). The Passion, the crucifix, and the Virgin were therefore brought together as a central devotional triumvirate. This was consolidated with the arrival of a new statue of the crucifixion, in 1636 (ibid.: 2). Within ten years, the dedication to the new crucifix had been institutionalized, with the establishment of the confraternity of the Holy Crucifix and the Passion of Christ, which is now responsible for taking care of the crucifix, the Good Friday procession, and the statues of the passion that are processed on that occasion.

The statue is powerful. It is carved from olive wood, and credited to a Sicilian Franciscan lay brother, Fra. Umile da Petralia Soprana, who sculpted a number of similar crucifixes in the early seventeenth century, alongside his brother, who was also a sculptor (ibid.: 5–6). The Valletta statue, though, is a particularly brutal and arresting depiction of the crucifixion. Standing life-size, the contorted and emaciated Christ oozes blood that pours down his torso in red lacquered rivulets against a parchment skin that has peeled off in places where he has been flogged, to reveal raw flesh beneath. The crown of thorns is a halo of six inch nails jagged into his scalp, with two puncturing downwards through his brow, and reappearing from the top of his eyelid and almost into his eye. On his chest, a blackened, open gash has blood cascading down. The blood on his shoulders mixes with his hair, to complete the depiction of the abject. It is queasily baroque, and the sheer corporeality of the image is a source of fascination for many Maltese. Rumor has it that inside Christ's mouth there is a thorn sticking down from the roof of his mouth to his tongue—which has presumably poked down through his head. But the fascination with the head of the crucifix does not stop there. It is also said that the head of the statue was completed by angels. Fra. Umile had carved the legs and torso of the Christ without incident. But when he came to the head, he fell into a trance, waking to find the head complete—the work of angels. The crucifix, then, is the result of direct holy intervention—miraculous in its creation.

As an artifact acknowledged to be miraculous, the crucifix is an index of power—*potentia*. Its very existence shows the power of the angels to intervene in the creative process. It also has an arresting power to command our attention. The depiction of pain and suffering, the mixture of sweat, hair, and blood, has the power to move even skeptical viewers of the statue. When I was conducting anthropological fieldwork in Valletta, in 1993, I was moved by the statue (Mitchell 1997). In the lead-up to the Easter procession, the niche that holds the crucifix is cleaned, including the glass at the front of the niche. The glass is important. Some locals suggest that it is there to protect the statue—not from environmental damage, but from supernatural attack from the glances of those with the evil eye.[9] Others suggest it is to contain the power of the statue itself—and to prevent people other than members of the confraternity from gaining access to that power. For, not only is the crucifix miraculous in its creation, it also possesses miraculous powers of healing. During the annual niche-cleaning, cotton wool wadding is dabbed onto Christ's bleeding wounds, to "soak up" this power. The wadding is then kept for circulation among the sick, to dab on their own wounds and heal them. After this was done in 1993, it was suggested that I should climb up into the niche and help clean the glass on the inside of the niche. Contact with the miraculous statue would help me after I left Malta. I climbed up next to the statue, and the glass was rolled back into place. I was trapped. In the heat and humidity the strong musty smell of the statue and its lacquers mixed with the cleaning fluids on the cloth I had been given, and as I started to wipe the glass, I became increasingly aware of the figure behind me. An intense feeling of excitement overcame me. My stomach tightened and I began to shake. My heart pounded, and I felt faint.

I discussed this experience at length with my friends and informants in Valletta. Although there were some skeptics, even among this dedicated group of confraternity members, who said it was the humidity and cleaning fluid, others were sure that what I had felt was the power of Christ. Such experiences were common, I was told, and were evidence of the statue's power to perform miracles. They were evidence of the presence—*praesentia*—of Christ. The statue was seen not merely as a depiction, or representation, of Christ, but an embodiment of his power, and evidence of his immanence. Perniola argues that Catholics live in an "enchanted world" (2003: 310), in which the presence of God and the saints is constantly making itself known. For Catholics, he argues, the power of God "lurks" (ibid.: 313) in the material world, such that "the experience of the world is an essential aspect of Catholicism" (ibid.: 311). In Malta, this world is populated by statues and other manifestations of the divine, and the feelings which go along with engagements with them, is commonplace. During rites of passage, such as the confirmation rite undertaken by 11- and 12-year-olds, when the Archbishop lays his hand on the heads of the initiands; and during the more regular ritual occasion of Holy Communion, God's power is felt. Informants reported an intense feeling or shock-wave emanating from the Archbishop's hand, and a feeling of warmth, or tingling sensation, when the consecrated host is ingested during Communion (see Mitchell and Mitchell 2008). Where Christ is present—in the host, in the crucifix worn round the neck as spiritual companion and protector, and in artifacts such as the Miraculous Crucifix—his power is felt.

The statue of the Miraculous Crucifix is not one that is performed with, but one that itself performs—acts of healing—and whose transcendent power is immanent in the world. His performances, although powerful, are nevertheless invisible. We know of the power because of its consequences— the inculcation of powerful feelings, or the healing of medical or social ills. However, other statues—such as the one bought by Angelik Caruana's wife—perform visible acts, of movement, bleeding, weeping.

Statues that perform

The power of the Miraculous Crucifix and the Passion radiates outwards through the performance of the Good Friday procession, but most particularly in the pilgrimage of Our Lady of Sorrows. The sorrowful Virgin is a realization, or culmination, of her maternal destiny, as she makes the ultimate sacrifice of hers and God's son for the good of humanity. She is depicted as a seated and haloed queen, holding the nails of the cross in her hands and gazing up to an empty cross, with a jewel-encrusted dagger thrust into her chest. Devotion to this Virgin is widespread, as manifest in the huge crowds of penitents that her pilgrimage attracts. However, it is Our Lady of the Immaculate Conception that holds a particular place in the popular Catholic imagination. If Our Lady of Sorrows represents the realization of the Virgin's destiny, then the Immaculate Conception is the point of origin—the devotion that allows the life of Mary, and her sacrifice, to unfold. As one Maltese informant, a member of the confraternity of the Holy Crucifix, and a man fiercely devoted to Our Lady of Sorrows, explained to me:

> For us Catholics, the Virgin Mary ... [*Il-Madonna*] ... is almost the most important. After all, she's the mother of Jesus—but not just a mother like your mother or my mother. No, she's the mother of the son of God. And she's immaculate. Do you know what that means? She has no sin, and is full of divine grace. That's why she is so important for us.

The doctrine of the Immaculate Conception of the Blessed Virgin Mary is central to modern Catholic visions such as those of Angelik at Borg-in-Nadur. The doctrine holds that, like the head of the Miraculous Crucifix, Mary herself was created by divine intervention. Although conceived through sexual intercourse, she was from the outset filled with divine grace and therefore free from any trace of sin. This doctrine was confirmed as infallible dogma by Pope Pius IX in his *Ineffabilis Deus* of 1854, four years before the vision of the Virgin at Lourdes. The central message of this vision was a confirmation of the dogma, as the Virgin told the young Bernadette Soubirous "I am the Immaculate Conception" (Marnham 1982: 29).

Carroll (1985: 65 ff.) has argued that there is reason to question the association of Bernadette's visions—which he calls "hallucinations"—with the Virgin Mary. Initially, Bernadette referred to the girl she saw as *Aquero*, meaning "her" or "that one," and it was only the reference to "penitence," and later, "I am the Immaculate Conception" that confirmed the presence of Our Lady. This was after a period of six weeks since the first apparition, after she had initially been punished for talking about the visions, and then attracted attention from local priests and others who made the suggestion that *Aquero* was in fact the Virgin. Carroll suggests that because of the regular Feast of the Immaculate Conception, and the recent local minting of a commemorative Medal of the Immaculate Conception, the notion of Immaculate Conception would have been familiar to Bernadette, even if she would probably have been ignorant of the details of the doctrine. It therefore served as a prototype for both the appearance and the identification of *Aquero*, once the suggestion had been made by these powerful figures around her, that the person she had seen was the Virgin Mary (ibid.: 70).

Carroll's interpretation points to the importance of existing imagery in the development of narratives of saintly visions (Zimdars-Swartz 1991). Like Bernadette before her, Angelik would certainly be aware of the centrality of the Immaculate Conception not only in Catholic doctrine and popular understandings of the Virgin, but also in the aetiology of visions. Lourdes is the most famous vision in Europe, with Medjugorje a close second, and partly because it was very early confirmed by the Church as a genuine vision, was able to grow into what is now a major commercial pilgrimage center (Kaufman 2005). Just as it is no surprise that his Virgin—appearing after a recent trip to Medjugorje—brings messages of peace, conversion and the family—all themes that Our Lady of Medjugorje has developed, it is also no surprise that the statue at the center of his visions is that of the Immaculate Conception.

Angelik's statue does not provide invisible performances of healing or intercession, it performs visible acts—crying blood, and secreting oils and other fluids. Since the initial appearance of blood in January 2006, fluid has been found secreted on a framed photograph of the statue, and on a set of rosary beads given to Angelik "by his guardian angel."[10] The statue was placed in a sealed glass box, and the photograph in two sealed plastic bags. Soon, the plastic bags showed signs of burning, while the glass case "burst," mixing broken glass and liquid on the floor of Angelik's house. Salt then began to appear at the base of the statue. A YouTube video of the statue and apparitions shows several gallons of liquid, which looks like oil that has been collected from the statue.

Conclusion

That statues should be capable of such dramatic material performances is in keeping with Perniola's understanding of Catholicism as a fundamentally material religion (2003). Statues are not merely artifacts, but are substantive embodiments of saintly presence, which are both conduits of spiritual power and agents of such power in and of themselves. They are agents, in the sense understood by Gell (1988), endowed with the capacity to act, and their presence is confirmed both through being performed with, and through their own performances. As such, they combine *praesentia* and *potentia*—presence and power—to unite transcendence and immanence. Writing of the moving statue of Our Lady at the Ballinspittle grotto in County Cork, Ireland, in the mid-1980s, Eipper argues:

> To say in these circumstances that stone is made spirit is not to suggest that masonry ceases to exist as matter—even in the minds of the most ardent of Our Lady's advocates. It *is* to suggest, however, that the laws of physics are answerable to those of metaphysics, an ulterior authority with the power to intervene (or not) at will … A material object behaving in a supernatural way both attracts attention to itself and beyond itself.
>
> (Eipper 2007: 225)

I have deliberately not delved into questions of "authenticity" in relation to the case of Angelik Caruana. This is partly because the Church and broader scientific community—including myself—are currently engaged in, but have not finished, a rigorous interrogation of the case. It is also partly because, as Eipper has pointed out (2007: 255–56), forms of iconoclasm that question "authenticity" effectively acknowledge the power they seek to question. Their power lies not merely in their meaning or symbolism, but in their materiality. So much so that two detractors of the Ballinspittle Virgin, bent on releasing the hold that the statue's cult had over local Catholics, were moved to smash the face of the statue with a hammer, in full view of her astonished and horrified devotees. That this attack did not shake the convictions of the cult's members is seen by Eipper as evidence that the statue was "merely an emblem of Her" (ibid.: 256). I am not so sure.

On the one hand, the transcendent power that manifests itself within such material artifacts can certainly appear elsewhere—the destruction of a particular Virgin will not shatter a devotee's commitment to "the Virgin." On the other hand, the immanence of the particular manifestations of this power—which has particular local and historical significances, linked to particular narratives, personalities and politics, cannot be overlooked. These tensions between the universal and the local, the transcendent and the immanent, are central to Catholic understandings of the world—indeed, to the very definition of Catholicism.

Notes

1   http://www.borgin-nadur.blogspot.com/ (accessed 2 March 2009).
2   Fourth message, received on 23 June 2006, at home. http://www.borgin-nadur.org/site/Il_Messaggi_Godda_tas_Sinjura.html (accessed 3 March 2009).
3   For example, in 1422, a vision of St. Paul appeared above the ramparts of the then Maltese capital, Mdina, which frightened off the Saracens who had besieged this Christian city (Cassar-Pullicino 1992: 125–26).
4   Doubts were cast on the accuracy of this story when a German theologian argued in the late 1980s that the Biblical *Melite*—the site of St. Paul's shipwreck—was not Malta, but Cephallonia. The debates that arose are discussed in Galea and Ciarló (1992), Mitchell (1998a, 2002c).
5   For a discussion of the significance of the inside–outside polarity in Maltese *festa*, see Mitchell (2004).
6   For a discussion of the significance of social space in performance more generally, and in *festa* in particular, see Mitchell (2006).
7   A confraternity is a lay brotherhood devoted to a particular saint, or devotion, such as the Sacred Heart, or in this case the Holy Crucifix. Historically, they often operated as trade guilds, but latterly have functioned as organizational committees for religious feasts, and key rites of passage in the lives of their members—and particularly funerals. Many have dedicated space for burials, and organize prayers to be said in perpetuity for the souls of deceased members.
8   "Behold the Man," the phrase used by Pilate when presenting Christ after his flagellation and coronation with thorns. It is an image of humiliation and bodily suffering.
9   For a more detailed treatment of the evil eye—*ghajn*—in Malta, see Mitchell (2002b).
10 http://www.youtube.com/watch?v=9L492NkTjVw&feature=related (accessed 2 March 2009).

WORKS CITED

Adams, Vincanne (2006) "Moral Orgasm and Productive Sex: Tantrism Faces Fertility Control in Lhasa, Tibet, China," in Vincanne Adams, and Stacey Leigh Pigg (eds.) *Sex and Development: Science, Sexuality and Morality in Global Perspective*, Durham, NC: Duke University Press.

AHDEL (1969) *American Heritage Dictionary of the English Language*, William Morris (ed.), Boston: Houghton Mifflin.

Al-Azraqi, Muhammad (1858) *Akhbar Makka wa ma ja'a fi-ha min al-athar*, 2 vols., Guttenberg: n.p.

Al-Batanuni, Muhammad (1911) *Al-Rihla al-Hijaziyya*, Cairo: al-Matba'a al-Jamal-iyya.

Al-Bukhari (1994) *Sahih al-Bukhari*, Abd al-Aziz Bin Baz (ed.) (8 vols), Damascus: Dar al-Fikr.

Al-Jarim, Muhammad (1923) *Adyan al-Arab fi al-Jahiliyya*, Cairo: Matba'a al-Sa'ada.

Allione, Tsultrin (1984) *Women of Wisdom*, Henley-on-Thames: Routledge & Kegan Paul.

Andrade, Maristela Oliveira de (2002) *500 anos de catolicismos & sincretismos no Brasil*, João Pessoa: Editoria Universitária UFPB.

Andrade, Maristela Oliveira de (2003) "O mito do Quinto Império na versão do Padre Antônio Vieira," in Maristela Oliveira de Andrade (ed.) *Milenarismos e utopias*, João Pessoa: Manufatura.

Anonymous (1901) "Une superstition de moins," *Mouvement Géographique*, 622–23.

Anonymous (1905) "La pêche à Mpala," *Missions d'Afrique (Pères Blancs)*, Paris edition, pp. 174–209.

Aquilina, Gorg (1986) *Il-Gimgha l-Kbira tal-Belt*, Valletta, Malta: Edizzjoni TAU.

Arweck, Elisabeth, and William Keenan (eds.) (2006) *Materializing Religion: Expression, Performance and Ritual*, Oxford: Ashgate.

Asad, Talal (1993) *Genealogies of Religion: Discipline and Reasons of Power in Christianity and Islam*, Baltimore, MD: Johns Hopkins University Press.

Atkinson, C. Harry (1956) *Building and Equipping for Christian Education*, New York: Bureau of Church Building of the National Council of Churches of Christ in the USA.

Ávila, Cristina (2001/2004) "O sermão—Imagem falada," *Barroco* 19: 43–70.

Babb, Lawrence, and Susan Wadley (eds.) (1995) *Media and the Transformation of Religion in South Asia*, Delhi: Motilal Banarsidass Publishers.

Bachelard, Gaston (1969) *The Poetics of Space*, Boston: Beacon Press.

Bal, Mieke (2003) "Ecstatic Aesthetics: 'Metaphoring' Bernini," pp. 1–30 in Claire Farago, and Robert Zwijnenberg (eds.) *Compelling Visuality: The Work of Art In and Out of History*, Minneapolis: University of Minnesota Press.

Ballard, Robert (1983) *Exploring Our Living Planet*, Washington, D.C.: National Geographic Society Press.

Barata, Mário (1955) *Azuleijos no Brasil*, Rio de Janeiro: Editora Jornal de Comércio.

Barker, John (2008) *Ancestral Lines: The Maisin of Papua New Guinea and the Fate of the Rainforest*, Ontario: Broadview Press.

Barker, John, and Anne Marie Tietjen (1990) "Women's Facial Tattooing among the Maisin of Oro Province, Papua New Guinea: The Changing Significance of an Ancient Custom," *Oceania* 60(3): 217–34.

Barnes, Ruth, and Joanne B. Eicher (eds.) (1992) *Dress and Gender: Making and Meaning in Cultural Contexts*, Oxford: Berg.

Barth, Fredrik (1990) *Cosmologies in the Making: A Generative Approach to Cultural Variation in Inner New Guinea*, Cambridge: Cambridge University Press.

Bataille, Georges (1986) *Erotism: Death and Sensuality*, San Francisco: City Lights Books.

Baten, Lea (2000) *Identifying Japanese Dolls: Notes on Ningyô*, Leiden: Hotei Publications.

Bates, Harold, and Bettie Currie (1963) "Balanced Facilities for Worship and Learning," pp. 33–47 in *Seattle Annual National Joint Conference on Church Architecture*, Church Architecture Guild of America and Department of Church Building and Architecture of the National Council of Churches of Christ in the USA.

Baumgarten, Alexander Gottlieb (1983) *Theoretische Aesthetik. Die grundlegenden Abschnitte aus der "Aesthetica" (1750–58)*, trans. and ed. Hans Rudolf Schweizer, Hamburg: Felix Meiner Verlag.

Baumgarten, Jens (2004) *Konfession, Bild und Macht: Visualisierung als katholisches Herrschafts- und Disziplinierungskonzept in Rom und im habsburgischen Schlesien (1560–1740)*, Hamburg: Dölling & Galitz.

Bax, Mart (1995) *Medjugorje: Religion, Politics and Violence in Rural Bosnia*, Amsterdam: Vreie Universiteit.

Bazin, Germain (1955) *L'architecture religieuse baroque au Brésil*, São Paulo: Museu de Arte de São Paulo.

Belting, Hans (2005) "Toward an Anthropology of the Image," pp. 41–58 in Mariät Westermann (ed.) *Anthropologies of Art*, Williamstown, MA: Sterling and Francine Clark Art Institute.

Belting, Hans (2007) *La vraie image. Croire aux images?*, trans. Jean Torrent. Paris: Gallimard.

Benjamin, Jessica (1995) *Like Subjects, Love Objects*, New Haven, CT: Yale University Press.

Benjamin, Walter (1968) "The Work of Art in the Age of Mechanical Reproduction," pp. 217–51 in Hannah Arendt (ed.) *Illuminations: Essays and Reflections*, New York: Schocken Books.

Bennett, Maxwell, Daniel Dennett, Peter Hacker, and John Searle (2007) *Neuroscience and Philosophy: Brain, Mind and Language*, New York: Columbia University Press.

Berger, Peter L. (1967) *The Sacred Canopy: Elements of a Sociological Theory of Religion*, Garden City, New York: Doubleday.

Binsbergen, Wim Van (1981) *Religious Change in Zambia*, London: Kegan Paul for the African Studies Center, Leiden, The Netherlands.

Blackman, Lisa, John Cromby, Derek Hook, Dimitris Papadopolous, and Valerie Walkerdine (2008) "Creating Subjectivities," *Subjectivity* 22(1): 1–27.

Blankenship, Lois (1959) "Building for Christian Education," pp. D1–6 in *Los Angeles National Guild Conference*, Church Architectural Guild of America and Department of Church Building and Architecture of the National Council of Churches in the USA.

Blankenship, Lois (1962) "Panel on 'Building for Christian Education,'" pp. 58–62 in *Cleveland Annual National Joint Conference on Church Architecture*, Church Architecture Guild of America and the Department of Church Building and Architecture of the National Council of Churches of Christ in the USA.

Blier, Suzanne Preston (ed.) (2004) *Art of the Senses: African Masterpieces from the Teel Collection*, Boston: MFA Publications.

Boie, Stan. Personal interview, 22 May 2007.

Bollas, Christopher (2009) *The Evocative Object World*, London: Routledge.

Bolt, Barbara (2004) *Art Beyond Representation: The Performative Power of the Image*, New York: I. B. Taurus.

Bolton, Lissant (2003) "Gender, Status and Introduced Clothing in Vanuatu," pp. 119–39 in Cloë Colchester (ed.) *Clothing the Pacific*, London: Berg Publishers.

Bonaventure (2000) *Minor Legends of Saint Francis*, in *Francis of Assisi: Early Documents*, vol. 2 of 3, Regis J. Armstrong, J.A. Wayne Hellmann, and William J. Short (eds.), New York: New City Press.

Bourdieu, Pierre (1970) "The Berber House, or the World Reversed," *Social Science Information* 9: 151–70.

Bourdieu, Pierre ([1972] 1977) *Outline of a Theory of Practice*, trans. Richard Nice, Cambridge: Cambridge University Press.

Bourdieu, Pierre (1980) "The Production of Belief: Contributions to an Economy of Symbolic Goods," *Media, Culture, and Society* 2: 261–93.

Bourdieu, Pierre (1984) *Distinction: A Social Critique of the Judgement of Taste*, London: Routledge.

Bourguignon, Erika (ed.) (1973) *Religion, Altered States of Consciousness, and Social Change*, Columbus, OH: Ohio State University Press.

Boyer, Pascal (2001) *Religion Explained*, New York: Basic Books.

Brennan, Teresa (2004) *The Transmission of Affect*, Ithaca, NY: Cornell University Press.

Brown, Daniel (2004) *A New Introduction to Islam*, Malden, MA: Blackwell.

Brown, Peter (ed.) (1982) *The Cult of the Saints: Its Rise and Function in Latin Christianity*, Chicago: University of Chicago Press.

Brückner, Wolfgang (2006) "Luther: heiliger Mann oder falscher Prophet? Legende und Antilegende zwischen 1517 und 1630," pp. 36–57 in Michael Neumann (ed.), *Mythen Europas. Schlüsselfiguren der Imagination*, Regensburg: Pustet.

Brunnholzl, Karl (2007) *Straight From the Heart: Buddhist Pith Instructions*, Ithaca, NY: Snow Lion Publications.

Burda-Stengel, Felix (2001) *Andrea Pozzo und die Videokunst. Neue Überlegungen zum barocken Illusionismus*, Berlin: Mann.

Burity, Glauce Maria Navarro (1988) *A presença dos Franciscanos na Paraíba através de Convento de Santo Antônio*, Rio de Janeiro: Bloch Editores.

Burton, Richard (1906) *Personal Narrative of a Pilgrimage to al-Madinah and Meccah* (2 vols.), London: George Bell & Sons.

Burton, W. F. P. (1961) "Luba Religion and Magic in Custom and Belief," *Annales* 35, Tervuren: Royal Museum of Central Africa.

Cabu, F. (1938) "Contribution à l'étude de la repartition des kwés au Katanga," *Annales du Musée Royal Belge* 1(4).

Cahill, James (1960) "Confucian Elements in the Theory of Painting," pp. 114–40 in Arthur F. Wright (ed.) *The Confucian Persuasion*, Stanford, CA: Stanford University Press.

Calabrese, Omar (1992) *The Neo-Baroque: A Sign of the Times*, Princeton, NJ: Princeton University Press.

Campbell, Heidi, Gordon Lynch, and Pete Ward (2009) "'Can You Hear the Army?' Exploring Public Discourse in Evangelical Youth Prayer Meetings," *Journal of Contemporary Religion* 24(2).

Carette, Jeremy (2005) "Religion Out of Mind: The Ideology of Cognitive Science and Religion," in Kelly Bulkeley (ed.) *Soul, Psyche, Brain: New Directions in the Study of Religion and Brain–Mind Science*, New York: Palgrave.

Carroll, Michael P. (1985) "The Virgin Mary at LaSalette and Lourdes: Whom Did the Children See?," *Journal for the Scientific Study of Religion* 24(1): 56–74.

Casey, Edward (1987) *Remembering: A Phenomenological Study*, Bloomington, IN: Indiana University Press.

Cassar-Pullicino, Joseph (1992) "Pauline Traditions in Malta," in Michael Galea, and John Ciarló (eds.) *St. Paul in Malta: A Compendium of Pauline Studies*, Valletta, Malta: published by the editors.

Caudill, William W. (1954) *Toward Better School Design*, New York: F.W. Dodge Corporation.

Caulfield, Mina (1972) "Culture and Imperialism: Proposing a New Dialectic," pp. 182–212 in Dell Hymes (ed.) *Reinventing Anthropology*, New York: Random House.

Centlivres, Pierre, and Micheline Centlivres-Demont (2005) "Une étrange rencontre: La photographie orientaliste de Lehnert et Landrock et l'image iranienne du prophète Mahomet," *Études photographiques* (Paris) 17: 5–15.

Centlivres, Pierre, and Micheline Centlivres-Demont (2006) "The Story of a Picture: Shiite Depictions of Muhammad," *ISIM Review* (International Institute for the Study of Islam in the Modern World, Leiden, the Netherlands) 17: 18–19.

Chamberlain, J. Gordon (1961) "Christian Education: Action and Meaning," pp. 48–52 in *Pittsburgh Annual National Conference on Church Architecture*, Church Architecture Guild of America and the Department of Church Building and Architecture of the National Council of Churches of Christ in the USA.

Chang, Garma C. (1992) *The Hundred Thousand Songs of Milarepa*, vols. 1 and 2, Boston: Shambhala Publications Inc.

Chidester, David (2005a) *Authentic Fakes: Religion and American Popular Culture*, Berkeley, CA: University of California Press.

Chidester, David (2005b) "The American Touch: Tactile Imagery in American Religion and Politics," pp. 49–65 in Constance Classen (ed.) *The Book of Touch*, Oxford and New York: Berg.

Chidester, David (2008) "Economy," pp. 83–95 in David Morgan (ed.) *Key Words in Religion, Media, and Culture*, London: Routledge.

Chidester, David, and Edward T. Linenthal (eds.) (1995) *American Sacred Space*, Bloomington, IN: Indiana University Press.

Cho, Insoo (2007) "Chosanghwareul boneun tto hanaui sigak (Anthropological Approach to the Portraiture in East Asia)," *Misulsa Hakbo* 29: 115–36.

Choi, Soon-guen (2001) "Sinjugo (A Study of Ancestor Tablet)," *Saenghwalmunmul yeongu* 2: 61–90.

Christ Church Lutheran (1960) *Christ Church Courier*, June, Minneapolis.

Christ Church Lutheran (1962) *Christ Church Courier*, 17 June, Education Building Dedication issue, Minneapolis.

Christian, William A. (1989a) *Apparitions in Late Medieval and Renaissance Spain*, Princeton, NJ: Princeton University Press.

Christian, William A. (1989b) *Local Religion in Sixteenth-Century Spain*, Princeton, NJ: Princeton University Press.

Christian, William A. (1992) *Moving Crucifixes in Modern Spain*, Princeton, NJ: Princeton University Press.

Christian, William A. (1996) *Visionaries: The Spanish Republic and the Reign of Christ*, Berkeley, CA: University of California Press.

Churchland, Patricia Smith (1986) *Neurophilosophy: Toward a Unified Science of the Mind/Brain*, Cambridge, MA: The MIT Press.

Classen, Constance (ed.) (2005) *The Book of Touch*, Oxford and New York: Berg.

Cohen, Thomas M. (1998) *The Fire of Tongues: António Vieira and the Missionary Church in Brazil and Portugal*, Stanford, CA: Stanford University Press.

Colchester, Cloë (2003) "Introduction," pp. 1–22 in Cloë Colchester (ed.) *Clothing the Pacific*, London: Berg Publishers.

Coleman, Simon (1996) "Words as Things: Language, Aesthetics and the Objectification of Protestant Evangelicalism," *Journal of Material Culture* 1(1): 107–28.

Collins, Steven (1997) "The Body in Theravāda Buddhist Monasticism," pp. 185–204 in Sarah Coakley (ed.) *Religion and the Body*, Cambridge: Cambridge University Press.

Corrigan, John (2002) *Business of the Heart: Religion and Emotion in the Nineteenth Century*, Berkeley, CA: University of California Press.

Cosentino, Donald (1995) "It's All for You, Sen Jak," pp. 242–65 in Donald Cosentino (ed.) *Sacred Arts of Haitian Vodou*, Los Angeles: UCLA Fowler Museum of Cultural History.

Cosentino, Donald (ed.) (1996) *Sacred Arts of Haitian Vodou*, Los Angeles: UCLA Fowler Museum of Cultural History.

Cosentino, Donald (1998) *Vodou Things: The Art of Pierrot Barra and Marie Cassaise*, Jackson: University of Mississippi Press.

Cosentino, Donald (2005) "Vodou in the Age of Mechanical Reproduction," *RES: Anthropology and Aesthetics* 47(Spring): 231–46.

Couliano, I. P. (1991) *Out of This World: Otherworldly Journeys from Gilgamesh to Albert Einstein*, Boston: Shambhala Publications.

Coupe, William A. (1998) "Iconographie de Luther. La publication des quatre-vingt quinze theses," pp. 187–96 in Michèle Ménard (ed.) *Histoire, image, imaginaire*, Le Mans: Presses de l'Université du Maine.

Crossley, Nick (2001) *The Social Body: Habit, Identity and Desire*, London: Sage.

Csordas, Thomas, J. (1990) "Embodiment as a Paradigm for Anthropology," *Ethos* 18(1): 5–47.

Daly, Gabriel (1980) *Transcendence and Immanence: A Study of Catholic Modernism and Integralism*, Oxford: Clarendon.

Damascus, St. John (2000) *On the Divine Images*, trans. David Anderson, Crestwood, NY: St. Vladimir's Seminary Press.

Damasio, Antonio (1994) *Descartes' Error: Emotion, Reason, and the Human Brain*, New York: Penguin.

Damasio, Antonio (1999) *The Feeling of What Happens: Body and Emotion in the Making of Consciousness*, San Diego: Harcourt.

Daniels, Inge (2003) "Scooping, Raking, Beckoning Luck: Luck, Agency and the Interdependence between People and Things in Japan," *Journal of the Royal Anthropological Institute* 9(4): 619–38.

Daniels, Inge (2008) "Japanese Homes Inside Out," *Home Cultures* 5: 115–40.

Daniels, Inge (2009a) "The 'Social Death' of Unused Gifts: Surplus and Value in Contemporary Japan," *Journal of Material Culture* 14(3): 385–408.

Daniels, Inge (2009b) "Seasonal and Commercial and Rhythms of Domestic Consumption: A Japanese Case Study," pp. 262–94 in Elizabeth Shove, Frank Trentmann, and Richard Wilk (eds) *Time, Consumption and Everyday Life: Practice, Materiality and Culture*, London: Routledge.

Daniels, Inge (in press) *The Japanese House: Material Culture in the Modern Home*, Oxford: Berg Publishers.

D'Aquili, Eugene G., Charles D. Laughlin, Jr., and John McManus (eds.) *The Spectrum of Ritual: A Biogenetic Structural Analysis*, New York: Columbia University Press.

Davis, Richard H. (1997) *Lives of Indian Images*, Princeton, NJ: Princeton University Press.

Dawson, Lorne (1989) "Otto and Freud on the Uncanny and Beyond," *Journal of the American Academy of Religion* 57(2): 283–311.

Day, Abby (in press) "Believing in Belonging: An Exploration of Young People's Social Contexts and Constructions of Belief," in Sylvia Collins-Mayo, and Ben Pink Dandelion (eds.) *Religion and Youth*, Aldershot: Ashgate.

Dean, Carolyn (1999) *Inka Bodies and the Body of Christ: Corpus Christi in Colonial Cuzco, Peru*, Durham, NC: Duke University Press.

Dean, Carolyn, and Dana Leibsohn (2003) "Hybridity and its Discontents: Considering Visual Culture in Colonial Spanish America," *Colonial Latin American Review* 12(1): 5–35.

Debeerst, Gustaaf (1894) "Essai de grammaire tabwa," *Zeitschrift für Afrika und Ocean Sprachen* 1–2.

Denny, Frederick (1985) "Pilgrimage and the History of Religions: Theoretical Approaches to the Hajj," pp. 63–77 in Richard Martin (ed.) *Approaches to Islam in Religious Studies*, Tucson, AZ: University of Arizona Press.

Descartes, René ([1649]1996) *Die Leidenschaften der Seele* (Französisch-deutsch), trans. And ed. Klaus Hamacher, Hamburg: Felix Meiner Verlag.

Dissanyake, Ellen (1992) *Homo Aestheticus: Where Art Comes From and Why*, New York: Free Press.

Dorje, Rinjing, and Ter Ellingson (1979) "'Explanation of the Secret Gcod Da Ma Ru': An Explanation of Musical Symbolism," *Asian Music* 10(2): 63–91.

Douglas, Mary ([1966] 2004) *Purity and Danger: An Analysis of Concepts of Pollution and Taboo*, London and New York: Routledge.

Dowman, Keith (1985) *Masters of Mahamudra*, Albany, NY: SUNY Press.

Drewal, Henry (1988) "Mami Wata Worship in Africa," *TDR, The Drama Review* 32(2): 160–85.

Drewal, Henry (2008a) "Introduction: Sources and Currents," pp. 22–69 in *Mami Wata: Arts for Water Spirits in Africa and Its Diasporas*, ed. Henry Drewal, Los Angeles: UCLA Fowler Museum.

Drewal, Henry (ed.) (2008b) *Sacred Waters: Arts for Mami Wata and Other Divinities in Africa and the Diaspora*, Bloomington, IN: Indiana University Press.

Drewal, Henry (ed.) (2008c) *Mami Wata: Arts for Water Spirits in Africa and Its Diasporas*, Los Angeles: UCLA Fowler Museum.

Drewal, Henry John, and Margaret Thompson Drewal (1983) *Gelede: Art and Female Power among the Yoruba*, Bloomington, IN: Indiana University Press.

Durkheim, Emile ([1912] 2001) *The Elementary Forms of the Religious Life*, Oxford: Oxford University Press.

Durkheim, Emile ([1965] 1995) *The Elementary Forms of the Religious Life*, trans. Karen E. Fields, New York: Free Press.

Edou, Jerome (1996) *Machig Labdron and the Foundation of Chod*, Ithaca, NY: Snow Lion Publications.

Edwards, Elizabeth, and Janice Hart (2004) "Introduction: Photographs as Objects," pp. 1–15, in Elizabeth Edwards, and Janice Hart (eds.) *Photographs, Objects, Things: On the Materiality of Images*, New York: Routledge.

Eicher, Joanne B. (ed.) (1995) *Dress and Ethnicity: Change across Space and Time*, Oxford: Berg.

Eickelman, Dale, and James Piscatori (1990) "Social Theory in the Study of Muslim Societies," pp. 3–28 in Dale Eickelman, and James Piscatori (eds) *Muslim Travellers: Pilgrimage, Migration, and the Religious Imagination*, Berkeley, CA: University of California Press.

Einstein, Mara (2008) *Brands of Faith: Marketing Religion in a Commercial Age*, London: Routledge.

Eipper, Chris (2007) "Moving Statues and Moving Images: Religious Artefacts and the Spiritualisation of Materiality," *The Australian Journal of Anthropology* 18(3): 253–63.

Eliade, Mircea (1959) *The Sacred and the Profane: The Nature of Religion*, trans. Willard R. Trask, New York: Harcourt, Brace and Company.

Eliade, Mircea (1992) *Shamanism: Archaic Techniques of Ecstasy*, Princeton, NJ: Princeton University Press.

Ellingson, Ter, and Rinjng Dorje (1979) "Explanation of the Secret Gcod Da ma ru.' An Exploration of Musical Instrument Symbolism," *Asian Music* 10(2) 63–91.

Encyclopedia of Islam (1999), CD-ROM edition, v.1.0, Leiden, the Netherlands: Brill.

Erdoes, Richard, and Alfonso Ortiz (eds.) (1984) *American Indian Myths and Legends*, New York: Pantheon.

Ernst, Carl (2003) *Following Muhammad: Rethinking Islam in the Contemporary World*, Chapel Hill: University of North Carolina Press.

Evens-Wentz , W. Y. (1967) *Tibetan Yoga*, Oxford: Oxford University Press.

Eves, Richard (1996) "Colonialism, Corporeality and Character: Methodist Missions and the Refashioning of Bodies in the Pacific," *History and Anthropology* 10(1): 85–138.

Fabrega, H. (1977) "Culture, Behavior, and the Nervous System," *Annual Review of Anthropology* 6: 419–55.

Faith United Protestant Church (1953) Building dedication bulletin, Park Forest Public Library.

Faith United Protestant Church (1991) *Our 40th: Forward from 40, Renewing the Vision*, Park Forest, Illinois.

Farago, Claire (ed.) (1995) *Reframing the Renaissance: Visual Culture in Europe and Latin America, 1450–1650*, New Haven, CT: Yale University Press.

Farrow, G. W. (1992) *The Concealed Essence of the Hevajra Tantra: With the Commentary Yogaratnamala*, Delhi: Motilal Banarsidass Publications.

Faure, Bernard (2004) "Buddhist Relics and Japanese Regalia," in David Germano and Kevin Trainor (eds.) *Embodying the Dharma: Buddhist Relic Veneration in Asia*, Albany, NY: SUNY Press.

Feeley-Harnik, Gillian (1989) "Cloth and the Creation of Ancestors in Madagascar," pp. 73–116 in Annette B. Weiner, and Jane Schneider (eds.) *Cloth and Human Experience*, Washington, DC: Smithsonian Institute.

Figal, Gerald (1999) *Civilization and Monsters: Spirits of Modernity in Meiji Japan*, Durham, NC: Duke University Press.

Fish, Stanley (1980) *Is There a Text in this Class? The Authority of Interpretive Communities*, Cambridge, MA: Harvard University Press.

Foucault, Michel (1979) *Discipline and Punish: The Birth of the Prison*, trans. A. Sheridan, New York: Vintage Books.

Frank, Georgia (2000) *The Memory of Eyes: Pilgrims to Living Saints in Christian Late Antiquity*, Berkeley, CA: University of California Press.

Fraser, Douglas, and Herbert M. Cole (eds.) (1972) *African Art and Leadership*, Madison, WI: University of Wisconsin Press.

Freedberg, David (1989) *The Power of Images: Studies in the History and Theory of Response*, Chicago: University of Chicago Press.

Freud, Sigmund (1995) "The Uncanny," in Sander L. Gilman (ed.) *Sigmund Freud: Psychological Writings and Letters*, New York: The Continuum Publishing Company.

Frey, Edward S. (1959) "Building for Christian Community," pp. 1–12 in *Los Angeles National Guild Conference*, Church Architectural Guild of America and Department of Church Building and Architecture of the National Council of Churches in the USA.

Frugoni, Chara (2004) "'Ad imaginem et similitudinem nostram.' Der Heilige Franziskus und die Erfindung der Stigmata," pp. 77–112 in B. Menke, and B. Vinken (eds.) *Stigmata*, Munich: Fink.

Galea, Michael, and John Ciarló (eds.) (1992) *St. Paul in Malta: A Compendium of Pauline Studies*, Valletta, Malta: published by the editors.

Gallagher, Shaun (2005) *How the Body Shapes the Mind*, Oxford: Clarendon Press.

Gaudefroy-Demombynes, Maurice (1954) "*Le Voile de la Ka'ba*," *Studia Islamica* 2: 5–21.

Gaudefroy-Demombynes, Maurice (1977) *Le Pélerinage à la Mekke: étude d'histoire religieuse*, Philadelphia, PA: Porcupine Press.

Gcod kyi chos skor (1978) New Delhi: Tibet House, pp. 10–410.

Geary, Patrick (1986) "Sacred Commodities: The Circulation of Medieval Relics," pp. 169–91 in Arjun Appadurai (ed.) *The Social Life of Things: Commodities in Cultural Perspective*, Cambridge: Cambridge University Press.

Geertz, Clifford (1973) *The Interpretation of Cultures*, New York: Basic Books.

Gell, Alfred (1998) *Art and Agency: An Anthropological Theory*, Oxford: Clarendon Press.

Gerbert, Elaine (2001) "Dolls in Japan," *Journal of Popular Culture* 35: 59–89.

Germano, David, and Kevin Trainor (eds.) (2004) *Embodying the Dharma: Buddhist Relic Veneration in Asia*, Albany, NY: SUNY Press.

Giddens, Anthony (1984) *The Constitution of Society*, Cambridge: Polity.

Giddens, Anthony (1991) *Modernity and Self-Identity*, Cambridge: Polity.

Goffman, Erving (1959) *The Presentation of Self in Everyday Life*, New York: Doubleday.

Good, Byron (1994) *Medicine, Rationality, and Experience: An Anthropological Perspective*, New York: Cambridge University Press.

Gougaud, Henri (1973) *Les Animaux magiques de notre universe*, Paris: Solar.

Grabar, Oleg (2002) "Les portraits du prophète Mahomet à Byzance et ailleurs," *Académie des Inscriptions et Belles-Lettres. Comptes rendus des séances de l'année 2002* (Paris) 4: 1431–445.

Graham, William (1987) *Beyond the Written Word: Oral Aspects of Scripture in the History of Religion*, Cambridge: Cambridge University Press.

Gray, David (2007) *The Cakrasamvara Tantra: A Study and Annotated Translation*, New York: American Institute of Buddhist Studies at Columbia University in the City of New York.

Griffith, R. Marie (2004) *Born Again Bodies: Flesh and Spirit in American Christianity*, Berkeley, CA: University of California Press.

Grimes, Ronald L. (2000) *Deeply into the Bone: Re-inventing Rites of Passage*, Berkeley, CA: University of California Press.

Grimes, Ronald L. (2006) *Rite Out of Place: Ritual, Media, and the Arts*, New York: Oxford University Press.

Grosso, Michael (1989) "UFOs and the Myth of the New Age," in Dennis Stillings (ed.) *Cyberbiological Studies of the Imaginal Component in the UFO Contact Experience*, *Archaeus* 5: 81–98.

Gruzinski, Serge (1988) *La colonisation de l'imaginaire. Sociétés indigènes et occi-dentalisation dans le Mexique espagnol XVIe–XVIIIe siècle*, Paris: Gallimard.

Gruzinski, Serge (1990) *La guerre des images de Christophe Colomb à "Blade Runner," 1492–2019*, Paris: Fayard.

Gruzinski, Serge (1991) *L'Amérique de la Conquête peinte par les Indiens du Mexique*, Paris: Flammarion.

Gruzinski, Serge (2004) *Les quatre parties du monde. Histoire d'une mondialisa-tion*, Paris: Martinière.

Gruzinski, Serge, and Carmen Bernand (1988) *De l'Idolâtrie. Une archéologie des sciences religieuses*, Paris: Seuil.

Gunning, Tom (1995) "Phantom Images and Modern Manifestations: Spirit Photography, Magic Theater, Trick Films, and Photography's Uncanny," in Patrice Petro (ed.) *Fugitive Images: From Photography to Video*, Bloomington, IN: Indiana University Press.

Gunning, Tom (2004) "Haunting Images: Ghosts, Photography and the Modern Body," pp. 8–19 in Alison Ferris (ed.) *The Disembodied Spirit*, Rhode Island: Meridian Printing.

Gyatso, Janet (1985) "The Development of the Gcod Tradition," pp. 320–41 in Barbara Nimri Aziz, and Matthew Kapstein (eds.) *Soundings of Tibetan Civilization*, New Delhi: Manohar.

Gyatso, Janet (2003) "One Plus One Makes Three: Buddhist Gender Conception and the Law of the Non-Excluded Middle," *History of Religions* 43(2): 89–115.

Hamburger, Jeffrey (1989) "The Use of Images in the Pastoral Care of Nuns: The Case of Heinrich Suso and the Dominicans," *The Art Bulletin* 71(1): 20–46.

Hansen, Karen Tranberg (2004) "The World in Dress: Anthropological Perspectives on Clothing, Fashion, and Culture," *Annual Review of Anthropology* 33: 369–92.

Harding, Sarah (2003) *Machik's Complete Explanation: Clarifying the Meaning of Chod, A Complete Explanation of Casting Out the Body as Food*, Ithaca, NY: Snow Lion Publications.

Harré, Rom (ed.) (1986) *The Social Construction of Emotions*, Oxford: Basil Blackwell.

Helliwell, Christine (1996) "Space and Sociality in a Dayak Longhouse," in Michael Jackson (ed.) *Things as They Are: New Directions in Phenomenological Anthropology*, Bloomington, IN: University of Indiana Press.

Hendrickson, Carol (1995) *Weaving Identities: Construction of Dress and Self in a Highland Guatemala Town*, Texas: University of Texas Press.

Henriques, Julian, Wendy Hollway, Cathy Urwin, Couze Venn, and Valerie Walkerdine (1998) *Changing the Subject: Psychology, Social Regulation and Subjectivity*, London: Routledge.

Hermann, Jacqueline (1998) *No reino do desejado. A construção do sebastianismo em Portugal séculos XVI e XVII*, São Paulo: Companhia das Letras.

Hermann, Jacqueline (2000) *1580–1600. O sonho da salvação*, São Paulo: Companhia das Letras.

Hermkens, Anna-Karina (2005) "Engendering Objects: Barkcloth and the Dynamics of Identity in Papua New Guinea," PhD dissertation, Radboud University, Nijmegen, the Netherlands.

Hermkens, Anna-Karina (2007a) "Church Festivals and the Visualization of Identity in Collingwood Bay, Papua New Guinea," *Visual Anthropology* 20(5): 347–64.

Hermkens, Anna-Karina (2007b) "Gendered Objects. Embodiments of Colonial Collecting in Dutch New Guinea," *Journal of Pacific History* 42(1): 1–20.

Herzfeld, Michael (2001) *Anthropology: Theoretical Practice in Culture and Society*, Oxford: Blackwell.

Hofmann, Werner (ed.) (1983) *Luther und die Folgen für die Kunst*, Munich: Prestel.

Holanda, Sergio Buarque de (1996) *Visão do Paraíso*, 6th edn., São Paulo: Brasiliense.

Hollier, Denis (1992) *Against Architecture: The Writings of Georges Bataille*, Cambridge, MA: MIT Press.

Hollywood, Amy (2002) *Sensible Ecstasy: Mysticism, Sexual Difference, and the Demands of History*, Chicago: University of Chicago Press.

Hoover, Stewart (2003) "Religion, Media and Identity: Theory and Method in Audience Research on Religion and Media," pp. 9–19 in Joylon Mitchell and Sophia Marriage (eds.) *Mediating Religion: Conversations in Media, Religion and Culture*, London: T&T Clark.

Hornby, Joan (2000) "Chinese Ancestral Portraits: Some Late Ming and Ming Style Ancestral Paintings in Scandinavian Museums," *Bulletin of Far Eastern Antiquities* 70: 173–271.

Hoskins, Janet (1989) "Why do Ladies Sing the Blues? Indigo Dyeing, Cloth Production, and Gender Symbolism in Kodi," pp. 141–73 in Annette B. Weiner, and Jane Schneider (eds.) *Cloth and Human Experience*, Washington, DC: Smithsonian Institution Press.

Hufford, David J. (1982) *The Terror That Comes in the Night: An Experience-Centered Study of Supernatural Assault Traditions*, Philadelphia, PA: University of Pennsylvania Press.

Hume, David (2000) *A Treatise of Human Nature*, David Fate Norton and Marty J. Norton (eds.), Oxford: Oxford University Press.

Hume, David (2007) *A Dissertation on the Passions* and *The Natural History of Religion: A Critical Edition*, ed. Tom L. Beauchamp, Oxford: Clarendon Press.

Hunt, Kate (2003) "Understanding the Spirituality of People Who Do Not Go to Church," in Grace Davie, Paul Heelas, and Linda Woodhead, *Predicting Religion: Christian, Secular and Alternative Futures*. Aldershot: Ashgate.

Ibn Battuta (1958) *The Travels of Ibn Battuta A.D. 1325–1354*, trans. H. A. R. Gibb, Cambridge: Cambridge University Press.

Ibn Ishaq (2004) *The Life of Muhammad: A Translation of Ibn Ishaq's "Sirat Rasul Allah,"* trans. Alfred Guillaume, New York: Oxford University Press.

Ibn Kathir (2002) *Tafsir al-Qur'an al-'Azim*, 4 vols, Cairo: Dar al-Taqwa li-l-Turath.

Ibn Muyassir (1981) *Akhbar Misr*, Ayman Fu'ad Sayyid, ed. Cairo: Institut Français d'Archéologie Orientale.

Ibn Taghri Bardi (1942) *Hawadith al-Duhur*, 8 vols., William Popper, ed. Berkeley, CA: University of California Press.

Imorde, Joseph (2004) *Affekt-Übertragung*, Berlin: Mann.

Ito, Mikuharu (1995) *Zôyokôkan no jinruigaku (An Anthropology of Gift Exchange)*, Tokyo: Chikuma.

James, Liz (1996) "'Pray Not to Fall into Temptation and Be on Your Guard': Pagan Statues in Christian Constantinople," *Gesta* 35: 12–20.

James, William ([1892] 1985) *Psychology: The Briefer Course*, ed. Gordon Allport, Notre Dame, IN: University of Notre Dame Press.

James, William (1961) *The Varieties of Religious Experience*, New York: Collier.

Jay, Martin (1988) "Scopic Regimes of Modernity," pp. 3–23 in Hal Foster (ed.) *Vision and Visuality*, Seattle: Bay Press.

Jeong, Duhui (1996) "Josang jesa munjewa Yun Jichung (Yun Jichung's Scandal on Ancestor Rites)," *Segyeui Sinhak* 33(Winter): 140–49.

Jewsiewicki, Bogumil (2008) "Mami Wata/Mamba Muntu Paintings in the Democratic Republic of the Congo," pp. 126–33 in *Mami Wata: Arts for Water Spirits in Africa and Its Diasporas* (ed.) Henry Drewal, Los Angeles: UCLA Fowler Museum.

Johnson, Frank (1914) "Here and There in Northern Africa," *National Geographic* 25(1): 1–132.

Johnson, Mark (2007) *The Meaning of the Body*, Chicago: University of Chicago Press.

Jomier, Jacques (1953) *Le Mahmal et la caravane Égyptienne des pèlerins de la Mecque (XIII–XX siècles)*, Cairo: Institut Français d'Archéologie Orientale.

Jomier, Jacques (1972) "Le *Mahmal* de Sultan Qanush al-Ghuri (début XVI siècle)," *Annales Islamologiques* 11: 183–88.

Jones, James (1991) *Contemporary Psychoanalysis and Religion: Transference and Transcendence*, New Haven, CT: Yale University Press.

Jordán, Manuel (1994) "Heavy Stuff and Heavy Staffs from Chokwe and Related Peoples of Angola, Zaire, and Zambia," in Allen F. Roberts (ed.) *Staffs of Life: Rods, Staffs, Scepters, and Wands from the Coudron Collection of African Art*, Iowa City: Project for Advanced Study of Art and Life in Africa and the University of Iowa Museum of Art.

Juhan, Deane (1987) *Jobs' Body: A Handbook for Bodywork*, New York: Station Hill Press.

Kaufman, Suzanne K. (2005) *Consuming Visions: Mass Culture and the Lourdes Shrine*, Ithaca, NY: Cornell University Press.

Kaufmann, Walter (1961) *Critique of Religion and Philosophy*, Garden City, New York: Anchor Books, Doubleday & Company.

Kawasaki, E., and M. Moteki (2002) *Seikatsu bunka wo kangaeru (Thoughts about the Culture of Everyday Life)*, Tokyo: Kanseikan.

Keane, Webb (1997) *Signs of Recognition: Powers and Hazards of Representation in an Indonesian Society*, Berkeley, CA: University of California Press.

Keane, Webb (2006) "Subjects and Objects: An Introduction," pp. 197–202 in Christopher Tilley *et al.*, *Handbook of Material Culture*, London: Sage.

Keane, Webb (2008) "The Evidence of the Senses and the Materiality of Religion," *Journal of the Royal Anthropological Institute* 14(April): 110–27.

Kieschnick, John (2003) *The Impact of Buddhism on Chinese Material Culture*, Princeton, NJ: Princeton University Press.

Kim, Bongryeol (2007) *Gim Bongryeolui Hanguk Geonchuk Iyagi 2*, Seoul: Dolbegae.

Klein, Frank (1953) "Education Building Dedication Bulletin for Faith United Presbyterian Church," Park Forest, Illinois.

Kohut, Heinz (1984) *How Does Analysis Cure?*, Chicago: University of Chicago Press.

Konaté, Yacouba, and Yaya Savané (1994) "Les artistes de la recupération à l'œuvre," pp. 64–77 in L. Ferera (ed.) *Ingénieuse Afrique: Artisans de la recupération et du recyclage*, Québec: Éditions Fides et le Musée de la Civilisation.

Kopytoff, Igor (1986) "The Cultural Biography of Things: Commoditization as Process," pp. 64–91 in Arjun Appadurai (ed.) *The Social Life of Things: Commodities in Cultural Perspective*, Cambridge: Cambridge University Press.

Kreamer, Christine Mullen, Mary Nooter Roberts, Elizabeth Harney, and Allyson Purpura (2007) *Inscribing Meaning: Writing and Graphic Systems in African Art*, Milan: 5 Continents Editions.

Kretschmer, Angelika (2000) *Kuyô in Contemporary Japan: Religious Rites in the Lives of Lay People*, Göttingen: Cuvillier Verlag.

Kretzmann, A. R. (1962) "Europe's Churches: A Theologian's Viewpoint," pp. 108–12 in *Cleveland Annual National Joint Conference on Church Architecture*, Church Architecture Guild of America and the Department of Church Building and Architecture of the National Council of Churches of Christ in the USA.

Kripal, Jeffrey J. (1995) *Kali's Child: The Mystical and the Erotic in the Life and Teachings of Ramakrishna*, Chicago: University of Chicago Press.

Krüger, Klaus (1992) *Der frühe Bildkult des Franziskus in Italien. Gestalt- und Funktionswandel des Tafelbildes im 13. und 14. Jahrhundert*, Berlin: Mann.

Krüger, Klaus (2001) *Das Bild als Schleier des Unsichtbaren. Ästhetische Illusion in der Kunst der frühen Neuzeit in Italien*, Munich: Fink.

Küchler, Susanne, and Walter Mellion (eds.) (1991) *Images of Memory: On Remembering and Representation*, Washington, DC: Smithsonian Institution Press.

Küchler, Susanne, and Graeme Were (eds.) (2005) *The Art of Clothing: A Pacific Experience*, London: Routledge Cavendish.

Lakoff, George (1987) *Women, Fire and Dangerous Things: What Categories Reveal About the Mind*, Chicago: University of Chicago Press.

Lakoff, George, and Mark Johnson (1980) *Metaphors We Live By*, Chicago: University of Chicago Press.

Lambek, Michael (1998) "Body and Mind in Mind, Body and Mind in Body: Some Anthropological Interventions in a Long Conversation," pp. 103–23 in Michael Lambek, and Andrew Strathern (eds.) *Bodies and Persons: Comparative Perspectives from Africa and Melanesia*, Cambridge: Cambridge University Press.

Lamp, Frederick (ed.) (2004) *See the Music, Hear the Dance: Rethinking African Art at the Baltimore Museum of Art*, Munich: Prestel.

Lane, Edward William (1989) *Manners and Customs of the Modern Egyptians*, Cairo: Livres de France.

Latour, Bruno (2005) *Reassembling the Social: An Introduction to Actor-Network Theory*, Oxford: Clarendon Press.

Laughlin, Jr., Charles D., and Eugene G. d'Aquili (1974) *Biogenetic Structuralism*, New York and London: Columbia University Press.

Laughlin, Jr., Charles D., John McManus, and Eugene G. d'Aquili (1993) *Brain, Symbol and Experience: Toward a Neurophenomenology of Human Consciousness*, New York: Columbia University Press.

Law, Jane (1997) *Puppets of Nostalgia*, Princeton, NJ: Princeton University Press.

Lawal, Babatunde (1996) *The Gelede Spectacle: Art, Gender, and Social Harmony in an African Culture*, Seattle and London: University of Washington Press.

Leach, Edmund (1954) *Political Systems of Highland Burma*, London: G. Bell & Sons.

Leinberger, Hugo ([1964] 1969) "Projecting Building Plans," pp. 81–89 in *For Church Builders: A Recall to Basics*, Valley Forge, PA: Religious Publishing Co.

Leiris, Michel (1952) "Notes sur l'usage de chromolithographies catholiques par les vodouisants d'Haiti," in *Les Afro-Américains*, Dakar: Institut Fondamental de l'Afrique Noire.

Lévi-Strauss, Claude ([1949] 1967) *Structural Anthropology*, trans. Claire Jacobson, and Brooke Grundfest Schoepf, Garden City, New York: Doubleday & Company, Inc.

Lévi-Strauss, Claude (1973) "Structuralism and Ecology," *Social Science Information* 12(1): 7–23.

Lévi-Strauss, Claude (1981) *The Naked Man*, trans. John and Doreen Weightman, New York: Harper & Row Publishers.

Lex, Barbara W. (1974) "Voodoo Death: New Thoughts on an Old Explanation," *American Anthropologist*, 76(4): 818–24.

Lex, Barbara W. (1979) "The Neurobiology of Ritual Trance," pp. 117–52 in Eugene G. d'Aquili, Charles D. Laughlin, Jr., and John McManus (eds.) *The Spectrum of Ritual: A Biogenetic Structural Analysis*, New York: Columbia University Press.

Li, Shujiang, and Karl W. Luckert (1994) *Mythology and Folklore of the Hui, a Muslim Chinese People*, Albany, NY: State University Press of New York.

Liljenberg, Karen (trans.) (2007) *The Longchen Nyingthig Chod Practice: "The Loud Laugh of the Dakini*," available at: www. zangthal.co.uk.

Lima, Luís Filipe Silvério (2004) *Padre Vieira. Sonhos proféticos, profecias oníricas. O tempo do Quinto Império nos sermões de Xavier dormindo*, São Paulo: Humanitas.

Lindquist, Galina, and Simon Coleman (2008) "Against Belief?" *Social Analysis* 52(1): 1–18.

Lingpa, Jigme (1970) *gCod-yul mKha' 'gro'i gad rgyangs*, in *Klong che snying thig*, Solukhumbu: n.p.

Looper, Matthew G. (2003) "From Inscribed Bodies to Distributed Persons: Contextualising Tairona Figural Images in Performance," *Cambridge Archaeological Journal* 13: 25–40.

Lopez, Jr., Donald S. (1998) "Belief," pp. 21–35 in Mark C. Taylor (ed.) *Critical Terms for Religious Studies*, Chicago: University of Chicago Press.

Löw, Martina (2001) *Raumsoziologie*, Frankfurt: Suhrkamp.

Luckmann, Thomas (1967) *The Invisible Religion*, New York: Macmillan.

Lundquist, L.-O., and U. Dimberg (1995) "Facial Expressions Are Contagious," *Journal of Psychophysiology* 9: 203–11.

Lundqvist, Daniel, and Arne Öhman (2005) "Caught by the Evil Eye: Nonconscious Information Processing, Emotion, and Attention to Facial Stimuli," pp. 97–122 in Lisa Feldman Barrett, Paula M. Niedenthal, and Piotr Winkielman (eds.) *Emotion and Consciousness*, New York: The Guilford Press.

Lutz, A., J. P. Dunne, and R. J. Davidson (2006) "Meditation and the Neuroscience of Consciousness: An Introduction," in P. D. Zelazo and E. Thompson (eds.) *The Cambridge Handbook of Consciousness*, Cambridge: Cambridge University Press.

Lutz, A., L. L. Greischar, N. B. Rawlings, M. Ricard, and R. J. Davidson (2004) "Long-term Meditators Self-induce High-amplitude Gamma Synchrony During Mental Practice," *Proceedings of the National Academy of Sciences of the United States of America* 101(46): 16369–73.

Lutz, Catherine, and Jane Collins (1993) *Reading National Geographic*, Chicago: University of Chicago Press.

Lynn, Robert W., and Elliott Wright (1980) *The Big Little School: Two Hundred Years of the Sunday School*, Birmingham, AL: Religious Education Press.

Lyon, Margot L. (1997) "The Material Body, Social Processes and Emotion: 'Techniques of the Body' Revisited," *Body & Society* 3(1): 83–101.

Lyon, M. L., and J. M. Barbalet (1994) "Society's Body: Emotion and the 'Somatization' of Social Theory," pp. 48–66 in Thomas J. Csordas (ed.) *Embodiment and Experience: The Existential Ground of Culture and Self*, Cambridge: Cambridge University Press.

McCauley, Robert N., and Harvey Whitehouse (2005) "New Frontiers in the Cognitive Science of Religion," *Journal of Cognition and Culture* 5(1/2): 1–13.

McCree, O. T. ([1964] 1969) "The Church Prepares for Architecture," pp. 90–149 in William S. Clark (ed.) *For Church Builders: A Recall to Basics*, Valley Forge, PA: Religious Publishing Co.

McCutcheon, Russell (2005) *Religion and the Domestication of Dissent*, London: Equinox.

McDannell, Colleen (1995) *Material Christianity: Religion and Popular Culture in America*, New Haven, CT: Yale University Press.

Mack, John (2007) *The Art of Small Things*, London: The British Museum Press.

McLagan, Meg (2002) "Spectacles of Difference: Cultural Activism and the Mass Mediation of Tibet," in Faye Ginsberg, Lila Abu-Lughod, and Brian Larkin (eds.) *Media Worlds: Anthropology on New Terrain*, Los Angeles: University of California Press.

McNaughton, Patrick (1979) "Secret Sculptures of the Komo: Art and Power in a Bamana (Bambara) Initiation Association," *Working Papers in the Traditional Arts* 4, Philadelphia, PA: Institute for the Study of Human Issues.

Maloy, John (2006) "Celebrating the *Mahmal*: The Rajab Festival in Fifteenth Century Cairo," pp. 404–24 in Judith Pfeiffer (ed.) *History and Historiography of Post-Mongol Central Asia and the Middle East*, Wiesbaden: Harassowitz.

Marks, Laura V. (2000) *The Skin of the Film: Intercultural Cinema, Embodiment, and the Senses*, Durham, NC: Duke University Press.

Marks, Laura V. (2002) *Touch: Sensuous Theory and Multisensory Media*, Minneapolis: University of Minnesota Press.

Marnham, Patrick (1982) *Lourdes: A Modern Pilgrimage*, New York: Image Books.

Martin, Bernice (2006) "The Aesthetics of Latin American Pentecostalism: The Sociology of Religion and the Problem of Taste," pp. 138–60 in E. Arweck, and W. Keenan (eds.) *Materializing Religion*, Oxford: Ashgate.

Marty, Martin E. (1963) "Building for the Christian Parish in a Secular Culture," pp. 9–15 in *Seattle Annual National Joint Conference on Church Architecture*, Church Architecture Guild of America and Department of Church Building and Architecture of the National Council of Churches of Christ in the USA.

Massimi, Marina (2001) "As paixões es seus 'remédios': um excursus pela literature jesuitica dos séculos XVI e XVII," pp. 17–34 in Marina Massimi, and Paulo José Carvalho da Silva (eds.) *Os olhos vêem pelo coração. Conhecimento psicológico das paixões na história da cultura brasileira dos séculos XVI a XVII*, Ribeirão Preto: Holos.

Massimi, Marina (2005) *Palavras, almas e corpos no Brasil colonial*, Ipiranga: Loyola.

Masuzawa, Tomoko (2005) *The Invention of World Religions, or, How European Universalism Was Preserved in the Language of Pluralism*, Chicago: University of Chicago Press.

Mauss, Marcel (1973) "Techniques of the Body," *Economy and Society* 2: 70–88.

Megiani, Ana Paula Torres (2003) *O jovem rei encantado. Expectativas do Messianismo régio em Portugal, séculos XIII a XVI*, São Paulo: Hucitec.

Megiani, Ana Paula Torres (2004) *O rei ausente*, São Paulo: Alameda.

Meissner, William (1984) *Psychoanalysis and Religious Experience*, New Haven, CT: Yale University Press.

Melton, J. Gordon (1995) "The Contactees: A Survey," pp. 1–13 in James R. Lewis (ed.) *The Gods Have Landed: New Religions from Other Worlds*, Albany, NY: State University of New York Press.

Menke, Bettine, and Barbara Vinken (eds.) (2004) *Stigmata. Poetiken der Körperinschrift*, Munich: Fink.

Merleau-Ponty, Maurice (1945) *Phénoménologie de la Perception*, Paris: Gallimard.

Merleau-Ponty, Maurice (1962) *Phenomenology of Perception*, trans. Colin Smith, London: Routledge.

Meyer, Birgit (1998) *Commodities and the Power of Prayer*, Amsterdam: WOTRO Netherlands Foundation for the Advancement of Tropical Research

Meyer, Birgit (2006) *Religious Sensations: Why Media, Aesthetics and Power Matter in the Study of Contemporary Religion*, Amsterdam: Vrije Universiteit.

Meyer, Birgit, and Peter Pels (eds) (2003) *The Magic of Modernity*, Stanford, CA: Stanford University Press.

Meyer, Birgit, and Jojada Verrips (2008) "Aesthetics," pp. 20–30 in David Morgan (ed.) *Key Words in Religion, Media and Culture*, London: Routledge.

Miller, Daniel (1987) *Material Culture and Mass Consumption*, Oxford: Blackwell.

Miller, Daniel (ed.) (2001) *Home Possessions*, Oxford: Berg.

Miller, Daniel (2005a) "Introduction," pp. 1–20 in Susanne Küchler and Daniel Miller (eds.) *Clothing as Material Culture*, Oxford: Berg.

Miller, Daniel (ed.) (2005b) *Materiality*, Durham, NC: Duke University Press.

Miller, Daniel (2008) *The Comfort of Things*, Cambridge: Polity.

Mills, Kenneth (1997) *Idolatry and Its Enemies: Colonial Andean Religion and Extirpation, 1640–1750*, Princeton, NJ: Princeton University Press.

Mills, Kenneth, and Anthony Grafton (eds.) (2003) *Conversions: Old Worlds and New*, Rochester, NY: University of Rochester Press.

Miranda, Maria do Carmo Tavares de (1969) *Os Franciscanos e a formação do Brasil*, Recife: Universidade Federal de Pernambuco.

Mitchell, Jon P. (1997) "A Moment with Christ: The Importance of Feelings in the Analysis of Belief," *Journal of the Royal Anthropological Institute* (n.s.) 3(1): 79–94.

Mitchell, Jon P. (1998a) "A Providential Storm: Myth, History and the Story of St. Paul's Shipwreck in Malta," in Frank Brinkhuis, and Sascha Talmore (eds.) *Memory, History and Critique: European Identity at the Millennium*, Utrecht: University for Humanist Studies.

Mitchell, Jon P. (1998b) "Performances of Masculinity in a Maltese *Festa*," pp. 68–92 in Felicia Hughes-Freeland and Mary Crain (eds.) *Recasting Ritual*, London: Routledge.

Mitchell, Jon P. (2002a) *Ambivalent Europeans: Ritual, Memory and the Public Sphere in Malta*, London: Routledge.

Mitchell, Jon P. (2002b) "The Devil, Satanism and the Evil Eye in Contemporary Malta," pp. 77–103 in Paul Clough, and Jon P. Mitchell (eds.) *Powers of Good and Evil: Social Transformation and Popular Belief*, Oxford: Berghahn.

Mitchell, Jon P. (2002c) "Modernity and the Mediterranean," *Journal of Mediterranean Studies* 12(1): 1–21.

Mitchell, Jon P. (2004) "Ritual Structure and Ritual Agency: 'Rebounding Violence' and Maltese *Festa*," *Social Anthropology* 12(1): 57–75.

Mitchell, Jon P. (2006) "Performance," in C. Tilley *et al.*, *Handbook of Material Culture*, London: Sage.

Mitchell, Jon P., and Hildi J. Mitchell (2008) "For Belief: Embodiment and Immanence in Catholicism and Mormonism," *Social Analysis* 52(1): 79–94.

Mitchell, Stephen (1988) *Relational Concepts in Psychoanalysis*, Cambridge, MA: Harvard University Press.

Mitchell, Stephen, and Lewis Aron (eds.) (1999) *Relational Psychoanalysis: The Emergence of a Tradition*, Hillsdale, NJ: Analytic Press.

Mitchell, W.J.T. (2005) *What Do Pictures Want? The Lives and Loves of Images*, Chicago: The University of Chicago Press.

Moore, R. Laurence (1994) *Selling God: American Religion in the Marketplace of Culture*, New York: Oxford University Press.

Morgan, David (1998) *Visual Piety: A History and Theory of Popular Religious Images*, Berkeley: University of California Press.

Morgan, David (2003) "Protestant Visual Piety and the Aesthetics of American Mass Culture," pp. 107–20 in Jolyon Mitchell and Sophia Marriage (eds.), *Mediating Religion: Conversations in Media, Religion and Culture*, London: T&T Clark.

Morgan, David (2005) *The Sacred Gaze: Religious Visual Culture in Theory and Practice*, Berkeley: University of California Press.

Morgan, David (2007) *The Lure of Images: A History of Religion and Visual Media in America*, London: Routledge.

Morgan, David (2009a) "The Look of Sympathy," *Material Religion* 5(2): 132–54.

Morgan, David (2009b) "Icon and Interface in the Visual Economy of the Sacred," unpublished paper.

Morphy, Howard (1991) *Ancestral Connections*, Chicago: University of Chicago Press.

Morse, John E. (1969) *To Build a Church*, New York: Holt, Rinehart and Winston.

Moser, Walter (2001) *Résurgences baroques: Les trajectoires d'un processus transculturel*, Brussels: La Lettre Volée.

Mrazek, Jan, and Morgan Pitelka (eds.) (2007) *What's the Use of Art? Asian Visual and Material Culture in Context*, Honolulu: University of Hawai'i Press.

Mrozik, Susanne (2007) *Virtuous Bodies: The Physical Dimensions of Morality in Buddhist Ethics*, New York: Oxford University Press.

Myers, Fred R. (2001) "Introduction: The Empire of Things," pp. 3–61 in Fred R. Myers (ed.) *The Empire of Things: Regimes of Value and Material Culture*, Santa Fe: School of American Research Press.

Nasir-i Khusraw (2001) *Book of Travels (Safarnama)*, trans. Wheeler Thackston, Costa Mesa, CA: Mazda Publishers.

Ndalianis, Angela (2004) *Neo-Baroque Aesthetics and Contemporary Entertainment*, Cambridge, MA: MIT Press.

Needham, Rodney (1972) *Belief, Language and Experience*, Oxford: Blackwell.

Niessen, Sandra, and Anne Brydon (1998) "Introduction: Adorning the Body," pp. ix–xvii in Anne Brydon and Sandra Niessen (eds.) *Consuming Fashion: Adoring the Transnational Body*, Oxford: Berg.

Nihon mingu gakkai (1997) *Nihon mingu jiten* [The Japanese mingu Dictionary], Tokyo: Gyôsei Shuppansha.

Nooter, Mary H. (1991) "Luba Art and Polity: Creating Power in a Central African Kingdom," PhD Dissertation for the Department of Art History and Archaeology, Columbia University, Ann Arbor, Michigan, University Microfilms.

Nooter, Mary H. (ed.) (1993) *Secrecy: African Art that Conceals and Reveals*, New York and Munich: The Museum for African Art and Prestel.

Norbu, Namkhai, and John Shane (eds.) (1986) *The Crystal and the Way of Light: Sutra, Tantra, and Dzogchen: The Teachings of Namkhai Norbu*, Philadelphia, PA: Taylor & Francis.

Nussbaum, Martha C. (2001) *Upheavals of Thought: The Intelligence of Emotions*, Cambridge: Cambridge University Press.

Nzongola-Ntalaja, Georges (ed.) (1986) *The Crisis in Zaire: Myths and Realities*, Trenton: Africa World Press.

Ohnuma, Reiko (2007) *Head, Eyes, Flesh, and Blood: Giving Away the Body in Indian Buddhist Literature*, New York: Columbia University Press.

Oliveira, Carla Mary S. (2003) *O Barroco na Paraíba*, João Pessoa: Editora O Livro.

Omura, Seigai (1931) *Chugoku bijutsu shi choso hen*, Tokyo: Kokusho Kankokai.

Orofino, Giacomella (2000) "The Great Wisdom Mother and the Gcod Tradition," pp. 396–416 in David Gordon White (ed.) *Tantra in Practice*, Princeton, NJ: Princeton University Press.

Orsi, Robert (2007) *Between Heaven and Earth: The Religious World's People Make and the Scholars Who Study Them*, Princeton, NJ: Princeton University Press.

Otto, Rudolf (1958) *The Idea of the Holy: An Inquiry into the Non-rational Factor in the Idea of the Divine and Its Relation to the Rational*, London: Oxford University Press.

Ouédraogo, Jean-Bernard (2002) *Arts photographiques en Afrique*, Paris: L'Harmattan.

Ouédraogo, Jean-Bernard (2008) *Identités visuelles en Afrique*, Nantes: Éditions Amalthée.

Ozawa-de Silva, Chikako (2002) "Beyond the Body/Mind? Japanese Contemporary Thinkers on Alternative Sociologies of the Body," *Body & Society* 8(2): 21–39.

Paden, William (1996) "Elements of a New Comparativism," *Method & Theory in the Study of Religion* 8(1): 5–14.

Pagels, Elaine (2003) *Beyond Belief: The Secret Gospel of Thomas*, New York: Random House.

Palmer, Susan Jean (1995) "Women in the Raelian Movement: New Religious Experiments in Gender and Authority," pp. 105–35 in James R. Lewis (ed.) *The Gods Have Landed: New Religions from Other Worlds*, Albany, NY: State University of New York Press.

Partridge, Christopher (2003) "Understanding UFO Religions and Abduction Spiritualities," in Christopher Partridge (ed.) *UFO Religions*, New York: Routledge.

Pascoli, Lione (1933) *Vite de' pittori, scultori ed architetto moderni, Rome 1736*, Rome: Facsimile-Ausgabe.

Pattison, Stephen (2007) *Seeing Things: Deepening Relations with Visual Artefacts*, London: SCM Press.

Pécora, Alcir (1994) *Teatro do sacramento. A unidade teológico–retórico–política dos sermões de Antono Vieira*, Campinas: Edunicamp.

Peirce, Charles Sanders (1992a) "The Fixation of Belief," in C.S. Peirce, *The Essential Peirce: Selected Philosophical Writings*, Nathan Houser and Christian Kloesel (eds.), 3 vols., Bloomington, IN: Indiana University Press, vol. 1: 109–23.

Peirce, Charles Sanders (1992b) "How to Make Our Ideas Clear," in C.S. Peirce, *The Essential Peirce*, Nathan Houser and Christian Kloesel (eds.), 3 vols., Bloomington, IN: Indiana University Press, vol. 1: 124–41.

Perniola, Mario (2003) "The Cultural Turn and Ritual Feeling in Catholicism," *Pargrana: Zeitschrift für historische Anthropologie* 12(1–2): 309–25.

Peters, Francis (1994) *The Hajj: A Muslim Pilgrimage to Mecca and the Holy Places*, Princeton, NJ: Princeton University Press.

Pink, Sarah (2006) *The Future of Visual Anthropology: Engaging the Senses*, London and New York: Routledge, Taylor & Francis.

Pinney, Christopher (2001) "Piercing the Skin of the Idol," pp. 157–79 in Christopher Pinney and Nicholas Thomas (eds.) *Beyond Aesthetics: Art and the Technologies of Enchantment*, Oxford and New York: Berg.

Pinney, Christopher (2004) *'Photos of the Gods': The Printed Image and Political Struggle in India*, London: Reaktion Books.

Pinney, Christopher, and Nicholas Thomas (eds.) (2001) *Beyond Aesthetics: Art and the Technologies of Enchantment*, Oxford: Berg.

Plate, S. Brent (2005) *Walter Benjamin, Religion, and Aesthetics: Rethinking Religion through the Arts*, New York: Routledge.

Plato (1992) *Republic*, trans. G.M.A. Grube, rev. C.D.C. Reeve, Indianapolis: Hackett Publishing Company.

Pompa, Cristina (2001) "As muitas línguas da conversão: missionários, Tupi e 'Tapuia' no Brasil colonial," *Tempo* 6(11): 27–44.

Pompa, Cristina (2002) *Religião como tradução: missionários, Tupi e Tapuia no Brasil colonial*, Bauru: EDUSC.

Pozzo, Andrea (1693) *Prospettiva de Pittori de Architetti d'Andrea Pozzo dell Compagnia di Giesù. Parte Prima. In cui s'igneva il modo più sbrigato di mettere in prospettiva tutti i disegni d'Architettura*, Rome.

Pozzo, Andrea (1700) *Prospettiva de Pittori de Architetti d'Andrea Pozzo dell Compagnia di Giesù. Parte Seconda*, Rome.

Primeiro, Fidelis M. de (1940) *Capuchinohos em Terras de Santa Cruz nos séculos XVII, XVIII e XIX*, São Paulo: Martins.

Primiano, Leonard Norman (1999) "Postmodern Sites of Catholic Sacred Materiality," pp. 187–202 in Peter W. Williams (ed.) *Perspectives on American Religion and Culture*, Oxford: Blackwell.

Prown, Jules David (1982) "Mind in Matter: An Introduction to Material Culture Theory and Method," *Winterthur Portfolio* 17(1): 1–19.

Pye, Elizabeth (ed.) (2007) *The Power of Touch: Handling Objects in Museum and Heritage Contexts*, Walnut Creek, CA: Left Coast Press.

Rabinovitch, Celia (2004) *Surrealism and the Sacred: Power, Eros, and the Occult in Modern Art*, Boulder, CO: Westview Press.

Rahimian, Muhammad Hasan (c. 1991) *Sayeh-i Aftab*, Teheran: Mu'assese Pasdar Islam.

Rambelli, Fabio (2007) *Buddhist Materiality: A Cultural History of Objects in Japanese Buddhism*, Stanford, CA: Stanford University Press.

Rampley, Matthew (2005) "Art History and Cultural Difference: Alfred Gell's Anthropology of Art," *Art History* 28(4): 524–51.

Rancière, Jacques (2007) *The Politics of Aesthetics*, trans. Gabriel Rockhill, New York: Continuum.

Randall, Gregory (2003) *America's Original G. I. Town: Park Forest, Illinois*, Baltimore, MD: Johns Hopkins University Press.

Rappaport, Roy (1999) *Ritual and Religion in the Making of Humanity*, Cambridge: Cambridge University Press.

Reader, Ian (1991) *Religion in Contemporary Japan*, London: Macmillan Press.

Reader, Ian, and George Tanabe (1998) *Practically Religious: Worldly Benefits and the Common Religion of Japan*, Honolulu: University of Hawai'i.

Reefe, Thomas Q. (1977) "Lukasa: A Luba Memory Device," *African Arts* 10(4): 48–50, 88.

Reefe, Thomas Q. (1981) *The Rainbow and the Kings: A History of the Luba Empire to 1891*, Berkeley, CA: University of California Press.

Renne, Elisha P. (1991) "Water, Spirits, and Plain White Cloth: The Ambiguity of Things in Bunu Social Life," *Man* 26(4): 709–22.

Reyna, Stephen P. (2002) *Connections: Brain, Mind and Culture in a Social Anthropology*, London: Routledge.

Rizzuto, Ana-Maria (1979) *The Birth of the Living God: A Psychoanalytic Study*, Chicago: University of Chicago Press.

Roberts, Allen (1984) "'Fishers of Men': Religion and Political Economy Among Colonized Tabwa," *Africa* 54(2): 49–70.

Roberts, Allen (1986) "Social and Historical Contexts of Tabwa Art," pp. 1–48 in Evan Maurer and Allen Roberts (eds.) *The Rising of a New Moon: A Century of Tabwa Art*, Seattle: University of Washington Press for the University of Michigan Museum of Art, Ann Arbor.

Roberts, Allen (1989) "History, Ethnicity and Change in the 'Christian Kingdom' of Southeastern Zaïre," pp. 193–214 in Leroy Vail (ed.) *The Creation of Tribalism in South and Central Africa: Studies in the Political Economy of Ideology*, Berkeley, CA: University of California Press.

Roberts, Allen (ed.) (1994) *Staffs of Life: Rods, Staffs, Scepters, and Wands from the Coudron Collection of African Art*, Iowa City: Project for Advanced Study of Art and Life in Africa and the University of Iowa Museum of Art.

Roberts, Allen (1996) "The Ironies of System D," pp. 82–101 in Charlene Cerny and Suzanne Seriff (eds.) *Recycled, Re-Seen: Folk Art from the Global Scrap Heap*, New York: Abrams for the Museum of International Folk Art, Santa Fe.

Roberts, Allen F., and Mary Nooter Roberts (2003) *A Saint in the City: Sufi Arts of Urban Senegal*, Los Angeles and Seattle: UCLA Fowler Museum of Cultural History and the University of Washington Press.

Roberts, Allen, and Mary Nooter Roberts (2008) "Flickering Images, Floating Signifiers: Optical Innovation and Visual Piety in Senegal," *Material Religion* 4(1): 4–31.

Roberts, Mary Nooter (1994) "Does an Object Have a Life?" in Mary Nooter Roberts and Susan Vogel (eds.) *Exhibition-ism: Museums and African Art*, New York: The Museum for African Art.

Roberts, Mary Nooter (2000) "Proofs and Promises: Setting Meaning before the Eyes," pp. 63–82 in John Pemberton, III, ed., *Insight and Artistry: A Crosscultural Study of Divination in West and Central Africa*, Washington, DC: Smithsonian Institution Press.

Roberts, Mary Nooter (2007) "Inscribing Identity: The Body," pp. 55–69 in Christine Mullen Kreamer, Mary Nooter Roberts, Elizabeth Harney, and Allyson

Purpura (eds.) *Inscribing Meaning: Writing and Graphic Systems in African Art*, Milan: Five Continents Editions.

Roberts, Mary Nooter (2008) "Exhibiting Episteme: African Arts Exhibitions as Objects of Knowledge," pp. 170–86 in Kenji Yoshida, and John Mack (eds.) *Preserving the Cultural Heritage of Africa: Crisis or Renaissance?* Woodbridge (Suffolk), Rochester, and Muckleneuk, South Africa: James Currey and Unisa Press.

Roberts, Mary Nooter, and Allen F. Roberts (1996) *Memory: Luba Art and the Making of History*, New York and Munich: The Museum for African Art and Prestel.

Roberts, Mary Nooter, and Allen Roberts (2007) *Luba: An Aesthetics of Efficacy*, Milan: Five Continents Press.

Roberts, Mary Nooter, and Susan Vogel (eds.) (1994) *Exhibition-ism: Museums and African Art*, New York: The Museum for African Art.

Roeder, Marge (2007) Personal interview, 7 July.

Rojcewicz, Peter M. (1989) "Signals of Transcendence: The Human–UFO Experience," pp. 65–79 in Dennis Stillings (ed.) *Cyberbiological Studies of the Imaginal Component in the UFO Contact Experience. Archaeus*, vol. 5, Saint Paul, MI: Archaeus Project.

Roof, Wade Clark (1999) *Spiritual Marketplace: Baby Boomers and the Re-making of American Religion*, Princeton, NJ: Princeton University Press.

Röwer, Basilio (1941) *Páginas de História Franciscana no Brasil*, Petrópolis: Vozes.

Röwer, Basilio (1947) *A ordem franciscana no Brasil*, Petrópolis: Vozes.

Rubial García, António (1996) *La hermana pobreza. El franciscanismo: de la Edad Media a la evangelización novohispana*, Mexico-City: UNAM.

Rubin, Arnold (1974) *African Accumulative Sculpture: Power and Display*, New York: Pace Gallery.

Rubin, Arnold (1988) *Marks of Civilization: Artistic Transformations of the Human Body*, Los Angeles: Museum of Cultural History, University of California, Los Angeles.

Ruel, Malcom (1982) "Christians as Believers," in John Davis (ed.) *Religious Organization and Religious Experience*, London: Academic Press.

Ruel, Malcolm (1997) *Belief, Ritual and the Securing of Life: Reflexive Essays on a Bantu Religion*, Leiden: E.J. Brill.

Rush, Dana (1999) "Eternal Potential: Chromolithographs in Vodunland," *African Arts* 32(4): 61–75, 94–5.

Saliba, John A. (1995) "Religious Dimensions of UFO Phenomena," pp. 15–64 in James R. Lewis (ed.) *The Gods Have Landed: New Religions from Other Worlds*, Albany, NY: State University of New York Press.

Sang, Charles (2008) Personal interview, 29 July.

Scarry, Elaine (1985) *The Body in Pain: The Making and Unmaking of the World*, Oxford: Oxford University Press.

Schattschneider, Ellen (2004) "Family Resemblances: Memorial Images and the Face of Kinship," *Japanese Journal of Religious Studies* 31(1): 141–62.

Schieffelin, Edward L. (1976) *The Sorrow of the Lonely and the Burning of the Dancers*, New York: St. Martin's Press.

Schieffelin, Edward L. (1998) "Problematizing Performance," pp. 194–207 in Felicia Hughes-Freeland, ed., *Ritual, Performance, Media*, London: Routledge.

Schimmel, Annemarie (1965) "Some Glimpses of the Religious Life in Egypt During the Later Mamluk Period," *Islamic Studies* 4(4): 353–92.

Schmich, Mary (2005) "Real or Not, Images Bring Us Together," *Chicago Tribune*, April 20, pp. 1, 7.

Schneider, Jane (1987) "The Anthropology of Cloth," *Annual Review of Anthropology* 16: 409–48.

Schneider, Jane (2006) "Cloth and Clothing," pp. 203–20 in Christopher Tilley *et al.*, *Handbook of Material Culture*, London: Sage.

Schofield Clark, Lynn (in press) "Mediatization and Media Ecology," in Knut Lundby (ed.) *Mediatization: Concepts, Changes, Consequences*, New York: Peter Lang.

Schoonover, Karl (2003) "Ectoplasms, Evanescence, and Photography," *Art Journal* 62(3): 31–43.

Schopen, Gregory (1991) "Archaeology and Protestant Presuppositions in the Study of Indian Buddhism," *History of Religions* 31: 1–23.

Schopen, Gregory (1997) *Bones, Stones, and Buddhist Monks: Collected Papers on the Archaeology, Epigraphy, and Texts of Monastic Buddhism in India*, Honolulu: University of Hawaii Press.

Schopen, Gregory (2005) "The Phrase 'sa pṛthivīpradeśaś caiyabhūto bhavet in the Vajracchedikā: Notes on the Cult of the Book in Mahāyāna," pp. 25–62 in *Figments and Fragments of Mahāyāna Buddhism in India: More Collected Papers*, Honolulu: University of Hawai'i.

Schreiner, Susan (2003) "Unmasking the Angel of Light: The Problem of Deception in Martin Luther and Teresa of Avila," pp. 118–37 in Michael Kessler and Christian Sheppard (eds.) *Mystics: Presence and Aporia*, Chicago: University of Chicago Press.

Sconce, Jeffrey (2000) *Haunted Media: Electronic Presence from Telegraphy to Television*, Durham, NC: Duke University Press.

Siggstedt, Mette (1991) "Forms of Fate: An Investigation of the Relationship between Formal Portraiture, Especially Ancestral Portrait, and Physiognomy (*xiangshu*) in China," pp. 713–48 in *International Colloquium on Chinese Art History*, Taipei: National Palace Museum, Taipei.

Sima, Guang (1725) *Shuyi*, Chap. 5, "Sangyi yi: hunpo," in *Wenyuange Siku quanshu*, vol. 142; reprint (1983–1986), Taipei: Shangwuyinshuguan.

Skolnick, Neil, and Susan Warshaw (1992) *Relational Perspectives in Psychoanalysis*, Hillsdale, NJ: Analytic Press.

Smith, Christian, and Melissa Lunquist Denton (2005) *Soul Searching: The Religious and Spiritual Lives of American Teenagers*, New York: Oxford University Press.

Smith, Jonathan (1987) *To Take Place: Toward Theory in Ritual*, Chicago: University of Chicago Press.

Smith, Jonathan (1993) *Map Is Not Territory*, Chicago: University of Chicago Press.

Smith, Robert (1974) *Ancestor Worship in Contemporary Japan*, Stanford, CA: Stanford University Press.

Smith, Wilfred Cantwell (1979) *Faith and Belief*, Princeton, NJ: Princeton University Press.

Sommer, Deborah A. (1994) "Images into Words: Ming Confucian Iconoclasm," *National Palace Museum Bulletin* 29(1–2): 1–24.

Sontag, Susan (1977) *On Photography*, New York: Anchor Books.

Sovik, Edward Anders (1967) "What is Religious Architecture?," *Faith and Form* 1 special inaugural issue: 8–9, 22–5.

Spyer, Patricia (1998) *Border Fetishisms: Material Objects in Unstable Places*, New York: Routledge.

Starrett, Gregory 1995) "The Political Economy of Religious Commodities in Cairo," *American Anthropologist* 97: 51–68.

Stoichita, Victor I. (1997) *Das mystische Auge—Vision und Malerei im Spanien des Goldenen Zeitalter*, Munich: Fink.

Stoller, Paul (1997) *Sensuous Scholarship*, Philadelphia, PA: University of Pennsylvania Press.

Strathern, Andrew J. (1996) *Body Thoughts*, Ann Arbor, MI: The University of Michigan Press.

Strong, John (2004) *Relics of the Buddha*, Princeton, NJ: Princeton University Press.

Strother, Z. S. (1998) *Inventing Masks: Agency and History in the Art of Central Pende*, Chicago: University of Chicago Press.

Suzuki, Shigefumi (2002), *Sumai wo mongataru* [Talking about Living], Tokyo: Kenchiku shiryo kenkyusha.

Synnott, Anthony (1993) *The Body Social: Symbolism, Self and Society*, London and New York: Routledge.

Tambiah, Stanley (1984) *The Buddhist Saints of the Forest and the Cult of Amulets*, Cambridge MA: Harvard University Press.

Tambiah, Stanley (1985) *Culture, Thought and Social Action: An Anthropological Approach*, Cambridge, MA: Harvard University Press.

Taussig, Michael (1992) *The Nervous System*, New York: Routledge.

Teilhet, Jehanne (1983) "The Role of Women Artists in Polynesia and Melanesia," pp. 45–56 in Sidney M. Mead and Bernie Kernot (eds.) *Art and Artists of Oceania*, Palmerston North: The Dunmore Press.

Teresa (1957) *The Life of Saint Teresa of Àvila by Herself*, New York: Penguin Books.

Teuber, Bernhard (2004) "Sichtbare Wundmale und unsichtbare Durchbohrung. Die leibhafte Nachfolge Christi als Paradigma des anhermeneutischen Schreibens," pp. 155–79 in B. Menke, and B. Vinken, eds., *Stigmata*, Munich: Fink.

Thagard, Paul (2006), in collaboration with Fred Kroon, Josef Nerb, Baljinder Sahdra, Cameron Shelley, and Brandon Wager, *Hot Thought: Mechanisms and Applications of Emotional Cognition*, Cambridge, MA: MIT Press.

Tha'labi, Abu Ishaq (2002) *'Ara'is al-Majalis fi Qisas al-Anbiya or "Lives of the Prophets*," William Brinner (ed. and trans.), Leiden: Brill.

Thomas, Julian (2006) "Phenomenology and Material Culture," pp. 43–59 in Christopher Tilley *et al.*, *Handbook of Material Culture*, London: Sage.

Thompson, Robert Farris (1983) *Flash of the Spirit: African and Afro-American Art and Philosophy*, New York: Random House.

Thompson, Robert Farris (1993) *Face of the Gods: Art and Altars of Africa and the African Americas*, New York and Munich: The Museum for African Art and Prestel.

Thomson, Ann (2008) *Bodies of Thought: Science, Religion, and the Soul in the Early Enlightenment*, Oxford: Oxford University Press.

Tilley, Christopher (2006) "Objectification," pp. 60–73 in Christopher Tilley *et al.*, *Handbook of Material Culture*, London: Sage.

Tilley, Christopher, Webb Keane, Susanne Küchler, Michael Rowlands, and Patricia Spyer (eds.) (2006) *Handbook of Material Culture*, London: Sage.

Tobin, Frank (ed.) (1989) *Henry Suso: The Exemplar, with Two German Sermons*, New York: Paulist Press.

"To Break Ground for Baptist Church" (31 January 1958) *Park Forest Star*, clipping in Park Forest Public Library History Collections.

Tocqueville, Alexis de ([1835/1840] 2003) *Democracy in America*, G. Bevan, trans., New York: Penguin Classics.

Traphagan, John (2004) *The Practice of Concern*, Durham, NC: Carolina Academic Press.

Trexler, Richard C. (2002) "The Stigmatized Body of Francis of Assisi: Conceived, Processed, Disappeared," pp. 463–97 in Klaus Schreiner (ed.), *Frömmigkeit im Mittelalter: politisch-soziale Kontexte, visuelle Praxis, körperliche Ausdrucksformen*, Munich: Fink.

Trinity Lutheran Church, Park Forest, Illinois (1960) Dedication book for second church, church archives.

Turner, Victor (1970) *The Forest of Symbols: Aspects of Ndembu Ritual*, Ithaca, NY: Cornell University Press.

Turner, Victor (1988) *The Anthropology of Performance*, New York: PAJ Publications.

Turner, Victor, and Edith Turner (1978) *Image and Pilgrimage in Christian Culture*, New York: Columbia University Press.

Tylor, Edward ([1873] 1891) *Primitive Culture*, vol. 2, London: John Murray.

Ulaymi, Abd al-Rahman (n.d.) *Uns al-Jalil bi-Ta'rikh al-Quds wa al-Khalil*, n.p.

Van der Leeuw, Gerardus (1963) *Religion in Essence and Manifestation*, trans. J.E. Turner, 2 vols., New York: Harper & Row.

Varela, Francisco (1992) *The Embodied Mind: Cognitive Science and Human Experience*, Boston: MIT Press.

Verrips, Jojada (1978) *En boven de polder de hemel. Een antropologische studie van een Nederlands dorp 1850–1971*, Groningen: Wolters-Noordhoff.

Verrips, Jojada (1980) "De genese van een godsdienstige beweging: Het Nieuwkerkse werk," *Tijdschrift voor sociale geschiedenis* 18: 113–39.

Verrips, Jojada (2008) "Offending Art and the Sense of Touch," *Material Religion* 4(2): 204–25.

Vieira, Antônio (1959) *Sermões*, Lisbon: Lello & Irmão, 16 vols.

Vieira, Antônio (2001) *Sermões*, vol. 2, org. by Alcir Pécora, São Paulo: Hedra.

Vinograd, Richard (1992) *Boundaries of the Self: Chinese Portraits, 1600–1900*, New York: Cambridge University Press.

Voas, David, and Alistair Crockett (2005) "Religion in Britain: Neither Believing nor Belonging," *Sociology* 39(1): 11–28.

Wagoner, Harold E. (1961) "Church Architecture: What Next?" in *Protestant Church Buildings and Equipment* (Feb.), reprinted by National Council of the Churches of Christ in the USA.

Wagoner, Harold E. *et al.* (1960) "Panel Discussion: Building for Christian Education—with Purpose and Beauty," pp. D4: 1–3 in *Minneapolis Annual National Guild Conference*, Church Architecture Guild of America and the Department of Church Building and Architecture of the National Council of Churches of Christ in the USA.

Waines, David (2001) *An Introduction to Islam*, New York: Cambridge University Press.

Warner, Marina (2006) *Phantasmagoria: Spirit Visions, Metaphors, and Media into the Twenty-First Century*, Oxford: Oxford University Press.

Warnke, Martin (1984) *Cranach's Luther. Entwürfe für ein Image*, Frankfurt: Fischer.

Watson, Sean (1998) "The Neurobiology of Sorcery: Deleuze and Guattari's Brain," *Body & Society* 4(4): 23–47.

Weiner, Annette B. (1989) "Why Cloth? Wealth, Gender, and Power in Oceania," pp. 33–71 in Annette B. Weiner, and Jane Schneider (eds.) *Cloth and Human Experience*, Washington, DC: Smithsonian Institute.

Weiner, Annette B. (1992) *Inalienable Possessions: The Paradox of Keeping-While-Giving*, Berkeley, CA: University of California Press.

Weiner, Annette B. (1994) "Cultural Difference and the Density of Objects," *American Ethnologist* 21(1): 391–403.

Westermann, Mariät (ed.) (2005) *Anthropologies of Art*, Williamstown, MA: Sterling and Francine Clark Art Institute.

Wheeler, Brannon (2006) *Mecca and Eden: Ritual, Relics, and Territory in Islam*, Chicago: University of Chicago Press.

White Fathers (1885–1940) "Diaire de la Mission de Mpala," typescript copy, Archives of the Kalemie-Moba Diocese, Kalemie, Democratic Republic of the Congo.

Whitehouse, Harvey (2002) "Modes of Religiosity: Towards a Cognitive Explanation of the Sociopolitical Dynamics of Religion," *Method and Theory in the Study of Religion* 14 (3/4): 293–315.

Whitmore, John (1995), "Religious Dimensions of the UFO Abductee Experience," pp. 65–84 in James R. Lewis (ed.) *The Gods Have Landed: New Religions from Other Worlds*, Albany, NY: State University of New York Press.

Whyte, William (1956) *The Organization Man*, New York: Simon and Schuster.

Wiebe, David (1996) "Is the New Comparativism Really New?," *Method & Theory in the Study of Religion* 8 (1): 21–9.

Willeke, Venancio (ed.) (1966) "Livro dos Guardiões do Convento de Santo Antônio de Paraíba," *Studia* 19: 173–207.

Williams, F.E. (1923) "The Vailala Madness and the Destruction of Native Ceremonies in the Gulf Division," *Territory of Papua Anthropology Report* 4.

Williams, Raymond, and Michael Orrom (1954) *A Preface to Film*, London: Film Drama Ltd.

Winnicott, Donald (1971) *Playing and Reality*, London: Routledge.

Woydack, Tobias (2005) *Der räumliche Gott. Was sind Kirchengebäude theologisch?*, Schenefeld: EB-Verlag.

Wuthnow, Robert (1998) *After Heaven: Spirituality in America Since the 1950's*, Berkeley, CA: University of California Press.

Yamada, Tokubei (1991) *Zusetsu—Nihon no Ningyôshi* [An Illustrated History of Japanese Dolls], Tokyo: Tokyodo Shuppan.

Yangita, Kunio (1951) *Minzokugaku Jiten (Folkore Dictionary)*, Tokyo: Tôyôdo.

Yates, Frances A. (1966) *The Art of Memory*, Chicago: The University of Chicago Press.

Yoshida, Kenji, and John Mack (2008) *Preserving the Cultural Heritage of Africa: Crisis or Renaissance?*, Woodbridge (Suffolk), Rochester, and Muckleneuk, South Africa: James Currey and Unisa Press.

Young, Leslie, E. Heather, and Ping-Ann Addo (2007) "Introduction. Pacific Textiles, Pacific Cultures: Hybridity and Pragmatic Creativity," *Journal of Pacific Arts* 3–5: 12–21.

Zhu, Xi (1725) *Yicheng yishu*, Chap. 22 in *Wenyuange Siku quanshu*, vol. 698; reprint (1983–1986), Taipei: Shangwuyinshuguan.

Zimdars-Swartz, Sandra L. (1991) *Encountering Mary: From La Salette to Medjugorje*, Princeton, NJ: Princeton University Press.

Zito, Angela (2008) "Can Television Mediate Religious Experience? The Theology of Joan of Arcadia," pp. 724–38 in Hent DeVries (ed.) *Religion: Beyond the Concept*, New York: Fordham University Press.

Index

Printed by Amazon Italia Logistica S.r.l.
Torrazza Piemonte (TO), Italy

11807941R00185